MIDDLE POWER IN THE MIDD

Canada's Foreign and Defence Policies in a Changing Region

Edited by Thomas Juneau and Bessma Momani

The Middle East has not, historically, been a first-order priority for Canadian foreign and defence policy. Most major Canadian decisions on the Middle East have come about through ad hoc decision-making rather than strategic necessity. Balancing international obligations with domestic goals, Canadian relations with this region try to find a balance between meeting alliance obligations and keeping domestic constituents content.

Middle Power in the Middle East delves into some of Canada's key bilateral relations with the Middle East and explores the main themes in Canada's regional presence: arms sales, human rights, defence capacity-building, and mediation. Contributors analyse the key drivers of Canada's foreign and defence policies in the Middle East, including diplomatic relations with the United States, ideology, and domestic politics. Bringing together many of Canada's foremost experts on Canada–Middle East relations, this collection provides a fresh perspective that is particularly timely and important following the Arab uprisings.

THOMAS JUNEAU is an associate professor at the University of Ottawa's Graduate School of Public and International Affairs and a non-resident fellow with the Sana'a Center for Strategic Studies.

BESSMA MOMANI is a professor of political science and assistant vice-president at the University of Waterloo, a senior fellow at the Centre for International Governance Innovation (CIGI), and a non-resident fellow of the Arab Gulf States Institute.

Middle Power in the Middle East

Canada's Foreign and Defence Policies in a Changing Region

EDITED BY THOMAS JUNEAU AND
BESSMA MOMANI

UNIVERSITY OF TORONTO PRESS
Toronto Buffalo London

© University of Toronto Press 2022
Toronto Buffalo London
utorontopress.com
Printed in the U.S.A.

ISBN 978-1-4875-2844-7 (cloth) ISBN 978-1-4875-2847-8 (EPUB)
ISBN 978-1-4875-2845-4 (paper) ISBN 978-1-4875-2846-1 (PDF)

Library and Archives Canada Cataloguing in Publication

Title: Middle power in the Middle East : Canada's foreign and defence policies
   in a changing region / edited by Thomas Juneau and Bessma Momani.
Names: Juneau, Thomas, editor. | Momani, Bessma, editor.
Identifiers: Canadiana (print) 20210393645 | Canadiana (ebook) 2021039370X |
   ISBN 9781487528447 (hardcover) | ISBN 9781487528454 (softcover) |
   ISBN 9781487528478 (EPUB) | ISBN 9781487528461 (PDF)
Subjects: LCSH: Canada – Foreign relations – Middle East. | LCSH:
   Middle East – Foreign relations – Canada. | LCSH: Canada – Relations –
   Middle East. | LCSH: Middle East – Relations – Canada.
Classification: LCC FC244.M53 M53 2022 | DDC 327.71056 – dc23

We wish to acknowledge the land on which the University of Toronto Press
operates. This land is the traditional territory of the Wendat, the Anishnaabeg,
the Haudenosaunee, the Métis, and the Mississaugas of the Credit First
Nation.

University of Toronto Press acknowledges the financial support of the
Government of Canada, the Canada Council for the Arts, and the Ontario Arts
Council, an agency of the Government of Ontario, for its publishing activities.

 Canada Council   Conseil des Arts
for the Arts   du Canada

ONTARIO ARTS COUNCIL
CONSEIL DES ARTS DE L'ONTARIO
an Ontario government agency
un organisme du gouvernement de l'Ontario

Funded by the   Financé par le
Government   gouvernement
of Canada   du Canada

Canadä

Contents

Acknowledgments vii

List of Acronyms ix

1 Introduction 3
THOMAS JUNEAU AND BESSMA MOMANI

2 Sleeping beside the Elephant: The United States in Canada's
Middle East Policy 14
FARZAN SABET

3 Being a Reliable Ally in a Politicized War: Canada's Fight
against the Islamic State 31
JUSTIN MASSIE AND MARCO MUNIER

4 Capacity Building and Training: Supporting Security Services in
Iraq, Jordan, and the Occupied Palestinian Territories 47
MIKE FLEET AND NIZAR MOHAMAD

5 Islamic State Foreign Fighters: Their Return and
Canadian Responses 67
AMARNATH AMARASINGAM AND STEPHANIE CARVIN

6 Humanitarian Foreign Policy and Refugees: Welcoming
Syrians in Crisis 85
NAWROOS SHIBLI

7 Supporting Civil Society: Jordan's Changing Development
Landscape 103
E.J. KARMEL

8 Dealing with an Illiberal Democracy: Turkey's Erdoğan Tests
   Bilateral Relations 122
   CHRIS KILFORD

9 Responding to Political Islam: Egypt's Muslim Brotherhood and
   Islam in Canada 138
   NERMIN ALLAM

10 Promoting Human Rights: Canada's Confused Policies
   in the Middle East 155
   DAVID PETRASEK

11 Selling Weapons: Saudi Arabia and the Trudeau Government's
   Feminist Foreign Policy 169
   JENNIFER PEDERSEN

12 Supporting Mediation: Canada as Peacemaker in the
   Middle East 188
   PETER JONES

13 Balancing Canada's Role in the Arab-Israeli Peace Process 206
   COSTANZA MUSU

14 Navigating Ideology and Foreign Policy: Canadian Prime
   Ministers and Israel 219
   FRÉDÉRIC BOILY

15 Conclusion 236
   NATHAN C. FUNK

Contributors 249

Index 255

Acknowledgments

This project started off as a phone conversation between the two editors, where we first discussed the idea of a collective book on Canada and the Middle East. After a meeting over coffee in the ByWard Market in Ottawa during which we further clarified our ideas, we started contacting individual chapter authors.

We wish to thank the Department of National Defence (DND) and its Mobilizing Insights in Defence and Security (MINDS) program for its generous support. It was a MINDS Targeted Engagement Grant that allowed us to organize a workshop in 2019 in Waterloo, during which chapter authors presented their papers to other authors, academics, as well as a group of practitioners. We thank in particular Veronica Kitchen, Melissa Finn, Rana Sweiss, Randa Slim, Cesar Jaramillo, Nader Hashemi, Howard Eissenstat, Amy Hawthorne, and Hussein Ibish, as well as officials from the Government of Canada for their valued participation in the workshop. Their comments and suggestions made each chapter stronger and helped ensure the book's overall coherence.

We are also thankful to the DND MINDS support for the Defence and Security Foresight Group, of which many of our chapter authors are team leads or members. This three-year network has also aimed to support emerging Canadian scholars of the Middle East through several events, to ensure that the next generations of experts in this field can continue to study and analyse this important region of the world for Canada's overall benefit.

At the University of Toronto Press we thank Dan Quinlan, Janice Evans, and Stephanie Mazza for their support and diligence in helping carry this project to the end. Very special thanks to Kersty Kearney and Lydia Callies for their administrative support, valuable insights, and formatting assistance. Kersty has been invaluable to the success of this book project, often well beyond the call of duty.

Finally, we wish to dedicate this book to the memory of David Petrasek, the author of one of the chapters in this book, who sadly passed away in May 2020. David was beloved by his colleagues at the University of Ottawa and elsewhere and was widely respected in the human rights community.

Acronyms

AKP	Justice and Development Party
BVORR	Blended Visa Office-Referred Refugees
CAF	Canadian Armed Forces
CB	capacity building
CBSA	Canada Border Services Agency
CCCEPV	Canada Centre for Community Engagement and Prevention of Violence
CCIQ	The Islamic Cultural Centre of Quebec City
CSDP	Common Security and Defence Policy
CTAT-J	Canadian Training Assistance Team-Jordan
CTCBP	Counter-Terrorism Capacity-Building Training Program
CVE	counter violent extremism
DND	Department of National Defence
EU	European Union
EUPOLL-COPPS	European Union Coordinating Office for Palestinian Police Support
FETÖ	Fetullah Terrorist Organization
FJP	Freedom and Justice party
FTO	foreign terrorist organization
GAC	Global Affairs Canada
GAR	government assisted refugee
GC	Government of Canada
HDP	Peoples' Democratic Party
IAF	Islamic Action Front
IDF	Israeli Defense Forces
IDTF	Interdepartmental Taskforce
IED	improvised explosive device
IMF	International Monetary Fund

IOM	International Organization for Migration
IPP	International Police Peacekeeping and Peace Operations
IRFAN-Canada	International Relief Fund for the Afflicted and Needy-Canada
IRGC	Islamic Revolutionary Guard Corps
IS	Islamic State
ISF	Iraqi Security Forces
ISIL	Islamic State of Iraq and the Levant
ISPI	Italian Institute for International Political Studies
JAF	Jordanian Armed Forces
JIPTC	Jordan International Police Training Centre
MAC	Muslim Association of Canada
MB	Muslim Brotherhood
MENA	Middle East and North Africa
MFA	Ministry of Foreign Affairs
MHP	Nationalist Movement Party
MLT	Ministerial Liaison Team
MoD	Ministry of Defence
MoI	Ministry of Interior
MP	member of Parliament
MTCP	Military Training and Cooperation Program
NATO	North Atlantic Treaty Organization
NMI	NATO Mission in Iraq
NSJOC	National Security Joint Operations Centre
OPT	Occupied Palestinian Territories
PA	Palestinian Authority
PASF	Palestinian Authority Security Forces
PCP	Palestinian Civil Police
PKK	Kurdish Workers Party
PMF	Popular Mobilization Forces
PNA	Palestinian National Authority
PSOP	Peace and Stabilization Operations Program
PSR	privately sponsored refugee
RAN	Radicalization Awareness Network
RCMP	Royal Canadian Mounted Police
RRP	Regional Response Plan
SDF	Syrian Democratic Forces
SSR	Security Sector Reform
START	Stabilization and Reconstruction Task Force
TGS	Turkish General Staff

UNEF	United Nations Emergency Force
UNHCR	United Nations High Commissioner for Refugees
USSC	United States Security Coordinator
WB	West Bank
YPG	People's Protection Units

MIDDLE POWER IN THE MIDDLE EAST

Canada's Foreign and Defence Policies
in a Changing Region

1 Introduction

THOMAS JUNEAU AND BESSMA MOMANI

Since the end of the Cold War, Canada has had a relatively easy run in managing its foreign and defence policy. It is sheltered by oceans on three sides and, to its south, by the United States, the most militarily powerful and economically prosperous country in the world. Canada's strong and cordial ties with its southern neighbour have brought it major benefits: as complicated as these bilateral relations often are, and as frustrating as they can be for Canadians and their governments, they have significantly contributed to the country's security and prosperity. Canada is also an active member of the North Atlantic Treaty Organization (NATO), arguably the most successful political-military alliance in history. Coddled by geography, Canada has remained far away from most of the world's conflicts.

This benign context has heavily shaped Canadian foreign and defence policy. When Canada has made major foreign and defence policy decisions during this period, such as intervening in an international conflict, it has been mostly as a result of choice, not necessity. Two key categories of variables have shaped these choices. First has been the priority of international alliance management: details vary from one issue to another, but Canada's foreign policy equation always ascribes important weight to relations with the United States and, to a lesser extent, other close allies, especially in NATO. Second, the relatively low level of direct threats to Canada's defence and security has implied that domestic variables, such as the ideology of the government of the day, diaspora politics, and other partisan considerations have also typically played an important role in shaping foreign and defence policy.

How has the interplay of these international and domestic priorities shaped Canadian foreign and defence policy in the Middle East? And during the past decade, how are the changes sweeping across the globe and through the Middle East, from the wave of Arab uprisings to the rise of more assertive rulers, affecting Canada's interests? These are some of the questions that this book explores.

Secure at Home When Engaged Abroad

Historically, the Middle East has not been a priority for Canadian foreign and defence policy. But developments in the region have repeatedly become important concerns in Ottawa, even if the direct impact on Canadian security and prosperity was limited. Whether in 1990–1 at the time of the first Gulf War, in 2002–3 in the run-up to the American invasion of Iraq, or since 2011 in the context of the Arab uprisings, the NATO intervention in Libya, or the fight against the so-called Islamic State (IS), Canadian foreign and defence policy has been preoccupied with decisions on whether or not to follow Washington's lead in the Middle East. Similarly, even if events in the region seldom affect Canada directly, they have consequences, and often important ones, for our closest allies – witness, for example, the refugee crisis in Europe produced by the war in Syria or American responses, domestically and abroad, to terrorist attacks launched by Al Qaeda and IS. More recently, repeated crises in Iraq and in US-Iran relations have also demonstrated how Canada is not sheltered from developments in the region: as tension between Washington and Tehran spiked in early 2020, for example, the government relocated a significant proportion of Canadian troops in Iraq to Kuwait, while a Ukrainian International Airlines flight was shot down by Iranian air defences hours after Iran lobbed missiles onto military bases used by American troops in Iraq, killing all 176 on board, including 138 with ties to Canada.

This is reflected in the reality that scholarship on Canadian foreign and defence policy has neglected the Middle East.[1] Of the limited academic work on the topic, the largest area of focus has been the Israeli-Palestinian conflict. Other works have studied Canada's role in the many US-led military interventions in the region, in Iraq in 2003,[2] Libya in 2011,[3] Syria since 2011,[4] and the coalition against IS.[5] In addition, a few authors have analysed Canada's response to changes emanating from the Arab uprisings since 2011[6] and Canada's bilateral relationships with Iran,[7] Saudi Arabia,[8] and Turkey.[9] Others, finally, have discussed domestic drivers of Canada's Middle East policies, such as diaspora groups[10] and electoral politics.[11]

Though the Middle East is not a first-order priority, it still matters to Canada. The region features prominently in debates in the media, and various issues – from decisions on whether to participate in US-led military interventions in the region to refugee policy and the repatriation of Canadian extremist travellers – rapidly become controversial political debates. It is in this context that we have prepared this collective book on Canada's policies in the Middle East. It proposes a comprehensive overview of the topic, integrating the key international aspects that often shape Canadian foreign and defence policies in the region with domestic drivers that can also affect them. Trying to balance these international and domestic forces has been the Canadian way, and as the global order is undergoing massive structural changes and the domestic Canadian political landscape is more polarized and uncertain, finding the optimal balance will further challenge subsequent Canadian governments.

Changing Global Order and the Middle East

If al-Qaeda's attack on the United States on 11 September 2001 led to the securitization of Western analysis on the Middle East and increased the American military footprint in the region, the Arab uprisings of 2011 changed the Middle East from within. As millions of mostly young people poured into the streets to call for the downfall of their autocratic regimes, many international relations and comparative politics scholars were baffled. Area specialists, who often base their research findings on empirical and field research, had not predicted such a wave of discontent. While many hoped that the Middle East would find a path of transition to democracy, akin to Eastern Europe or Latin America earlier, the post-Arab uprisings reality has instead included heightened security state structures and the rise of new, and often younger, rulers who have increased repression and stifled dissent. Moreover, state centralization of the economy, high inequality, illiteracy, prevalence of religiosity, and lack of a demonstration effect of a successful Arab democracy all contributed to explanations of authoritarian resilience. As a result, rather than a transition to democracy, autocratic resilience and continued regional insecurity seem more probable in the medium term.

Persistently seeing the region through a security lens has had a great impact on Canadian foreign and defence policy as well. As this volume discusses, it is difficult to avoid important security issues when examining the Middle East, as the region has experienced conflict, failed states, refugee exodus, and radicalization, both after 9/11, since the Arab uprisings, and in most recent years. Predictably then, the region is also the largest importer of weapons in the world, while many countries, from Lebanon to Iraq, are in great need of professionalizing their armed forces. All these regional dynamics put pressure on Canadian foreign and defence policy, often seeping into domestic debates about how to engage in the world.

Moreover, while the Middle East looks increasingly volatile, so does the global order. The rise of populism and illiberal democracies, a global pandemic that has tested international cooperation, a crushing economic downturn that has seen a reversal of globalization, the rise of autocratic China, and an intransigent Trump administration in the United States have all chipped away at the rules-based and liberal edifice of the global order. Despite this instability, Canadian security will continue to depend on international cooperation, multilateralism, and a transparent rules-based order. By our very nature as an exporting middle power, a rules-based order ensures that the most powerful are kept in check – be it the United States, a rising China, or an assertive Russia. Understanding how Canadian foreign and defence policy navigate these international, domestic, and regional forces is why this book is needed.

Canada cannot afford to retreat and ignore the Middle East, yet our foreign and defence policy of years past will be tested by these changes. Conflict in the Middle East rarely stays contained within the region. Civil wars, failed states, and repressive autocracies can spill over and affect Canadian interests. Prior to the COVID-19 pandemic, global migration had reached its highest peak in history, leading to increased demands on Canada to do its share. In addition to refugees and asylum-seekers from the Middle East, Canada's growing quest for global talent will mean that more immigrants will want to leave the Middle East while Canada will want to capitalize on this brain gain. This new pattern of global migration may change domestic conversations on our priorities in the Middle East.

Canadians' transnational ties to the Middle East have also accelerated as migration from the region has increased significantly since the 1990s. These interests and connections to the Middle East are significant, and while they have often been dismissed in our formulation of Canadian foreign and defence policy, this may also change. With Canada home to a growing Middle Eastern diaspora, the influence of these communities upon policy towards the region will likely increase.

The fourteen chapters in this volume explain how Canadian foreign and defence policies in the Middle East have typically tried to balance international priorities with domestic concerns. This book is not meant to cover the gamut of bilateral relationships with each Middle Eastern state; rather, we chose important themes that display the delicate balancing act that Canadian policy in the Middle East has had to perform. Historically and more recently, Canada has played a limited role in the region, as one should realistically expect from a distant mid-sized country, as demonstrated in particular by low bilateral trade numbers. Moreover, when Canada makes important decisions on the Middle East, one dominant variable in its calculus is its relationship with the United

States – and not its direct regional or bilateral interests, as discussed in the chapter by Farzan Sabet. Similarly, as Justin Massie and Marco Munier further explain – in their case in the context of Canada's role in the coalition against IS – Canada's chief interest is to be, and to be seen as, a reliable ally. A middle power, Canada can also selectively choose boutique issues, such as supporting the capacity-building and training of partner regional security services as a way to punch above its weight, as Mike Fleet and Nizar Mohamad explain.

A third element to understand in Canadian policy is geography: much more than its European allies, Canada is mostly shielded from instability in the region. Yet spillover from Middle Eastern conflicts can still affect Canada, as demonstrated in the chapters by Amarnath Amarasingam and Stephanie Carvin on how Canada has dealt with the return of foreign fighters who joined IS and by Nawroos Shibli on how Canada responded to multilateral efforts to settle Syrian refugees. In both cases, Canada's responses were crafted by taking into consideration domestic interests as well as its role as a responsible stakeholder of multilateralism.

Canadian policies in the Middle East have not remained static, constantly adjusting to realities in the region and to evolutions in the domestic balance of electoral power. Prime ministers' decisions at critical junctures have steered policy in specific directions. A hypothetical Prime Minister Stephen Harper in 2003, for example, would likely have agreed to participate in the US-led coalition to invade Iraq, contrary to what Prime Minister Jean Chrétien actually decided, while Prime Minister Justin Trudeau's decision in 2015 to initially accept 25,000 Syrian refugees may not have materialized had the Conservatives remained in power. Moreover, as Nermin Allam notes in her chapter, Canada's response to the electoral success of the Muslim Brotherhood in Egypt was very much shaped by the Harper government's own negative views of political Islam. For his part, Chris Kilford explains in his chapter how Canada has adapted to the growing illiberalism of the Erdogan government in Turkey.

The chapters in this volume also show that there are many common misperceptions about Canada's Middle East policies. The chapters by David Petrasek and Peter Jones, for example, explain how the notion cherished by many Canadians that their country promotes human rights and acts as an honest broker in the region are, at most, only partly true. Similarly, chapters by Jennifer Pedersen and E.J. Karmel demonstrate how Canada's rhetoric on human rights and democracy promotion is unmatched by the reality of its arms sales in the region, especially to Saudi Arabia, and its support of civil society organizations that help uphold undemocratic governments. Frédéric Boily's chapter breaks down another myth, the common view that Conservative governments are far closer to Israel than Liberal ones – with the chapter by Costanza Musu providing more background on the evolution of Canada's approach to the Israeli-Palestinian conflict.

Plan of the Book

In the first part of the book, we look at international factors shaping Canadian foreign and defence policy in the Middle East. Living in the shadow of the United States, the most powerful military and economic power in the world, is a key determinant of Canadian policy. To that end, we begin with Farzan Sabet in chapter 2 as he looks at American influence on Canada's Middle East policy since 2006. He synthesizes the literature on US-Canada relations and on Canadian Middle East policy to conceptualize how the United States influences Canada's regional policies, using two case studies: the campaign against IS and relations with Iran. Canada can support, remain neutral, or oppose American diplomatic initiatives and military interventions in the region, though it rarely chooses the last option. However, the United States is seldom the only factor in Canadian decisions, partly because it rarely applies strong pressure on Canada. Because Canada has few strong security and economic interests in the region, at least four other factors matter: maintenance of a rules-based international order; management of other alliances; bilateral relations with regional states; and electoral coalition and political ideology of the ruling party. Once a decision is made, American pressure can nudge Canada but rarely changes its course entirely.

We then turn to how alliances can shape Canadian foreign and defence policy towards the Middle East. In chapter 3, Justin Massie and Marco Munier explain how and why Canada's military contribution to the Global Coalition against the Islamic State has varied since 2014. What began as a swift but limited contribution to assist Kurdish forces against the startling expansion of the Islamic State under US leadership evolved into a long-term, region-wide, multidimensional mission to defeat the movement. They argue that the politicization of the war during the 2015 federal election as well as alliance considerations principally account for Canada's changing behaviour. They conclude that even though Canada's military contribution has fluctuated, an unshakable concern with preserving Canada's reputation as a reliable ally is observable throughout the conflict.

Indeed, being a reliable ally is a function of Canada's position as a middle power that cannot exercise the kind of hard power that the United States and, to varying extents, some other NATO allies can exercise in the Middle East. In this context, Canada's decision to support capacity building of partner governments has been a way to punch above its weight. As Mike Fleet and Nizar Mohamad discuss in chapter 4, Canada has trained police and security forces of Iraq, Jordan, and the Palestinian Authority. This boutique approach allows Canada to play a valued role while committing limited numbers of Canadian Armed Forces (CAF) personnel. This low-cost, high-return strategy has gained recognition, especially with NATO's 2018 decision to have Canada lead its training centre in Baghdad. But Canada's broader strategic goals remain unclear and dependent on other allies, while its limited engagement could provoke blowback when the CAF appear to be complicit with unpopular governments.

In keeping with the discussion of Canada's role in the coalition against IS, a key issue has been the challenge of Canadians who fought for the terrorist group in Iraq and Syria. As Amarnath Amarasingam and Stephanie Carvin explain in chapter 5, Canada, like many other Western countries, has generally tried to avoid domestic debates on how to repatriate foreign fighters. Yet an immigrant-rich country like Canada must contend with the response of diaspora communities to conflicts that originate in their homelands. While the numbers of Canadian foreign fighters are generally limited, especially when compared to those of some European allies, the fear of their return and their potential proclivity towards radicalization and violence is of great concern and ought to provoke more public debate.

While debates on Canada's role in the fight against IS have been prominent, the decision by the Trudeau government to accept approximately 50,000 Syrian refugees also garnered global attention. As Nawroos Shibli details in chapter 6, Canada's intake was modest when compared to regional countries who have hosted millions of refugees. Nevertheless, the international profile of the Trudeau government's decision to welcome refugees during a time of rising populism and closed doors to immigration was noteworthy. This was in keeping with the Trudeau government's foreign policy that also emphasized humanitarian support instead of a solely military role in addressing the consequences of the Syrian civil war.

Turning a critical lens on Canadian support for civil society organizations (CSOs), E.J. Karmel looks in chapter 7 at how Canada's support for CSOs is often securitized and neoliberalized. Like many Western donors, Canada has invested in CSOs that foster good governance, but this support has often been framed as forms of democratization while devolving responsibility to CSOs instead of governments to deliver policy. Using the case of Jordan, Karmel notes how the royal family pressures many CSOs to dull their political impact and their critique of the ruling order.

There is dwindling space for CSOs to provide needed services and understand local needs when they are increasingly professionalized as they adopt Western lingo and meet highly bureaucratized and demanding reporting requirements. Canada's support for CSOs in Jordan encapsulates this balancing act that Western donors face in delivering development aid in limited democratic political spaces.

How Canada handles these thorny foreign policy issues while remaining a champion of human rights will be a continued challenge. With the rise of illiberal democracies around the globe, some of which are allies like Turkey, Chris Kilford examines in chapter 8 how Canada has navigated these choppy waters. Turkish President Recep Tayyip Erdoğan's increased illiberalism has been years in the making, putting Canada in the uncomfortable position of managing this bilateral relationship with a NATO ally. Between Turkey's growing military footprint throughout the region and the human rights violations of its forces in Kurdish regions in its fight against the PKK, Ottawa's bilateral relationship with Ankara has become increasingly difficult.

While Canada's bilateral ties with Turkey and Egypt have historically been limited, there has been spillover of their domestic turmoil in Canada. As Nermin Allam discusses in chapter 9, the 2011 uprising in Egypt and the subsequent rise and fall of the Muslim Brotherhood had an important impact on Canada's domestic conversation about the role of political Islam. Egypt's Muslim Brotherhood represented one of the few cases where Islamist politics were allowed to compete and win in free elections, yet the framing of this 2012 electoral win was highly politicized by the Harper government. When Islamist politics are discussed in Canadian political debates, it is often framed from the perspective of increased Islamization of Western society and can spiral into Islamophobic discourses, Allam warns.

We then turn to how Canada's foreign and defence policy is often shaped by factors at home. Canada's balancing act of engaging with the world to feel secure at home is evident in tough choices Canadian governments have had to make about the Middle East. Since the 1970s, all governments have claimed that promotion of human rights is a key foreign policy goal. This rhetorical position is so entrenched that it is rarely challenged. Yet even to casual observers, it is obvious that promotion of human rights abroad is contingent on Canada being able to do so in ways that do not undermine other objectives, including trade, security, and relations with allies. David Petrasek explains in chapter 10 that this is perhaps especially true in the Middle East. The result is a muddle. Canada has frequently stated its commitment to promote human rights, but actually putting it into practice in an unstable region where our foreign policy often pursues competing objectives and where Canada can have little impact is, at best, difficult. Nevertheless, Petrasek discerns underlying drivers of Canada's human rights policies in the Middle East.

The challenges inherent to championing human rights in an unstable region of convenient partners has been most evident in Canada's handling of its dispute with Saudi Arabia. In chapter 11, Jennifer Pedersen examines the Trudeau government's approach to arms sales to Saudi Arabia, with a particular focus on the $15 billion contract to supply the kingdom with light armoured vehicles (LAVs). She argues that the government's rhetoric on arms sales did not match its actions. Between 2015 and 2019, the government's handling of the relationship with Saudi Arabia was met with intense criticism from human rights activists, civil society, and some political opponents: why would Canada continue to supply weapons to a country with such an abysmal human rights record? This issue became a tricky foreign policy challenge, particularly as the Trudeau government promoted its feminist foreign policy and respect for human rights.

No other Middle East issue has occupied foreign policy discourse like the Israeli-Palestinian conflict. Here, Canada has long prided itself on playing a helpful role in the search for peace. Its approach has taken many forms, including peacekeeping, facilitating the refugee working group within the Madrid process, and supporting informal dialogue. In chapter 12, Peter Jones identifies and explores three eras of Canadian Middle East peacemaking. He argues that Canada's actions have been tentative, relatively small in scale, and motivated largely by a desire to be seen as a good ally of the United States and other NATO members. Moreover, while Canada's supposed impartiality has been a key element of its acceptability as a peacemaker, it has not been impartial in the outcomes it has sought. The chapter explores meanings of the term "impartial" as they pertain to peacemaking, and develops an analytical framework for the issue.

In chapter 13, Costanza Musu analyses Canada's policy towards the Arab-Israeli conflict. She places Canada's policy towards the Middle East in the context of its broader foreign policy priorities, particularly its relations with the United States and other important allies. The chapter then analyses the instruments at Canada's disposal. Musu sees the result as an essentially contradictory policy. On the one hand, Canada has tried to contribute to the peace process. It has established cordial relations with the Palestinian Authority and strong ties with Israel, while working on increasing its relationships in the broader Middle East. On the other hand, its initiatives are crafted to minimize negative impacts on its far more important relations with the United States. Even accounting for the variations in policies and rhetoric between successive Conservative and Liberal governments, Musu argues that this balancing act remains at the core of Canada's policy and will continue to limit the potential for further Canadian involvement.

Frédéric Boily examines the ideological and non-ideological foundations of Canadian policy towards Israel in chapter 14. Looking at Justin Trudeau and his four predecessors, Boily seeks to draw out Canada's motivations. While the issue is not of primary concern for Canada's major political parties, it differentiates them from each other and reinforces their identity. The chapter discusses the importance of political leaders in determining policy towards Israel by proposing an analytical framework that identifies four distinct ideal-type positions. It then provides a brief historical overview of the positions of Prime Ministers Brian Mulroney, Jean Chrétien, and Paul Martin, followed by a comparison of the positions of the two most recent prime ministers, Stephen Harper and Justin Trudeau.

Finally, in the conclusion, Nathan C. Funk questions whether it might be more useful to understand the Middle East as a study in continuities and constraints. Noting how Canadian defence and foreign policy decisions on the Middle East can sometimes strike an independent tone that is different from its allies, he also pushes us to consider that Canadian Middle East policy is not infinitely malleable, nor are policy choices free of political costs. However, Funk questions if Canada could manifest a larger strategic vision than currently framed. To do so, Canada may need to be more proactive and invest in niche activities such as public and track two diplomacy. As many of the chapters in this volume noted, Canada clearly has a stake in a stable and prosperous Middle East, and Funk suggests that new forms of engagement may be necessary to help the region achieve such a reality.

NOTES

1 Paul Heinbecker and Bessma Momani, *Canada and the Middle East: In Theory and in Practice* (Kitchener-Waterloo: Wilfrid Laurier University Press, 2007).
2 Srdjan Vucetic, "Why Did Canada Sit Out the Iraq War? One Constructivist Analysis," *Canadian Foreign Policy Journal* 13, no. 1 (May 2011): 133–53.
3 Andrew Cooper and Bessma Momani, "The Harper Government's Messaging in the Build-up to the Libyan Intervention: Was Canada Different than Its NATO Allies?," *Canadian Foreign Policy Journal* 20, no. 2 (August 2014): 176–88.
4 Thomas Juneau, "The Civil War in Syria and Canada's Containment Policy," *International Journal* 70, no. 3 (September 2015): 471–88.

5 Stéfanie von Hlatky and Justin Massie, "Ideology, Ballots, and Alliances: Canadian Participation in Multinational Military Operations," *Contemporary Security Policy* 40, no. 1 (2019): 101–15.

6 Marie-Joëlle Zahar, "Navigating Troubled Waters: Canada in the Arab World," in *Elusive Pursuits: Lessons from Canada's Interventions Abroad*, ed. Fen Osler Hampson and Stephen Saideman, 35–58 (Waterloo, ON: CIGI, 2015).

7 Thomas Juneau, "A Story of Failed Re-engagement: Canada and Iran, 2015–18," *Canadian Foreign Policy Journal* 25, no. 1 (2019): 39–53.

8 Thomas Juneau, "A Surprising Spat: The Causes and Consequences of the Saudi-Canadian Dispute," *International Journal* 74, no. 2 (2019): 313–23.

9 Chris Kilford, "The Development and Future of Canada-Turkish Relations," *Canadian Foreign Policy Journal* 22, no. 1 (May 2015): 69–83.

10 Sami Aoun, "Muslim Communities: The Pitfalls of Decision-Making in Canadian Foreign Policy," in *The World in Canada: Diaspora, Demography, and Domestic Politics*, ed. David Carment and David Bercuson, 109–22 (Montreal and Kingston: McGill-Queen's University Press, 2008).

11 Donald Barry, "Canada and the Middle East Today: Electoral Politics and Foreign Policy," *Arab Studies Quarterly* 32, no. 4 (Fall 2010): 191–216.

2 Sleeping beside the Elephant: The United States in Canada's Middle East Policy[1]

FARZAN SABET

This chapter looks at American influence on Canada's Middle East policy since 2006. It synthesizes the literature on US-Canada relations and Canada's Middle East foreign policy to conceptualize how the United States influences Canadian policy in the region using two case studies: the campaign against the so-called Islamic State (IS) and the Iran nuclear deal. The chapter finds that the United States often shapes the context of Canadian regional policy as a driver of diplomatic initiatives and military interventions in the region. Canada can support, remain neutral, or oppose US policy. However, the United States is seldom the decisive factor in Canadian decisions on the Middle East, partly because it chooses not to apply strong pressure on Canada. Because Canada has few strong economic and security interests in the region, at least four other factors usually play a larger or equal role in shaping its decision-making: maintenance of a rules-based international order; alliance management; bilateral relations with regional states; and the ruling party's electoral coalition and political ideology. Once a decision is made, US pressure can nudge Canada but rarely change its course entirely. US influence on Canada's Middle East policy is explored here through interviews with a half-dozen current and former Canadian government officials and experts, as well as content analysis of documents, media articles, and the academic and policy literature.

Most scholars of Canadian foreign policy agree that it was highly consistent during the Cold War.[2] The Canadian government under Prime Minister William Lyon Mackenzie King (1935–48) embraced a "functional principle," whereby Canada could maximize its global impact by engaging on issues in which it already possessed the greatest expertise and was an active participant.[3] Canada helped to create a number of international institutions during this period, including the United Nations, North Atlantic Treaty Organization, and Bretton Woods system.

Canada's global engagements, almost always conducted multilaterally and spanning a wide range of issues, included the establishment of the first UN peacekeeping force in the military arena; helping defuse the Suez Crisis in the diplomatic domain; pursuing open global trade and investment regimes in the economic realm; and accepting large numbers of immigrants and refugees, promoting rights, and providing aid to impoverished nations in the humanitarian, human rights, and development spheres.

Comparing Liberal and Conservative Policies in the Middle East

The Canadian foreign policy consensus, implemented by successive Liberal and Progressive Conservative governments, began to decay with the end of the Cold War. This led to a transformation of Canadian foreign policy that started becoming apparent under Liberal Prime Minister Paul Martin (2003–6) and culminated with the paradigm shift that accompanied the election of Conservative Prime Minister Stephen Harper (2006–15).

Scholars have assigned several attributes to Harper's foreign policy: a more selective approach to international organizations and multilateralism; a larger focus on economic diplomacy and the linkage of foreign aid to this diplomacy; a greater willingness to deploy Canadian troops abroad in combat missions as a symbol of Canadian martial prowess and national pride; and a move away from a neutral "honest broker" diplomacy towards a more explicitly ideological "megaphone diplomacy."[4] Marcin Gabryś and Tomasz Soroka frame this as Canada's move away from a "middle power" towards a "selective power," defined as an issue-structured, highly selective and result-oriented approach to international relations based on the primacy of effectiveness and an economic cost-benefit calculation. This has entailed, among other things, a departure from traditional multilateralism and placed more weight on unilateralism and autonomous actions in specific states and regions.[5]

While this framework allows little variation based on the characteristics of the ruling party, I argue that there are important distinctions between Liberal and Conservative foreign policies, especially related to the Middle East. The gap between the two parties is one of both substance and tone. The Trudeau Liberals' 2015 slogan, "Canada is back," was meant to create a contrast with the Harper Conservatives by signalling Canada's return to its supposed traditional role as a multilateralist "honest broker" willing to engage like-minded Western allies as well as less compatible non-Western adversaries.[6] But the idea, sometimes raised by critics, that the Harper Conservatives had abandoned multilateral diplomacy is misplaced. It is more accurate to say that their foreign policy engaged in a selective multilateralism that prioritized cooperation on Canada's economic interests and collaboration with like-minded Western allies. However, this meant a stance, ranging from neglect to hostility, towards certain international organizations. On the other hand, the Harper Conservatives did largely abandon "honest broker" diplomacy. They instead promoted what some call "megaphone diplomacy," emphasizing a foreign policy said to centre on the values of "freedom, democracy, human rights and the rule of law."[7] Nowhere has this been more marked than in the Middle East, where the Harper Conservatives further embraced Israel and cut ties with Iran.

But even this embrace of Israel was not unreserved. Canada remained steadfast to much of the Western consensus on the Israeli-Palestinian conflict, like opposition to Israeli settlement policies in the West Bank. And in places where Canada has more economic and security interests, the Harper Conservatives' early boldness was tempered by experience, such as ties with China.[8] Any change to Canada's post-1991 foreign policy thus also reflects broader transformations of the international system and American power, and Liberal and Conservative policies remain constrained by Canada's economic and security interests (see the Musu and Boily chapters in this volume). This still leaves room for each party's idiosyncrasies to express themselves in foreign policy. For example, John Ibbitson has focused on the unique nature of the Harper Conservatives' electoral coalition. This points to each party's diverging economic, geographic, and demographic constituencies, and the way their respective material interests and ideology differ on foreign policy.[9] Therefore, where Canada's hard interests are limited, idiosyncrasies of a ruling party, linked to its coalition and ideology, can exercise more pull in foreign policy, with the Middle East being a prime example.

Canadian Foreign and Defence Policy under the Shadow of the United States

Before diving into Canadian Middle East policy, it is worth understanding how the United States factors into Canadian foreign policy more generally. Brian Bow and Adam Chapnick organize the literature on this topic around three main debates. First, should Canada and the United States be considered together as paired components of a distinctive North American continental relationship, or as complementary but still individual contributors to a wider global community? Second, should the US-Canada relationship be defined as a partnership between independent equals, mutually constrained interdependence, or a strict hierarchy?

Finally, to what degree has the relationship been characterized by cooperation versus conflict?[10]

Scholars emphasize three events that shaped current US-Canada relations. Denis Stairs has argued that Canadian territory lessened in significance for US strategic defence against the Soviet Union after the early 1960s and fell further with the end of the Cold War. This was not unique to Canada, but part of a pattern of decreased importance of allies for the United States after it was left standing as the world's sole superpower.[11] The terrorist attacks of 11 September 2001 and the resulting US-led global war on terrorism may have renewed the old strategic interdependence of the early Cold War, but the bilateral tensions of the 2000s suggest the effects were limited. The end of the Cold War therefore inaugurated strategic divergence, while 9/11 facilitated re-convergence where there is transatlantic consensus on common threats like militant political Islam as well as challenges posed by traditional adversaries like Russia and new ones like China. The third event, the implementation of the North American Free Trade Agreement (NAFTA) in 1994, brought Canada and the United States even closer.

With this basic history in mind, the United States and Canada can be viewed as being in a relationship of "asymmetrical interdependence," with deep economic and social ties, that establishes the basic power dynamic between them. The leverage each side wields in bilateral bargaining differs widely, depending on the issue. Moreover, the relationship is characterized by a pattern of conflict and cooperation that moves between crisis and correction, and neither side has shown much interest in reciprocal concessions that would unlock the intensive cooperation seen during the early Cold War.[12] Each has its own leverage, deriving from a range of factors such as economic interdependence and legal and institutional constraints.[13] Thus, in studying the US factor in Canadian Middle East policy, we must tease out just how Canada exercises its limited autonomy in this asymmetrical interdependence.

Canada has no strong economic and security interests in the Middle East, nor a high capacity to exert influence there. For these and other reasons, the United States seldom applies strong direct pressure on Canada over Middle East policy. Yet it still exerts enormous clout, mainly through two mechanisms. First, the United States can shape Canadian Middle East policy through its role as the historically main extra-regional actor driving diplomatic initiatives and military interventions in the region. Other states must often choose to support, remain neutral, or oppose American policies in the region. Canada usually accedes to US initiatives and interventions. In some cases, such as the decision by the Chrétien Liberals not to join the invasion of Iraq in 2003, it appears to remain neutral. Canada rarely strongly publicly opposes American policies. As this study reveals, however, while the United States shapes the environment for Canadian Middle East policy, it is rarely the primary factor behind the decision the Canadian government makes. As noted above, and explored in greater depth in the next section, usually a combination of other factors play the primary role, and US factor is secondary.

Second, the deeply intertwined geographies, societies, economies, security, and culture(s) of North America in the context of this asymmetrical interdependence allow the United States to exert other forms of indirect influence on Canadian Middle East policy. Strong pressure on Canada in priority areas can spill over into regional policy. For example, after 9/11 the United States pressed Canada to adopt more forceful measures on counterterrorism, intelligence-sharing, border security, and customs and immigration, in line with new American standards and expectations, with some consequences for its approach to the Middle East and its peoples.[14] One senior Canadian official closely involved in immigration and refugee policy in the late 2000s noted that while he and his colleagues avoided using the term "harmonization," they did engage in close "cooperation" with the United States at the bureaucratic, if not political, level.[15] US secondary and extraterritorial sanctions also limit the Canadian government's ability to deepen economic ties with sanctioned jurisdictions. While Canadian governments are theoretically free to set their own bilateral economic relations, American sanctions affect the risk calculation of Canadian private companies by presenting them with the choice of doing business with the massive US economy or smaller sanctioned jurisdictions. This can scare away Canadian companies from doing business with sanctioned jurisdictions such as Iran and Syria, denying the government a key tool of economic statecraft. A final example of this indirect mechanism of US influence on Canadian Middle East policy is the diffusion of laws, policies, and concepts through transnational policy and lobbying networks.

This last example hints at broader US-Canada political and cultural ties and cross-national policy convergence. Put simply, like-minded governments in the United States and Canada are more likely to agree and cooperate on policies than non-like-minded governments. Although party politics in the United States and Canada cannot be precisely equated, broad analogies between the left-liberalism and right-conservatism can be drawn. The left and right in Canada, based on their electoral coalitions and political ideologies, fall on different sides of the spectrum on a wide range of policy and stylistic issues. Two prominent examples of this divide in foreign policy in Canada are multilateralism and diplomatic style. On the former, Liberals prefer broad multilateralism versus Conservatives' selective multilateralism. On diplomatic style, while Liberals generally prefer "honest broker" diplomacy versus Conservatives' megaphone diplomacy, the parties can selectively apply the opposite style, depending on the issue. The distinction between their respective foreign and defence policy paradigms are not always stark and can often be one of degree or tone. The debate over the Kyoto Protocol provides a good example. The Chrétien and Martin Liberals supported the protocol but did relatively little to implement it. The Harper Conservatives withdrew from it with great fanfare. While this represented a symbolically significant divergence between the parties, the substantive difference is debatable.[16] Such left-right divides can, again generally speaking, be projected onto American politics. The Democratic and Liberal parties have shown comparable preferences for multilateralism and "honest broker" diplomacy. In contrast, the Republican and Conservative parties have shown a proclivity towards more selective multilateralism and megaphone diplomacy that, in the case of the Middle East, villainizes anti-Western authoritarian regimes and militant political Islam. It therefore stands to reason that when like-minded governments are in power in the United States and Canada, they are more likely to agree and cooperate on Middle East policy. We can expect the following pattern in US-Canada relations based on this framework: Chrétien-Martin Liberal / Bush Republican divergence (2000–6); Harper Conservative / Bush Republican convergence (2006–9); Harper Conservative/Obama Democratic divergence (2009–15); Trudeau Liberal / Obama Democratic convergence (2015–17); and Trudeau Liberal / Trump Republican divergence (2017–21). The limited but interesting evidence to support this notion is explored in the final section. In the next section, we first incorporate insights from the academic and policy literature on Canadian Middle East policy into our framework.

Canadian Foreign and Defence Policy in the Middle East

The post–Cold War Canadian foreign policy consensus decay and partisan polarization has spilled over into Middle East policy. Since Prime Minister Pierre Elliott Trudeau (1968–79 and 1980–4), successive governments have sought to advance Canadian interests in the region through the expansion of diplomatic representation and trade relations.[17] In more recent years, the events of 9/11, and the US military interventionism that followed, the election of the Harper Conservatives, and Arab uprisings and civil wars since 2010 have been critical junctures that heralded changes to Canadian Middle East policy. Yet Canadian interests in the region remain limited. According to Thomas Juneau, despite numerous conflicts, Canadian security is not directly affected by regional developments.[18] Bessma Momani and Agata Antkiewicz have argued that while Canadian business activity in the Middle East has produced worthwhile economic benefits, "Canada–Middle East economic relations have clearly not been a top priority for Canada and are never going to be under any reasonable scenario."[19] Canada does not import significant amounts of oil, nor has it been the beneficiary of large arms and investment deals to the same degree as other Western states.

One former senior Canadian official with extensive experience in the region went so far as to say that no Canadian government had ever declared the Middle East a foreign policy priority. However, he also noted that while major disruptions to regional energy exports might not affect Canada directly, they would affect Canadian partners in Western Europe and East Asia, which in turn could have important economic and security knock-on effects for Canada.[20] Costanza Musu has also highlighted how the region can be of importance to Canada: "The region matters because of its potential impact on political and social instability, the uncontrolled migration flows generated by the scarcity of jobs and by economic underdevelopment, the presence of vast energy resources, the possibility that countries in the area might prove to be a fertile breeding ground for terrorism, and the unresolved Arab-Israeli conflict, which is a constant source of tension and instability."[21]

This absence of direct threats from the Middle East and of major economic interests means that poor decisions are unlikely to impose major costs on Canada. And while the United States can shape Canadian choices in the region,[22] it rarely chooses to impose strong and direct pressure over Canada's Middle East policy, meaning that the US factor plays a limited role in Canadian decision-making on specific issues. This gives Canadian governments a considerable margin of manoeuvre in regional policy and increases the importance of other factors in determining the course of Canadian Middle East policy: maintenance of a rules-based international order; alliance management; bilateral relations with regional states, particularly the special relationship with Israel; and the ruling party's electoral coalition and political ideology.

While the first three factors are self-explanatory, the last requires elaboration. The Israeli-Palestinian conflict is a good example of how a party's electoral coalitions and political ideology can shape policy (see also the chapters by Boily and Musu). Canada has historically had a strong relationship with Israel, nourished by Canadians' sympathy for the Jewish people's tragedy in the Holocaust, and by the perception of Israel as an outpost of Western civilization surrounded by hostile non-Western and illiberal actors. This close relationship has been tempered by disagreements, particularly surrounding Palestine. For example, Canada has consistently opposed Israeli settlement construction in Palestine and supported a two-state solution to the conflict. Until the 2000s, Canada's voting record on the Israeli-Palestinian peace process at the United Nations was guided by a desire to have a fair and balanced approach, highlighting the legitimacy of Israel's security needs, while supporting Palestinian aspirations for national self-determination. However, a shift away from Canada's prior UN voting pattern towards more open support for Israel was already underway by 2004 under the Martin Liberals (2003–6). Under the Harper Conservatives, support for Israel surged to include more diplomatic initiatives and stronger public rhetoric. Scholars' explanations emphasize Conservatives' desire to woo historically liberal Canadian Jews and conservative Evangelicals.[23] These communities constitute better organized voting blocs, in contrast to, for example, Canadian Arabs, who are far less organized around the Palestinian cause. The political ideology of the Harper Conservatives, in part a function of Stephen Harper's strong personal support for Israel, was also a key driver of Canadian foreign policy becoming more pro-Israel.[24] With this background in mind, how the US factor operates in practice is illustrated with two case studies in the next section. Beyond shaping the context of Canadian policy, the United States rarely plays a primary role in the choices Canadian decision-makers make on Middle East policy, often because Washington chooses not to exert strong direct pressure on Canada. However, in combination with other, more important factors, the US–Canada relationship can nudge Canadian regional policy in one direction or another.

The US Factor in Canadian Middle East Policy

Canadian Participation in US Military Interventions in the Middle East since 9/11

Since 9/11, Canada has faced the choice to join at least four US-led military interventions in the greater Middle East and North Africa, including the Afghanistan War (2001–21); the Iraq War (2003–11); the campaign against the regime of Muammar Qaddafi in Libya (2011); and the campaign against the Islamic State (2014–present). Canada has overtly participated in all these interventions except the Iraq War. The instances in which Canada chose to participate, and those in which it did not, reveal Canada's calculus and how the United States factors in.[25] When Canada joined a US-led intervention, there was a NATO, UN, or international mandate. Canada's participation in the Afghanistan War and Libya intervention were under NATO, while the intervention in Iraq and Syria against the Islamic State is centred on a US-led Global Coalition against the Islamic State, which includes an even broader grouping of states (see the chapter by Massie and Munier). Although these conflicts only indirectly implicate Canadian security, there were a range of reasons for Liberal and Conservative governments to join. The two interrelated reasons that consistently arose across all three conflicts in interviews and secondary sources was the desire of Canadian governments to uphold a rules-based international order and to be perceived as a member in good standing by like-minded allies.[26] To the extent the United States is at the centre of the contemporary international order, NATO, and the Global Coalition, it certainly shaped the context for Canadian interventions. But upholding international order and managing alliances was framed as providing a range of indirect security and non-security benefits for Canada, not simply placating the United States. Bilateral relations with regional states and their stability were also a factor in these interventions, but not a primary one.

Beyond these commonalities, the motivation for participation differs somewhat between Conservatives and Liberals. Electoral coalitions did not appear to be a strong factor, but party ideology may have been. The Harper Conservatives seemed more motivated by a desire to demonstrate Canadian martial prowess and fight militant political Islam and anti-Western authoritarian regimes,[27] while Trudeau Liberals have been less motivated by these factors. Canada's participation in the Coalition against the Islamic State since 2014 is a good example of the difference that ideology can make, but also how American influence makes itself felt. The Harper Conservatives eagerly joined the Coalition against the Islamic State. The centrepiece of the Canadian contribution was six CF-18 Hornet fighter aircraft deployed in a combat role, as well as support aircraft and a train, advise, and assist mission. Justin Trudeau in his 2015 Canadian electoral platform promised to end Canada's air combat role and did so once in power.[28] As mentioned above, Canada's security interests were only indirectly implicated in the campaign against the Islamic State, and its contribution was not make-or-break for the coalition. There also does not appear to have been great pressure on Canada to join from regional states, or groundswell during the election campaign for Canada to end its combat role in Iraq and Syria. The decision by the Trudeau Liberals to end the air combat mission seems to have been influenced instead by ideology, specifically the desire to cast themselves in the supposedly traditional mantle of Canadian diplomacy and peace-keeping, rather than war fighting, to differentiate themselves from the Harper Conservatives.

However, as noted in the previous section, the difference that ideology makes in Canadian policy can often be one of degree. While the

Trudeau Liberals ended the air combat role in Iraq and Syria, they maintained or expanded Canada's military presence in other ways. Canada increased its contribution of military personnel, including the deployment of troops along the front lines to mark targets and call in airstrikes; continued the presence of support aircraft for surveillance and refuelling allied planes; furnished a more robust train, advise, and assist mission to local partners (see the chapter by Fleet and Mohamad); bolstered the presence of medical personnel to support Canadian troops and their allies and to advise Iraqi security forces; and boosted the provision of military supplies to Kurdish Peshmerga in northern Iraq. This increased military effort was combined with a more vigorous diplomatic presence in the region and over $1.1 billion in humanitarian and development aid over three years. This included funds for water, food, shelter, health care, hygiene and sanitation, protection and education, and financial and capacity-building support to refugee-hosting countries in the region and Europe to address refugees' basic needs, maintain and repair infrastructure, promote employment and economic growth, and foster good governance.[29] The Trudeau Liberals' approach to the campaign against the Islamic State has thus been different from their predecessors' but continues to have a strong military component. One interviewee indicated that American displeasure likely pushed Canada to maintain a military role in the campaign. Concerns may have been that Canadian "defection" would reduce its perceived reliability as an international security partner and lead other smaller actors to leave the coalition.[30] The Trudeau Liberals thus kept their election promise by ending the air combat mission but adapted to US displeasure through a compensatory strategy that increased counterterrorism cooperation, training, and relief aid. The United States thus shaped the context of the Canadian intervention, but US pressure was not the primary factor inducing Canada to join the campaign against the Islamic State or end its air combat role. However, once the Trudeau Liberals made their decision, US pressure nudged them to adopt a compensatory strategy.

Another important case of possible Liberal-Conservative divergence over military intervention in the region is the decision by the Chrétien Liberals not to join the invasion of Iraq in 2003, despite strong American pressure. The official reason given by Prime Minister Jean Chrétien focused on the lack of a UN mandate for the invasion.[31] Stephen Harper, leader of the Opposition and of the Canadian Alliance party at the time, called for Canada to join the invasion to advance freedom and non-proliferation of WMD. This divergence could be explained by ideology taking precedence over the US factor, but this interpretation has shortcomings. For example, in 1998 the Chrétien Liberals supported an

Anglo-American bombing campaign against Iraq without explicit backing from the UN Security Council. A more recent study suggests that electoral politics may have also been at play: the Chrétien Liberals did not want to antagonize the historically anti-war Québécois in the lead-up to the provincial elections there in April 2003. The Québécois, a key Liberal constituency, were the most opposed to war, while Albertans, a key Alliance/Conservative base, were most in favour.[32] Finally, a former senior Canadian official with knowledge of these matters indicated there was a lack of consensus on the veracity of US claims in the internal debates of the Chrétien government, and thus on whether there were grounds for military action.[33] It thus appears that the decision by the Chrétien Liberals not to publicly support the Iraq War was motivated by a mix of uncertainty about the validity of American justifications for the war, ideology, and the Liberal party's electoral coalition.

However, three caveats should be kept in mind. First, while the Liberals did not want to be publicly associated with the war for lack of political cover, it was later revealed that they offered covert and token support for the invasion and occupation.[34] One former senior Canadian official well versed on this issue even claimed that Canada ended up having one of the largest unofficial contingent of troops in the coalition through secondments.[35] Second, we must consider that had the Harper-led Alliance party been in power in 2003 and forced to hold together a broader coalition, it may have taken a similar position to the Liberals. Finally, we should not completely dismiss the US factor. Months before the war, Canada committed a relatively large military contingent to the Afghanistan War. This may have been calculated as a show of support for the United States and to tie down military assets in the hope of dampening American displeasure with Canada's absence from Iraq.

The US Factor in Canada-Iran Relations since 2006

Canada-Iran relations since 2006 have had their own dynamics, at once distinct but also invariably tied up with the US context. One factor shaping Canada's Iran policy has been the perceived challenge posed by the Islamic Republic to Middle East peace and security through nuclear proliferation and support for militant non-state actors against local and extra-regional states. This may pose little direct threat to Canada but occupies government bandwidth as a result of domestic lobbying by interest groups, and diplomatic pressure from friendly regional states like Israel and the Arab monarchies of the Persian Gulf. A second factor shaping Canada's Iran policy is the Iranian diaspora in Canada. The Islamic Republic's treatment of Iranian-Canadians, including their arrest, torture, and killing on Iranian soil, as well as the Iranian government's actions inside Canada, have been irritants in Canada-Iran relations since the 2000s. Iranian-Canadians' views of their former homeland have been another factor, particularly the divide between those who support and those who oppose engagement with the Islamic Republic. Iranian-Canadians have not been a force uniformly in favour or against improvement of ties with the Islamic Republic but can be part of Liberal or Conservative electoral coalitions.[36] In this context, the United States plays a similar role in Canada-Iran relations, as in the first case study above. Similar dynamics are also at play in the Harper Conservatives' decision to cut diplomatic relations with Iran in 2012 and the Canadian government's subsequent stance towards the Iran nuclear negotiations and the deal that followed in 2015.

The decision by the Harper Conservatives to cut ties with the Islamic Republic in 2012, the subsequent campaign pledge by the Trudeau Liberals to restore ties, and their failure to do so have been well covered in the secondary literature and news media. The Harper Conservatives' decision to cut relations was timed to coincide with the coming into force of the Justice for Victims of Terrorism Act (JVTA). This law, along with changes to the State Immunity Act, allows victims of terrorism to sue perpetrators and their listed state backers for loss or damage caused by a terrorist act committed anywhere in the world since 1985. The immediate official reason for severing ties was a fear of the state-sponsored takeover of the Canadian embassy in Tehran due to tensions over the JVTA. It was a reasonable concern, given the violent takeover of the British embassy in Tehran a year earlier, and a longer history of threats to diplomatic facilities in Iran going back to 1979. However, this action also came against the backdrop of fluctuating Canada-Iran bilateral relations since the mid-1990s, the Harper Conservatives' animus towards militant political Islam and anti-Western authoritarian regimes, the special relationship with Israel, and budding ties with the Persian Gulf Arab monarchies.

Interestingly, according to at least one senior Canadian government official working on Canada-Iran relations at the time, the Obama administration expressed its concerns to the Canadian government. The embassy in Tehran was an important conduit of information for the US government during the Iran nuclear negotiations, because there was no American diplomatic presence on the ground.[37] But whatever US pressure the Canadian government may have felt, it does not appear to have changed its chosen course of action. Instead, embassy security, bilateral relations with Iran and regional states, as well as their election coalition and party ideology appear to have been more important factors.

The US factor also seems not to have been a major one in the Trudeau Liberals' campaign pledge to restore ties with Iran. Instead, party ideology – in this case the notion of returning to so-called traditional Canadian foreign policy values – and intra-party electoral competition with the Harper Conservatives appear to have been larger considerations. By 2018, however, complications created by the JVTA, continuing bilateral tensions over consular issues, lack of prioritization of this issue by both sides, and a split in the Liberal Party over the issue convinced the Trudeau government to suspend its efforts to restore ties.[38] Iran's shooting down of Ukraine International Airlines Flight 752 in January 2020, with 138 passengers headed to Canada and 63 Canadians onboard, has created a new layer of complication in bilateral ties.[39]

Similarly, while the United States, as a leading party in the Iran nuclear negotiations, shaped the context of Canadian policy towards the talks and subsequent Joint Comprehensive Plan of Action (JCPOA), agreed to in 2015, it did not determine the Canadian position. According to a senior Canadian official with direct knowledge of the issue, the efficacy of the JCPOA, and its implications for Israeli and regional security, were larger considerations for Harper Conservatives and Trudeau Liberals. The official said that when the JCPOA was signed, Canadian officials expressed concerns about parts of the deal that would expire and that the Obama administration was exaggerating its non-nuclear benefits. However, the official said the Canadian government was satisfied with the deal because it generally upheld a rules-based international order and was beneficial for regional security. President Donald Trump's later withdrawal from the JCPOA in 2018 was therefore viewed with alarm in Ottawa. Nevertheless, the Trudeau Liberals continue to support the deal, and Canada is a leading sponsor of International Atomic Energy Agency inspections of Iranian facilities, which allow for greater transparency and verification of its nuclear program.[40] The interviewee expressed concern that this access would be lost. When asked whether the Canadian government might have responded differently to the Trump withdrawal if Conservatives were in power, the official said this could have created a "different calculus."[41]

The United States has shaped the context of Canada-Iran relations in at least two other important ways. First, Canadian legislation like the JVTA, which some view as a poison pill against the restoration of Canada-Iran relations deliberately inserted by the Harper Conservatives, is often inspired by similar legislation in the United States or imported into Canada by transnational policy and lobbying networks.[42] Second, American extraterritorial economic sanctions – given the high level of US-Canada economic integration and that sanctions deter business with

Iran globally – also decrease economic incentives for Canadian business and government to re-engage with Iran.[43] A former senior Canadian official emphasized that the downturn in bilateral ties, combined with sanctions, had taken Iran from being one of Canada's top regional trading partners to among the bottom.

Conclusion

This chapter has yielded several insights on the US factor in Canadian Middle East policy. American diplomatic initiatives, such as the Iran nuclear negotiations, and military interventions, such as the campaign against the Islamic State, often create the policy environment to which Canada responds. Canada usually supports these initiatives and interventions, even if its material contribution is limited, and only sometimes does not, as with the 2003 Iraq War. The United States can also influence Canadian legislation by its example and through transnational networks. Moreover, the high level of US-Canada economic integration and the long arm of US extraterritorial sanctions limit opportunities for Canada to deepen relations with US-sanctioned jurisdictions in the Middle East such as Iran and Syria, should it want to. However, once it has shaped the context, the United States is seldom the primary factor shaping Canadian Middle East policy, nor does it typically exercise strong pressure on Canadian governments to fall into line, because it often does not care to do so. Furthermore, Canada lacks strong economic and security interests in the region. This gives it relative autonomy and raises the importance of other factors in policymaking, including upholding a rules-based international order; alliance management; bilateral relations with regional states; and the ruling party's coalition and ideology.

That said, US pressure can nudge Canadian governments once a decision is made. In the Iraq War context, pressure from the Bush administration may have pushed Canada to offer discrete and token support for the war and to boost its involvement in the Afghanistan War. In the campaign against the Islamic State, the displeasure of the Obama administration may have been a factor that led the Canadian government to increase its military role and provision of relief aid, even as the Trudeau Liberals kept their campaign pledge of withdrawing Canada's fighter aircraft. Finally, cross-national ideological congruence may indicate an increased likelihood of Canadian governments supporting American policies. That is, Liberal governments are more likely to support Democratic policies, and Conservative governments Republican ones. Several examples, including two counterfactual scenarios, provide limited evidence for this. First, indicators suggest that had the Harper Conservatives been in power at the outset of the Iraq War, they may have publicly supported the Bush administration and sent military forces. Second, the Conservatives did not prioritize the Obama administration's concerns about Canada cutting ties with Iran over their own security concerns and ideological proclivity to do so. Third, the Trudeau Liberals have not ceased support for the JCPOA since the Trump administration withdrew from the deal in May 2018. However, had the Conservatives been in power when Trump withdrew, at least one well-placed interviewee suggests Canadian policy may have differed. These findings open avenues for further research into Canadian Middle East policy, the US-Canada asymmetrical interdependence, and how Canada's exercise of power on the global stage continues to evolve under a range of new and old conditions.

NOTES

1 This chapter is directly based on a project headed by Grégoire Mallard that received funding from the European Research Council under the European Union's Horizon 2020 research and innovation programme (Grant Agreement PROSANCT, "Bombs, Banks and Sanctions" Project 716216). The author thanks all the interviewees who participated in the research.

2 John Ibbitson, *The Big Break: The Conservative Transformation of Canada's Foreign Policy* (Waterloo, ON: Centre for International Governance and Innovation, 2014), 6, www.cigionline.org/sites/default/files/cigi_paper_29.pdf.

3 Duane Bratt, "Stephen Harper and the Transformation of Canadian Foreign Policy," in *Europa World Online* (Abingdon, UK: Routledge, 2017), s. 490.

4 Bratt, "Stephen Harper," 488–9.

5 Marcin Gabryś and Tomasz Soroka, *Canada as a Selective Power: Canada's Role and International Position after 1989* (Kraków: Archeobooks, 2017), 14.

6 Daryl Copeland, "'Canada's Back': Can the Trudeau Government Resuscitate Canadian Diplomacy?," *Canadian Foreign Policy Journal* 24, no. 2 (2018): 243–52.

7 Gabryś and Soroka, *Canada as a Selective Power*, 149.

8 Ibbitson, *Big Break*.

9 Ibbitson, *Big Break*, 7–8.

10 Brian Bow and Adam Chapnick, "Teaching Canada-US Relations: Three Great Debates," *International Journal* 71, no. 2 (2016): 293.

11 Denis Stairs, "Myths, Morals and Reality in Canadian Foreign Policy," *International Journal* 58, no. 2 (2003): 239–56.

12 Bow and Chapnick, "Teaching Canada-US Relations," 308.

13 Bow and Chapnick, "Teaching Canada-US Relations," 304–5.

14 Costanza Musu, "Canada and the MENA Region: The Foreign Policy of a Middle Power," *Canadian Foreign Policy Journal* 18, no. 1 (2012): 71.

15 Senior Canadian official 02, interviewed by Farzan Sabet on Skype, 20 August 2019.

16 Ibbitson, *Big Break*, 12; Bratt, "Stephen Harper," 489.

17 Musu, "Canada and the MENA Region," 70.

18 Thomas Juneau, *Canada and the Middle East* (Calgary: Canadian Global Affairs Institute, 2016), 1–5, https://www.cgai.ca/canada_and_the_middle _east.

19 Bessma Momani and Agata Antkiewicz, "Canada's Economic Interests in the Middle East," in *Canada and the Middle East: In Theory and Practice*, ed. Paul Heinbecker and Bessma Momani, 161–84 (Waterloo, ON: Wilfrid Laurier University Press, 2007).

20 Ex-senior Canadian foreign policy official 01, interviewed by Farzan Sabet in Toronto, Canada, 20 June 2019.

21 Musu, "Canada and the MENA Region," 65.

22 Musu, "Canada and the MENA Region," 70; Marie-Joëlle Zahar, "Talking One Talk, Walking Another: Norm Entrepreneurship and Canada's Foreign Policy in the Middle East," in *Canada and the Middle East: In Theory and Practice*, ed. Paul Heinbecker and Bessma Momani, 45–72 (Waterloo, ON: Wilfrid Laurier University Press, 2007).

23 Musu, "Canada and the MENA Region": Donald Barry, "Canada and the Middle East Today: Electoral Politics and Foreign Policy," *Arab Studies Quarterly* 32, no. 4 (2010): 191–217; Jonathan Malloy, "Bush/Harper? Canadian and American Evangelical Politics Compared," *American Review of Canadian Studies* 39, no. 4 (2009): 352–63.

24 Jordan Michael Smith, "Reinventing Canada: Stephen Harper's Conservative Revolution," *World Affairs* 174, no. 6 (2012): 21–8.

25 This part of the analysis is based on interviews with three current and former senior Canadian officials with direct knowledge of and involvement in government decision-making in one or more of these interventions, as well as other primary and secondary sources.

26 Ex-senior Canadian foreign policy official 01; and senior Canadian official 02.

27 Ibbitson, *Big Break*, 10; Roland Paris, "Are Canadians Still Liberal Internationalists? Foreign Policy and Public Opinion in the Harper Era," *International Journal* 69, no. 3 (2014): 274–307.

28 The Current, "Trudeau Pulls Jets Out from Coalition against ISIS to Mixed reviews," CBC, 12 November 2015, https://www.cbc.ca/radio/thecurrent /the-current-for-october-23–2015–1.3285264/trudeau-pulls-jets-out-from -coalition-against-isis-to-mixed-reviews-1.3285292.

29 Daniel Leblanc, Michelle Zilio, and Laura Stone, "Canada's Changing Role in the Fight against the Islamic State," *Globe and Mail*, 12 November 2017, https://www.theglobeandmail.com/news/canadas-changing-role -in-the-fight-against-islamicstate/article28659664/.

30 Senior Canadian official 02.

31 Srdjan Vucetic, "Why Did Canada Sit Out of the Iraq War? One Constructivist Analysis," *Canadian Foreign Policy Journal* 13, no. 1 (2006): 133–53.

32 Joseph Fiorino, "Why Canada Really Didn't Go to Iraq in 2003," NATO Association of Canada, 9 June 2015, natoassociation.ca/why-canada-really-didnt-go-to-iraq-in-2003/.

33 Ex-senior Canadian foreign policy official 01.

34 Greg Weston, "Canada Offered to Aid Iraq Invasion: WikiLeaks," CBC News, 16 May 2011, www.cbc.ca/news/politics/weston-canada-offered-to-aid-iraq-invasion-wikileaks-1.1062501.

35 Ex-senior Canadian foreign policy official 01.

36 Thomas Juneau, "A Story of Failed Re-engagement: Canada and Iran, 2015–18," *Canadian Foreign Policy Journal* 25, no. 1 (2019): 39–53.

37 Ex-senior Canadian foreign policy official 01.

38 Juneau, "Story of Failed Re-engagement."

39 Staff, "Timeline: Canada's Diplomatic Relationship with Iran," Canadian Press, 9 January 2020, https://globalnews.ca/news/6389129/timeline-canada-iran-relationship/; Justin Trudeau, "Canadian Report Blames Iranian Recklessness for Shoot-Down of Ukraine International Airlines Flight 752," 24 June 2021, https://pm.gc.ca/en/news/statements/2021/06/24/canadian-report-blames-iranian-recklessness-shoot-down-ukraine.

40 Adam Austen, "Canada Supports Diplomatic Efforts Established for Iran to Return to Full Implementation of Joint Comprehensive Plan of Action," Global Affairs Canada, 14 January 2020, https://www.canada.ca/en/global-affairs/news/2020/01/canada-supports-diplomatic-efforts-established-for-iran-to-return-to-full-implementation-of-joint-comprehensive-plan-of-action.html.

41 Senior Canadian official 04, interviewed by Farzan Sabet in Brussels, Belgium, 6 November 2019.

42 Ex-Canadian parliamentary staffer 03, interviewed by Farzan Sabet on Skype, 19 June 2019.

43 Grégoire Mallard, Farzan Sabet, and Jin Sun, "The Humanitarian Gap in the Global Sanctions Regime: Assessing Causes, Effects, and Solutions," *Global Governance: A Review of Multilateralism and International Organizations* 26, no. 1 (2020): 121–53; ex-senior Canadian foreign policy official 01.

3 Being a Reliable Ally in a Politicized War: Canada's Fight against the Islamic State

JUSTIN MASSIE AND MARCO MUNIER

Canada's military contribution to the Global Coalition against the Islamic State (IS) has varied considerably since IS began seizing territorial control of several Iraqi and Syrian cities in 2014. What began as a swift but limited contribution to assist Kurdish forces against the startling expansion of the IS under US leadership has evolved into a sizable, long-term, region-wide, multidimensional mission aimed at defeating IS in the Middle East. While Canada was the first US ally to strike IS in Syria, it was also the first coalition member to withdraw altogether from combat operations. Canada's Operation Impact is extended until 31 March 2022,[1] but much depends on the future of US and NATO involvement in Iraq. As of 11 April 2021, there were 500 Canadian troops in Iraq, out of the 850 authorized by the federal government, to train, advise and assist Iraqi security forces and support the NATO Mission in Iraq.[2] The war against the Islamic State is expected to become Canada's second-longest war participation after Afghanistan (2001–14).

This chapter analyses Canada's military contribution to the counter-IS coalition from its commencement in August 2014 to its taking command of the NATO training mission in Iraq in 2018. It seeks to explain the considerable variations in the nature and level of military assistance provided to the war against IS. We argue that the politicization of the war during the 2015 federal election and alliance considerations principally account for Canada's inconstant behaviour towards the coalition.[3] We conclude that even though Canada's military contribution has fluctuated as a result of domestic electoral calculations, an unshakable concern with preserving Canada's reputation as a reliable ally is observable throughout the conflict. As such, Canada has remained a steadfast ally despite significant variation in the size and nature of its military involvement, including its premature withdrawal from combat operations following the election of Justin Trudeau's government.

Joining the War

On 7 August 2014, President Barack Obama announced his decision to conduct targeted airstrikes to stop the Islamic State's rapid expansion in Iraq. "We can act, carefully and responsibly, to prevent a potential act of genocide," he declared, but cautioned against a large-scale military intervention: "I will not allow the United States to be dragged into fighting another war in Iraq. And so even as we support Iraqis as they take the fight to these terrorists, American combat troops will not be returning to fight in Iraq, because there's no American military solution to the larger crisis in Iraq."[4] The Harper government immediately expressed its support to "all efforts, including United States supply drops and airstrikes, to protect civilians."[5] It committed two transport aircraft to help carry military supplies from Europe to Kurdish forces in Iraq, alongside its American, British, French, and Australian allies. Prime Minister Harper invoked humanitarian and security objectives to justify Canada's military involvement while approving Obama's limited containment strategy in Iraq.[6]

Canada was the first ally to formally commit troops alongside US forces to the anti-IS coalition formed on the sidelines of the September 2014 NATO summit in Wales. While other Western allies expressed their readiness to take part in the coalition, Prime Minister Harper announced the deployment of 50 to 100 special forces operatives to northern Iraq for an initial thirty-day mission, with a mandate to "provide strategic and tactical advice to Iraqi forces before they commence tactical operations."[7] Although Canada's training contribution was announced first, it appeared small relative to other allies' commitments. Spain deployed 300 military advisors, Italy 280, Australia 200, Denmark 140, and the Netherlands 130. In fact, Canada was the twelfth-greatest contributor to the Iraq training mission amongst the sixteen troop-contributing Western nations (see the chapter by Fleet and Mohamad in this volume).[8] Whilst relatively small, Canada's military contingent was formed of highly valued special operations forces (SOF) working close to the frontlines, which contrasted with most allies' deployment of regular soldiers to the Building Partner Capacity training program of Iraqi forces.[9] Canadian SOF's mission consisted of advising and assisting Iraqi Kurdish troops, notably by directing airstrikes against ground targets, firing anti-tank missiles at IS, engaging in gun battles, and using sniper fire to fend off enemy attacks at the front lines.[10] Reporting from Bashiqa Mountain in Iraq, a journalist wrote, "Canada is the only nation in the US-led coalition that has regularly sent teams of military spotters far forward to identify ISIL targets and the only country whose observers have used lasers to pinpoint those targets for coalition warplanes to destroy."[11] In other words, despite their relatively small number, Canadian SOF offered a critical contribution to the coalition because of their permissive rules of engagement.

The decision to swiftly commit SOF to the US-led "advise and assist" mission was essentially made on the basis of alliance considerations. While Prime Minister Harper stated that IS posed "a threat to millions of innocent people" and "an even greater threat to the security of Canada and its allies," he insisted that his government was acting at the request of the United States.[12] Harper was surprisingly candid when he explained that his government's decision was typical of any other Canadian government: "The position the government of Canada has generally taken in those kinds of situations is where there is a common threat to ourselves and our allies, and where particularly our major allies – the United States and also the United Kingdom, France – are willing to act, the general position of the government of Canada is that we're also willing to act and prepared to play our full part."[13] Willingness of the alliance to follow a leader was thus key to the Harper government's rapid deployment of SOF advisers to Iraq. As Harper's spokesperson summarized it, "We have been asked to contribute military advisers and we have done that."[14]

In contrast, domestic political considerations may explain why the Harper government was unhurried to commit Canadian forces to ground combat operations against the Islamic State. Both the Liberals and the NDP opposed Canadian involvement in combat operations. The Trudeau-led Liberals supported the government's decision to commit trainers as long as Canadian SOF were not expected to fight,[15] while the NDP opposed any Canadian military involvement in the conflict, linking it to the 2003 invasion of Iraq.[16] According to a senior government official, the Harper government avoided taking part in a ground combat mission for fear "to see Canadian forces captured and then paraded in orange jumpsuits before getting their heads cut off."[17]

But alliance considerations led the Harper Conservatives to commit to air combat operations against the Islamic State, albeit in a relatively low-risk fashion. On 15 September 2014, over thirty countries met in Paris to discuss strategy and allot roles to combat IS. The day before the meeting, Australia announced it had agreed to a US request to take part in an airstrike mission with up to eight Super Hornets, an AWACS and a refuelling aircraft, as well as 200 military trainers (including special forces) to "advise and assist" Kurdish Peshmerga fighters. In contrast, the Canadian government received a US request on 19 September, and Prime Minister Harper stressed that his government needed time to weigh its response.[18] But ahead of the debate in Cabinet, Harper made clear he favoured taking part in the airstrike mission, explaining, "We do not stand on the sidelines and watch. We do our part. That's always been how this country has handled its international responsibilities, and as long as I'm Prime Minister that's what we will continue to do."[19] He then announced on 3 October that Canada would commit six CF-18 fighter aircraft, as well as a transport, a refuelling, and two surveillance aircraft, and would renew the SOF training mission. This was days after the Dutch had announced their participation in the US-led combat mission on 24 September, followed by the British, the Danes, and the Belgians on 26 September.

The Conservative rationale for taking on a combat role stressed that the Islamic State posed a direct threat to Canada, but Prime Minister Harper was remarkably forthright when he pointed out, "While the mission is evidently necessary, we do not have to be the ones doing it because others will." The real motivation to take part in airstrikes was a desire to uphold Canada's reputation as a reliable ally. As Harper put it, "When our allies recognize and respond to a threat that would also harm us, we Canadians do not stand on the sidelines. We do our part."[20]

The Harper government nevertheless issued several caveats. The mission would not involve ground combat, it would be "easy to end," it would not pursue "regime change," and strike operations would be circumscribed to Iraqi territory because Canada did not have "the clear support" of the Syrian government to conduct strikes against IS in Syria.[21] The Conservatives took pains to argue that Canada would not become entangled in a costly, regime-changing, long-term war in the Middle East with no exit strategy. These cautionary remarks were reportedly aimed at assuaging Liberal opposition to the combat mission.[22] However, with only one exception, Liberal MPs joined their NDP colleagues in voting against the combat mission. The Liberal leader, Justin Trudeau, hoped that a war-weary electorate would reward him in the upcoming federal election.[23] More importantly, in the absence of an open-ended, large-scale combat commitment by the United States itself, the Harper government had no reason to commit the CAF to a longer and wider mission. The only discrepancy between the Canadian and American commitments (besides the size of the military contingent, of course) pertained to Harper's decision not to broaden the scope of Canada's operations to Syria. However, this discrepancy would last only six months.

Expanding the War to Syria

In March 2015, Prime Minister Harper renewed Canada's mission against IS for one year and audaciously expanded the scope of the airstrike mission to eastern Syria. Canada was thus the first Western country other than the United States itself to strike IS in Syria. Ottawa did not, however, (officially) deploy SOF in Syria. The decision to expand Canada's airstrike mission to Syria was justified on the basis of changes on the ground. Ahead of the debate in the House of Commons, Defence Minister Jason Kenney stated that IS "appears to be increasingly on the defensive in Iraq, and as I've mentioned before, they have apparently begun moving some of their heavier equipment back into Syria. And so we need to be flexible as we consider our options in the future."[24] In the House, Harper added that IS's "power base" was in Syria, and that Islamic jihadists "must cease to have any safe haven in Syria."[25] However, Canadian airstrikes in Syria were not necessary to the coalition's goal of preventing the Islamic State from having a safe haven in Syria. First, as a Canadian military official acknowledged, IS's Syrian "power base" could still be targeted by other members of the coalition, such as Jordan, Saudi Arabia, Turkey, the United Arab Emirates, and the United States.[26] Second, Canada's airstrikes in Syria were actually scarce. Despite an expanded zone of operation, the RCAF struck IS in Syria only five times between 8 April 2015 and the end of the combat mission in February 2016, for less than 0.2 per cent of coalition strikes in that country.[27]

While not necessary to the coalition's military success, Canadian airstrikes in Syria buttressed Canada's reputation as a steadfast ally of the United States. Defence Minister Jason Kenney stated that Canada had been asked by American authorities to expand the scope of its air combat operations to eastern Syria because, unlike other nations bombing Syria, it had precision-guided munitions and an expertise in dropping them against dynamic targets with limited civilian casualties. Chief of the Defence Staff Tom Lawson later clarified that other nations bombing IS in Syria also used advanced precision-guided munitions.[28] This nevertheless illustrated that Canada's expanded mission scope aimed to fulfill US requests for additional partners in targeting terrorists in Syria. As Kenney put it, "We had ongoing discussions with the Americans and our other allies, and they indicated that it would be useful for Canada, for the Canadian air force to do strikes against ISIL targets in eastern Syria."[29]

By making Canada the first Western country to join the United States in striking IS in Syria, Canada demonstrated its solidarity with the United States and bolstered its reputation as a leading military ally while minimizing its costs. Indeed, when assessing the renewal of Canada's military commitment, the Harper government considered several options.[30] These included increasing the number of CF-18s committed to the mission, but this option would have proven difficult given the RCAF's concurrent deployments in Eastern Europe in 2014.[31] A second option, which was embraced by Australia, consisted in expanding the training mission to Iraq's conventional army units.[32] This would have necessitated deploying a regular army contingent in a second theatre of operation, without the added value of SOF's "advise and assist" mission near the frontlines of the war. A third option involved boosting Canada's SOF contingent advising and assisting Kurdish Peshmerga forces, as suggested by a former commander of Canada's Joint Task Force 2.[33] However, this last option was readily rejected by the defence minister.[34] The Harper government chose a less costly option: the expansion of Canada's bombing mission to Syria without any increase in personnel or equipment deployed. This decision was aimed at satisfying the US request for additional help without compromising the government's fiscal objective of achieving a balanced budget ahead of the October 2015 election. By making Canada the first US Western ally to strike in Syria, the decision would also put pressure on other coalition members to follow.[35] Indeed, Canada was later joined by Australia (15 September 2015), France (27 September 2015), Britain (3 December 2015), and the Netherlands (29 January 2016) in conducting airstrikes in Syria.

Debating War: The 2015 Federal Election and Its Consequences

Foreign and defence policy is seldom an important issue at the ballot box in Canada, and it is rarely subject to intense electoral debate. However, the war against IS became an electoral wedge issue and was the subject of the first Munk debate in September 2015 focused solely on foreign policy. Two main factors led to this unique situation. First, the crisis in the Middle East was made salient when photographs of three-year-old Alan Kurdi's lifeless body lying face down on the beach captured the world's attention. It further became an electoral issue when it was revealed that Kurdi and his family were trying to flee Syria to join relatives in Vancouver.[36] This transformed a complex foreign situation into a domestic electoral issue. Second, the Conservatives made keeping Canada safe from foreign terrorists a key theme in their electoral campaign strategy and adopted a singular position on how to deal with the crisis in the Middle East. While the NDP and Liberals seized the Kurdi incident to call for Canada to open its borders to refugees, the Conservatives framed the issue as a security problem rather than a humanitarian concern. Prime Minister Harper vowed to attack IS as the root cause and chastised his opponents for ignoring the security threat posed by hordes of refugees. He further ridiculed Mulcair and Trudeau's opposition to striking the Islamic State, stating, "If your policy is humanitarian assistance without military support ... all you're doing is dropping aid on dead people.

That's not acceptable."[37] During the Munk debate, Harper claimed his government had a "balanced approach" towards the Middle East situation with a "generous but responsible refugee policy," the provision of humanitarian assistance, and "direct military action" against IS.[38]

The Conservatives had a good reason to try to make the war against IS an electoral wedge issue: most Canadians supported their position. A few weeks before the October election, a strong majority (61 per cent) of Canadians continued to support Canada's military participation in the war against IS, including prospective Conservative (87 per cent), Liberal (52 per cent), and NDP (46 per cent) voters. Harper's stance on the war thus appealed to his voting base and beyond.[39] According to pollsters, the terrorist attacks in Ottawa and Saint-Jean-sur-Richelieu (south of Montreal) in October 2014, as well as those in Paris in January 2015, "have all coalesced to produce a very significant shift in public fears about security. These are strongly evident in the diagnostic indicators tracking these issues and Mr. Harper has been seen as effectively responding to these as a strong and decisive leader."[40] Conservative strategists painted a picture of Harper as a strong leader with the experience and resolve to guarantee Canadians' security, while contrasting this image with that of a pacifist NDP leader and an inexperienced Liberal leader. They went as far as testing a negative ad that incorporated IS video into its message about Trudeau's perceived lack of commitment to fighting terrorism.[41]

Despite the Conservative narrative's resonance with many Canadians, the low popular salience of the war limited its actual electoral gains. While Harper's tough stance on the Middle East was initially rewarded in the polls, the issue mattered little to most Canadians at the ballot box. The war's importance to Canadians actually decreased during the campaign, despite increased media attention and political clashes on the issue; it ranked only ninth when Canadians were asked about their most important voting issues.[42] Therefore, while some have alleged that the Liberals won an election by campaigning on values, including the alleged risk posed by Muslim immigrants, the war against IS was not a major concern for most Canadians.[43]

Nevertheless, the politicization of foreign policy issues led to electoral promises (for more on the interplay of domestic politics, party ideology, and Middle East policy, see the chapter by Boily in this volume). Among the most important ballot pledges made was Trudeau's commitment to withdraw from combat operations against IS. The Liberals' electoral platform promised to "end Canada's combat mission in Iraq" (and Syria) and to "refocus Canada's military contribution in the region on the training of local forces, while providing more humanitarian support and immediately welcoming 25,000 more refugees from Syria."[44] Once elected, Trudeau's first foreign policy decision was thus to tell President Obama, during his call to congratulate Trudeau for the electoral victory, that he would carry out the promise to withdraw Canadian CF-18s from airstrike operations in Iraq and Syria. Just hours before, the White House had expressed hope that Canada would remain involved in the war. But Trudeau stated that the American president understood his electoral commitment and promised to withdraw "in an orderly fashion."[45]

Indeed, Canada's jets ended airstrike operations four months later, in February 2016, making it the first ally to withdraw altogether from combat operations. Only Belgium and Denmark had temporarily suspended their airstrike missions as a result of budgetary and logistical issues. Furthermore, the Trudeau government sought to compensate by committing additional capabilities to the war. Prime Minister Trudeau tripled the number of SOF trainers, augmented intelligence and headquarters personnel, deployed three helicopters, and maintained Canada's surveillance and refuelling aircraft in support of the coalition's airstrike operations. This led to an increase of Canada's overall military contingent from 630 to 830 troops. This enlarged commitment was deemed the price to pay to fulfill an electoral promise while maintaining Canada's reputation as a reliable ally.

On the one hand, the Liberals had promised to end the combat mission in order to score electoral points by adopting a position distinct from Harper's pro-war and Mulcair's no-war stances. As Trudeau put it during the Munk debate, "Mr. Mulcair has said he doesn't think we should be in this fight at all. Mr. Harper hasn't seen a fight in the Middle East that he hasn't wanted to send Canadian troops into, starting with 2003 in George W. Bush's Iraq War. The Liberal Party, as we have in the past, know that Canada has an important role to play on the world stage and should be a strong partner in this coalition, but we disagree with Mr. Harper about the best way to do it in terms of dropping bombs." The best way Canada could help fight IS, he added, was "by doing more of the kind of training of infantry troops on the ground that we developed tremendous capacities to do in Afghanistan and in other places."[46] This position was intended to distinguish the Liberal Party from its political adversaries, not to assuage domestic pressures. Indeed, a majority of Canadians – and Liberal voters – believed their party should maintain Canada's combat operations against the Islamic State.[47] Following the announcement of the new mission, however, most Canadians rallied around the change.[48]

On the other hand, the newly elected Trudeau government faced considerable pressure from its allies to boost its commitment to the war against IS. France and Australia had expanded their combat mission to

Syria in September 2015. Following the November 2015 terrorist attacks in Paris, France and the United States announced an intensification of airstrikes against IS targets, which was quickly followed by the UK, Germany, Italy, and the Netherlands. In December 2015, US Secretary of Defense Ashton Carter asked coalition participants to enhance their contributions to the war, including strike and reconnaissance aircraft, as well as special operations forces.[49] While Defence Minister Harjit Sajjan acknowledged that allies had requested Canada's CF-18s to remain in the fight, he claimed his government felt "no pressure" to increase its contribution to the war.[50] Yet Canada's defence minister was not invited to a meeting in Paris of the leading contributors to the anti-IS coalition.

A few days after the Paris gathering, Prime Minister Trudeau unveiled a refurbished military mission focused on training, which would increase the number of ground troops to 830, including over 200 SOF. Trudeau acknowledged that "there is a role for bombing" in the fight against IS, but claimed Canada had specific advantages, including "hard-earned abilities on training local troops that we gained through ten years in Afghanistan and other theatres."[51] The new mission would involve greater risks for Canadian troops, since more SOF would be deployed on the front lines of the war in Iraq and would support Kurdish soldiers in offensive operations against IS insurgents.[52] However, it would strike a balance between an electoral promise to end combat operations and allied pressures for a strengthened commitment to the war against the Islamic State. As a memorandum by Global Affairs Canada put it in preparation for a counter-IS coalition meeting in Italy in February 2016, "Canada's objectives at this meeting are to reiterate to Coalition partners our ongoing commitment to the objective of the Coalition to degrade and defeat ISIL ... while at the same time fulfilling the electoral commitment to withdraw the CF-18 fighter aircraft from the Coalition military operations."[53]

The Trudeau government's foreign policy objective in the Middle East remained "to complement US efforts" in the war against IS, with the hope of satisfying what "the US values in terms of meaningful military contributions from partners in the Middle East and globally."[54] In that spirit, Prime Minister Trudeau announced at the NATO summit in Brussels in July 2018 that Canada would assume command of NATO's training and capacity-building mission in Baghdad. Up to 250 Canadian troops would serve, including advisors, trainers, headquarters staff, and force protection personnel. This brought Canada's military commitment in the Middle East to 850 CAF personnel, including the continued deployment of three Griffon helicopters, two tactical airlift aircraft, twenty engineers specialized in explosive devices, training assistance teams in

Jordan and Lebanon, and 200 SOF members. The Trudeau government remained committed to Canada's Operation Impact in Iraq, renewing the mission to at least March 2022, despite the drawdown of some of its air operations with the withdrawal of the surveillance and refuelling aircraft in December 2017 and January 2019 respectively. While Canada's command of the NATO training mission in Iraq was expected to last only one year, it was extended to November 2020, in part for lack of a willing replacement nation. Justifying his decision, Trudeau emphasized Canada's historical support of NATO and to the advancement of peace and security.

Indeed, Canada has taken part in every NATO operation since its creation, with the notable exception of Operation Resolute Support in Afghanistan, aimed at training, advising, and supporting Afghan security forces. While he acknowledged having been requested to redeploy Canadian troops to Afghanistan following Canada's military withdrawal in 2014, Defence Minister Sajjan explained that other nations would need to step forward. Canada's military priority, he claimed, was to defeat IS; it would therefore only provide financial support to Afghan security forces.[55] The Trudeau government's decision to focus its military engagement abroad to the Middle East (as well as Eastern Europe, with operations Reassurance and Unifier) rather than Central Asia owes more to the 161 Canadian casualties suffered in Afghanistan than to anything else. It serves to demonstrate that while alliance considerations overwhelmingly explain Canada's military involvement abroad, domestic considerations constrain the nature and scope of its operations.

Conclusion

Canada's military involvement in Iraq has been marked by both continuity and change. It has evolved from a relatively small but valuable commitment that included combat operations to a more substantial but restricted mission excluding the offensive use of force. The political importance of contributing meaningfully to the counter-IS coalition has not weakened, however. In light of the decisions examined in this chapter, the best possible explanation for this inconstant but enduring military commitment is the interaction of alliance considerations and domestic political calculations.

Both the Conservative and Trudeau governments responded positively to allied requests for military assistance against IS. They emphasized the importance of supporting Canada's allies and defeating a source of threat to Canada. While the Harper government was much more open in explaining the nature and scope of Canada's military commitment (aptly clarifying that Canada's specific military contribution was not essential to defeating IS), the Trudeau government did not embellish the reasons it remained committed to war or seek to downplay the overwhelming importance of sustaining Canada's reputation as a reliable ally. Trudeau's preference for military operations in Iraq, Latvia, and Ukraine over Afghanistan and Mali, however, have not been properly defended publicly.

This difference between the two governments is due primarily to electoral considerations. Despite a common commitment to NATO, the Harper and Trudeau governments displayed significant differences on the use of force. The politicization of the war against IS during the 2015 election led to the crafting of distinctive positions, attractive to their specific electoral constituencies. The Harper Conservatives emphasized leadership in protecting Canadians from external threats by taking a strong stance in favour of combat operations and security screening of refugees, which pleased its right-leaning electorate. The Trudeau Liberals, in contrast, emphasized Canada's role as a good international citizen, dismissing both a non-military engagement and combat operations.

The future of Canada's military involvement in the Middle East (as elsewhere) will be shaped by both alliance and electoral considerations. While decisions in Washington, London, and Paris will continue to determine whether or not Canada will be active militarily abroad, electoral strategies will determine the precise contours of Canada's military commitment.

NOTES

1 National Defence, "Operation IMPACT," Government of Canada, 30 June 2021, https://www.canada.ca/en/department-national-defence/services /operations/military-operations/current-operations/operation-impact.html.

2 Lee Berthiaume, "Canadian Special forces Supported Major Iraqi Military Assault on ISIS Last Month," *CTV News*, last modified 11 April 2021, https://www.ctvnews.ca/canada/canadian-special-forces-supported -major-iraqi-military-assault-on-isis-last-month-1.5383073.

3 Justin Massie, "Why Canada Goes to War: Explaining Support to US-Led Coalition Operations," *Canadian Journal of Political Science* 52, no. 3 (2019): 575–94, https://doi.org/10.1017/S0008423919000040; Stéfanie von Hlatky and Justin Massie, "Ideology, Ballots, and Alliances: Canadian Participation in Multinational Military Operations," *Contemporary Security Policy* 40, no. 1 (2019): 101–15, https://doi.org/10.1080/13523260.2018.1508265; Laura Pelletier and Justin Massie, "La guerre en élection: Dynamiques électorales de la participation du Canada à la guerre contre Daech," in *Démocratie et*

politiques publiques , ed. Jérôme Couture and Steve Jacob, 21–51 (Quebec City: Presses de l'Université Laval, 2019); Laura Pelletier and Justin Massie, "Role Conflict: Canada's Withdrawal from Combat Operations against ISIL," *International Journal* 72, no. 3 (2017): 298–317, https://doi.org /10.1177/0020702017723357..

4 Barack Obama, "Statement by the President," Speeches & Remarks, The White House, last modified 7 August 2014, https://obamawhitehouse .archives.gov/the-press-office/2014/08/07/statement-president.

5 Josh Wingrove, "Canada Stops Short of Offering Humanitarian Aid to Iraq," *Globe and Mail*, 9 August 2014, A3.

6 Stephen Harper, "Statement by the Prime Minister of Canada Announcing Further Canadian Support to the People of Iraq," Statements, Government of Canada, 15 August 2014, https://www.canada.ca/en/news/archive/2014/08 /statement-prime-minister-canada-announcing-further-canadian-support -people-iraq.html; Steve Rennie, "Harper Draws Parallels between Taliban and Islamist Militants in Iraq, Syria," *Globe and Mail*, 21 August 2014, last modified 12 May 2018, https://www.theglobeandmail.com/news/politics /harper-draws -parallels-between-taliban-and-islamist-militants-in-iraq-syria /article20158700/.

7 Stephen Harper, "PM Announces the Deployment of Canadian Armed Forces to Iraq," Office of the Prime Minister, 5 September 2014, https:// www.canada.ca/en/news/archive/2014/09/pm-announces-deployment -canadian-armed-forces-iraq.html.

8 Kathleen J. McInnis, "Coalition Contributions to Countering the Islamic State," Congressional Research Service, 4 August 2015, 3–5.

9 Operation Inherent Resolve's BPC training sites were located in Erbil, Alasad, Camp Taji, and Besmaya. The Americans, British, French, and Australians also deployed special forces to Iraq.

10 Steven Chase, "Canadian Soldiers Engage in Iraq Combat," *Globe and Mail*, 20 January 2015, A1.

11 Matthew Fisher, "'The Canadians Are among Our Most Important Guys': Peshmerga Praise Elite Commandos in Fight against ISIL," *National Post*, last modified 28 April 2015, https://nationalpost.com/news/within -shouting-distance-of-isil-755418.

12 Stephen Harper, "PM Delivers Closing Remarks at the NATO Summit," Speeches, Government of Canada, 5 September 2014, https://www.canada .ca/en/news/archive/2014/09/pm-delivers-closing-remarks-nato-summit .html.

13 Campbell Clark and Steven Chase, "Canada Is 'Willing to Act,'" *Globe and Mail*, 4 September 2014, A6.

14 Tim Harper, "Harper's Phoney 30-Day Iraq Timeline Absurd," *Toronto Star*, 12 September 2014, A4.

15 Joan Bryden, "NDP Refuses to Back Canadian Military Mission in Iraq," *Toronto Star*, last modified 17 September 2014, https://www.thestar.com /news/canada/2014/09/17/ndp_refuses_to_back_canadian_military _mission_in_iraq.html.

16 Parliament of Canada, "House of Commons Debates," *Hansard* 147, no. 110 (Ottawa: Parliament of Canada, 16 September 2014): 7464; see also Bryden, "NDP Refuses to Back Canadian Military Mission."

17 Peter Mansbridge, "Andrew Doiron's Colleagues Held Fire When Kurds Turned Guns on Them," CBC News, 12 March 2015, https://www.cbc.ca /news/politics/andrew-doiron-s-colleagues-held-fire-when-kurds -turned-guns-on-them-1.2993010.

18 Susana Mas, "Stephen Harper Considers US Request for Further Military Help in ISIS Fight," CBC News, last modified 25 September 2014, http:// www.cbc.ca/news/politics/stephen-harper-considers-u-s-request-for -further-military-help-in-isis-fight-1.2776585.

19 Steven Chase, "Harper's Cabinet to Debate Combat Role against the Islamic State," *Globe and Mail*, 26 September 2014, last modified 12 May 2018, http://www.theglobeandmail.com/news/politics/harper-says-no -reluctance-to-help-us-battle-islamic-state/article20802288/.

20 Stephen Harper, "House of Commons Debates," *Hansard* 147, no. 122 (Ottawa: Parliament of Canada, October 3, 2014): 8227 and 8828.

21 Harper, "House of Commons Debates," 8827.

22 Chase, "Harper's Cabinet to Debate Combat Role."

23 Tim Harper, "War Vote Carries Risks for Justin Trudeau," *Toronto Star*, last modified 5 October 2014, https://www.thestar.com/news/canada/2014/10/05 /war_vote_carries_risks_for_justin_trudeau_tim_harper.html.

24 Lee Berthiaume, "Ban on Fighting ISIL in Syria Not a Problem, Military Says," *Ottawa Citizen*, last modified 20 March 2015, http://ottawacitizen .com/news/politics/ban-on-fighting-isil-in-syria-not-a-problem-military-says.

25 Stephen Harper, "House of Commons Debates," *Hansard* 147, no. 188 (Ottawa: Parliament of Canada, 24 March 2015): 12208.

26 Berthiaume, "Ban on Fighting ISIL in Syria."

27 Based on data compiled by Airwars, 29 December 2016, http://airwars.org/.

28 David Pugliese, "Lawson Now Admits Allies Using Smart Bombs on Raid," *Ottawa Citizen*, 1 April 2015, A8.

29 Question Period, "Interview with Jason Kenney," CTV Television, 29 March 2015.

30 Canadian Press, "Five Possibilities for Canada's Extended Mission against Jihadists," *Vancouver Sun*, 17 March 2015, B2.

31 Matthew Fisher, "Canada's Complex Path to Iraq," *National Post*, 8 October 2014, A9.

32 Daniel Hurst, "Australia to Send 300 Extra Troops to Iraq on Joint Training Mission with NZ," *Guardian*, last modified 3 March 2015, https://www

.theguardian.com/australia-news/2015/mar/03/australia-to-send-300 -extra-troops-to-iraq-on-joint-training-mission-with-nz; Australian Government, "Minister for Defence – Transcript – 7:30 Report Interview with Leigh Sales," Transcripts, Department of Defence Ministers, last modified 14 April 2015, https://www.minister.defence.gov.au/minister/kevin-andrews /transcripts/minister-defence-transcript-730-report-interview-leigh-sales.

33 David Pugliese, "Canada Mulls More Troops for Iraq," *Ottawa Citizen*, 10 March 2015, A1.

34 Canadian Press, "ISIS Mission: Jason Kenney Says Extending Iraq Mandate Won't Add Troops," CBC News, last modified 12 March 2015, http://www .cbc.ca/news/politics/isis-mission-jason-kenney-says-extending-iraq -mandate-won-t-add-troops-1.2991781.

35 Thomas Juneau, "Yes, with Conditions, to Iraq Mission," *National Post*, 24 March 2015, A10.

36 Christopher Dornan, "The Long Goodbye: The Contours of the Election," in *The Canadian Federal Election of 2015*, ed, Jon H. Pammett and Christopher Dornan (Toronto: Dundurn, 2016), 16–18.

37 Canadian Press, "Stephen Harper Slams Liberal, NPD ISIL Strategy as 'Dropping Aid on Dead People,'" The National, last modified 11 August 2015, https://nationalpost.com/news/politics/rivals-isil-stance-like-dropping -aid-on-dead-people-harper.

38 *Maclean's*, "Tale of the Tape: Transcript of the Munk Debate," last modified 28 September 2015, http://www.macleans.ca/politics/ottawa /tale-of-the-tape-transcript-of-the-munk-debate-on-the-refugee-crisis/.

39 Angus Reid Institute, "Election 2015: Canadians Profess Decline in International Reputation in Last Decade by Margin of 2:1," 28 September 2015, http://angusreid.org/election-2015-foreign-policy/. A similar level of support was expressed at the beginning of the combat mission in October 2014. See Ipsos, "Two Thirds (64%) Support Use of Canadian Forces Fighter Jets in Airstrikes against ISIL Targets in Iraq," 3 October 2014, https://www.ipsos.com/en-ca/two-thirds-64-support-use-canadian-forces -fighter-jets-airstrikes-against-isil-targets-iraq.

40 Ekos Politics, "Conservatives Now Polling Higher Than in Final Stages of 2011 Campaign," last modified 5 February 2015, http://www.ekospolitics .com/index.php/2015/02/conservatives-now-polling-higher-than-in-final -stages-of-2011-campaign/.

41 Faron Ellis, "Stephen Harper and the 2015 Conservative Campaign: Defeated but Not Devastated," in *The Canadian Federal Election of 2015*, ed. Jon H. Pammett and Christopher Dornan (Toronto: Dundurn, 2016), 40.

42 Pelletier and Massie, "La guerre en élection."

43 Mark Kennedy, "Liberal Values Won Election, Says Poll," *Ottawa Citizen*, 19 November 2015, A12.

44 Liberal Party of Canada, *A New Plan for a Strong Middle Class* (2015), 71.

45 Alexander Panetta, "Trudeau Tells Obama He's Sticking to Plan to Wind Down Canada's Mideast Combat," Global News, last modified 21 October 2015, https://globalnews.ca/news/2287899/world-leaders-congratulate-trudeau-win/.

46 *Maclean's*, "Tale of the Tape."

47 Bruce Anderson and David Coletto, "Canada's Mission against ISIL: What Comes Next?," Abacus Data, February 2015, https://abacusdata.ca/canadas-mission-against-isil-what-comes-next/; Angus Reid Institute, "Election 2015"; Angus Reid Institute, "Mission against ISIS: Three-in-Five Canadians Say Government Should Maintain or Increase Bombing," 18 November 2015, http://angusreid.org/canada-isis-mission-november.

48 Lorne Bozinoff, "One Half Approve of Mideast Mission Reset," *The Forum Poll*, last modified 20 February 2016, http://poll.forumresearch.com/post/2461/one-half-prefer-a-non-combat-role/.

49 Secretary of Defense Ash Carter, "Statement on the Counter-ISIL Campaign before the Senate Armed Services Committee," US Department of Defense, last modified 9 December 2015, https://www.defense.gov/News/Speeches/Speech-View/Article/633510/statement-on-thecounter-isil-campaign-before-the-senate-armed-services-committ/.

50 Chris Hall, "'Of Course' Allies Want Canada's Fighter Jets to Stay, Says Defence Minister," CBC Radio, last modified 16 January 2016, www.cbc.ca/radio/thehouse/when-dark-economic-clouds-overshadowthe-political-agenda-1.3403555/of-course-allies-want-canada-s-fighter-jets-to-stay-says-defenceminister-1.3403789; CBC News, "Canada Feels 'No Pressure' to Agree to the US Request on ISIS Mission," last modified 15 December 2015, www.cbc.ca/news/politics/canada-isis-mission-us-letter-carter-1.3366185.

51 Justin Trudeau, "News Conference – Canada's ISIS Mission," CPAC, 8 February 2016, https://www.cpac.ca/episode?id=47ba0303-53ad-4f3b-a8f7-55f2d6f3a600.

52 Murray Brewster and CBC News, "Canadian Troops Spending More Time at Front Lines in Iraq as Future of Mission Is Unclear," CBC News, last modified 6 October 2016, www.cbc.ca/news/politics/iraqcanada-troops-1.3794722.

53 Deputy Minister of Foreign Affairs Daniel Jean, "Memorandum for Action," Global Affairs Canada, Access to Information Act, A-2015-02211, 21 January 2016.

54 James McNee, "USS Meeting with Brett McGurk, US Special Presidential Envoy to the Global Coalition to Counter ISIS," IDR Division, Government of Canada, Access to Information Act, A-2017-00148, 16 March 2017.

55 Thomas Gibbons-Neff, "Canada Won't Redeploy Troops to Afghanistan as NATO Promises More Soldiers," *National Post*, last modified 29 June 2017, https://nationalpost.com/news/world/canada-wont-redeploy-troops-to-afghanistan-as-nato-promises-more-soldiers; Chris Hall, "Afghanistan Looks to Canada for More Training Support," CBC News, last modified 19 November 2017, https://www.cbc.ca/news/politics/afghanistan-training-support-1.4409506.

4 Capacity Building and Training: Supporting Security Services in Iraq, Jordan, and the Occupied Palestinian Territories

MIKE FLEET AND NIZAR MOHAMAD

On 28 August 2014, the Canadian Armed Forces (CAF) delivered the first military supplies to Iraqi security forces, whose northern defences had collapsed in the face of a swift offensive launched by the Islamic State (IS) six weeks earlier. Alarmed at the rate at which the militant group was able to capture territory in Syria and Iraq, the US-led Global Coalition against IS was launched in September. That same month, Canada approved the deployment of up to 100 troops from its Special Operations Forces to "advise and assist" Iraq's security forces, primarily the Kurdish Peshmerga. CAF deployment with the Peshmerga was intended to develop their capacity and assist in intelligence gathering and the execution of operations, while excluding direct combat. Since 2014, Canada has remained engaged in Iraq as part of Operation IMPACT, which constitutes its contribution to the coalition.

Beyond Iraq, Canadian personnel are deployed in seven other countries in the Middle East, performing a range of functions from tactical support to active training.[1] At the same time, Canada has expanded the scope of its Middle East Strategy budget, investing over $2 billion from 2016 to 2019, and committing an additional $1.39 billion in 2019's federal budget over two years.[2] So what could this mean? Is Canadian foreign policy towards the Middle East undergoing an evolution marked by greater engagement? If so, how is Canada pursuing its own objectives in the region? Is it doing so effectively? And what are the long-term implications?

This chapter complements the chapter by Massie and Munier: whereas the latter focused on the more kinetic aspects of Canada's contribution to the coalition against IS, this one discusses security force capacity building (CB) as part of a broader current within Canadian foreign and defence policy in the Middle East. To do so, we examine Canada's role in training the police and security forces of Iraq, Jordan, and the

Palestinian Authority in Israel-Palestine, namely the Occupied Palestinian Territories (OPT). We draw on three cases: Operation IMPACT (2014–19) in Iraq and Jordan,[3] and Operations PROTEUS and EUPOL-COPPS in the OPT (2005–19). These cases were selected to highlight the models of Canadian engagement that are applied across different political and security contexts, as well as to examine the different strategic goals guiding Canada's involvement in these operations. On the basis of these cases, we argue that Canada's CB efforts in the Middle East reflect a Canadian trend to utilize multilateral security engagements to respond to complex regional events and in doing so, expand its footprint and further its interests in the region. Such efforts demonstrate a relatively new adaptation of an older foreign policy dynamic driven by the logic of middle power manoeuvring.

The Middle Power Rationale and Capacity Building

As a middle power, Canada has long had a history of pursuing foreign and defence policy objectives through multilateral diplomacy.[4] Among other things, this has included a proclivity to maintain relationships with powerful allies while encouraging them to act within the framework of multilateral institutions. This rational commitment to multilateralism has enabled Canada to pursue its strategic interests by adopting an internationalist orientation.[5] Canada's foreign policy in the Middle East likewise follows this logic. Contrary to the notion that Canada's peace-keeping legacy in the region has historically been driven by a sense of altruism, up until the Suez Crisis, Canadian politicians viewed the Middle East with reservation. However, in response to the dangerous escalation of the crisis, Canada's perspective changed, and its involvement in peacekeeping operations effectively transformed it into a regional stakeholder. Canada's part in establishing the United Nations Emergency Force (UNEF), the first peacekeeping deployment in history, along with its subsequent emphasis on such missions, therefore "provided Canada with a distinct and useful global role that went beyond its status as a junior partner in the US-led Western alliance."[6]

Canadian CB contributions represent a modern adaptation of this historic trend. The role of Canada in CB operations, as a middle power, has been principally to augment US, UK, and NATO initiatives in the Middle East in order to manage its relationships with key allies, particularly the United States.[7] This strategy has been pursued through "tactical"-level programs, which enable Canada to leverage multilateral frameworks to enhance these relationships while expanding its presence in the region. As such, Canada's efforts to reinforce these initiatives bolster its own

Table 4.1. Current Canadian Military Operations outside of North America, 2019

	Central and South America	Europe	Africa	Middle East	Asia-Pacific
Operation title (Y/N multilateral; Y/N capacity building)	CARIBBE (Y/N)	IGNITION (Y/N)	EDIFICE (N/Y)	ARTEMIS (Y/N)	NEON (Y/N)
		KOBOLD (Y/N)	CROCODILE (Y/N)	CALUMET (Y/N)	RENDER-SAFE (Y/N)
		OPEN SPIRIT (Y/N)	FREQUENCE (N/N)	FOUNDATION (Y/N)	DRIFTNET (N/N)
		REASSURANCE (Y/N)	NABERIOUS (N/Y)	IMPACT (Y/Y)	
		SNOWGOOSE (Y/N)	PRESENCE (Y/N)	JADE (Y/N)	
		UNIFIER (Y/Y)	PROJECTION (varies)	PROTEUS (Y/Y)	
			SOPRANO (Y/N)		

Source: Department of National Defence, "Current Operations List," 6 August 2020, https://www.canada.ca/en/department-national-defence/services/operations/military-operations/current-operations/list.html.

foreign policy objectives while CB operations, including security sector reform (SSR), suit the Canadian tendency to view its actions on the world stage as focused upon "human security." Yet through the framework of CB, Canada is able to move beyond the era of classical peacekeeping to assert its presence in the region and beyond in ways previously unseen.

As table 4.1 demonstrates, Canada's military deployment in the region illuminates a distinct pattern of engagement: most operations are non-kinetic, a growing number focus on CB, and all are multilateral. This is largely mirrored globally: of its twenty-three operations worldwide, most deployments constitute contributions to multinational missions, are non-kinetic, and several focus on CB or assistance.

These operations highlight two discernible Canadian goals: (1) alliance management and (2) leveraging limited resources to strategically expand Canada's footprint, which differs by region. Bound by the constraints of a middle power, Canada's strategic interests are best served when it works in concert with its partners and pursues its foreign and defence policy through such frameworks. It is therefore not surprising that Canada's 2017 defence policy, *Strong, Secure, Engaged*, references the word "multilateral" 11 times, "alliance" 15 times, and "partner" 115 times.[8]

The Canadian Calculus: Engagement as a Low-Cost, High-Return Investment?

Through a combination of multilateralism, CB, and SSR, Canada has attempted to reinvigorate its presence on the regional stage. However, given its limited resources, Canada has consistently sought to engage in a manner that is measured and calculated. By tying security to aid, Canada has used its reputation as an "honest broker" to begin developing a larger footprint in places like Iraq, Jordan, and Israel-Palestine. This has been achieved without over-exerting Canadian personnel, who have played an active, albeit largely supportive, role in security development.

Compared to combat, training missions are cheaper, pose less risk, and are easier to sell domestically. Performing CB functions in the security sector therefore offers an avenue through which Canada can be engaged while avoiding kinetic operations, which are often costly and politically contentious. Through the framework of "security aid," Canada can market its engagement as "technical" or delivering "value-added expertise" in order to improve visibility to donor beneficiaries and rationalize its military presence throughout the insecure landscapes of the Global South.[9] This enables Canada to develop pathways for partnerships on defence and security, particularly as the CAF, with their distinctly high levels of cultural awareness, often have a competitive edge in training in countries with diverse and complex contexts.[10] Canadian Forces have even begun to lead on training initiatives. In this regard, security aid is viewed as an efficient means for Canada to leverage its resources in order to expand its presence internationally.

As we will see, in all three cases, Canada's involvement constitutes a strategic low-cost, high-return investment that, while imperfect, has allowed it to carve out a regional character separate from its American and European counterparts. However, these returns vary by case, particularly if we are to define them as presenting cohesive long-term political objectives beyond alliance management.

Israel-Palestine

Canada's deployment in Israel-Palestine began in 2005 and stems from its desire to commit to the Middle East peace process (for more background on this, see the chapter by Musu in this volume). In March 2005, the United States Security Coordinator (USSC) was established. Conceived in the aftermath of the Second Intifada, the USSC was intended to guide the US-led multinational Roadmap to Peace that framed the resumption of Israeli-Palestinian peace talks, mainly by reforming the security institutions of the Fatah-led PA in order to strengthen its relations with the State of Israel. One month later, the USSC helped integrate myriad overlapping security forces and militias into three main organizations under the auspices of the Palestinian National Authority (PNA): the Internal Security Forces, the National Security Forces, and the General Intelligence Organisation.[11] On 1 January 2006, the EU followed suit by launching EUPOL-COPPS, an EU Common Security and Defence Policy (CSDP) mission, to support Palestinian police and justice reform.

By late January 2006, Hamas assumed control of Gaza through democratic elections, but by June 2007 had moved to coercively consolidate its authority after an attempted US-backed coup by political rival Fatah. The United States, Israel, and the PA strategically converged on their desire to curb Hamas, producing common grounds for the Israeli and Palestinian governments for the first time since the Oslo Accords.[12] Running in tandem with Palestinian Prime Minister Salam Fayyad's "state-building" project, the formulation of a professional Palestinian security force became the cornerstone of the policy's mandate to develop the institutions of statehood. Its top priority: the establishment of a Palestinian government that would reliably coordinate with Israel on all matters related to security.

To complement these initiatives, Canada's mission focuses on training the security and police forces of the PA, collectively referred to as the PASF. In 2005, Canada deployed its first senior CAF officer to Israel-Palestine through PROTEUS, a Canadian operation comprising Canada's contribution to the USSC. This marked the start of its contribution to Palestinian CB and SSR. By 2008, Canada expanded its involvement by deploying two officers to EUPOL-COPPS to contribute to Palestinian police and SSR. While different in ownership and focus, both operations emanate from the broader US-spearheaded "peace through security" initiative. Through PROTEUS, Canadian personnel work primarily in conjunction with their US and UK counterparts to develop training and logistics systems meant to professionalize the PA's security institutions, as well as "encourage" joint Israeli-Palestinian security coordination via confidence-building measures. Through EUPOL-COPPS, Canadians help develop the Palestinian Civil Police (PCP), criminal justice system, prosecution-police interactions, and coordination of external donor aid to the Palestinian Police. Although their operational demarcation line isn't always clear, they have collectively employed members of the CAF, the RCMP, and CBSA, in addition to civilian staff.

During the Second Intifada, the Israeli Defense Forces (IDF) had destroyed most of the Palestinian Authority Security Forces (PASF) defence and security infrastructure, as several recruits had partaken in the uprising. Accordingly, PROTEUS augmented US-led efforts to rebuild the PASF by combining training with the construction of security facilities. Under the USSC's multinational umbrella, Canadian officers contributed to the training of 18,029 PASF personnel between 2008 and 2016 at the US-led Jordan International Police Training Centre (JIPTC),[13] located near Amman. From 2006 to 2016, GAC provided $500 million in development assistance, and from 2010 to 2011, "Canadians oversaw the construction of several new Joint Operations Centers, designed and developed several courses on Operational Planning and Command and Control (at both the operational and tactical levels) and then delivered them to over 600 PASF personnel."[14] In July 2013, Canadian RCMP officers began supporting the design and delivery of the Palestinian Officers' Academy in Jericho where they train cadets in the fundamentals of leadership, such as logistics, de-escalation techniques, and the proper use of force.[15] That year, the first cohort produced 112 graduates, 30 of whom were women. Today, PROTEUS comprises twenty CAF personnel and one officer who provide "technical policing expertise"[16] – the largest contingent of any USSC partner state.

Officers in both operations are deployed under the mandate of Canada's International Police Peacekeeping and Peace Operations (IPP) program. This program aims to regionally "bridge the gap" between police and military in support of whole-of-government development. Under the IPP, an average of two officers per rotation – seventeen to date – have also been deployed to EUPOL-COPPS to advise, assist, and train the Palestinian Civil Police to develop their capacity "based on the principles of democratic policing, neutrality and community service."[17] The officers' role includes assisting in accountability and oversight, criminal investigations, as well as building or enhancing "public order training," command systems, the Ministry of the Interior, and even traffic programs. Additionally, in 2010, Canada pledged a maximum budget of $54,091,754 to construct courthouses in Tulkarem (now complete) and Hebron,[18] expected to run until 2021. It has since trained judges, enhanced public prosecution systems, supported forensic science services, and assisted the Office of the Attorney General.[19] These efforts ostensibly align with Canada's aim to help "establish a law-based, peaceful, and prosperous society that can ultimately become a state for the Palestinians, and a stable and secure neighbour for Israel."[20]

Canada's supportive role was instrumental in the training of the PASF. In a 2009 keynote address, the former head of the USSC, Lieutenant

General Keith Dayton, emphasized that Canadian and British personnel served as his "eyes and ears." Canadians, whom Dayton referred to as "road warriors," conducted daily visits to PASF leaders within the West Bank, provided English-Arabic translators, liaised between PROTEUS and EUPOL-COPPS, and coordinated training for the Palestinian Presidential Guard, which was tasked with "manning borders." Canadian personnel played an important role in facilitating the logistics needed to carry out the training and coordination on which the operation rested. Since, unlike their American counterparts, Canadians do not face travel restrictions in the West Bank, they are able to move freely, "gauging local conditions, and working with real Palestinians in order to sense the mood on the ground."[21] Canadian officers also helped develop a police code of conduct for the Palestinian Civil Police, expanding their presence across twelve districts in the occupied West Bank. Retired US Marine Colonel P.J. Dermer, who headed PROTEUS in its earlier years, has stressed the role of Canadians in augmenting the American effort. "Hands down, it simply would not have happened without the Canadians," he said. "You really cannot commend them enough."[22]

Iraq

Canadian security force CB in Iraq has been a consistently central theme from its involvement in Operation IMPACT within the Global Coalition against IS to the current NATO Mission-Iraq (NMI). This is not the first time Canadians have trained Iraqi security personnel: in 2004 Canadian police officers (along with personnel from sixteen other countries) trained Iraqi police in the Jordan International Police Training Centre.[23] The broader package of Canadian CB is split into three separate but overlapping areas: (1) training conducted by the CAF under the mandate of the DND, (2) training conducted in partnerships through GAC's Peace and Stabilization Operations Program (PSOP) and Counter-Terrorism Capacity Building Training Program (CTCBP), and (3) police training conducted by the RCMP in coordination with the Ministerial Liaison Team (MLT) of the Global Coalition and under the direction of the Italian carabinieri. Much of the history of Operation IMPACT, however, is covered in the chapter by Massie and Munier.

By 2015, up to 600 CAF members were deployed to train the Peshmerga as part of IMPACT. Aside from requiring training in "equipment use, maintenance and repair; ground navigation; battlefield skills; communications; command and control; and combat medical care," the Peshmerga also "need[ed] direct advice and assistance with strategic and tactical planning, particularly when it [came] to integrating the air support provided by the international coalition."[24] In spite of their short-comings, however, Canadian policymakers viewed the Kurdish force as a more reliable partner than the Iraqi military. Conservative MP Jason Kenney, for example,[25] considered them demonstrably more effective to train than the Baghdad-based Iraqi Army.

After the 2015 Canadian federal election, IMPACT underwent a drastic change. Prime Minister Justin Trudeau committed to his campaign promise to end air operations in Iraq and shift IMPACT towards training and support, increasing the numbers of approved CAF members to upwards of 850 – to be deployed across Iraq, Jordan, Lebanon, Kuwait, and Qatar. In line with its training strategy, Canada led in instructing security forces in Iraq by heading the Ministerial Liaison Team and CJ-7 (director of training) from its inception in March 2016. This position serves to coordinate with the Global Coalition and the Iraqi ministries of Defence, Interior, Health, and the Peshmerga, as well as the national security advisor and the Prime Minister's National Operations Centre. This coincided with the approval of the deployment of up to twenty RCMP officers as of August 2016 to train the Iraqi National Police at the Iraqi police training academy based in Baghdad – training intended to focus on community policing, as well as gender, human rights, and policing of vulnerable populations. After 2016, the "train-the-trainer" methodology became the centrepiece for CB.

By 2017, the Kurdish independence referendum resulted in Iraqi federal forces reclaiming the disputed territories of Iraq, including the city of Kirkuk, which was taken by Kurdish forces when they had repelled IS in the summer of 2014. The Canadian position, while silent, supported a unified Iraq. In October 2017, Canada ceased training operations with the Peshmerga and reoriented its focus towards training the Iraqi national army. The 200 CAF personnel in Erbil then reallocated their efforts to securing Mosul, while training operations shifted primarily to Baghdad.[26] During this period IMPACT deployed twenty CAF engineers to Besmaya for explosive threat training, such as IED detection and dismantlement. In April 2018, NATO announced that it would begin its Train-the-Trainer mission by July, although training officially began in January 2017. While this was stipulated as part of the Defence and Related Security Capacity Building package that was requested by Iraqi Prime Minister Haidar al-Abadi and confirmed in July 2015, Iraq's central government requested that NATO expand its training mandate to include a long-term mission in Baghdad involving the Ministry of Defence and staff colleges.[27] At the 2018 NATO Brussels Summit, Trudeau announced that Canada would lead this mission in concurrence with IMPACT by committing an additional 250 CAF members.[28]

Headquartered in Baghdad and focusing on the Iraqi national army, the NMI now functions under a singular operational command, as Canada led the mission from 2018 to 2020.[29]

The operation works in two principle areas: advice to the national security advisor and the Ministry of Defence, and capabilities, the latter meant to streamline formalizing leaders in tactical, operational, and strategic areas.[30] It is further divided into three components: increasing the number of trainers, enhancing the military training system, and SSR. To address these areas, the operation works with Iraqi authorities on three SSR subcommittees – critical infrastructure, democratic institutional oversight and accountability, and defence and internal security strategy – and does so only with forces under the "direct and real control" of the Iraqi government. On 18 March 2019, Canadian Defence Minister Harjit Sajjan announced that Canada would extend both IMPACT and the NATO mission to 2021, with Canadian Brigadier-General Jennie Carignan assuming leadership in the fall of 2019. Denmark then replaced Canada as leader of the NMI in November 2020.

Jordan

The template for the Canadian CB in Jordan differs from the one applied for the mission in Iraq. Jordan has been a member of the NATO Mediterranean Dialogue since 1994 and a partner in the Military Training and Cooperation Program (MTCP) since 1998.[31] Under this program's mandate, Canada has a defence attaché in Jordan who (in concert with Jordanian military officers) facilitates yearly courses in English/French, staff officer training, and professional development. The program has trained around 450 Jordanians. In 2009 Jordan had its first Individual Cooperation Program, and in 2016 became part of the Enhanced Opportunities Partners.

Coinciding with these NATO initiatives, Canada and Jordan signed an MoU for CB projects in Jordan on 5 May 2016. Following the Liberal government's pivot towards aligning Canadian programming to strategically competitive CB projects, Canada decided to expand IMPACT into Lebanon and Jordan in order to enhance their forces' ability to repel spillover from the Syrian war and the rise of IS. This includes addressing increased refugee flows and processing at key junctures (such as airports and borders), border security, and improving skillsets and reaction time of military units. These projects were administered by GAC and led by the Counter-Terrorism Capacity Building Training Program and the Stabilization and Reconstruction Task Force (START). After conducting a needs assessment, Canada approved deploying the RCMP and the Counter-Terrorism Capacity Building Training Program under IMPACT in November 2017. Intended to support training in border patrol, security infrastructure, and soldier equipment usage and maintenance, the CB deployment was implemented in December 2017.[32]

In response to a request from the Jordanian government, the RCMP now trains a contingent of women police officers from the Jordanian Gendarmerie. The RCMP provides tactical training that tackles riot control and child soldiers, in addition to fulfilling the country's need for female police officers, whose primary function is to search other women, respecting personal privacy and in accordance with socio-religious customs. This is mirrored by the training conducted by the CAF as part of the Counter-Terrorism Capacity Building Training Program programming of the Female Engagement Team Platoon of the Jordanian Special Forces' Mohammed Bin Zaïd Quick Reaction Brigade, which was created in December 2017 as part of Jordan's policy to raise the number of women in the armed forces to 3 per cent.[33] Additionally, on 8 April 2019, the Jordan Border Road Rehabilitation Project officially began; the project ran for two years and repaired around sixty-three kilometres of road and border posts in tandem with other stretches of border with Syria and Iraq that are under the assistance of partner countries such as the United States and United Kingdom. This work aimed to further the Jordanian military's infrastructural capacity to patrol their border, as well as provide training zones for the quick reaction forces.[34]

Defining Returns in the Middle East: The Challenges of Engagement in a Complex Environment

In all three cases, Canada has had to navigate complex political and security environments. Defining success in these cases depends on how Canada outlines its objectives. What is meant to come of these operations? Each case offers a different result.

Canada's involvement in Israel-Palestine is perhaps the most problematic of the three. First, it occurs primarily in territories that the international community (including Canada, the United States, and the EU) consider to be illegally occupied by Israel. Even Israel maintains as its official policy a two-state solution negotiated along the 1967 lines, although many have become sceptical, as numerous Israeli politicians have rejected the Palestinian right to self-determination and the division of Jerusalem, particularly since the ascendance of former prime minister Benjamin Netanyahu and the corresponding shift in Israeli politics to the right. As a result, critics of Canada's security involvement in the West Bank claim that Canada is complicit in the subcontracting of Israel's occupation of Palestinian land. This criticism is made more pronounced when considering the expansion of Israel's illegal settlements in the

OPT, which, in spite of the internationalization of the Roadmap to Peace and the training of the PASF, have proliferated unabated and today have a settler population that has quadrupled since the signing of the Oslo Accords.[35] Observers therefore commonly claim that Oslo is dead, and along with it the prospect of a two-state solution.[36] By participating in these operations, Canada can be seen as legitimizing the occupation and denying, rather than affirming, the Palestinian right to self-determination and the creation of a sovereign Palestinian state. This view is made more prevalent in the wake of multiple Israeli governments that have campaigned on the rejection of the 1967 lines and the complete annexation of the West Bank. And while Canada promoted the two-state solution through the Madrid Process, its work in the OPT has failed to respond to shifting realities and has instead consistently followed its 1993 aid model. It has therefore pursued a stagnant policy that perpetuates the status quo as opposed to addressing it.

Second, despite efforts to professionalize the PASF, they still suffer from a crisis of legitimacy. While meant to comprise the security sector of an area that was intended to facilitate the transition into Palestinian self-rule, the PASF at best enjoy limited authority in the OPT. In the West Bank, the PASF exercise no authority in Area C and only limited authority in Area B.[37] In Area A, where (on paper) they exercise full control, the PASF's credibility is undermined by their capitulation in the face of IDF incursions and attacks by settlers against the Palestinian population whose security they are entrusted to uphold. This hinders their capacity to execute proper policing functions and deal with crime.[38] But the crux of this crisis is the accusation that the PASF merely act as the repressive wing of a political body that perpetuates the Israeli occupation by silencing its critics and stifling dissent. The accusation is that Israel's security arrangement with the PA has allowed it to outsource operations to produce a more efficient occupation, effectively subcontracting the burdens of governance, including repression. Even a preliminary review of the PASF's human rights record points to widespread abuses where dissent, both against Israel and the PA, is not tolerated.[39] Many have labelled it a "police state" because the presidential mandate of Mahmoud Abbas expired in 2009, yet he has continued to rule unopposed with a combination of repression and corruption. The "Palestinian Authority" is therefore viewed within the OPT as a misnomer, used to describe an authoritative political body that, "Palestinians sometimes bitterly joke, neither serves Palestinian interests nor exercises political authority."[40] Revealingly, when in 2012 the Harper government threatened to discontinue Palestinian security aid in retaliation for their bid to upgrade their UN status, Israel reportedly urged them not to.[41]

Third, the mission prioritizes Israel's security over that of the Palestinians. Belonging to the "Security First" paradigm, the multinational mission emphasizes Israel's security as a precondition for any manoeuvres to build and reform the PASF. For instance, in an analysis of eighty reports by the top nine donor countries to the OPT, Canadians and Americans stood out as being fundamentally "preoccupied with providing security for Israel from Palestinian violence."[42] In a revealing demonstration of its position, a leaked Canadian briefing note stresses the importance of maintaining calm for Israel, boasting that training the PASF allowed it to reduce its incursions into once-turbulent cities like Jenin by roughly 40 per cent.[43] Lieutenant-General Dayton himself is on record stating, "We don't provide anything to the Palestinians ... unless it has been thoroughly coordinated with the State of Israel and they agree to it,"[44] including prior screening of cadets by Shin Bet, Israel's domestic intelligence agency. However, acquiescence to Israeli directives has often stalled reform of the Palestinian Civil Police. Canada's own International Police Peacekeeping and Peace Operations program evaluation affirms this: in addition to lacking control over territory, borders, and funding, Palestinian police even faced "challenges" obtaining Israel's authorization for equipment and forensic chemicals. Meanwhile, the PA's security institutions have failed to protect Palestinians from their main source of insecurity – the Israeli occupation – and have instead criminalized all forms of resistance as "insurgency" or "instability."[45]

Similar to its involvement in Israel-Palestine, Canadian engagement in Iraq followed a pattern of responding to regional events while attempting to manage its relationships in an alliance. Canada perceived IS as a threat to Canadians abroad and domestically, but the politics of alliance management encouraged Ottawa's policymakers to lead in the NMI. By 2015, Canada used counterterrorism CB to assist in defeating IS, stemming the flow of foreign fighters, and countering extremism – with low-cost programming. As the operation began, Canada placed itself within the fold of the Global Coalition and conducted short-mission air operations (as to avoid mission creep and over-commitment) while delivering limited training to the Peshmerga. Upon assuming office, the Trudeau government ceased all air operations and instead began to develop a more robust training role. This shift in direction was accompanied by playing a more assertive role in the Global Coalition via the Ministerial Liaison Team and CJ-7 director of training in 2016 and onwards, as well as the RCMP conducting training, although to a far more limited extent, sending very few officers.

After the Kurdish referendum in September 2017, Canada prioritized its relationship with Baghdad and shifted operations towards exclusively training the Iraqi national army and Federal Police Force. While working with the Peshmerga was a pragmatic choice in 2014, given the metastasis of IS, it became an awkward position when these same forces were accused of abuses in areas recaptured while beating back the militant group, and then again when they turned on Baghdad during the referendum and in its aftermath.[46] This dilemma was compounded by the fact that the Kurdistan Regional Government's (KRG) security forces are fractured by party loyalties, dissent from which is met with repressive and/or punitive economic measures. Since the Iraqi army had largely regrouped by 2017, Canada transferred operations to Baghdad as its confidence in their value as training partners grew. Work in Erbil, however, remained focused on clearing mines in Mosul and providing health services and support to the coalition.[47] By July 2018, US President Donald Trump began openly questioning the value and purpose of NATO, including ridiculing the monetary commitment of its members. Canada seized the opportunity to head the NMI, which complemented Canadian training operations under IMPACT while pleasing Iraqis, who purportedly preferred Canadian Forces over their American, British, and Turkish counterparts. The quick pivot towards Baghdad's national military and police force through NMI helped Canada avoid exacerbating tensions and becoming entangled in a political dispute between its competing Iraqi partners.[48] Nonetheless, the Canadian presence in NMI has been drastically reduced, highlighting again an objective underscored by limited interests focused primarily on alliance management. In 2021 the Canadian contribution to NMI was reduced from around 200 Canadians to 17.[49] Further, the security situation throughout 2020, paired with the COVID-19 pandemic, resulted in the majority of NMI staff being withdrawn to Kuwait from Union III base in Baghdad, shuttering most activity from January to August 2020. The mission declared that it returned to full operational capacity on 31 October, 2020, preceding the change in command from Canada to Denmark, although many challenges remain.[50]

While in Israel-Palestine Canadian personnel have had to navigate between a constrained PASF and an intransigent occupying power, in Iraq they have had to balance between actors with competing agendas. Since the NMI incorporates SSR, Canada may encounter further issues. For example, Canada has explicitly stated that it will not participate in any operations with which the Popular Mobilization Forces (PMF) are affiliated, as several factions have been implicated in human rights abuses, and some enjoy close relations with Iran's Islamic Revolutionary Guard Corps-Qods Force (IRGC-QF).[51] Although IMPACT and NMI both have their own vetting process meant to ensure that they exclusively train personnel under the command of the Iraqi government, disentangling

Iraq's militiamen from the state's coercive apparatus will prove to be difficult, as many are embedded in the ISF's rank-and-file.[52] Moreover, patrol gaps between Baghdad and Erbil in disputed territories create security voids that the Islamic State exploits. Coupled with the hostile security environment created by several Iran-aligned militias incorporated into the PMF that inhibit the ability of the coalition to conduct training and support operations to the ISF, these issues challenge Canada's goal of fostering a secure, unified, and democratic Iraqi state, especially as they are intrinsically domestic.

There are no such major predicaments in Jordan, where the military, aside from having prior experience training with the CAF, is the country's dominant security force. In Jordan, Canadian operations mirrored NATO's policy recommendations for the country, but were performed separately. While Canada's Military Training and Cooperation Program had easier access as a result of DND and GAC familiarity with the Jordanian Army, the broader operation within IMPACT supported NATO's Mediterranean Dialogue and efforts with other partner countries like the United States and the United Kingdom in Jordan to strengthen border control. This made it easier for Canada to send a team to work with the JAF to develop a training program suitable for Jordanians. And although Canada was initially reluctant to accommodate the JAF's request for expensive weapons and equipment, Canada's contribution to CB and skills training has greatly improved the effectiveness of JAF units.[53] That said, the kingdom's human rights profile is far from perfect, with its police and security forces implicated in widespread prison torture, cracking down on free speech, and detaining political activists.

Through programs like the Military Training and Cooperation Program, Canada has enhanced its bilateral ties with Jordan. Initiatives like the training of the country's female engagement team and women in the gendarmerie garnered greater success in large part as a result. Moreover, in line with its propensity to multilateralism, Canada led the creation of the Amman-6, formalizing a partnership between the states that provide the main military assistance programming in Jordan into a group that develops complementary CB programming. While humanitarian, stabilization, and (to a lesser extent) development projects have matured, the organizational process underlining this military CB approach was novel. Through Canadian leadership, the Amman-6 later adopted the Women, Peace, and Security agenda as part of their programming.[54]

Conclusion

While Canada's contributions to security sector CB are modest in comparison to allies like the United States, engagement remains the option best-suited for Canada's strategic interests. Given its middle power limitations, a focus on tactical-level programs performed through multilateral frameworks affords Canada a unique advantage with which it can accomplish its objectives. In order to succeed, however, Canada must adopt a broad political strategy (beyond sectoral projects) that articulates a clear, cohesive, and *adaptive* vision of what it wishes to achieve – not just what it can accomplish via programming. Otherwise, it will remain a strategy consumer.

In Israel-Palestine, Canada pragmatically utilized the peace process to deepen its relations with its allies, strengthen bilateral ties with Israel, and establish a foothold in the OPT. However, it suffered strategic drift; its failure to adapt its mission in light of Israeli rejectionism resulted in a deployment void of its original purpose. In contrast, in Jordan and Iraq, Canada acted adaptively and resourcefully, translating meaningful military operations into sustainable political gains, such as enhanced bilateral relationships through the Military Training and Cooperation Program.

But the tumultuous events of 2019 and 2020 have highlighted significant gaps in Canada's Middle East engagement, amplifying critiques centred on enabling occupation, sustaining authoritarianism, and vulnerability to American unilateralism. In Iraq, an anti-government protest movement sparked in October 2019 that called for an end to corruption and the overhaul of the *muhassasa* (ethno-confessional quota) system was met with repression by Iraqi forces and Iran-aligned militias. On 3 January 2020, four months into the unrest, the Trump administration began the year by assassinating, on Iraqi soil, General Soleimani and Jamal Ja'afar "Abu Muhandis" al-Ibrahim – leader of the IRGC-QF and the PMF chief of staff, respectively. With one directive, the United States escalated military tensions in one of the world's most volatile regions and placed Canadian Forces in harm's way. They now face heightened risks of retaliation by Iran-aligned militias, whose targeting of coalition bases have increased in frequency and intensity ever since. It also jeopardized Ottawa's mission, as politicians in Baghdad, citing Iraq's territorial integrity, reflexively passed a non-binding resolution aimed at expelling foreign forces.[55]

Weeks later, Israel's "Deal of the Century" was unveiled at the White House. Crafted with Washington's assistance, it superimposed on the Palestinians a proto-state under Israeli control – one that flagrantly violates the international consensus on the two-state solution and institutionalizes "perpetual occupation, cynically rebranded as statehood."[56] And in Amman, security forces continued down a repressive road, arresting over 1,000 teachers in the August 2020 crackdown on union activists.[57] How Canada plans to rectify these contradictions – the looming reality of annexation with the purported goal of "supporting a two-state solution," the repression of teachers with the empowerment of women, and the potential to be seen as occupying forces by angry governments – is yet to be seen. Such issues, if unaddressed, are likely to be problematic for Canada's global branding. Without a clear articulation of Canada's broader strategy beyond the anti-IS mission or the failing peace process, its efforts and presence become fragile and dependent on the unpredictability of US actions, or in the case of Israel, the intransigence of Tel Aviv's leadership.

But strategic foreign policy considerations and critiques aside, a Canadian presence in the region can effect real change. With its CB programs, Canada is uniquely positioned to leverage its reputation in order to cultivate an improved institutional culture within the region's security sectors. Working to professionalize security forces to be more cognizant of human rights, gender equality, and community policing can mitigate risks and abuses that, in a region as tumultuous as the Middle East, could lead to larger problems down the line. Said differently, Canada's engagement, while imperfect, gives it the opportunity to professionalize these forces in a manner aimed at democratizing them – even if this starts with fostering orderly and transparent chains of command. This would align strategy with principles in a manner that ultimately leaves a footprint consistent with Canada's global image. However, for Canada to optimize its efforts, Canadian leaders must define Canadian interests in the Middle East at both regional and bilateral levels beyond alliance management.

NOTES

1 These countries include Jordan, Lebanon, Israel/Palestine, Kuwait, Egypt, Bahrain, and Qatar.

2 Department of Finance Canada, "Renewing Canada's Middle East Strategy," in *Investing in the Middle Class: Budget 2019*, tabled in the House of Commons by William Francis Morneau, Minister of Finance, 19 March 2019, https://www.budget.gc.ca/2019/docs/plan/chap-04-en.html#Renewing-Canadas-Middle-East-Strategy. This funding is front-end loaded, directed at continuing Canada's humanitarian and stabilization programming as well as its training operations.

3 Notably, while Iraq is the primary focus of IMPACT, Jordan has been engaged as a partner country with the Military Training and Cooperation Program since 1998, as well as a member of NATO's Mediterranean Dialogue since 1995.

4 For a discussion on Canada's history of multilateralism, see Thomas Keating, *Canada and World Order: The Multilateralist Tradition in Canadian Foreign Policy*, 3rd ed. (Don Mills, ON: Oxford University Press, 2013).

5 It has even been argued that the emphasis on Canada's "relative capability" as a middle power in the international system bears the conceptual hallmarks of realism but is often blurred by the normative assessments underpinning the label "middle-powermanship." See David G. Haglund, "The Paradigm That Dare Not Speak Its Name: Canadian Foreign Policy's Uneasy Relationship with Realist IR Theory," *International Journal* 72, no. 2 (2017): 230–42.

6 Greg Donaghy, "The Politics of Accommodation: Canada, the Middle East, and the Suez Crisis, 1950–1956," *International Journal* 71, no. 2 (2016): 325–26.

7 Despite US pressure to join in the 2003 invasion of Iraq, Canada stated that its involvement would be contingent on the formation of a multinational UNSC-endorsed coalition, underlining Canada's aim of reinforcing multilateral frameworks. See Timothy Sayle, "Taking the Off-Ramp: Canadian Diplomatic Intelligence, and Decision-Making before the Iraq War," in *Australia, Canada, and Iraq: Perspectives on an Invasion*, ed. Ramash Thakur and Jack Cunningham, 210–27 (Toronto: Dundurn, 2015).

8 Canada, Canadian Armed Forces, Department of National Defence, *Strong, Secure, Engaged: Canada's Defence Policy* (2017), 6–106, http://dgpaapp.forces .gc.ca/en/canada-defence-policy/docs/canada-defence-policy-report.pdf.

9 See Jeffrey Monaghan, *Security Aid: Canada and the Development Regime of Security* (Toronto: University of Toronto Press, 2017), 4; and Monaghan, "Security Development and the Palestinian Authority: An Examination of the 'Canadian Factor,'" *Conflict, Security & Development* 16, no. 2 (2016): 133.

10 DND interview 28 March 2019; GAC 12 April 2019.

11 Roland Friedrich and Arnold Luethold, eds., *Entry-Points to Palestinian Security Sector Reform* (Geneva: Geneva Centre for the Democratic Control of Armed Forces, 2007), 22, https://www.dcaf.ch/sites/default/files /publications/documents/Entry-Points(EN).pdf.

12 See Steven White and P.J. Dermer, "How Obama Missed an Opportunity for Middle East Peace," *Foreign Policy*, 18 May 2012, https://foreignpolicy .com/2012/05/18/how-obama-missed-an-opportunity-for-middle-east-peace/.

13 US Department of State, *Second FY 2016 Report to Congress on US Assistance for Palestinian Security Forces and Benchmarks for Palestinian Security Assistance Funds*, case no. F-2016-03467, 12 April 2017, 2, https://fas.org/irp/world /palestine/fy16-assistance.pdf.

14 Regan Legassie, "In Harm's Way," in *The Comprehensive Approach: Perspectives from the Field* (Kingston, ON: Canadian Defence Academy Press, 2015), 140–1.

15 Royal Canadian Mounted Police, "Current Operations," 17 April 2020, http://www.rcmp-grc.gc.ca/en/current-operations.

16 Global Affairs Canada, "Evaluation of the Canadian Police Arrangement and the International Police Peacekeeping and Peace Operations Program," 21 January 2019, https://www.international.gc.ca/gac-amc /publications/evaluation/2018/cpaipp_apcpip18.aspx?lang=eng.

17 Royal Canadian Mounted Police, "Current Operations."

18 Global Affairs Canada, "Project Profile: Courthouses Construction Project, 2020, https://w05.international.gc.ca/projectbrowser-banqueprojets /project-projet/details/z020917001.

19 Representative Office of Canada to the Palestinian Authority, Canada-West Bank/Gaza Strip Relations, Government of Canada, 26 October 2016, https://www.canadainternational.gc.ca/west_bank_gaza-cisjordanie_bande _de_gaza/bilateral_relations_bilaterales/canada-wbg-cg.aspx?lang=eng.

20 Representative Office of Canada to the Palestinian Authority.

21 Keith Dayton, "Peace through Security," speech, Soref Symposium, Washington Institute for Near East Policy, Washington, DC., 7 May 2009, https:// www.washingtoninstitute.org/policy-analysis/peace-through-security -americas-role-development-palestinian-authority-security.

22 Tom Blackwell, "Canada Training Palestinian Troops as Part of Controversial Plan to Create a Security Force in the West Bank," *National Post*, 2 June 2013, https://nationalpost.com/news/world/israel-middle-east /canada-training-palestinian-troops-as-part-of-controversial-program.

23 Martin Patriquin, "Coalition of the Sort-of Willing Canada Iraq Police," *Walrus*, 26 May 2020, https://thewalrus.ca/2005-03-security/.

24 Canada, Parliament, House of Commons, Standing Committee on National Defence, *Minutes of Proceedings*, 2nd sess., 41st Parliament, meeting no. 45, 2015, http://www.ourcommons.ca/DocumentViewer/en/41–2 /NDDN/meeting-45/evidence

25 For a complete description, see Canada, Parliament, House of Commons, Standing Committee on National Defence, *Minutes of Proceedings*, 2nd sess., 41st Parliament, meeting no. 63, 2015, https://www.ourcommons.ca /DocumentViewer/en/41–2/NDDN/meeting-63/evidence.

26 Rudaw, "Canada Ends Training Mission with Peshmerga, Turns Focus to Mosul," *Rudaw*, Kurdistan Region: Erbil, 6 August 2018, http://www .rudaw.net/english/kurdistan/080620181.

27 GAC interview, 12 April 2019.

28 Justin Trudeau, "Canada to Assume Command of New NATO Training Mission in Iraq," Belgium, 11 July 2018, https://pm.gc.ca/eng/news/2018 /07/11/canada-assume-command-new-nato-training-mission-iraq.

29 Trudeau, "Canada to Assume Command." This includes force protection of about 100 people (one company) and transport.

30 CAF interview, 5 July 2019.

31 DND interview, 28 March 2019.

32 GAC interview, 12 April 2019; National Defence, "Border Road Rehabilitation Project Ground Breaking Ceremony in Jordan," news release, 8 April 2019, https://www.canada.ca/en/department-national-defence /news/2019/04/border-road-rehabilitation-project-ground-breaking -ceremony-in-jordan.html.

33 Bessma Momani, "On the Ground with Canadian Armed Forces in Jordan," *Canada and the World Podcast*, episode 32 (15 March 2019).

34 GAC interview, 12 April 2019.

35 Khalil Shikaki, "Do Palestinians Still Support the Two-State Solution?," *Foreign Affairs*, 12 September 2018, https://www.foreignaffairs.com/articles /middle-east/2018–09–12/do-palestinians-still-support-two-state-solution. See also B'Tselem, "Statistics on Settlements and Settler Population," Israeli Information Centre for Human Rights in the Occupied Territories, 1 January 2011, last modified 16 January 2019, https://www.btselem.org/settlements /statistics. This number is likely much higher if we factor in East Jerusalem as well as outposts not technically, but often tacitly, sanctioned by the state.

36 See Daniel Levy, "The Oslo Accords Are Dead, but There Is Still a Path to Peace," *Foreign Policy*, 13 September 2018, https://foreignpolicy .com/2018/09/13/the-oslo-accords-are-dead-but-there-is-still-a-path -to-peace-israeli-palestinian-arafat-rabin-clinton.

37 The West Bank is divided into three areas: Areas A and B, consisting of Palestinian inhabitants, and Area C, which is home to Jewish settlers who reside in illegal settlements.

38 Blackwell, "Canada Training Palestinian Troops."

39 For a detailed report on human rights contraventions by both the Palestinian Authority and Hamas, see Human Rights Watch, "Two Authorities, One Way, Zero Dissent: Arbitrary Arrest & Torture under the Palestinian Authority & Hamas," October 2018, https://www.hrw.org/sites/default/files /report_pdf/palestine1018_web4.pdf.

40 Nathan J. Brown and Daniel Nerenberg, "Palestine in Flux: From Search for State to Search for Tactics," Carnegie Endowment for International Peace, 19 January 2016.

41 Post Media New, "Israel Urged Canadian Government Not to Cut Aid to Palestinians over UN Vote: Documents," *National Post*, 9 July 2013, https:// nationalpost.com/news/politics/israel-urged-canadian-government -not-to-cut-aid-to-palestinians-over-un-vote-documents.

42 Jeremy Wildeman, "Donor Aid Effectiveness and Do No Harm in the Occupied Palestinian Territory," Aid Watch Palestine, 2019, 20, https:// www.researchgate.net/publication/338149823_Donor_Aid_Effectiveness _and_Do_No_Harm_in_the_Occupied_Palestinian_Territory_An_Oral _and_Documentary_Analysis_of_Western_Donor_Perceptions_of _Development_and_Peacebuilding_in_their_Palestinian_Aid_Pro.

43 Jeffrey Monaghan, "Security Development and the Palestinian Authority: An Examination of the 'Canadian Factor,'" *Conflict, Security & Development* 16, no. 2 (2016): 142.

44 Keith Dayton, keynote address, 7 May 2009.

45 Alaa Tartir, "The Palestinian Authority Security Forces: Whose Security?," *Al Shabaka*, 16 May 2017, https://al-shabaka.org/briefs/palestinian -authority-security-forces-whose-security/.

46 David Zucchino, "Iraqi Forces Sweep into Kirkuk, Checking Kurdish Independence Drive," *New York Times*, 16 October 2017, https://www.nytimes .com/2017/10/16/world/middleeast/kirkuk-iraq-kurds.html

47 GAC interview, 12 April 2019; Rudaw, "Canada Ends Training Mission." See also Ayub Nuri, *Being Kurdish in a Hostile World* (Regina: University of Regina Press, 2017). Nuri details Canada's important role in responding to the issues that Iraqi Kurds faced in the aftermath of the fall of Mosul's and ISIS's encroachment on Erbil.

48 GAC interviews, 12 April 2019.

49 Lee Berthiaume, "Canada to Face Pressure to Reverse Withdrawal of Troops from NATO Mission in Iraq," CP24, 17 February 2021, https://www .cp24.com/news/canada-to-face-pressure-to-reverse-withdrawal-of -troops-from-nato-mission-in-iraq-1.5312124.

50 Peter Dahl Thruelson, "Misaligned in Mesopotamia: Conflicting Ambitions in NATO Mission Iraq," War on the Rocks, 16 September 2021, https:// warontherocks.com/2021/09/misaligned-in-mesopotamia-conflicting -ambitions-in-nato-mission-iraq/. As Thruelson notes, NMI suffered from both strategic communication and objective misalignment between NATO command and Iraqi stakeholders in 2021.

51 Amnesty International, "Iraq: Turning a Blind Eye: The Arming of the PMU," 3 January 2017, https://www.amnestyusa.org/reports/iraq-turning -a-blind-eye-the-arming-of-the-pmu/.

52 CAF interview, 5 July 2019.

53 GAC interview, 31 May 2019.

54 GAC interview, 31 May 2019.

55 Lee Berthiaume, "Canada Will Withdraw from Iraq If Government Expels All Foreign Troops: Defence Minister," Global News, 17 January 2020, https://globalnews.ca/news/6428640/canada-iraq-government-troops/.

56 Nizar Mohamad, "The 'Deal of the Century,' an Architecture of Exclusion," Mondoweiss, 5 February 2020, https://mondoweiss.net/2020/02 /the-deal-of-the-century-an-architecture-of-exclusion/.

57 Michael Safi, "Jordan Arrests 1,000 Teachers in Crackdown on Union," *Guardian*, 19 August 2020, https://www.theguardian.com/world/2020 /aug/19/jordan-arrests-1000-teachers-in-crackdown-on-union?CMP=share _btn_tw.

5 Islamic State Foreign Fighters: Their Return and Canadian Responses[1]

AMARNATH AMARASINGAM AND STEPHANIE CARVIN

From April to June 2018, Rukmini Callimachi, a reporter who formerly covered national security issues with the *New York Times*, published a ten-part podcast series discussing her reporting on Islamic State (IS) fighters as well as her numerous trips to Syria and Iraq. The podcast has apparently been downloaded over twenty-five million times.[2] Many in the Canadian public were shocked to hear the voice of a young Canadian on the podcast, who claimed to have fought for IS and then returned home to Canada. "Abu Huzayfah," his *kunya* or nom de guerre, at times sounded reflective and regretful but at other times seemed to betray his ongoing admiration of jihadism and the IS caliphate. Even worse, he admitted to Callimachi that he had carried out executions while a member of IS. Inevitably, the Canadian political establishment erupted.[3]

"The media are reporting this individual is in Toronto, right now, as we speak," said Conservative House leader Candice Bergen in the House of Commons, demanding answers from the Liberal Party of Canada. "Can the government confirm it? Why isn't this government doing something?" she asked to the applause of her party members.[4] While the Canadian government had been quietly finding ways to address the "returnee issue" behind closed doors, this was the first time it erupted into the public sphere, with many Canadians accusing the ruling Liberal Party of being soft on terrorism. A similar national debate was sparked when journalist Stewart Bell and one of the authors of this chapter (Amarasingam) travelled to Syria in October 2018 and interviewed three Canadian members of IS who were then in the custody of the Syrian Democratic Forces (SDF).[5]

As of mid-2020 there were believed to be forty-five Canadians overseas in Kurdish detention camps and prisons, of which twenty are adults and twenty-five are children. Media and NGO reports suggest that these camps are unhealthy, dangerous places, without proper medical care or adequate housing.[6] For instance, Al-Hol camp in north-eastern Syria houses around 70,000 people, of whom 43,000 are children (most under the age of twelve).[7] Slightly over a dozen countries have taken some steps to repatriate their citizens, and even then the process has been choppy – Trinidad, Australia, and Nigeria took a few of their orphans back, while countries like the United States have selectively taken back citizens for whom they have enough evidence to charge.[8] Parts of Al-Hol camp have become hotbeds of pro-IS activity already. Kurdish guards looking after the annex of the camp, where the foreign families are living, avoid entering the section for months at a time in response to several instances of stabbing and rock throwing.[9] On social media apps like Telegram and Hoop Messenger, there are several channels dedicated to the plight of individuals in Kurdish custody.

Nevertheless, Western governments, including Canada, have done little to retrieve their citizens. This raises a moral dilemma: although the adults in these camps have been associated with one of the most dangerous terrorist movements in modern history, their children have done nothing to deserve their fate. In addition, it places a burden on Kurdish forces, who are left in the difficult position of monitoring Western violent extremists with little support. Turkey's incursion into northern Syria in November 2019 further exposed the risks of the Al-Hol camp breaking down.

This chapter examines the fallout of the end of the war against the so-called IS caliphate, particularly through the lens of transnational mobilization of foreign fighters and the ongoing debates on the repatriation of captured fighters and families. The Syrian conflict, from even the moment of initial protest mobilization, had important ripple effects around the world with young Muslims. Human rights violations and chemical attacks by the Syrian regime, and the rise of a militant response by a variety of armed groups, galvanized members of the Muslim community around the world. A small subset of the population, particularly after the militant mobilization became jihadist in flavour, travelled in droves to fight with these organizations against the Assad regime.[10]

This chapter provides an overview of Canada's foreign fighter and returnee problem and the national security concerns they raise. Next, using findings based on extensive field research, the chapter provides an overview of Canadian foreign fighters and returnees. Data are based on interviews conducted by Amarasingam with foreign fighters themselves as well as friends and family over the last seven years.[11] The second half of the chapter highlights current policies to address this issue and the difficulties with their implementation.

Muslim Youth, Transnational Identity, and Foreign Fighter Mobilization

Much scholarship has examined the issue of migration flows and transnational identity over the last several decades.[12] While the transnational mobilization literature generally focuses on remittances, protest movements, and fundraising in a particular "hostland" for the benefit of "homeland" politics, we argue here that foreign fighter mobilization can also be understood from the perspective of transnational activism. Most contemporary youth, in Canada and elsewhere, live transnationally, in constant communication with friends and family in other parts of the world, fundraising for causes they have only heard about online, and moving quite fluidly between international and local issues. Academics have been slow to fully understand this shift in consciousness because of our "methodological nationalism" in which "the idea of the nation-state has been so thoroughly internalised as the standard reference point for the consideration of political community."[13] Indeed, "modes of social and political life defined and practiced solely within the container of the nation-state are today the exception rather than the rule."[14]

Interviews in the Canadian Muslim community from 2013 onwards made it clear that the fight against the Assad regime in Syria was causing some youth in Canada to wrestle with deep theological and religious questions. Many noted that in the face of such injustice in Syria, they were genuinely concerned that they would be questioned by God about "what they did" to help the situation for their Muslim brothers and sisters. Some thought it was enough to attend protests, lobby their member of Parliament, and engage in social media awareness campaigns. A minority of young people, in Canada and elsewhere, came to the conclusion that more needed to be done, that it was their religious duty to go directly to the aid of those suffering abroad. They questioned their parents and religious leaders about jihad, about whether there was a religious obligation to fight and sacrifice themselves, and debated with their friends about which militant or jihadist organization was on the righteous path. Starting in late 2012, they started to hop on flights to Turkey and found smugglers to take them into the Syrian war zone.

While there has been some confusion in the public sphere, at times exacerbated by government officials themselves, on exactly how many Canadians travelled to Iraq and Syria[15] and how many have returned, the 2019 threat assessment from Public Safety Canada provides some clarification. It notes that the Canadian government is aware of at least 190 individuals "with a nexus to Canada [who] are currently abroad, including Syria and Iraq, Turkey, Afghanistan, Pakistan, and North and East Africa."[16] It further clarifies that of the 190, "approximately half" are in

Turkey, Syria, or Iraq. That puts the number of Canadian foreign fighters – or "extremist travellers" as the Canadian government calls them[17] – in Turkey, Syria and Iraq at between 95 and 100. This is very much in line with our own research.

The threat assessment notes that an *additional* sixty individuals with a nexus to Canada have returned to Canada. Of these, "only a relatively small number" have returned from Turkey, Iraq, or Syria.[18] As we will show below, it is not only the number of returnees that is important, but also how they have been defined, and what this might mean for better understanding their potential threat at home.

For this chapter, we have included eighty-one Canadians in the analysis (see figure 5.1). Inclusion of extremist travellers in this report means that at least four pieces of information are known about them in addition to their real name or *kunya* (nom de guerre). This information could have been obtained from open source journalistic reports or our own interviews and research in the community. For most of those men and women included in this study, we have their real name, ethnicity, year of birth, year of departure, province of origin, whether they are converts to Islam, and/or a reasonable sense of their current fate. It should be noted that we are aware of other individuals, rumours of whom have circulated in Muslim communities around Canada or have been mentioned to the authors of this chapter by journalists or law enforcement officials. However, since at least four pieces of information could not be verified about their identity – or, in some cases, whether they even exist – they were not included in this chapter.

There are two significant findings in our dataset about Canadian foreign fighters. First, while the number of Canadians travelling to Syria has been relatively low, compared to other Western countries like the United Kingdom or Belgium, Canadian fighters have been quite prominently featured by the English-language Al Hayat Media Centre of the Islamic State. André Poulin, from Timmins, Ontario, was the first Canadian to appear in Islamic State propaganda materials. The slickly produced video, using stock footage of ski slopes and skyscrapers, runs for eleven minutes and shows Poulin (known as "Abu Muslim") speaking directly to the camera. "Before Islam I was like any other regular Canadian," he says. "I watched hockey. I went to the cottage in the summertime. I loved to fish." As the video depicts, Poulin died in August 2013 during an attack on Mennegh Military Airport in Aleppo.[19]

Another Canadian featured in early 2014 is Farah Shirdon from Calgary, Alberta. Shirdon, known as "Abu Usamah," can be seen burning his Canadian passport and threatening Western powers. Shirdon, whose present status is unknown, achieved greater fame when he conducted

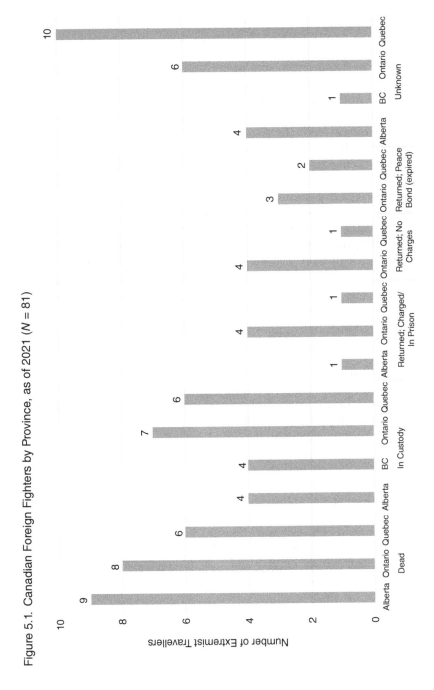

Figure 5.1. Canadian Foreign Fighters by Province, as of 2021 (*N* = 81)

a Skype interview with Vice News in 2014.[20] There is also John Maguire from Ottawa, who, much like Poulin, implores Muslims in the West to make *hijrah*, or emigrate, to the Islamic State. In the interim between the Poulin and Maguire videos, the Canadian government joined the coalition of countries seeking to militarily dismantle the Islamic State. Accordingly, Maguire's video is more confrontational, lambasting the Canadian government for its military aggression and arguing that the attacks in Ottawa and Montreal in October 2014 should be seen as a natural consequence. Even more remarkable, there is "Abu Ridwan al-Kanadi," who was captured by the Kurdish forces in January 2019, who worked with the media apparatus of the Islamic State and voiced their numerous English-language releases for several years.[21]

Second, travel patterns suggest that many Canadian foreign fighters were the product of local "clusters" within major Canadian cities, especially Calgary, Montreal, and Windsor. Individuals in these clusters appeared to have made the decision to mobilize together and subsequently left at similar times to join the fighting in Syria together, although they may have separated once they arrived. This finding generally highlights the social aspect of violent extremist activity in Canada.[22] As is clear from figure 5.1, at least twenty-three of those individuals who travelled abroad have been killed, and little is known about the current status of an additional twenty-one people, some of whom may have been killed in the final stages of the anti-IS campaign or have managed to escape out of Syria and Iraq.

When we discuss the issue of returnees, definitions matter. For the purposes of this chapter, we define a returnee as anyone who left Canada with the intent to join a proscribed terrorist entity. To be included in our database, they need not have been successful. Several individuals made it to Egypt or Turkey, were intercepted by local law enforcement, and were sent home.[23] We count them as returnees in this chapter. There are also several individuals who are currently in Turkish or Syrian-Kurdish custody. We similarly count them in the returnee data, under the assumption that they will eventually make it back to Canada. Even while casting such a large definitional net, the Canadian returnee problem consists of thirty-seven men and women (see figure 5.1, excluding the dead and unknown categories). Of the eighty-one foreign fighters, fifty-nine were men and twenty-two were women.[24]

The Canadian Security and Policy Dilemma

Western security agencies have been concerned about the potential threat of returnees from Syria and Iraq since at least 2014. Media reports indicate that the RCMP have been preparing for a "flood of foreign fighters" to return to Canada as the conflict dynamics in Syria and Iraq change and evolve.[25] As late as February 2017, some foreign intelligence services were predicting that the number of returnees was likely to increase dramatically.[26] An overriding concern was that a wave of battle-hardened and ideologically committed men and women could make their way into Europe or North America to launch a series of Paris- and Brussels-style attacks.[27] This phenomenon of extremist travellers from conflict zones returning to their home countries in order to conduct attacks is often described as "blowback." Yet research and evidence suggests that so far it is not as common as may have been feared.[28] This finding raises two key issues.

First, few of the fighters are actually returning. Studies cite two "waves" of returnees to Europe in 2013/14 (after infighting between jihadist groups in Syria began) and 2015 (as IS began to face severe counterterrorism pressure from the allied coalition).[29] In July 2017 Europe's Radicalization Awareness Network (RAN) estimated that the average percentage of foreign fighters returning to European countries is around 30 per cent. However, despite IS's loss of territory, it appears that the tide of returnees has stemmed significantly since 2016.[30] That there was not a surge in returnees to Canada during this time is confirmed by Public Safety Canada's 2018 *Public Report on the Terrorist Threat*, which kept the number in Canada at sixty, the same as the 2015–18 period.[31] As is clear below, our numbers suggest the rate in Canada is approximately 30 per cent, in line with other countries, depending on how one defines "returnee."

Second, where there were expectations for a wave of attacks by or linked to returnees, especially after 2015, open-source information suggests that the risk of terrorism remains primarily with homegrown violent extremists. One study by the Italian Institute for International Political Studies (ISPI) notes that of fifty-one "jihadist inspired" attacks carried out in the West between June 2014 and 2017, only 18 per cent of perpetrators (twelve out of sixty-five) had travelled to "jihadist-controlled territories."[32] (Of this dataset, three attacks were by Canadians, none of whom were foreign fighters, although they might be considered "thwarted" travellers.) An earlier study by Thomas Hegghammer and Petter Nesser, which looked at the period of 2011–15, came to a similar conclusion, suggesting that sixteen of sixty-nine plots (or 23 per cent) involved at least one returnee from Syria but also from Afghanistan, Pakistan, and Yemen.[33] Given that the authors of these studies used different criteria to create their databases, a perfect comparison is not possible. However, this information does suggest that there has not been a sudden and dramatic increase in attacks perpetuated by returnees. Rather, these attacks have been perpetuated by individuals inspired or encouraged by IS, not fighters they have trained and dispatched abroad.

Nevertheless, there is good reason why returnees rank high on the agenda of national security agencies: their attacks are more lethal than those carried out by homegrown perpetrators. Of the twelve attacks conducted by returnees identified by ISPI, the average death toll was thirty-five people, versus seven for attacks carried out by individuals who had not travelled to conflict zones. In the Hegghammer and Nesser study, the ratio was 7.3 deaths per attack when carried out by returnees as opposed to 1.2 deaths per attack conducted by homegrown violent extremists.[34] In this sense, returnees may be statistically less likely to conduct attacks, but when they do, the results are far more deadly, as is clear from the May 2014 attack on a Jewish Museum in Brussels, the November 2015 Paris attacks, as well as the March 2016 attacks on an airport and metro station in Brussels. Another study by David Malet and Rachel Hayes, which examined 230 jihadi returnees to Western countries, noted that "among foreign fighter returnees who do become or attempt to become domestic terrorists, the median lag time between return and plot or arrest is less than six months for most returnees, the majority of attacks occur within one year, and nearly all attempts occur within three years."[35] After this point, they argue, the risk decreases substantially.

Further, the threat of terrorism to the West is constantly evolving. The good news is that the numbers of extremist travellers going to conflict zones across the West, including Canada, appears to be dropping dramatically, likely as a result of the loss of Islamic State territory and improvements in policies aimed at preventing departures. However, this means that individuals returning from Iraq/Syria will have been away and living in a conflict zone for several years – if they have not travelled to another country in between.

In this sense, future returnees from this area present a unique series of challenges for the West. For example, they may be more "ideologically hardened" and/or emotionally traumatized from their time abroad. Dutch intelligence assesses that men who have been in the region for this time will have almost certainly received some kind of weapons training, and it is likely that women and children over the age of nine will have as well.[36] However, there is also a range of non-violent activities that returnees may engage in: radicalization, financing and facilitation, and travel.

First, radicalization is a process whereby individuals come to hold extremist beliefs. Although there is no agreement on how, exactly, radicalization works, there is consensus that the process is highly individualized, variable, and influenced by a variety of personal and environmental circumstances. Holding radical beliefs alone is insufficient to constitute a crime under Canadian law. Rather, a threat-dimension emerges only when individuals who are radicalized decide to act violently on their beliefs. Returnees are known to have engaged in radicalization activities in Canada. Their experience on the ground may provide them with a more "authentic" voice with which to appeal to potential recruits. Having been on the ground in conflict zones can allow these individuals to portray themselves as having fought for a worthy cause overseas. This credibility can be used to convince others of the worthiness of the cause or press the need to engage in violence.

Second, having developed networks overseas, returnees are known to have provided funds and/or materials to terrorist organizations. Further, while these networks can be used to smuggle money and goods, they can also be used to assist violent extremists in their efforts to travel abroad to conflict zones or to carry out terrorist attacks.

Third, ironically, one of the most frequent threat-related activities returnees engage in is travel. In other words, they aspire to return to the conflict zones they left. As discussed below, where the return was involuntary, the returnee may be seeking to return to the conflict zone, even if he or she is under scrutiny.

Having gone abroad, there are several reasons why individuals may return: they can become disillusioned or feel a sense that they have done their duty and are ready to move on with their lives. Alternatively, they can be captured by security forces and turned over to authorities from their country of origin, seek medical treatment, or attempt to obtain further equipment, money, or support. These latter reasons are more problematic and suggest the individual may desire to re-engage in the threat-related activities outlined above.[37] In a worst-case scenario, an individual may return to Canada to carry out an attack.

The Canadian government has been vague about its returnee policy. Government officials have consistently stated that, given the security situation on the ground, the government's ability to provide consular assistance or repatriation in any part of Syria is extremely limited. While true, visits to the camps by journalists and humanitarian aid workers make it clear that these claims are exaggerated. Moreover, it is clear that in 2018 the Trudeau government was taking some steps towards developing policies. They include documents noting that "investigating, arresting, charging and prosecuting any Canadian involved in terrorism or violent extremism is the government's main strategy and priority."[38] Additionally, from information gained from media reports, interviews with returnees, and government statements, we know that the government is preparing options, even if they have not unveiled them at time of writing.[39]

It is not unusual for extremist travellers to make their intentions to return known to government authorities before they actually do so. Travellers to Iraq/Syria have frequently had their documents confiscated or destroyed by the groups they have joined. In other cases, the government may have cancelled their travel documents if they believe the individual has gone overseas for an extremist cause. In either scenario, travellers will require consular assistance to return home. The government is obliged to provide assistance for Canadian citizens to return home, although not necessarily get them out of prison if they are being held captive. Although some countries have been able to strip their citizens of citizenship, even making them stateless, this would be a difficult option for Canada, given that citizenship protections fall under the Charter of Rights and Freedoms.[40]

In these circumstances the government can prepare for the arrival of returnees, who may be interviewed by consular and national security officials (typically Global Affairs Canada [GAC], RCMP, and possibly also CSIS) overseas. Individuals may also come to the attention of authorities if they are a "listed person" under the Secure Air Travel Act or wanted on another outstanding charge/warrant. In these cases, authorities may be alerted via the flight manifest that such individuals are returning, or when they physically show up at the border.

Once it is learned that an individual plans to return, the matter is managed by two government bodies. First, the High-Risk Returnee Interdepartmental Taskforce (IDTF), led by GAC, "is activated" to identify what the government might do to mitigate any threat a returnee may pose. This includes facilitating information sharing, coordination, managing the travel of the returnee back to Canada, post-arrival actions, and gathering evidence.[41] Other members of the IDTF include GAC, the RCMP, Canada Border Services Agency, CSIS, Passport Canada, Public Safety Canada, and Transport Canada.[42] Second, the RCMP's National Security Joint Operations Centre (NSJOC) coordinates the RCMP's "High-Risk Traveller" operations with several government departments, including CBSA, CSIS, Immigration, Refugees and Citizenship Canada, the Communications Security Establishment, and the Canadian Armed Forces.[43] Like the IDTF, the NSJOC helps to facilitate information sharing and deconfliction (i.e., preventing overlapping operations) within the RCMP and with its partners.

Depending on the risk, the RCMP may use undercover officers to engage with returnees to collect evidence and/or monitor them on the way home.[44] Identified returnees may also be interviewed at their port of entry. During these interviews, government officials try to gather information on why individuals wish to return, what they did while they were abroad, and if they pose a security threat to Canada. Shortly thereafter, a decision will have to be made on how the government should respond: lay charges, investigate further, refer to a counter-violent extremism (CVE) program, or nothing.

First, should there be enough evidence that individuals have committed a terrorist offence, they may be charged under Canada's terrorism legislation. As of September 2021, only five of the sixty identified returnees have been convicted of terror offences. (Three others have been charged in absentia and another trial is ongoing. Two individuals were acquitted and two others had charges stayed/withdrawn.)[45]

Second, where it is suspected that individuals may continue to pose a threat to the security of Canada, they may be monitored by security services, particularly CSIS and/or the RCMP. In this case security services would investigate individuals under national security legislation to find out further information about their activities overseas and to assess if they pose an ongoing security threat. In particular, there would be concerns if it was believed that the individuals had received training or the capacity to re-engage in threat-related activity, particularly planning a sophisticated attack. However, other than enhanced foreign ties, this would not necessarily be different from national security investigations of domestic/homegrown violent extremists. However, it should be noted that this is also one of the most expensive options, given the costs of national security investigations. Moreover, CSIS and the RCMP have limited capacity in an increasingly complex global threat environment. Dedicating these scarce resources to this issue at a time of rising espionage, cyber-threats, as well as growth in other areas of violent extremism (far right and incels, for example) is a serious challenge and a difficult balance to make.

Third, as criminal prosecutions have not been possible, the government has had to turn to other policy options. One is peace bonds (technically, "recognizance with conditions"[46]), for which individuals may have certain conditions imposed upon them by a judge when it is "believed on reasonable grounds that a terrorist activity may be carried out" and that such conditions would prevent the act from occurring. Canada is unique in having such an approach to violent extremism – it is a measure between doing nothing and a full-scale prosecution. Importantly, it does not solve the larger issue of an individual's proclivity to violence (or supporting it), but it creates the space for authorities to try other measures, short of arrest, to prevent a terrorist act. These can include restrictions on liberty, including the wearing of a GPS bracelet, restricting or prohibiting use of the internet or interactions with certain people, and/ or staying in a certain location. For a while it seemed as if peace bonds were a preferred option for the government. However, as of mid-2020, there were no active peace bonds in Canada.

Fourth, since 2016, individuals returning to Canada may be referred to CVE programs of which there are several throughout the country (the most well-known in Calgary, Montreal and, to a lesser extent, Toronto). CVE programs in Canada are at least partially supported and coordinated by the Canada Centre for Community Engagement and Prevention of Violence.[47] Typically, these programs are designed to provide an individually tailored CVE program based on individuals' experiences and needs and to assist them with disengaging from violence. While Canadian CVE programs were not initially based on providing support to returnees, they have been adapting where necessary.[48] These programs are multi-agency and may include local police forces, mental health experts, social workers, and community/religious institutions.

Although CVE has become a controversial topic in Canada, there is a consensus among experts that some kinds of programs are required to prevent individuals from re-engaging in (or supporting) violent extremist activities. Even if Canada can charge and successfully prosecute returnees with crimes, they will not be in prison forever. Having programs that work towards lessening the danger of these individuals once they leave prison is in Canada's interest.

Conclusion

Returnees represent a serious national security threat to Canada. Statistical analysis demonstrates that their attacks tend to be deadlier than those caused by homegrown violent extremists. At the same time, they may not represent the large-scale threat that had been envisioned by national security agencies. Although Europe has seen thousands of returnees, there has not been a corresponding increase in the number of attacks. Further, it is not clear that returnees are forming "sleeper cells." As a report by the Egmont Institute notes, the Kouachi brothers who conducted the 2015 Charlie Hebdo attack in Paris are outliers among violent extremists, in that they were able to lie low for a number of years.[49]

It is important to recognize that IS has been more successful at inspiring individuals already in Western countries to conduct attacks, rather than dedicating its resources to a campaign of out-of-area operations.[50] In this sense, Canada already has experience in investigating and countering the major and most likely threat posed by IS in the coming years.

Unfortunately, the discussion about returnees is driven largely by fear rather than by fact. Concerns about returnees have crossed into political debates over immigration policy, multiculturalism, and refugees.[51]

This situation has not been helped by politicians and journalists who have consistently (or perhaps deliberately) gotten the actual numbers and policies wrong. References to "sixty ISIS foreign fighters" returning to Canada have been made by Cabinet ministers, politicians, and even the prime minister.[52] While a nuanced breakdown of these numbers has been provided in the 2018 and the 2019 Public Safety Threat reports, it is unlikely that most regular Canadians are reading such specialized reports.

A second major conflation is between programs that are designed to "prevent" and those that are designed to "disengage." Programs created to help communities combat extremism by helping them deal with the pressures of integration and multiculturalism have been characterized by accusations that the government is trying to "deradicalize" by reading IS returnees poetry.[53] Prevention and disengagement programs have their place in a comprehensive policy to counter violent extremism, but they are separate, serving different needs and audiences, and should not be conflated.

It is not clear why the media and politicians consistently get the numbers and policies wrong on Canadian extremist travellers, but misinformation can be exploited by actors who seek to create mistrust and discord for their own political ends. Moreover, it serves to discredit one of the few counterterrorism tools we have. Nearly every study of returnees cited in this chapter suggests that a CVE triage, supported by agencies across different levels of government, is essential to protecting countries from the threat of violence. There is also no evidence that CVE strategies take away from more muscular counterterrorism policies and strategies – on the contrary, they are complementary. In Canada, our CVE strategies are based largely on research initially funded by the Harper government through its Kanishka program and is now being put into practice. Addressing the problems of foreign fighters and returnees will require a toolkit of flexible and agile options. As it is likely there will be foreign fighters in the future, it makes sense to prioritize developing these tools now.

Finally, it is probable that the foreign fighter issue will loom large in Canada's Middle East policy for years, but the status quo policy of trying to ignore the situation is untenable. While Canadians may think they are safer if our foreign fighters are detained abroad, they continue to pose a risk to the region and possibly Canada in the long run. It is worth remembering that the Islamic State got its start in a prisoner camp during the 2003 Iraq War. In Camp Bucca, Abu Bakr al-Baghdadi was able to form the networks that would eventually enable him to revive an insurgency in Iraq to deadly results.

Moreover, abandoning Canada's foreign fighter problem to the Kurds, a stateless people who are involved in their own fight for survival, is unsustainable and unfair. As a nation that respects the rule of law, Canada should gather evidence of war crimes, repatriate its foreign fighters, and prosecute them at home.

NOTES

1 All dates and data current to August 2020.
2 Personal communication, Rukmini Callimachi, December 2018.
3 Canadian Press, "Tories Want Action against Self-Confessed ISIS Recruit Reportedly Living in Toronto," 11 May 2018, https://www.ctvnews.ca /politics/tories-want-action-against-self-confessed-isis-recruit-reportedly -living-in-toronto-1.3926046.
4 Canadian Press, "Tories Want Action against Self-Confessed ISIS Recruit Reportedly Living in Toronto," CTV News, 11 May 2018, https://www.ctvnews .ca/politics/tories-want-action-against-self-confessed-isis-recruit-reportedly -living-in-toronto-1.3926046.
5 Stewart Bell, "Islamic State: 'I Just Want to Go Back': Canadian ISIS Fighter Captured in Northern Syria Speaks Out," Global News, 10 October 2018, https://globalnews.ca/news/4528417/canadian-isis-fighter-captured -in-northern-syria-speaks-out/.
6 Sirwan Kajjo, "Canada Urged to Repatriate IS Suspects, Relatives Held in Syria," VOA, 1 July 2020, https://www.voanews.com/extremism-watch /canada-urged-repatriate-suspects-relatives-held-syria.
7 Save the Children, "Syria: Thousands of Foreign Children in Al Hol Camp Must Be Repatriated Given Coronavirus Fears," 11 May 2020, https://www .savethechildren.ca/article/syria-thousands-of-foreign-children-in-al-hol -camp-must-be-repatriated-given-coronavirus-fears/.
8 Ruth Sherlock, "Trinidadian Mom Reunites with Kids Taken by Their Father to ISIS," NPR, 26 January 2019, https://www.npr.org/2019/01 /26/688326707/trinidadian-kids-taken-away-to-isis-reunite-with -mom-thanks-to-help-from-a-rock-.
9 Bethan McKernan, "Inside al-Hawl Camp, the Incubator for Islamic State's Resurgence," *Guardian,* 31 August 2019, https://www.theguardian.com /world/2019/aug/31/inside-al-hawl-camp-the-incubator-for-islamic -states-resurgence.
10 Charles Lister, *The Syrian Jihad* (New York: Oxford University Press, 2015).
11 Lorne Dawson and Amarnath Amarasingam, "Talking to Foreign Fighters: Insights into the Motivations for Hijrah to Syria and Iraq," *Studies in Conflict & Terrorism* 40, no. 3 (2016): 191–210; Amarnath Amarasingam and Lorne

Dawson, "'I Left to Be Closer to Allah': Learning about Foreign Fighters from Family and Friends," ISD Report (2018), https://www.isdglobal.org /isd-publications/i-left-to-be-closer-to-allah-learning-about-foreign-fighters -from-family-and-friends/.

12 Peter Mandaville, "Transnational Muslim Solidarities and Everyday Life," *Nations and Nationalism* 17, no. 1 (2011): 7–24; Amarnath Amarasingam, *Pain, Pride, and Politics: Social Movement Activism and the Sri Lankan Tamil Diaspora in Canada* (Athens: University of Georgia Press, 2015).

13 Peter Mandaville, "Muslim Transnational Identity and State Responses in Europe and the UK after 9/11," *Journal of Ethnic and Migration Studies* 35, no. 3 (2009): 496.

14 Mandaville, "Muslim Transnational Identity," 496.

15 To keep things straightforward, we do not focus here on the dozens of individuals who have fought and returned to Canada from previous conflicts such as Afghanistan, Lebanon, Libya, and Somalia. We limit the discussion in this chapter to Canadians who have joined Sunni rebel and jihadist groups – such as Ahrar al-Sham, Jabhat al-Nusra, and the Islamic State – in Syria and Iraq since around 2012. In the second half of the report, we explore the key policy challenges Canada faces as well as what is known about its response so far. In developing policy recommendations, it looks at the response of its allies and makes recommendations for the future.

16 Public Safety Canada, *2018 Public Report on the Terrorist Threat to Canada*, April 2019, https://www.publicsafety.gc.ca/cnt/rsrcs/pblctns/pblc-rprt -trrrsm-thrt-cnd-2018/index-en.aspx.

17 Public Safety Canada, "Mitigating the Threat Posed by Canadian Extremist Travellers," 20 December 2020, https://www.publicsafety.gc.ca/cnt /ntnl-scrt/cntr-trrrsm/cndn-xtrmst-trvllrs/index-en.aspx.

18 Public Safety Canada, *2018 Public Report*.

19 Amarnath Amarasingam, "Canadian Foreign Fighters in Syria: An Overview," Jihadology, 4 March 2015, https://jihadology.net/2015/03/04 /the-clear-banner-canadian-foreign-fighters-in-syria-an-overview/.

20 Vice News, "Islamic State Member Warns of NYC Attack, 25 September 2014, https://www.youtube.com/watch?v=j8TLu514EgU.

21 Stewart Bell, "As Fate of ISIS Prisoners in Syria Grows More Unpredictable, RCMP Has Still Not Charged Any of the Canadians," Global News, 15 October 2019, https://globalnews.ca/news/6027248/kurdish-forces-rcmp -canadians/. See also Amarnath Amarasingam's discussion on Twitter: https://twitter.com/AmarAmarasingam/status/1085602370707427329.

22 Amarnath Amarasingam, "Canadian Foreign Fighters in Syria: An Overview," Jihadology, 4 March 2015, https://jihadology.net/2015/03/04 /the-clear-banner-canadian-foreign-fighters-in-syria-an-overview/.

23   See Stewart Bell, "How RCMP Officers Tracked Three Canadian Girls in Egypt," *National Post*, 15 April 2015, https://nationalpost.com/news/canada/how-rcmp-tracked-canadian-girls-in-egypt-before-they-could-join-isis-in-syria.

24   If we include the at least eighteen children currently being held by the YPG in Syrian camps, this number increases to forty-nine.

25   Colin Clarke and Amarnath Amarasingam, "Where Do ISIS Fighters Go When the Caliphate Falls?," *Atlantic*, 6 March 2017; Stewart Bell, "Dealing with Foreign Fighters: Document Reveals RCMP Strategy for Possible 'Flood of Foreign Fighters' Returning to Syria," *National Post*, 27 October 2016.

26   General Intelligence and Security Service (AIVD), *Focus on Returnees*, February 2017, 5.

27   AIVD, *Focus on Returnees*, 5; RAN, *Manual Responses to Returnees: Foreign Terrorist Fighters and Their Families*, July 2017, 20.

28   Caveats to this research into the foreign fighter/returnee phenomenon are still nascent and hampered by access to open source information about plots only.

29   Thomas Renard and Rik Coolsat, eds., *Returnees: Who Are They, Why Are They (Not) Coming Back and How Should We Deal with Them*, Egmont Paper 101, February 2018. See also a similar assessment made in Radicalization Awareness Network, *RAN Manual Responses to Returnees: Foreign Terrorist Fighters and Their Families*, July 2017, 20.

30   RAN, *RAN Manual*, 15.

31   Public Safety Canada, *2018 Public Report on the Terrorist Threat to Canada*, April 2019.

32   Lorenzo Vidino, Francesco Marone, and Eva Entenmann, *Fear Thy Neighbour: Radicalization and Jihadist Attacks in the West* (Milan: Italian Institute for International Political Studies, 2017), 37–61.

33   Thomas Hegghammer and Petter Nesser, "Assessing the Islamic State's Commitment to Attacking the West," *Perspectives on Terrorism* 9, no. 4 (2015): 14–30.

34   Hegghammer and Nesser, "Assessing the Islamic State's Commitment."

35   David Malet and Rachel Hayes, "Foreign Fighter Returnees: An Indefinite Threat?" *Terrorism and Political Violence* 13 (2018): 1–19.

36   AIVD, *Focus on Returnees*, 4–5.

37   AIVD, *Focus on Returnees*, 5–6; RAN, *Manual*, 18–20.

38   Canada Centre for Community Engagement and Prevention of Violence, "National Strategy on Countering Radicalization to Violence," Public Safety Canada, 2018, 36. See also Public Safety Canada, "Mitigating the Threat Posed by Canadian Extremist Travellers," 11 December 2018, https://www.publicsafety.gc.ca/cnt/ntnl-scrt/cntr-trrrsm/cndn-xtrmst-trvllrs/index-en.aspx.

39 See Stewart Bell, "Exclusive: Canada's Plan for Managing the Return of ISIS Fighters Revealed in Documents," Global News, 14 May 2018, https://globalnews.ca/news/4205480/canadas-plan-freturn-isis-fighters/.

40 Citizenship is governed under section 6 of the charter and states, "Every citizen of Canada has the right to enter, remain in and leave Canada." While it is subject to section 1 where the government can justify limits as reasonable in a free and democratic society, section 6 is not subject to the section 33 notwithstanding clause. The government would not be able to appeal a Supreme Court decision on the matter. Sean Fine, "How Law to Strip Terrorists of Citizenship Fits into Global Picture," *Globe and Mail*, 2 October 2015, https://www.theglobeandmail.com/news/politics/how-law -to-strip-terrorists-of-citizenship-fits-into-global-picture/article26640140/. For a summary of legal and practical issues related to stripping Canadian citizenship, see the testimony of Craig Forces to the Senate Committee on Social Affairs, Science and Technology, Standing Committee on Social Affairs and Technology, 16 February 2017, https://sencanada.ca/Content /SEN/Committee/421/SOCI/pdf/16issue.pdf. That this is the view of the government was confirmed in documents obtained by Stewart Bell under the Access to Information Act: Public Safety Canada, "Briefing Note for the Minister: Canada's Approach to Terrorism and Violent Extremism" (RDIMS #2382669, n.d.).

41 PowerPoint presentation obtained by Stewart Bell under the Access to Information Act: Federal Policing Criminal Operations, "Terrorism and the National Security Environment: LinCT Regional Workshop," PowerPoint, *RCMP*, slide 32, 6 April 2017.

42 Documents obtained by Bell under the Access to Information Act, "Briefing Note for the Minister"; "17-002092 Input to Scenario Note: Counter Terrorism, South East Asia Region Law Enforcement Coordination Meeting, Singapore July 26–27, 2017."

43 Documents obtained by Stewart Bell under the Access to Information Act: RMCP, "Issue: Countering Terrorism and Countering Radicalization to Violence" (n.d.); PowerPoint presentation obtained by Bell under the Access to Information Act, "Terrorism and the National Security Environment," slide 37.

44 Documents obtained by Bell under the Access to Information Act, "Briefing Note for the Minister."

45 Information from Michael Nesbitt and Harman Nijjar, "Table of Canadian Terrorism Cases to Date," 17 June 2021. https://static1.squarespace.com /static/59b99154bce176cf26878ef3/t/60cb6861e998f20eb0b6acb6 /1623943265837/IntrepidBlog_TerrorismChargesData.pdf.

46 Section 83.3 of the Criminal Code of Canada.

47 Mubin Shaikh, Hicham Tiflati, Phil Gurski, and Amarnath Amarasingam, "Turning the Page on Extremism: Deradicalization in the North American

Context," in *Routledge Handbook of Deradicalization and Disengagement*, ed. Stig Jarle Hansen and Stian Lid, 312–25 (London: Routledge, 2020).

48 See Stephanie Carvin and Craig Forcese, "An Intrepid Podcast Special Part 3: Foreign Fighters and Counter Violent Extremism Interventions," Intrepid, episode 84, 2019, https://www.intrepidpodcast.com/podcast/2019/4/11/ep-84-an-intrepid-podcast-special-part-3-foreign-fighters-and-counter-violent-extremism-interventions.

49 Renard and Coolsat, *Returnees*, 16.

50 Hegghammer and Nesser, "Assessing the Islamic State's Commitment."

51 Amarnath Amarasingam, "Is There a Terrorist Threat to Canada from Syrian Refugees?," *Canadian Diversity* 14, no. 3 (2017): 19–21, https://www.academia.edu/36385963/Is_There_a_Terrorist_Threat_to_Canada_from_Syrian_Refugees.

52 CBC.ca, "Goodale Confirms 60 ISIS Fighters in Canada," 2017, https://www.cbc.ca/player/play/1100118595721; Brad Trost, "Reintegration of ISIS Fighters in Canada," BradTrost.ca, 24 November 2017, http://bradtrost.ca/reintegration-of-isis-fighters-in-canada/.

53 Evan Dyer, "Federal Government Not Tracking Interventions with Returning ISIS Fighters," CBC, 23 November 2017, http://www.cbc.ca/news/politics/deradicalization-canada-isis-fighters-program-1.4414999; Cheryl Gallant, "Question to the Minister of Public Safety," Public Safety Committee, 30 November 2017, https://openparliament.ca/committees/public-safety/42–1/88/cheryl-gallant-7/.

6 Humanitarian Foreign Policy and Refugees: Welcoming Syrians in Crisis

NAWROOS SHIBLI

This chapter outlines Canada's role in resettling and assisting Syrian refugees in the context of the Syrian civil war and analyses the implications for Canadian foreign policy in the Levant. The social, political, and economic changes that followed the eruption of the Arab uprisings in the Middle East and North Africa (MENA) had significant consequences on power dynamics in the region, but nowhere have the effects of the popular uprisings and state responses been more severe or potent than in the Syrian Arab Republic. Embroiled in a civil war since 2011, Syria has held the rapt attention of the international and regional community, resulting in international policies and actions in response to one of the most substantial corollaries of the war: the refugee crisis.

What was Canada's response to the Syrian refugee crisis, and how did it fit with its strategy for the Middle Eastern conflict? Why did the Trudeau government respond to calls for greater humanitarian involvement in the region? How did Canada's role in the resettlement of refugees compare to that of other members of the international community? What factors prompted the change in policy towards what was effectively the greatest occurrence of forced migration since the Second World War?[1] And what are the impacts of the resettlement initiative on Canadian foreign policy more broadly? These are some of the questions that will be addressed. This chapter argues that Canada's Syrian refugee resettlement initiative was an integral part of its response to the Syrian civil war writ large, marking a shift in Canadian foreign policy back to its traditional humanitarian roots. Canada led at the international level in accepting Syrian refugees, signalling its commitment to a rules-based international order and the importance of international legal obligations.

Syrian Refugees

The Syrian civil war precipitated one of the worst humanitarian crises since the mid-twentieth century. What began with popular protests and demonstrations of widespread discontent against a repressive government during the Arab uprisings ended in a civil war complicated by non-state actors and proxies influenced by external governments. The civil war resulted in the destruction of cities, villages, and vital infrastructure, damage to critical transportation routes, heightened insecurity, increased violence, and internal displacement of Syrians. The situation was exacerbated by the onslaught of the Islamic State (IS), which wreaked havoc across the region introduced by a brutally archaic governance apparatus through which state boundaries were punctured, intensifying the mass exodus of people into the bordering countries of Iraq, Turkey, Jordan, Lebanon, and Egypt. These countries have experienced the highest number of refugees and migrants.

To put this into perspective, of the twenty-three million Syrians living in the country pre-2011 civil war, more than half have been displaced, and over thirteen million require humanitarian assistance internally.[2] As of April 2018, the United Nations High Commissioner for Refugees (UNHCR) estimated that 6.6 million Syrians have been internally displaced with upwards of five million more on the move externally, seeking refuge across the MENA and beyond.[3] This number does not account for migrants who remain unregistered and unable to access UNHCR services as a result of the precariousness of their movement in the midst of conflict and insecurity.[4] Presumably these numbers also neglect to account for those who died during their migrant journey through mountain crossings, on dinghies across perilous waters, or under wartime fire and bombings towards their final destinations.[5] With roughly sixty million refugees in the world today, a harrowing one in ten hail from Syria.[6] With borders getting tighter against the flood of refugees seeking safety, millions of people find themselves in a position of statelessness.

Given these staggering statistics and unimaginable realities, how did the surrounding countries in the MENA and abroad react to the need emanating from Syria and its population? And how did Canada's response compare?

A Survey of the International Responses to the Crisis

To appreciate what would be a deviation from international norms at this time with Canada's response to the Syrian refugee crisis, a summary of the regional and international responses is useful.

The UNHCR 2014 Syria Regional Response Plan (RRP) initially called on the international community for US$4.2 billion in monetary assistance to meet the needs of the 4.1 million people affected by the conflict in Syria that year.[7] With a primary focus on protecting refugees by providing asylum, ensuring food provisions, education, shelter, basic needs, sanitation, and health services, the RRP's requests for funds were intended for three particular population groups: refugees living in camps, refugees living in informal settlements outside of camps, and the communities hosting the arriving refugees.[8] Although the RRP was amongst the only concerted international efforts addressing the humanitarian aspect of the Syrian emergency, it was criticized for not being holistic in its approach: "It illustrates a containment paradigm that is unsustainable and dangerous, rather than an approach that more equitably shares the responsibility towards the individual refugees among the wider community of states outside the current host region."[9] In response, the UNHCR ultimately expanded its RRP to include humanitarian admissions, asking members of the international community to accept up to thirty thousand of the most vulnerable Syrian refugees for resettlement by the end of 2014.[10] Eventually Canada would meet these requests.

In the meantime, however, countries in Syria's immediate neighbourhood were overwhelmed by the sheer number of refugees crossing their borders. Since the beginning of the crisis, Turkey has received and accepted the highest number of Syrians into the country with 3.6 million registered refugees by 2019 in Turkish cities and in the twenty-two refugee camps spanning ten provinces.[11] With an initial open-door policy, Syrians were able to cross into Turkey from Syria at designated entry points with little trouble.[12] The Turkish government has since revised this policy by tightening border controls and increasing security at checkpoints to deal with the large volumes of irregular migration.[13] The government's principle measure to oversee the migration crisis, the Temporary Protection Regulation, precludes recognition of forced migrants as refugees and inhibits pathways to permanent residency and integration, instead promising limited short-term sanctuary with variable access to social and economic benefits, including health care, education, social assistance, and the labour market.[14] The international community has favourably viewed Turkey's management of the issue as an efficient way to meet obligations under the 1951 Refugee Convention and address the immediate needs of displaced Syrians. Recent reports from Human Rights Watch, however, have indicated that, contrary to Turkey's temporary protection initiative, nine of the ten provinces surrounding the Turkish-Syrian border have suspended registration of Syrian asylum seekers, no longer allowing newly arrived Syrians to register for temporary protection, and in some cases forcibly deporting them.[15] This is all part of an effort to deter Syrians from seeking refuge in an overwhelmed Turkey and to essentially keep Syrians in Syria. Though these concerning instances do not diminish the country's substantial response to the refugee crisis, it does highlight systemic issues with the current refugee policies in the region.

Lebanon hosts the second-largest Syrian refugee population within its borders with approximately 930,000 registered refugees.[16] The country's "no camp policy" has resulted in increased insecurity for displaced persons: approximately one in five people in Lebanon is a refugee, of which half are children, living in informal settlements in northern urban centres.[17] With common occurrences of insurgent fighting along the border and an already substantial and historically situated Palestinian refugee demographic, the influx of Syrians has overwhelmed Lebanon's capacity to provide for and protect newly arrived refugees,[18] especially since the country – like Syria and Jordan – is not party to the 1951 Refugee Convention or Protocol and thus has ad hoc refugee laws that do not facilitate permanent residency and instead underscore eventual resettlement elsewhere.[19] In effect, the state does not intend to allow for its Syrian refugee population to remain within its borders or to integrate as full members of Lebanese society.

Jordan's shared border with Syria has similarly resulted in a substantial inflow of refugees, with more than 600,000 registered Syrian refugees.[20] While over 80 per cent of these men, women, and children reside outside of camps, and just over 120,000 live in camps such as Za'atari and Azraq, roughly 93 per cent of refugees in Jordan live in poverty.[21] Like Turkey, Jordan had an open-border policy for Syrians fleeing violence in their home country, but after shouldering the socio-economic responsibility for so long, its policies have been pulled back in an effort to constrict the flow of migrants into Jordan's already strained camps and on its drained financial resources.[22] The gradual closure of the shared border has been further aggravated by the practice of refoulement whereby, contrary to international legal norms, the Jordanian government has deported droves of Syrians back to war-torn areas where the risk of death is high.[23] The kingdom also does not facilitate permanent integration into society and provides no avenue with which to gain permanent residency, though refugees do have access to education, health care, and other basic services.[24] Underscoring the dire living conditions and lack of legal recourse and work, many have repatriated to Syria despite the ongoing conflict, with sentiments that they would "rather die in Syria than live in a camp."[25] Nevertheless, Jordan – like Turkey and Lebanon – has borne the brunt of the Syrian refugee crisis and has often resorted to the coercive and premature collective return of refugees as a result of security concerns and insufficient international assistance in the face of a long-term economic burden.

Of course, other surrounding countries like Iraq and Egypt have also hosted a significant number of refugees.[26] Having experienced uprisings of its own and an economic depression and new political regime that followed, the situation in Egypt has not been kind to incoming Syrian refugees, especially since the only options available to them are voluntary repatriation or resettlement in a third country.[27] Iraq's own volatile political and economic situation, in a post-IS conflict phase, has resulted in challenging circumstances for Iraq's own population and Syrians seeking safety. The upsurge of refugees in the already drained and fragile Iraq amplified the growing humanitarian needs in the country; the closure of eight camps in February 2019 complicated the dire conditions faced by Syrian refugees and internally displaced Iraqis, which has caused premature returns and additional displacement.[28]

These cases demonstrate that the Syrian humanitarian crisis has most directly affected the MENA region, despite popular renderings of the crisis as an exceptional emergency affecting Europe the most.[29]

Still, many of the aforementioned neighbouring countries are considered transit countries for many Syrians. Because of the limited or non-existent pathways to permanent residency and integration in the MENA and with no end in sight in the Syrian civil war and thus little probability of a safe, dignified return home, many refugees have chosen to take the risk and extend their journey through irregular and undocumented means towards Europe in hopes of finding stability and security. However, the European Union (EU) has notoriously securitized its borders with strict interdiction policies on land and at sea, while some states have even offshored their detention camps for incoming migrants, asylum-seekers, and refugees. These strict border controls, an illustration of the EU's desire to police who can and cannot cross Europe's external and internal points of entry, have resulted in thousands of preventable deaths, including the drowning of entire refugee families who crossed unpredictable Mediterranean waters in hopes of reaching safe lands. A product of increased border regulations and severe migration policies, 2262 migrants drowned at sea in an attempt to reach European coasts in 2018 alone, with upwards of 3000 dying at sea in the four consecutive years prior.[30] In 2019 alone, roughly 124,000 people risked the treacherous journey to Europe, the majority by crossing the Mediterranean Sea, while 1336 were feared to have drowned or went missing en route.[31] It was the image of a child – one who had risked the perilous journey by boat with his family and countless others – drowned and face down on a Turkish beach, that would stir the international community, including Canada, into action.

Canada's Response: From Harper to Trudeau

At a time when most countries were tightening their immigration policies and closing their borders against the perceived instability emanating from the Middle East in the bodies of Syrian migrants, Canada veered from the global trends of containment and paved its own path in response to the dire resettlement needs of the families, women, and children fleeing war and persecution. What precipitated this sudden shift in Canada's position on the Syrian conflict?

It cannot be understated that 2015 was a critical election year. Prior to Justin Trudeau's Liberals coming to power, the incumbent Conservative government held a stern stance on the Syrian issue in the latter half of 2015: Prime Minster Stephen Harper not only supported exclusionary immigration and refugee policies; he and members of his party also adopted dangerous public discourses linking Syrian refugees and Muslim asylum seekers with terrorism.[32] The emphasis was on national security, rigorous and discriminatory immigration screening processes that included selective prioritization of ethno-religious minorities such as Yazidis and Christians (thereby precluding the vulnerable Muslim populations, which comprised the majority of fleeing Syrians, and also contravening norms of non-discrimination as per international refugee laws), and active military support in Syria.[33] Under Harper, Canada took in a minimal number of refugees for resettlement through an extensive vetting process and limited public services upon their arrival because these people – many of whom were alleged "bogus refugees" (undercover IS extremists either parading as deserving refugees in order to assault Canada and the United States by stealth or fraudulently seeking to use and abuse the Canadian welfare state) – could very well represent a security threat to the country.[34] This politically charged, fear-inciting rhetoric was espoused by many right-leaning politicians to galvanize public opinion against intervention in the crisis, including at times by Harper himself. A spring 2015 Environics Institute survey reflected this when it revealed that only 37 per cent of Canadian respondents rejected the statement that "most people claiming to be refugees are not real refugees."[35]

Trudeau's election pledge juxtaposed that of the Conservatives. His policy was not one of restriction and insular exclusion, but rather one that assumed a whole-of-government approach that reflected not only Canada's national identity as a welcoming, multicultural society, but also its international liberal identity as a compassionate, peacekeeping, responsible global citizen.[36] His proposed directives were to "enhance security and stability, provide vital humanitarian assistance, and help partners deliver social services, rebuild infrastructure and good governance."[37] On the 2015 campaign trail, the Liberal Party leader promised that, if elected, Canada would resettle 25,000 Syrian refugees by the end of the year,[38] compared to the 10,000 Syrian and Iraqi refugees Harper committed to resettling over the next four years if re-elected, in addition to a previous pledge made in January 2015 of admitting 10,000 refugees.[39]

During this time, Canadians held favourable views on immigration, with 57 per cent stating that there was not too much immigration in Canada and 82 per cent agreeing that immigration was economically beneficial for the country.[40] Still, in an Ipsos poll conducted in November 2015 shortly after the horrific Paris attacks, 60 per cent of Canadians opposed Trudeau's plan to accept 25,000 Syrian refugees into Canada, citing security as their primary concern,[41] and a similar survey conducted at this time by the Angus Reid Institute highlighted that 54 per cent of Canadians disapproved of the government's original plan with similar concerns about too-short timelines and security anxieties.[42] Of the respondents surveyed by Ipsos, 67 per cent agreed with the "bogus refugee" theory that terrorists disguised as refugees would infiltrate Canadian borders; 75 per cent believed that Canada was vulnerable to an attack similar to that in Paris, up from the 61 per cent who thought an assault on home territory represented a real threat to Canadians in a poll taken a month earlier.[43] The Paris attacks heightened Canadians' anxiety about a possible terrorist threat from the Middle East, but despite these enhanced fears, 67 per cent of Canadians disagreed that the country's borders should be completely closed down.[44]

Interestingly, an Ipsos poll taken a month later in December 2015 showed a thaw in Canadian public opinion towards the refugee crisis and the government's role in it: 54 per cent of Canadians now favourably viewed plans to resettle Syrian refugees.[45] This increase in support was due in part to the way Trudeau personally handled the arrival of the first Syrian refugees by warmly receiving them at Toronto Pearson Airport,[46] remarking, "Tonight they step off the plane as refugees, but they walk out of this terminal as permanent residents of Canada."[47] The diminishing number of trustworthy proponents citing evidenced-based security concerns damaged the credibility of the "bogus refugee" theory, which in turn helped soften the public's stance towards welcoming Syrians to the country and the government's plan to facilitate the mass resettlement.[48]

In early 2016, 52 per cent of Canadians supported Trudeau's plan to resettle 25,000 Syrian refugees,[49] with the majority of the public being amenable to the plan so long as appropriate security requirements were not compromised.[50] This figure sits in contrast to earlier polls, which indicated that a majority of Canadians originally opposed the Liberal Party's refugee promise. This reversal of public opinion could be ascribed to the revised program deadlines, which alleviated worries that the original timeline was too short and would undermine the immigration security screening process and public safety.[51] The decision to extend the original timeline is attributed to the Paris attacks and the public's new sensitivities towards potential terrorist threats and perceived security risks.[52] This shifted the country's foreign policy in a direction that reflected public sentiment and national self-perceptions of Canada as doing the right thing.

The heartbreaking image of three-year-old Syrian refugee Alan Kurdi lying lifeless in the sands of a Turkish beach stimulated the debate even further, nationally and internationally. Having so strongly captured the attention of the global public and the media, the Syrian humanitarian emergency – embodied by the small, limp body of a drowned boy – finally precipitated change in refugee policies at home and abroad.[53] Prior to Alan's death on 2 September 2015 and the extensive circulation of his image worldwide, the international community addressed the plight of Syrians with folded arms and cold shoulders. It was not until after this tragedy and the associated eruption of crisis discourse in media and political circles that countries more cohesively mobilized in response to the repercussions of the Syrian conflict. A "macabre catalyst for progressive change,"[54] Kurdi's tragic and wholly preventable death brought to bear questions, criticisms, and changes within Canada on the country's role in Syria. When it was later uncovered that Kurdi's aunt in Vancouver had previously tried and failed to privately sponsor her family and bring them to Canada (her sponsorship claim had been rejected), the incumbent government's unforgiving immigration processes were publicly scrutinized, with allegations that Canada was partially responsible for a tragedy that could have been avoided.[55] It was at this point that both Trudeau and Harper responded with promises to resettle 25,000 Syrians and an additional 10,000 Syrian and Iraqi refugees, respectively.

Election fever and rhetorical fervour aside, the refugee policies proposed by the Tories and the Liberals were substantively similar in content, though not in detail, breadth, or discourse. All of Canada's major political parties enjoined similar stances on the Syrian refugee crisis in establishing that it must expand its overall response to the humanitarian emergency and broaden its commitment to resettling Syrian refugees, with policies ranging from sparing to generous. The disparities between Trudeau's and Harper's positions must not be overstated, as they were generally comparable, despite significant rhetorical differences. The most notable distinction in their views was in volume and process: they agreed that Canada should and would welcome those fleeing war and persecution in Syria, but they disagreed on how many refugees Canada should accept, the period of time in which to admit them, and their demographic makeup. As the polls ultimately indicated, however, Trudeau's empathetic plan for refugee resettlement spoke most closely to the spirit of Canadians at the time. Interestingly, with changes to the initial refugee program, including revised deadlines and a shift in the composition of those admitted, Trudeau's ambitious promise turned out to be quite similar to the plans outlined by the Harper government.

For comparative purposes, it is helpful to note the total number of refugees admitted to Canada. Table 6.1 features the volume of permanent residents, including traditional resettled refugees (those who have arrived through government, private, or blended sponsorship) and protected persons (asylum seekers who applied for and were granted refugee status) into Canada each year. It underlines parallels between Stephen Harper's and Justin Trudeau's stances on refugees more generally. Harper's refugee acceptance rates were consistent over his nine years in office. While the 2015 refugee levels are unequally split under the management of both Harper and Trudeau, the 2016 numbers represent Trudeau's first full year overseeing immigration policy, with the steep increase due to the Syrian refugee resettlement program, which was well underway by that time. Although the dip from 2017 onwards provokes the question of whether Trudeau's benevolent refugee rates can be sustained over the longue durée, the data confirm the large number of refugees welcomed into Canada, as per his 2015 election promise.

Canada took big strides in leading the way on the refugee crisis. On 24 November 2015, the newly elected Liberal government declared its commitment to resettling a record number of Syrian refugees in Canada.[56] The new initiative was facilitated in a three-pronged model consisting of government-assisted refugees (GAR), privately sponsored refugees (PSR), and blended Visa Office-referred refugees (BVORR) programs, all of which require medical, criminal, and security screenings. While GARs are sponsored entirely by the government and PSRs are sponsored by private groups, BVORRs are jointly sponsored by civil organizations and the government.[57] Trudeau made good on his 2015 campaign promise: between September 2015 and February 2016, with a mixture of GARs (15,000), PSRs, and BVORRS (13,000 across the latter two categories), Canada resettled more than 28,000 Syrian refugees across the country.[58]

Table 6.1. Canadian Admissions of Resettled Refugees by Immigration Category, Citizenship World Area, and Landing Year

Immigration category and world area of citizenship	Annual average 2004–12*	2013	2014	2015	2016	2017	2018	January–June 2019
Africa & Middle East	0	120	140	720	4,250	1,210	1,065	340
Americas	0	10	30	10	30	35	40	0
Asia & Pacific	0	55	45	75	150	35	40	5
Europe	0	0	0	0	–	–	0	0
Stateless	0	0	–	5	5	10	10	40
United States	0	0	0	0	0	–	0	0
Blended sponsorship refugee total	**0**	**185**	**215**	**810**	**4,435**	**1,295**	**1,155**	**385**
Africa & Middle East	3,326	4,215	6,225	8,155	22,830	7,920	7,565	4,075
Americas	1,089	310	205	160	150	340	185	90
Asia & Pacific	2,167	885	1,020	1,010	525	285	315	240
Europe	214	10	20	20	10	50	–	–
Stateless	29	–	45	50	30	35	15	30
United States	0	0	0	0	–	0	0	0
Not stated	2	–	0	0	0	0	0	0
Government-assisted refugee total	**6,827**	**5,425**	**7,515**	**9,400**	**23,545**	**8,630**	**8,085**	**4,435**
Africa & Middle East	2,911	5,390	3,830	7,825	16,785	14,475	16,235	6,895
Americas	89	30	–	5	10	15	10	–
Asia & Pacific	982	1,000	685	1,455	1,410	1,960	2,055	1,685
Europe	13	5	–	10	20	10	25	–
Stateless	43	35	70	40	130	225	205	80
United States	0	0	0	–	5	10	35	5
Not stated	0	–	0	0	0	0	0	0
Privately sponsored refugee total	**4,038**	**6,460**	**4,590**	**9,340**	**18,360**	**16,700**	**18,570**	**8,670**
Total	**10,865**	**12,070**	**12,320**	**19,550**	**46,340**	**26,620**	**27,810**	**13,490**

Source: IRCC, Permanent Residents, June 2019 data. Data request tracking number RE-19-0416.
Note: Data are preliminary estimates and are subject to change. Values between 0 and 5 are shown as "–" to prevent individuals from being identified when IRCC data are compiled and compared to other publicly available statistics. All other values are rounded to the closest multiple of 5 for the same reason; as a result of rounding, data may not sum to the totals indicate.
* Rounded to nearest whole number.

Indeed, between November 2015 and December 2018, Canada admitted 61,955 Syrian refugees for resettlement,[59] a number far surpassing the initial pledge of 25,000 people.

Of course, Canada's Refugee and Humanitarian Resettlement Program was not the only addition to its revamped foreign policy towards Syria. The government made other changes in line with this humanitarian focus: Trudeau recalled the Canadian air force from its combat missions in Syria and Iraq (see the Massie and Munier chapter in this volume), emphasized diplomatic relationship-building, and increased Canada's contributions to development projects in the affected MENA region as a result of the Syrian conflict.[60] As of early 2018, Canada dedicated over C$1.6 billion towards humanitarian aid, development funding, and security initiatives – including financial support, health and medical provisions, educational assistance, technical training, protection, and capacity-building projects to major refugee camps in Jordan, Lebanon, and surrounding areas.[61] Canada was among the most generous contributors to the Syria Emergency Relief fund with a contribution of C$31.8 million between September 2015 and February 2016, with Jordan receiving the bulk of Canada's humanitarian relief assistance and development aid.[62] Given its commitment to the Syrian crisis and considering its experience with resettling large numbers of refugees, Canada has been well-suited to export its knowledge and expertise to the Middle Eastern countries most affected by the civil war.[63]

Having led on the Syrian refugee issue, the government of Canada was internationally commended for its commitment and contribution in the resettlement processes. The government's Syrian initiatives, its private sponsorship program in particular, have been so successful that both the United Kingdom and Australia have piloted similar programs in order to create a Canadian-esque "culture of welcome," alluding to the slogan for Canada's Syrian initiative, "Welcome Refugees."[64] Both the former head of the International Organization for Migration (IOM) and the former UN high commissioner for refugees praised Canada for its advocacy on behalf of the most vulnerable refugee populations and its stance against the ever-growing tides of xenophobia that continue to mark the immigration policies of many states.[65] Canada's trailblazing position on the refugee crisis, in comparison to the hostile and hesitant reactions of much of the world, fortified its standing on the international stage.[66] The change in foreign policy that accompanied Trudeau's ascendance to government reflected well on Canada's international reputation as a humanitarian, liberal, and progressive country.

To further appreciate Canada's divergence from the prevailing foreign policy responses to the Syrian situation, it is helpful to situate it in contrast to that of the United States. As close partners, the Canadian and American worldviews are often in sync; both countries have worked in concert in different foreign policy arenas on the Middle East in the past. But the Syrian situation represented a shift in this status quo. Although President Obama's plan to resettle 10,000 Syrian refugees in 2016 was reached, with proposed plans of an additional 25,000 for 2017, this commitment to international burden-sharing in the Syrian conflict was halted with the ascendance of the Trump administration.[67] Instead of answering the UNHCR's calls for international support for displaced Syrians, President Trump issued an executive order in 2017 that imposed a travel ban on Muslim majority countries such as Syria and Iraq, affecting the admission of refugees. Public responses from the Canadian prime minster and the American president further underscored this departure from traditionally aligned foreign policy approaches: Trudeau personally greeted the first Syrian refugees to arrive as part of the government's new commitment, welcoming them with new winter coats and the assurance, "You're safe at home now,"[68] while Trump spewed rhetoric likening Syrian refugees to IS terrorists, warning citizens to be vigilant and "lock your doors."[69] Despite the American response to the refugee situation, under Trudeau's leadership Canada tailored its policy to fit the perceptions of the Canadian body politic, public sentiments, and Canadian values.

Conclusion

Understanding the shift in Canada's response through its Syrian resettlement initiative illustrates a new direction in the country's foreign policy towards the Middle East more broadly, a nod to its traditional humanitarian roots, and an indication of a different course for the future. A central focus of the 2015 federal elections, Canada's involvement in the Syrian civil war and its response to the flood of Syrian refugees seeking asylum was a critical aspect of the Liberal and Conservative election campaigns. It was also an issue of primary concern for Canadians who wished to see their country shake off the vestiges of a closed, unsympathetic, insular foreign policy under the previous Harper government, which they felt did not reflect Canada's welcoming, inclusive, and multicultural history, identity, and image. Indeed, on the Syrian refugee crisis, the Liberal party platform hearkened back to Canada's history of relieving the suffering of vulnerable peoples and assisting refugees in need, with references to the Hungarian refugees in the 1950s, Ismaili Muslim refugees of the 1970s, and the boat people of Southeast Asia in the 1970s and 1980s,[70] in the last of which Prime Minister Pierre Trudeau played an important role. This intentional reference to humanitarian moments in Canadian history underlines the fact that the proposed, and now current, refugee resettlement program is simply an extension of traditional, compassionate immigration and refugee policies intrinsic to Canada's spirit of internationalism and hospitality.

The Syrian Refugee and Humanitarian Resettlement Program was but one small element of Canada's response to the Syrian conflict overall, as well as in its larger involvement in the Middle East. The new policy in Iraq, Syria, and the region demonstrates a turn in Trudeau's foreign policy to that of a principled middle power in the MENA. Canada's soft power potential as highlighted through its financial, material, and capacity-building support in the areas bordering the conflict zones indicates a renewed commitment to regional cooperation, international security, and humanitarian relief. That other countries around the world look to Canada as a global example for resettlement expertise further hints at Canada's growing soft power prowess in the international arena. This pivot away from hard power strategies and active military entanglements in war zones towards standard-setting humanitarian assistance and traditional Canadian diplomacy has added metaphorical gold coins to Canada's bank of goodwill in the region and has positioned Canada as a trailblazer in refugee resettlement by a third country as well as a reliable leader during times of human crisis. As such, the Canadian government's pledge to resettle 25,000 vulnerable Syrian asylum seekers and its overachievement of this promise embodies the country's true involvement in the Syrian civil war, cementing Canada as a pivotal, principled player paving its own path in world affairs.

NOTES

1   International Organization for Migration, "A New Home: Resettling Syrian Refugees in Canada" (Geneva, 2017), 8, https://publications.iom.int /books/new-home-resettling-syrian-refugees-canada.
2   Nergis Canefe, "Introduction: Syrians Are Coming? Reframing the Syrian Refugee Crisis," *Refugee Watch* 48 (May 2017): 1; United Nations High Commissioner for Refugees, "Syria Emergency," 19 April 2018, https:// www.unhcr.org/syria-emergency.html.
3   Canefe, "Introduction," 1; Michaela Hynie, "Canada's Syrian Refugee Program, Intergroup Relationships and Identities," *Canadian Ethnic Studies* 50, no. 2 (2018): 1; United Nations High Commissioner for Refugees, "Syria Emergency."
4   United Nations High Commissioner for Refugees, "Syrian Regional Refugee Response," Operational Portal: Refugee Situations, accessed 32 July 2019, https://data2.unhcr.org/en/situations/syria.

5 Canefe, "Introduction," 4.

6 Canefe, "Introduction," 4; René Houle, "Results from the 2016 Census: Syrian Refugees Who Resettled in Canada in 2015 and 2016," Statistics Canada: Insights on Canadian Society (Ottawa, 2019): 2, https://www150.statcan .gc.ca/n1/en/pub/75-006-x/2019001/article/00001-eng.pdf?st=i5sviJVW.

7 Sarah Bidinger, Aaron Lang, Danielle Hites, Yoana Kuzmova, and Elena Noureddine, "Protecting Syrian Refugees: Laws, Policies, and Global Responsibility Sharing" (Boston, 2015): 1, https://www.bu.edu/law/files /2015/08/syrianrefugees.pdf.

8 United Nations High Commissioner for Refugees, "2014 Syria Regional Response Plan: Strategic Overview," 2014, 7, https://www.unhcr.org /syriarrp6/docs/Syria-rrp6-full-report.pdf.

9 Bidinger et al., "Protecting Syrian Refugees," 1.

10 United Nations High Commissioner for Refugees, "2014 Syria Regional Response Plan," 31; Bidinger et al., "Protecting Syrian Refugees," 2.

11 United Nations High Commissioner for Refugees Turkey, "Syrian Refugee Camps and Provincial Breakdown of Syrian Refugees Registered in South East Turkey," 30 July 2018, https://reliefweb.int/sites/reliefweb.int/files /resources/UNHCR_Syrian-Refugee-Camps-and-Provincial-Breakdown -of-Syrian-Refugees-Registered-in-South-East-Turkey-August-2018-1.pdf; United Nations High Commissioner for Refugees, "Syrian Regional Refugee Response."

12 Bidinger et al., "Protecting Syrian Refugees," 96.

13 Ayşegül Akdemir, "Syrian Refugees in Turkey: Time to Dispel Some Myths," Conversation, 26 September 2017, http://theconversation.com /syrian-refugees-in-turkey-time-to-dispel-some-myths-80996.

14 Suzan Ilcan, Kim Rygiel, and Feyzi Baban, "The Ambiguous Architecture of Precarity: Temporary Protection, Everyday Living and Migrant Journeys of Syrian Refugees," *International Journal of Migration and Border Studies* 4, no. 1/2 (2018): 58; Human Rights Watch, "Turkey Stops Registering Syrian Asylum Seekers: New Arrivals Deported, Coerced Back to Syria," 16 July 2018, https://www.hrw.org/news/2018/07/16/turkey-stops-registering -syrian-asylum-seekers.

15 Human Rights Watch, "Turkey Stops Registering Syrian Asylum Seekers: New Arrivals Deported, Coerced Back to Syria." This includes Adana, Gaziantep, Kahramanmaraş, Kilis, Mardin, Mersin, Osmaniye, and Şanlıurfa province; Istanbul has also halted the registration of Syrians as of February 2018.

16 United Nations High Commissioner for Refugees, "Syrian Regional Refugee Response."

17 Bidinger et al., "Protecting Syrian Refugees," 29; International Organization for Migration, "New Home," 11.

18 Thomas Juneau, "The Civil War in Syria and Canada's Containment Policy," *International Journal* 70, no. 3 (2015): 475.

19 Bidinger et al., "Protecting Syrian Refugees," 29, 34.

20 United Nations High Commissioner for Refugees, "Syrian Regional Refugee Response."

21 United Nations High Commissioner for Refugees, "Syria Emergency"; United Nations High Commissioner for Refugees, "Syrian Regional Refugee Response."

22 Sarah El Deeb, "Aid Groups Urge Jordan to Open Border to Fleeing Syrians," *Washington Post*, 27 June 2018, https://www.washingtonpost.com /world/middle_east/aid-group-urges-jordan-to-open-border-to -displaced-syrians/2018/06/27/3da0f270-79e2-11e8-ac4e-421ef7165923 _story.html?utm_term=.bf5d3995b4f8.

23 Alice Su. "Why Jordan Is Deporting Syrian Refugees," *Atlantic*, 20 October 2017, https://www.theatlantic.com/international/archive/2017/10/jordan -syrian-refugees-deportation/543057/; Human Rights Watch, "'I Have No Idea Why They Sent Us Back': Jordanian Deportations and Expulsions of Syrian Refugees," 2017, https://www.hrw.org/report/2017/10/02/i-have-no-idea -why-they-sent-us-back/jordanian-deportations-and-expulsions-syrian.

24 Bidinger et al., "Protecting Syrian Refugees," 56.

25 Bidinger et al., "Protecting Syrian Refugees," 56.

26 United Nations High Commissioner for Refugees, "Syrian Regional Refugee Response."

27 Bidinger et al., "Protecting Syrian Refugees," 76.

28 USA for United Nations High Commissioner for Refugees, "Iraq Refugee Crisis: Aid, Statistics and News," 2018, https://www.unrefugees.org /emergencies/iraq/.

29 Canefe, "Introduction," 2.

30 Samantha Raphelson, "More Than 3,100 Migrants Died Crossing Mediterranean in 2017," The Two-Way, NPR, 2017, https://www.npr.org /sections/thetwo-way/2018/01/06/576223035/more-than-3-100 -migrants-died-crossing-mediterranean-in-2017; United Nations High Commissioner for Refugees, "UNHCR Appalled at News of Refugee and Migrant Deaths on Mediterranean Sea," 19 January 2019, https://www.unhcr.org /news/press/2019/1/5c41e8a04/unhcr-appalled-news-refugee-migrant -deaths-mediterranean-sea.html.

31 United Nations High Commissioner for Refugees, "Refugee & Migrant Arrivals to Europe in 2019 (Mediterranean)," UNHCR, 2019, https://data2 .unhcr.org/en/documents/download/74670.

32 Petra Molnar, "The Boy on the Beach: The Fragility of Canada's Discourse on the Syrian Refugee 'Crisis,'" *Connection: The Multidisciplinary Journal of Social Protest* 4, no. 1–2 (2016): 70.

33 Xavier Léger Guest, "Narratives on Arrival: The Framing of the Syrian Refugee Crisis in Canadian Parliamentary Debates" (University of Ottawa, 2018), https://ruor.uottawa.ca/handle/10393/37992; Canadians for Justice and Peace in the Middle East, "2015 Election Guide: Syrian Refugee Crisis," 2015, https://www.cjpme.org/an_2015_10_15_election_guide_syrian _refugees_crisis.

34 Victoria M. Esses, Leah K. Hamilton, and Danielle Gaucher, "The Global Refugee Crisis: Empirical Evidence and Policy Implications for Improving Public Attitudes and Facilitating Refugee Resettlement," *Social Issues and Policy Review* 11, no. 1 (2017): 105; Molnar, "Boy on the Beach," 70.

35 Melissa Carlier, "Explaining Differences in the Canadian and American Response to the Syrian Refugee Crisis," *Virginia Policy Review* 9, no. 2 (2016): 61.

36 Anne-Marie Mcmurdo, "Causes and Consequences of Canada's Resettlement of Syrian Refugees," *Forced Migration Review* 52 (2016): 82.

37 Léger Guest, "Narratives on Arrival," 49.

38 Esses, Hamilton, and Gaucher, "Global Refugee Crisis," 105.

39 Carlier, "Explaining Differences," 68; Hynie, "Canada's Syrian Refugee Program," 4; Laura Payton, "Election Issues 2015: A Maclean's Primer on Syrian Refugees," *Maclean's*, 3 September 2015, https://www.macleans.ca /politics/ottawa/refugees-primer/.

40 Carlier, "Explaining Differences," 68.

41 Andrew Russell, "60% of Canadians Disagree with Liberal Plan to Accept Syrian Refugees: Ipsos Poll," Global News, 20 November 2015, https:// globalnews.ca/news/2352983/60-of-canadians-disagree-with-liberal-plan -to-accept-syrian-refugees-ipsos-poll/.

42 Angus Reid Institute, "Canadians Divided on Legacy of Syrian Refugee Resettlement Plan," 19 February 2016, http://angusreid.org/canada -refugee-resettlement-plan/.

43 Russell, "60% of Canadians Disagree."

44 Russell, "60% of Canadians Disagree."

45 Andrew Russell, "Canadians' Support for Taking in Syrian Refugees Is Increasing: Ipsos Poll," Global News, 30 December 2015, https:// globalnews.ca/news/2426553/canadians-support-for-taking-in-syrian -refugees-is-increasing-ipsos-poll/.

46 Russell, "Canadians' Support for Taking in Syrian Refugees."

47 Ian Austen, "Syrian Refugees Greeted by Justin Trudeau in Canada," *New York Times*, 11 December 2015, https://www.nytimes.com/2015/12/12 /world/americas/syria-refugees-arrive-in-canada.html.

48 Russell, "Canadians' Support for Taking in Syrian Refugees."

49 Angus Reid Institute, "Canadians Divided on Legacy."

50 Carlier, "Explaining Differences," 63.

51 Angus Reid Institute, "Canadians Divided on Legacy."

52 Léger Guest, "Narratives on Arrival"; Angus Reid Institute, "Canadians Divided on Legacy"; Yannis Behrakis, "Canada's New Refugee Plan: What We Know (and Don't Know) so Far," *Globe and Mail*, 25 November 2015, https://www.theglobeandmail.com/news/politics/canadas-new-refugee -plan-what-we-know-and-dont-know-sofar/article27476421/.

53 Kim Rygiel, "Dying to Live: Migrant Deaths and Citizenship Politics along European Borders: Transgressions, Disruptions, and Mobilizations," *Citizenship Studies* 20, no. 5 (2016): 545.

54 Molnar, "Boy on the Beach," 73.

55 Jennifer Hyndman, William Payne, and Shauna Jimenez, "The State of Private Refugee Sponsorship in Canada: Trends, Issues, and Impacts," 20 January 2017, 4, http://jhyndman.info.yorku.ca/files/2017/05/hyndman _et-al.-RRN-brief-Jan-2017-best.pdf; Hynie, "Canada's Syrian Refugee Program," 5; Barbara J. Messamore, "Justin Trudeau and Canada's 2015 Election," *Round Table* 105, no. 1 (2016): 82.

56 Houle, "Results from the 2016 Census," 2; David Delacrétaz, Scott Duke Kominers, and Alexander Teytelboym, "Refugee Resettlement," 8 November 2016, 5, www.t8el.com/jmp.pdf.

57 Joseph Garcea, "The Resettlement of Syrian Refugees: The Positions and Roles of the Federation of Canadian Municipalities and Its Members," *Canadian Ethnic Studies* 48, no. 3 (2016): 151.

58 Garcea, "Resettlement of Syrian Refugees," 152.

59 Immigration Refugees and Citizenship Canada, "Canada: Admissions of Syrian Refugees by Province/Territory and Census Metropolitan Area (CMA) of Intended Destination and Immigration Category, November 4th, 2015 – December 31st, 2018" (Ottawa: IRCC – Open Government, 2019), https:// open.canada.ca/data/en/dataset/4a1b260a-7ac4-4985-80a0-603bfe4aec11.

60 Stuti Banerjee, "Canada and the Liberal Government: One Year After," Indian Council of World Affairs, 30 May 2017, 3, https://icwa.in/show _content.php?lang=1&level=3&ls_id=5034&lid=752.

61 Banerjee, "Canada and the Liberal Government," 6; International Organization for Migration, "New Home," 10; Government of Canada, "Canada's Response to the Conflict in Syria," 2018, https://international.gc.ca/world -monde/issues_development-enjeux_developpement/response_conflict -reponse_conflits/crisis-crises/conflict_syria-syrie.aspx?lang=eng.

62 Juneau, "Civil War in Syria," 484, 486; Government of Canada, "Canada's Response to the Conflict in Syria."

63 Hyndman, Payne, and Jimenez, "State of Private Refugee Sponsorship," 9.

64 Hyndman, Payne, and Jimenez, "State of Private Refugee Sponsorship," 9.

65 Les Perreaux, "After Syria Initiative, UN Looks to Canada as a Refugee Haven," *Globe and Mail*, 3 November 2017, https://www.theglobeandmail.com /news/politics/after-syria-initiative-un-looks-to-canada-as-a-refugee-haven

/article36836631/; Vappu Tyyskä, Jenna Blower, Samantha DeBoer, Shunya Kawai, and Ashley Walcott, "Canadian Media Coverage of the Syrian Refugee Crisis: Representation, Response, and Resettlement," *Geopolitics, History and International Relations* 10, no. 1 (2018): 12.

66 Jonathan Kay, "Why Canada's Refugee Policy May Actually Be Doing More Harm Than Good," *National Post*, 8 September 2017, https://nationalpost.com/news/canada/jonathan-kay-why-canadas-refugee-policy-may-actually-be-doing-more-harm-than-good.

67 Haeyoun Park and Rudy Omri, "US Reaches Goal of Admitting 10,000 Syrian Refugees. Here's Where They Went," *New York Times*, 31 August 2016, https://www.nytimes.com/interactive/2016/08/30/us/syrian-refugees-in-the-united-states.html; Hanne Beirens and Susan Fratzke, "Taking Stock of Refugee Resettlement: Policy Objectives, Practical Tradeoffs, and the Evidence Base," Migration Policy Institute Europe, 2017, 2.

68 Austen, "Syrian Refugees Greeted."

69 Esses, Hamilton, and Gaucher, "Global Refugee Crisis," 105, 87.

70 Liberal Party of Canada, "2015 Platform: Syrian Refugees."

7 Supporting Civil Society: Jordan's Changing Development Landscape

E.J. KARMEL[1]

The promotion of democracy remains a stated foreign policy objective of the Canadian government,[2] but it has been largely subsumed under the banners of good governance and stability and is often given diminished priority in more vulnerable contexts. Indeed, a striking aspect of "Canada's Middle East Engagement Strategy" is that, while it emphasizes stabilization and the achievement of good governance, it does not mention the promotion of democracy.[3] The shift in focus towards governance and stability is not a uniquely Canadian flavour of foreign policy; it reflects a general move towards neoliberalism and, building on this neoliberal foundation, the more recent securitization of development aid among donor countries. The effects of these combined trends were palpable in the Middle East in the immediate aftermath of 11 September 2001, but they took on a new significance in the wake of the Arab uprisings. This chapter focuses on the impacts these changes have provoked for civil society in the Middle East by focusing on a specific class of civil society – intermediary organizations – that has expanded within this new development paradigm. Drawing on the case of Jordan, the chapter explores how the shift in development aid has reoriented civil society organizations (CSOs) that had previously focused on democracy, transforming them into intermediary organizations by recasting civil society as a tool for supporting good governance and stabilization.

This chapter is based on the author's observations while working for more than two years with an intermediary organization in Jordan in the mid-2010s as well as subsequent work in Jordan with international development organizations focused on governance, stability, and security.[4] It is also based on interviews conducted in Amman between February and July 2019 with members of intermediary organizations, international donors, including members of Global Affairs Canada (GAC), and international and national implementers of Canadian programming.

Civil Society and Foreign Aid

Canada's engagement with civil society in the Middle East (and beyond) over the last three decades has been guided in large part by the neoliberalization and subsequent securitization of its foreign aid. These dynamics reflect general shifts in the international aid paradigm, which have been pushed by large international donors (namely the United States) and supported – and legitimized – by mid-sized countries like Canada. The neoliberal paradigm, including its more recent securitized incarnations, has resulted in donors funnelling significant development aid through civil society; however, it has also contributed to the transformation of civil society landscapes, at least in some donor recipient countries, reorienting CSOs and limiting their scope of potential interventions.

The Neoliberalization of Aid

Neoliberalism emerged as the dominant development paradigm for donor countries in the 1980s. While Canada was not a central mover behind this shift, neoliberalism has been central to its foreign policy,[5] and the country has, in turn, supported neoliberalism's growing prevalence. Just as Canada's influence as a middle power, as Neufeld shows, legitimates the post-war Pax Americana by positioning Canada as an ostensive honest broker and moral compass,[6] Canada supported the rise of neoliberalism through the same middle-power role as well as its subsequent turn to a human security agenda.[7] As Crosby argues, Canada's "discourse and practice of human security can be understood as an informal conditioning framework for the pursuit of neo-liberal economic interests and processes in that human security is about security *within the context* of global market forces and the on-going efforts by the state to enforce them."[8]

Neoliberalism took hold in development practice in the wake of the international debt crisis of the 1970s. Responding to the ostensive failures of central planning, neoliberal "solutions" were introduced to reduce fiscal deficits, liberalize trade and investment, and deregulate domestic markets.[9] These policies were central to what became known as the "Washington consensus" and its Structural Adjustment Programs (SAPs) that increasingly guided development policy into the 1980s. However, facing economic shocks in the mid- to late 1990s, a new "post-Washington consensus" began to emerge that advocated a "softer" neoliberalism.[10] In this revised neoliberalism, good governance became a primary development focus, underpinned by a theoretical link between democracy and economic growth,[11] whereby it was hoped that improved *governance* – as opposed to *government* – could provide a means to correct market imperfections.

The role of civil society in development grew significantly in the offloading of government services onto non-governmental actors. As a result, funding to civil society – particularly non-governmental organizations (NGOs) – vastly increased in the 1980s, acquiring a "pedestal status" within development discourse and practice.[12] As government was brought back into vogue in the new, softer neoliberalism as a crucial – but not the *only* – actor for realizing good governance, attention partly turned away from civil society.[13] Nonetheless, civil society remained centre stage in development policy. With a focus on introducing a wider range of actors to address the problems previously created by government, civil society was identified as a key partner that could work alongside government to foster good governance.[14]

Donor countries have framed good governance as a democratic project. In the Trudeau government's Feminist International Assistance Policy, for instance, the promotion of "democracy and political participation" is included under the title of "inclusive governance."[15] In practice, however, donors have approached the realization of good governance as a technical rather than a political process.[16] Cast as a central actor for fostering good governance, civil society has likewise been viewed as playing a technical role, employed to enhance state accountability, efficiency, and stability. In this context, the key legitimizing capacity of CSOs became the mastery of standard management practices.[17] These requirements have translated into significant impacts on the kinds of CSOs with which donors will work. In response, CSOs strive to satisfy these requirements and thereby acquire top-down legitimacy in a global system (rather than bottom-up legitimacy from their beneficiaries).[18] This has led to their growing professionalization and reinforced international isomorphism, whereby CSOs all over the world increasingly resemble one another, applying uniform buzzwords such as "empowerment" and "participation,"[19] relying on similar organizational forms,[20] and employing standardized best practices in their project management.[21] In this sense, the international system provides organizations with normative ideas of appropriate goals and required project management approaches, with the innocuous implementation of workshops, trainings, and organizational development processes becoming the mechanisms of their realization.[22]

The rise of civil society alongside neoliberalism in international development has mirrored the interplay between neoliberalism and the voluntary sector at home in Canada. On the one hand, the rising influence of neoliberalism in domestic policy and the consequent shift away from government has increased the role of the voluntary sector in Canadian governance. On the other hand, this role has expanded primarily in policy delivery, not policy formulation.[23] For instance, Laforest has demonstrated that the rising prominence of Canada's voluntary sector has occurred at the cost of a significant transformation within the sector itself.[24] As funding priorities and mechanisms have changed, with the state placing greater responsibility on the voluntary sector to deliver services and reduce core funding (thereby requiring compliance with the requirements of other funding sources), voluntary organizations have been forced to respond. They have not only placed greater emphasis on organizational professionalism, but they have also focused more on the requested services and research than other activities that had been crucial to their mandates, particularly advocacy. At the same time, prominent, professionalized organizations, which were given funding preference, contributed to the framing of the sector as a willing partner in Canadian governance. As a result, NGOs were increasingly institutionalized and depoliticized, becoming part of a unified governance system rather than a separate (and even, at times, opposing) pillar to the government.

The Securitization of Aid

At the global level – and in the Middle East, in particular – the effects of neoliberalism have been augmented by the securitization of foreign policy over the past two decades, yielding what Klassen has termed "armoured neoliberalism."[25] In the wake of 11 September 2001, security concerns moved to centre stage for donors, often eclipsing the focus on the Millennium Development Goals to which countries had agreed only a year before al Qaeda's attack.[26] Against the backdrop of the "War on Terror," the aid programming of donor countries began to shift, resulting in a (further) instrumentalization of development aid for national security interests.[27] The consequent securitization of aid has been broadly represented by two trends that have emerged among donors. First, donors are increasingly implementing medium-term, development-assistance programming in countries that are in the midst of conflict or its immediate aftermath. Second, new models for development assistance have emerged that target the improvement of security in recipient countries by supporting security-sector reform (SSR).

Following 11 September, consecutive Canadian governments reshaped the country's diplomatic and security priorities. "In quick succession, these governments built a national security apparatus, and reorganized the foreign policy agencies around the military project of combatting terrorism, failed states, and weapons of mass destruction."[28] These new policies were designed alongside US grand strategies and formulated to secure Canada's regional interest. Over the last two decades, therefore,

Canadian governments have formalized a new foreign policy approach that reflects the geopolitical interests of the state.

Within the region, a key focus of Canada's Middle East Strategy is stability,[29] with Canada offering security and stabilization assistance in conflict and post-conflict environments, such as Syria and Iraq, and supplying SSR support in several countries (see Fleet and Mohamad chapter in this volume). Even though Jordan is considered to be a more stable country in the region with a functioning economy and governmental systems, and Canada's programming in the country therefore concentrates on development and humanitarian assistance to address the effect of the Syrian refugee influx (see Shibli chapter), Canada is nonetheless providing support in the security sector (albeit comparatively less), including the deployment of Canadian forces through train-and-assist teams. Moreover, given the focus of Canada's strategy in the region, security and stability concerns are reflected in the way that all of Canada's aid is delivered in Jordan.

Like neoliberalization before it, the securitization of aid policies has resulted in significant changes to the space available for civil society and the roles in which donors and northern NGOs have cast CSOs. Out of the context of the "War on Terror," civil society in the Middle East has faced increased scrutiny of its programming and financing. GAC officials and interviewed representatives of other donor countries indicated that there has been increased emphasis on ensuring that civil society funding does not end up in the hands of terrorist organizations. So more regulations have been introduced, with the result that funding is delayed and, at least in Jordan, there is further government interference. At the same time, states have been re-centred in the new stabilization focus – particularly in ally countries, such as Jordan – and desirable parts of civil society have consequently been co-opted into the security and counterterrorism agendas.[30] In both cases, donors have placed increased emphasis on working with established, professionalized organizations in the region that can maintain positive relationships with their respective governments.

The Infiltration of Civil Society in Jordan

Scholars of the Middle East have provided fruitful studies highlighting why civil society has not performed the same crucial role in democratic transitions in the Middle East that it has in other regions. In Jordan, this research has focused primarily on the bureaucratic restrictions used by the government to limit opportunities for civil society engagement. For instance, Wiktorowicz has produced excellent research on how CSOs become "embedded in a web of bureaucratic practices and legal codes which allow those in power to monitor and regulate collective activities,"[31] with the result that "civil society does not act as a conduit of freedom," and instead "further extends the state's control over its citizens."[32] While these bureaucratic tactics are central to understanding the limited engagement of civil society in Jordan, scholars have highlighted a further strategy used by the Jordanian government to control civil society: the infiltration of civil society space by establishing regime-controlled NGOs. Crucially, some authors pursuing this avenue of research have turned their attention to the role played by donors in these dynamics, focusing particularly on the infiltration of society by demonstrating how regime-controlled organizations disguised as independent civil society have become key recipients of donor funding. In doing so, this research has helped to highlight the political and funding dynamics that have emerged – due in large part to neoliberalization and securitization – and resulted in international support for government-controlled organizations. Discussed in the following section, this research provides a basis for understanding donor engagement with intermediary organizations in the prevailing paradigm.

Across the Middle East, governments have attempted to infiltrate civil society spaces through "NGOs in disguise,"[33] which are commonly referred to as (semi-) governmental NGOs (GONGOs) or regime NGOs (RENGOs). These organizations have materialized in diverse forms, but a number of authors have noted that, as a result of the monarchy's prominent role in politics in Jordan, the most common manifestation of these regime NGOs in the kingdom is royal NGOs (RONGOs). RONGOs are founded by and remain under the patronage of a member of the royal family.[34] They focus on the same issue areas as other organizations in Jordan and are also officially registered, but, because of their unique positions, they typically enjoy special privileges (which can allow for lower operational costs than competitors) and enhanced access to the government.[35] RONGOs are spared much of the legal limitations and bureaucratic hoop-jumping that confine more independent organizations, and many are provided with core funds by the state.[36]

Despite receiving state funding, RONGOs in Jordan also compete with other CSOs for international funding; indeed, some scholars suggest that the raison d'être for RONGOs is the capture of international funds earmarked for civil society as a way to bypass the state.[37] These organizations have been very successful in this regard. RONGOs have become favoured partners of international donors (and received a significant portion of donor funds) for two key reasons.[38] First, their core funds ensure professionalized staff who can compile strong proposals and subsequently deliver effective projects. Second, the funding of RONGOs enables donors to maintain good relations with the Jordanian government, mitigating potential offences to members of the royal family. In this vein, Wiktorowicz argues that the growing prominence of RONGOs has enabled the government to "slowly establish hegemony over the direction of NGO activities," thereby allowing the state to benefit from "the best of both worlds – it continues to receive international aid (through NGOs controlled by the regime) while reducing formal state expenditures, thus fulfilling neoliberal requirements of structural adjustment and privatization."[39] By funding these organizations, donors have, perhaps inadvertently, enabled the Jordanian government to exert its control over civil society and allowed government affiliates to absorb a significant share of international funds.

It is easy to fault donors for their support to RONGOs, but donors are operating within a complex funding environment. They seek to assist civil society while also supporting a key ally that, in turn, supports donors' geostrategic interests but is increasingly hostile towards domestic civil society. Attempting to navigate this delicate political landscape, donors naturally remained cautious about the kinds of organizations they are willing to support. Not wanting to offend or risk destabilizing their allies in the region, donors have largely played by the rules of host governments and respected their red lines, and therefore contributed sometimes to the closing space available to civil society. Of course, donors are not ignorant of the politics surrounding civil society. In fact, most donors, including Canada, have endeavoured to support more independent forms of civil society to perform the roles that would otherwise be played by RONGOs. However, these efforts have themselves resulted in the growth of a new class of organizations with its own adverse consequences for Jordan's civil society landscape.

The Closing Space for Democratic Civil Society in Jordan

Research has highlighted the dynamics that have resulted in international support for RONGOs. However, less attention has been paid to how these dynamics have contributed to the growth of a related but distinct class of organizations that has received significant donor funding but limited attention in the literature – in Jordan or beyond. Variously referred to as "intermediary NGOs,"[40] "bridging organizations,"[41] and "support organizations"[42] in the small body of work focusing explicitly on these organizations, intermediaries occupy a space between local groups, national bodies, and international institutions. They perform functions such as organizational capacity building, training, research and advocacy, collection and dissemination of information, and networking.[43] In

Jordan, these intermediary organizations have emerged as key recipients of development funding. They have the potential to play a positive role, but, like RONGOs, they have contributed to a closing space for democratic civil society in Jordan.

The Role of Intermediary Organizations in Jordan

Intermediary organizations in Jordan have become favoured partners for donors and northern NGOs because, at the same time as they are perceived to be active members of Jordanian civil society, they also constitute organizations with which it is easy to partner. This is, in part, a function of their being well known and easily identifiable. Intermediary organizations in Jordan do not account for a large number of organizations, but they include some of the best-known in the kingdom. These organizations have typically produced well-disseminated research or monitoring reports that are published on their websites, making the organizations easy to find online. Intermediaries are also located in Amman – usually in the west of the city close to donors and northern NGOs – thereby facilitating visits and coordination.

The ease of partnership with these organizations is also aided by their relative professionalism and their extensive experience with donor-funded projects. In addition to publications, the websites of intermediary organizations offer track records (of varying quality), demonstrating that they have carried out projects that follow rigorous and well-established donor compliance and reporting processes. In combination with reputations that precede the intermediaries within the donor community, these track records render due diligence a simpler process, highlighting that intermediary organizations are capable. They signal that the organizations can write effective proposals, manage project activities and finances, and provide satisfactory reports. This assures partners that the project cycle will be relatively easy to manage, reducing the program risks of donors and northern NGOs. In this sense, intermediaries have the isomorphic qualities of development organizations that are offered by RONGOs. Thus, while these organizations are non-governmental, their professionalism and experience allow them to compete – with some success – with RONGOs and GONGOs and perform key project roles.

Interviewed members of intermediary organizations as well as donors (including Canada) and northern NGOs indicated that intermediaries have been cast in two primary roles. These roles consist first of supplying the typical services that intermediary organizations perform in other contexts, including organizational capacity building, training and staff development, research, collection and dissemination of information, and networking.[44] Second, intermediaries have also been cast as suppliers of information, often serving as a key source of information for the design of contextually sensitive programming.[45] Intermediary organizations are seen as able to perform these functions because they occupy a unique space of conceptual ambiguity between the amorphous imagined communities of local and transnational civil society. In this sense, whereas the government's co-option of civil society blurs the boundary between civil society and the state,[46] intermediaries blur the boundary between national and international civil society.

Despite their possession of the desired isomorphic NGO qualities, intermediary organizations are able to maintain a claim to the "local," in part because of their demographics. RONGOs and GONGOs are staffed (at least in their upper echelons) by elite Jordanians who, in more recent generations, attended private schools in Jordan and then pursued their post-secondary education abroad. By contrast, much of the staff in intermediary organizations come from humbler backgrounds. In this regard, their acquisition of the requisite knowledge to navigate international development spaces is a function of their working within the aid system rather than their social backgrounds. The staffs of intermediary organizations typically remain on the peripheries of these cosmopolitan spaces, regarded by members of these spaces primarily as representatives of the local rather than the transnational. Furthermore, RONGOs and GONGOs have staff who move not only in and out of high-level positions in Jordan's public and private sectors, but also northern NGOs. In contrast, staff working for intermediary organizations do not move as fluidly into international organizations, remaining more firmly "local." However, this dynamic seems to be changing, especially for senior staff members of the most prominent intermediary organizations.

Intermediary organizations have also maintained a claim to the "local" sphere because the concept of "local" carries an ambiguous meaning in the development diction, referring to Jordanian organizations generally, as well as to community-level organizations more specifically.[47] Intermediaries are cast as key partners with which donors and northern NGO partners can cooperate in order to address their knowledge and legitimacy deficits, which means that these organizations are sometimes able to "capture" their international audiences and provide them with a filtered picture of "local" situations. Donors and northern NGOs also partner with these organizations to comply with the prevailing development maxims of locally led and owned programming. This in no way suggests that donors and northern NGOs cannot differentiate between civil society actors. Instead, strong reliance on intermediaries reflects an assumption that has been observed with NGOs elsewhere:[48] because intermediaries are seen as key actors for strengthening civil society, their funding is often approached as being equivalent to building civil society.

The Genesis of Intermediary Organizations

It is important to point out that donors and northern NGOs did not simply identify intermediary organizations in Jordan that were sufficiently professionalized to facilitate effective partnerships. As in other contexts, this class of organizations has been forged within the international aid system itself. The main cohort of organizations that now make up Jordan's intermediary organizations emerged, albeit with some earlier exceptions, in the 1990s and 2000s. Reflecting a general opening in the region as governments attempted to "selectively redefine liberties,"[49] Jordan witnessed a controlled political opening in the late 1980s and early 1990s.[50] This opening led to an expansion of civil society activity and an increase in the number of NGOs.[51] With a greater available space for civil society, these organizations began to advocate for reforms salient to their own operations and many of the key concerns that were vocalized by local protestors, called *hirak*, during the Arab uprisings protests in Jordan.[52] In this sense, they were quite political, coordinating with ephemeral social movements and working at the boundaries of government red lines.

These organizations consequently represented active members of a still-under-developed civil society in the kingdom. Thus, when donors devoted increased attention to working with civil society in the region in the 1990s,[53] these organizations were seized upon because they constituted some of the most promising civil society actors in the country. Support was consequently provided to help build their capacities to scale up their impact and strengthen the wider civil society sector. Donor efforts have yielded significant effects, mirroring dynamics that have been observed in development contexts. In particular, it has resulted in the professionalization of these democracy-focused organizations. Reflecting the isomorphism of civil society discussed above, the organizations increasingly adopted the standardized management practices shared by development NGOs the world over.

The effects of aid dynamics on these (formerly) democracy-focused organizations have been potent in Jordan because of the shift in the funding environment in the country. When these organizations first attracted funding, their relationship with donors was led by demand, allowing organizations to design program priorities.[54] While not wanting to rock any boats and therefore pursuing incremental rather than radical democratic reform, the donors nonetheless permitted a degree of contentiousness, supporting civil society advocacy for key political reforms. As in many contexts, however, the donor–civil society relationship has become more supply-led in Jordan. The relationship has become more unidirectional, with aid channelled to programs that have specific goals set by donors, and CSOs acting as mere implementers that supply services and produce information.[55] In response to the suggestion that funding in Jordan had become more supply-led, one senior GAC official noted that Canada's programming in Jordan remains demand-led in that it follows the needs identified by the Jordanian government. Another GAC official elaborated, indicating that Canada does not blindly follow the wish list provided by the Jordanian government, but it tries to respond to the needs of its partner. Responding to the demands of the government may mean that Canadian programming is "locally" driven, but it provides limited space for civil society engagement.

Interviewed members of intermediaries emphasized a significant shift away from demand-led projects since the mid-2010s. However, interviewees described different ways in which this shift has manifested itself. For instance, one prominent director of an intermediary organization explained that "donors do not tell you what to do, but they specify their own objectives and goals, which do not always sit with our long-term goals." Along with other interviewees, he indicated that organizations must now fit within these goals if they want to continue receiving funds. At the same time, other interviewed members of intermediaries indicated that they have also been increasingly approached by donors and northern NGOs that are looking for "suppliers" to deliver specific, pre-formulated projects.

This shift from a demand-led to a supply-led relationship occurred in the context of the neoliberalization and securitization of foreign aid. The effects of this shift have increasingly been felt across the region since 2001 and have only intensified in the wake of the Arab uprisings. In Jordan, they took on new significance as a result of the Syrian war (and the consequent refugee crisis) and the growing threat of IS in the region. The Jordanian government responded to the emerging crises by further confining the space available to civil society – especially its more contentious manifestations. Civil society representatives noted a palpable shift in permissible discourse and programming, particularly around human rights, in this period. These changes yielded significant impacts on democracy-focused organizations, limiting their ability to exploit legal "grey areas" that had facilitated their more contentious repertoires.[56]

However, interviewed members of intermediaries indicated that the Jordanian government's heightened restrictions on civil society were not the only factor that impeded their ability to engage; they stressed that the loss of international financial support for democracy promotion was crucial in their change of foci.[57] Indeed, many asserted that continued advocacy would have been possible if international support remained – but this support also declined. In the midst of regional crises, the geo-strategic importance of Jordan expanded. Even though donors and the Jordanian government had already shared mutual interests that had contributed to the robustness of the government,[58] the crises pushed donors to place increased emphasis on ensuring the stability of the kingdom and, what one GAC official called, its "friendly government." As a result, donors grew cautious of supporting contentious civil society engagement – because it was contrary to their perceived interests in the region and because it would risk damaging their relationship with a key ally and alienate the government and undermine its legitimacy to the benefit of potentially hostile forces.[59] In this context, donors have consequently placed increasing emphasis on helping to safeguard the stability of the Jordanian government.

With increased emphasis on good governance and stability, the support available for democracy-focused organizations has grown smaller. One civil society representative identified a declining focus on democracy among donors starting around 2014. Interviewed GAC officials also acknowledged that the focus on democracy has become less prevalent in Jordan (and the Middle East more broadly), even though it remains a greater focus for Canada in other contexts, such as Latin America. They indicated that, given the immediate threats to stability and the nature of the issues being faced, there was a need to first address these issues. Thus, funding in this area has been limited. One GAC official clarified that emphasis on stability does not mean that democratization has been abandoned completely, but it is instead being approached in a slower way that focuses on the gradual strengthening of governance institutions and the long-term fostering of a more amenable political culture. While this reflects the approaches of softer neoliberalism and securitization, the GAC official noted that it also reflects experiences with limited success from focusing on democratization through shorter-term strategies that focus more on democratic institutions, such as electoral reform.

In response to changes in funding across the donor community, democracy-focused organizations have been pushed away from their more political ambitions and have reoriented to support good governance and stability. These organizations have positioned themselves not only as being able to conduct the activities donors require, but also as experts in the technical areas that are important to donors. In this sense, just as changes to government funding for Canadian civil society transformed organizations in the sector, professionalizing and reorienting them, and bringing them closer to the government, so too have democracy-focused organizations in Jordan been brought closer to their donors and northern NGO partners – and, as a result, the Jordanian government. Given their growing integration into the aid system as well as a more regulated role for civil society in it, these organizations have become less able to assert their independence, while, at the same time, their connections to grassroots constituencies have loosened, alienating them from the organizational centres of decision-making.[60] As has been discussed in other contexts, these organizations have consequently emerged as a "human face" of neoliberalism.[61] As a result, a pillar of democracy promotion in Jordan has been lost.

Conclusion

The focus of Canada's current Middle East Strategy is stabilization. However, as a result of Jordan's relative stability, Canada has placed greater emphasis on development in the country. This focus allows for a larger space to engage with civil society than is feasible in more fragile contexts in the region. As GAC officials acknowledged, not all areas of stabilization engagement provide an opportunity for engagement with civil society, but there is much more space for cooperating with and supporting civil society on the development side. As such, while constituting a relatively recent entrant to the provision of support to civil society in Jordan and therefore playing a more minor role in the transformation of the civil society landscape discussed in this chapter, Canada now provides significant support to Jordanian civil society within the current landscape. With this enlarged role and Canada in the midst of revising its strategy for the Middle East, it is important to take stock of Canada's engagement with Jordanian civil society and consider what this should look like in the future.

It is worth reviewing the continued effectiveness of cooperating with intermediary organizations for the supply of information and projects. Yet the more crucial question is Canada's long-term objectives and how working with different kinds of civil society contributes to them. If, despite the current focus on stabilization, democratization remains a long-term goal for Canada, as its foreign policy continues to suggest and GAC officials have articulated, to what extent does supporting intermediary organizations contribute to (or undermine) the realization of this objective? And what other kinds of civil society should be engaged and in what way? Of course, GAC is aware of the importance of distinguishing between and supporting different kinds of civil society. Thus, while its funding requirements prevent the Canadian Embassy in Amman from supporting non-institutionalized forms of civil society, GAC offers mechanisms through which the embassy can support smaller CSOs. A key framework in this regard is the Canada Fund for Local Initiatives (CFLI), which supports "local groups that may not otherwise qualify for funding from larger donors," thereby "helping local civil-society organizations to flourish and succeed."[62] Interviewed GAC officials emphasized the potential of the CFLI to reach beyond the usual suspects for funding, noting that they even focus on providing first-time funding to nascent CSOs.

However, it is important to consider *how* CFLI and similar mechanisms offered by Canada and other donors support these emerging organizations. Is the support provided to these organizations actually enabling them to carry out their own goals, or is it simply contributing to the genesis of the next generation of professionalized intermediary organizations? Canada's current emphasis may be on supporting civil society to enable the gradual strengthening of governance institutions, but, as has been demonstrated elsewhere in the region, the ability of civil society to foster gradual political change can be limited when civil society becomes enmeshed in local and international power structures.[63] It is also important to bear in mind that professionalization is a double-edged sword. Professionalization is necessary for large-scale support, to build a strong reputation and establish relationships; but it can also lead to tensions between organizations' activities and their overarching mission for lasting change, which often require a different set of capacities, relationships, and metrics.[64] In many of Jordan's democracy-focused organizations, changes in the aid environment (and the consequent professionalization of CSOs to engage therein) have resulted in a transformation of their substantive goals. Donors therefore need to be careful that by helping to build capacities and providing support for supply-driven projects, they are not inadvertently undermining the long-term democratic development of the countries in which they are working.

NOTES

1   The author would like to acknowledge the contribution of Janine A. Clark for her guidance and support throughout the research and writing of this chapter. He would also like to thank the editors, Bessma Momani and Thomas Juneau, as well as Rana Sweis, Haitham Abdalla, and Benjamin Schuetze for their helpful feedback on the chapter. Finally, he would like to thank the numerous participants, especially members of Jordanian civil society and Global Affairs Canada, for the invaluable insights they provided.

2 See Government of Canada, "Canada's Feminist International Assistance Policy," 2017, https://www.international.gc.ca/world-monde/issues _development-enjeux_developpement/priorities-priorites/policy-politique .aspx?lang=eng#1.

3 This chapter was written while "Canada's Middle East Strategy" for 2016–19 was in place, which was formulated in the context of Canada's contribution to the Global Coalition against Daesh. A new strategy has since replaced it but continues to omit democracy (except in relation to the Iraq country strategy). For the current strategy, see Global Affairs Canada, "Canada's Middle East Engagement Strategy," https://www.international.gc.ca/world -monde/international_relations-relations_internationales/mena-moan /strategy-strategie.aspx?lang=eng#a3.

4 While this chapter does not explicitly identify any intermediary organizations in Jordan, this connection is noted because the intermediary organization for which the author worked no longer exists.

5 Cranford Pratt, "Ethical Values and Canadian Foreign Aid Policies," *Canadian Journal of African Studies/La Revue canadienne des études africaines* 37, no. 1 (2003): 85.

6 Mark Neufeld, "Hegemony and Foreign Policy Analysis: The Case of Canada as a Middle Power," *Studies in Political Economy* 48 (1995): 7–29; and Neufeld, "Democratization in/of Canadian Foreign Policy: Critical Reflections," *Studies in Political Economy* 58, no. 1 (1999): 97–119.

7 Cranford Pratt, "Competing Rationales for Canadian Development Assistance: Reducing Global Poverty, Enhancing Canadian Prosperity and Security, or Advancing Global Human Security," in *Readings in Canadian Foreign Policy: Classic Debates and New Ideas*, ed. Duane Bratt and Christopher Kukucka, 306–23 (Don Mills, ON: Oxford University Press, 2007).

8 Ann Denholm Crosby, "Myths of Human Security Pursuits: Tales of Tool Boxes, Toy Chests, and Tickle Trunks," in *Readings in Canadian Foreign Policy: Classic Debates and New Ideas*, ed. Duane Bratt and Christopher Kukucka (Don Mills, ON: Oxford University Press, 2007), 270.

9 Craig Johnson, *Arresting Development: The Power of Knowledge for Social Change* (London: Routledge, 2009), 6.

10 David Craig and Doug Porter, *Development beyond Neoliberalism? Governance, Poverty Reduction and Political Economy* (New York: Routledge, 2006), chap. 3.

11 Sylvia Bergh, *The Politics of Development in Morocco: Local Governance and Participation in North Africa* (New York: I.B. Tauris, 2017), 3. See also Janine Clark, *Local Politics in Morocco and Jordan: Strategies of Centralization and Decentralization* (New York: Columbia University Press, 2018).

12 Ben Fine, "They F**k You Up Those Social Capitalists," *Antipode* 34, no. 4 (2002): 796.

13 Nicola Banks, David Hulme, and Michael Edwards, "NGOs, States, and Donors Revisited: Still Too Close for Comfort?," *World Development* 66 (2015): 708.

14 Craig and Porter, *Development beyond Neoliberalism?*, chap. 3.

15 Government of Canada, "Canada's Feminist International Assistance Policy."

16 Craig and Porter, *Development beyond Neoliberalism?*, chap. 3.

17 Tiina Kontinen and Anja Onali, "Strengthening Institutional Isomorphism in Development NGOs? Program Mechanisms in an Organizational Intervention," *Sage Open* (2017): 2.

18 Oliver Edward Walton, Thomas Davies, Erla Thrandardottir, and Vincent Charles Keating, "Understanding Contemporary Challenges to INGO Legitimacy: Integrating Top-Down and Bottom-Up Perspectives," *Voluntas: International Journal of Voluntary and Nonprofit Organizations* 27 (2016): 2764–86.

19 Andrea Cornwall, "Buzzwords and Fuzzwords: Deconstructing Development Discourse," *Development in Practice* 17 (2007): 471–84.

20 Terje Tvedt, *Angels of Mercy or Development Diplomats? NGDOs and Foreign Aid* (Oxford: Africa World Press, 1998).

21 Ron Kerr, "International Development and the New Public Management: Projects and Logframes as Discursive Technologies of Governance," in *The New Development Management*, ed. Sadhvi Dar and Bill Cooke, 91–110 (London: Zed Book, 2008).

22 Kontinen and Onali, "Strengthening Institutional Isomorphism."

23 See Bryan Evans and John Shields, "Nonprofit Engagement with Provincial Policy Officials: The Case of NGO Policy Voice in Canadian Immigrant Settlement Services," *Policy and Society* 33 (2014): 117–27; and Yves Vaillancourt, "Social Economy in the Co-construction of Public Policy," *Annals of Public and Co-operative Economics* 80, no. 2 (2009): 275–313.

24 Rachel Laforest, *Voluntary Sector Organizations and the State* (Vancouver: UBC Press, 2011).

25 Jerome Klassen, *Joining Empire: The Political Economy of the New Canadian Foreign Policy* (Toronto: University of Toronto Press, 2014), chap. 6.

26 Brown, "Canadian Aid Enters the Twenty-First Century," in *Struggling for Effectiveness: CIDA and Canadian Foreign Aid*, ed. Stephen Brown, 3–23 (Montreal and Kingston: McGill-Queen's University Press, 2012).

27 Liam Swiss, "Gender, Security, and Instrumentalism: Canada's Foreign Aid in Support of National Interest?," in Brown, *Struggling for Effectiveness*, 135–58.

28 Klassen, *Joining Empire*, 14.

29 As per the GAC website, the overarching focus of Canada's 2016–19 Middle East strategy is to enhance regional security and stability, to provide vital humanitarian assistance, to help host communities build resilience, and to increase diplomatic engagement in Iraq, Syria, Jordan, and Lebanon. GAC

officials, however, highlighted the centrality of security and stabilization, noting that it informs engagements even when they do not explicitly fall under security and stabilization.

30 Jeremy Lind and Jude Howell, *Civil Society under Strain: Counter-Terrorism Policy, Civil Society, and Aid Post-9/11* (Hartford, CT: Kumarian, 2010).

31 Quintan Wiktorowicz, "Civil Society as Social Control: State Power in Jordan," *Comparative Politics* 33, no. 1 (2000): 43. See also Wiktorowicz, "The Limits of Democracy in the Middle East: The Case of Jordan," *Middle East Journal* 53, no. 4 (1999): 606–20; and Wiktorowicz, "The Political Limits to Nongovernmental Organizations in Jordan," *World Development* 30, no. 1 (2002): 77–93.

32 Wiktorowicz, "Civil Society as Social Control," 58.

33 Felia Boerwinkel, "The First Lady Phenomenon in Jordan: Assessing the Effect of Queen Rania's NGOs on Jordanian Civil Society," Knowledge Programme Civil Society in West Asia; working paper 19, University of Amsterdam and Hivos, 2010, 24.

34 Given the prominence of RONGOs led by Jordan's queens, several authors have drawn specific attention to first lady NGOs (FLANGOs). See Boerwinkel, "First Lady Phenomenon in Jordan"; and Mayssoun Sukarieh, "The First Lady Phenomenon: Elites, States, and the Contradictory Politics of Women's Empowerment in the Neoliberal Arab World," *Comparative Studies of South Asia, Africa and the Middle East* 35, no. 3 (2015): 575–87.

35 Wiktorowicz, "Political Limits to Nongovernmental Organizations in Jordan," 86.

36 Janine A. Clark and Wacheke M. Michuki, "Women and NGO Professionalisation: A Case Study of Jordan," *Development in Practice* 19, no. 3 (2009): 331–2.

37 Wiktorowicz, "Political Limits to Nongovernmental Organizations in Jordan," 85.

38 Amy Hawthorne, "Is Civil Society the Answer?" in *Unchartered Journey*, ed. Thomas Carothers and Marina Ottaway, 81–114 (Washington, DC: Carnegie Endowment for International Peace, 2005); Laurie A. Brand, *Women, the State, and Political Liberalization* (New York: Columbia University Press, 1998).

39 Wiktorowicz, "Political Limits to Nongovernmental Organizations in Jordan," 86.

40 Thomas Carroll, *Intermediary NGOs: The Supporting Link in Grassroots Development* (Hartford, CT: Kumarian, 1992).

41 L. David Brown, "Bridging Organizations and Sustainable Development," *Human Relations* 44, no. 8 (1991): 807–31.

42 L. David Brown and Archana Kalegaonkar, "Support Organizations and the Evolution of the NGO Sector," *Nonprofit and Voluntary Sector Quarterly* 31, no. 2 (2002): 231–58.

43   Paromita Sanyal, "Capacity Building through Partnership: Intermediary Nongovernmental Organizations as Local and Global Actors," *Nonprofit and Voluntary Sector Quarterly* 35, no. 1 (2006): 67.

44   Sanyal, "Capacity Building through Partnership," 67.

45   Several GAC officials noted that intermediaries also constitute a key source of information for Canada's direct bilateral advocacy, but that the organizations were less likely to receive funds in this area.

46   Ozlem Altan-Olcay and Ahmet Icduygu, "Mapping Civil Society in the Middle East: The Cases of Egypt, Lebanon and Turkey," *British Journal of Middle Eastern Studies* 39, no. 2 (2012): 157–79.

47   A number of studies have highlighted the problematic nature of the concept of "local" in development and civil society. See Ann Armbrecht Forbes, "The Importance of Being Local: Villagers, NGOs, and the World Bank in the Arun Valley, Nepal," *Identities* 6, no. 2–3 (1999): 319–44; and Lori Ann Thrupp, "Legitimizing Local Knowledge: From Displacement to Empowerment for Third World People," *Agricultural and Human Values* 6, no. 3 (1989): 13–24.

48   Claire Mercer, "NGOs, Civil Society and Democratization: A Critical Review of the Literature," *Progress in Development Studies* 2, no. 1 (2002): 7–10.

49   Eberhard Kienle, "Civil Society in the Middle East," in *The Oxford Handbook of Civil Society*, ed. Michael Edwards, 146–58 (Oxford: Oxford University Press, 2011).

50   Glenn E. Robinson, "Defensive Democratization in Jordan," *International Journal of Middle East Studies* 30, no. 3 (1998): 387–410.

51   Wiktorowicz, "Civil Society as Social Control," 47.

52   Curtis Ryan, *Jordan and the Arab Uprisings: Regime Survival and Politics beyond the State* (New York: Columbia University Press, 2018).

53   Amy Hawthorne, "Middle Eastern Democracy: Is Civil Society the Answer," Carnegie Papers: Middle East Series, no. 44, 2004, 3–24; and Altan-Olcay and Icduygu, "Mapping Civil Society in the Middle East."

54   Kelly Krawczyk, "The Relationship between Liberian CSOs and International Donor Funding: Boon or Bane?," *Voluntas* 29 (2018): 296–309.

55   Alnoor Ebrahim, "Accountability Myopia: Losing Sight of Organizational Learning," *Nonprofit and Voluntary Sector Quarterly* 34, no. 1 (2005): 56–87.

56   Sameer Jarrah, "Civil Society and Public Freedom in Jordan: The Path of Democratic Reform," Saban Center for Middle East Policy, Working Paper No. 3, July 2009, 6.

57   Beyond a general change in the kind of projects and organizations that donors are supporting, interviewed members of intermediaries also believed that donors were abandoning them when they faced political or legal problems.

58 Martin Beck and Simone Hüser, "Jordan and the 'Arab Spring': No Challenge, No Change?," *Middle East Critique* 24, no. 1 (2015): 89.

59 Guilain Denoeux, "Promoting Democracy and Governance in the Arab World: Strategic Choices for Donors," in *NGOs and Governance in the Arab World*, ed. Sarah Ben Néfissa, Nabil Abd al-Fattah, Sari Hanafi, and Carlos Milani (Cairo: American University in Cairo Press, 2005), 90.

60 David Hulme and Michael Edwards, eds., *NGOs, States and Donors: Too Close for Comfort?* (London: Macmillan, 1997); and Banks, Hulme, and Edwards, "NGOs, States, and Donors Revisited."

61 Ronaldo Munck, "Global Civil Society: Royal Road or Slippery Path?" *Voluntas: International Journal of Voluntary and Nonprofit Organizations* 17 (2006): 328.

62 Government of Canada, "The Canada Fund for Local Initiatives," https://www.international.gc.ca/world-monde/funding-financement/cfli-fcil/index.aspx?lang=eng.

63 Altan-Olcay and Icduygu, "Mapping Civil Society in the Middle East."

64 Banks, Hulme, and Edwards, "NGOs, States, and Donors Revisited," 713.

8 Dealing with an Illiberal Democracy: Turkey's Erdoğan Tests Bilateral Relations

CHRIS KILFORD

Using modern-day Turkey as a case study, this chapter examines Turkey's current political situation and its government, led by President Recep Tayyip Erdoğan and the Justice and Development Party (AKP). The chapter continues with a discussion focused on contemporary Canada-Turkey relations and then highlights the importance of understanding Turkey's history to better contextualize current events, especially when crafting policy options.

Why should Canada and Canadians care about Turkey? While Canada and Turkey have had diplomatic relations since the 1940s, the two countries have little in common, apart from membership in international organizations such as the UN, NATO, and the G20. In trade, Canada's exports to Turkey were only $1.6 billion in 2019, just slightly above exports to Singapore.[1] In general, relations between Ankara and many Western capitals have also cooled recently as the result of Turkey's weakening democratic checks and balances and the government clampdown following a failed military coup in 2016. One indicator of these changes is that between 2017 and 2019, Turkey was the primary source of political refugees given asylum in Canada.[2]

Nevertheless, Turkey remains a major economic and security power situated in one of the most volatile areas of the world. What happens there, and in the Middle East, where Turkey is also a key player, often affects Canada. One example is the arrival of almost 65,000 Syrian refugees in Canada since the start of the 2011 Syrian revolution turned civil war (see the chapter by Shibli in this volume). In addition, Canada is participating in Operation IMPACT (see the chapter by Fleet and Mohamad), and was a founding member of the coalition of countries that joined in 2014 to defeat the Islamic State (IS) in Iraq and Syria and is now helping to rebuild the Iraqi security services. As part of the latter effort, Canada took command of the Baghdad-based NATO training mission in October 2018, and Canadian troops will remain in Iraq until at least 31 March 2022.[3]

Turkey's Tenuous Democratic Underpinnings and the Rise of Illiberalism

Between October 1923, when it was founded, and its first democratic election in July 1946, Turkey was a one-party state. Then, when a religiously conservative party came into power following the first free and fair election in 1950, it was overthrown by a portion of Turkey's armed forces in 1960. From that point forward, whenever a religiously based political party ran afoul of the Turkish military, it was removed from power. In 2002, many Turks turned to Recep Tayyip Erdoğan and the AKP in the hope that decades of economic mismanagement and frequent political meddling by the military would finally come to an end.

During his first years as prime minister, Erdoğan confronted many of the issues that had dogged past governments. He launched campaigns against corruption and human rights abuses and attempted to limit the military's role in Turkish society. His government also quickly moved to reign in frequent budgetary deficits, reduce inflation, and lower unemployment. Other reforms included liberalizing tax legislation that proved attractive to foreign investors and privatizing many state-owned enterprises. In this sweeping effort to resuscitate Turkey's economy, he was assisted by loans from the International Monetary Fund (IMF) and continued with economic reforms introduced by his predecessor, Bülent Ecevit. The commencement of accession talks with the EU in 2005 told of Turkey's economic turnaround.

Cautiously, and often in secret, Erdoğan also sought an end to the long-standing conflict with the Kurdish Workers Party (PKK) and reconciliation with Turkey's Kurdish minority.[4] Along the way, many Turks endorsed his vision of a confident, prosperous country playing a leading political and economic role regionally and internationally. In line with political and economic reforms introduced by the AKP during its first mandate, *Freedom House* almost declared Turkey "free" in 2005. This remained so until 2013, when Turkey's overall rankings slipped for many reasons, including the government's "arbitrary prosecutions of rights activists and other perceived enemies of the state."[5]

The 2002 election of the AKP sent shock waves through Turkey's secular establishment. There would also be many confrontations between the military and government, which came to a head in 2007, when the Turkish General Staff (TGS) published a memorandum on their website threatening the government that if Abdullah Gül, an AKP politician with a headscarf-wearing wife, were to be elected president, they would react accordingly. "It should not be forgotten," the memorandum said, "that the Turkish armed forces are a side in this debate and are a staunch defender of secularism. They will display their attitude and act openly and clearly whenever necessary."[6] Facing a potential military coup, Erdoğan called national elections forward from November to July 2007, and 46.7 per cent of Turks voted for the AKP – 13 per cent greater than in 2002. Gül was subsequently elected as Turkey's new president.

In many ways, the failure of the military to intimidate the AKP government signalled its declining hold over Turkish politics. In the decades after the 1960 coup, effectively until 2007, Turkish politicians remained under the military's watch or aware that the military might leave the barracks if provoked by the rise of religiosity and decline of secularism. Indeed, after the 1960 coup, the military removed elected governments in 1971, 1980, and 1997. And between 1980 and 1983 it ruled the country directly. The armed forces also implemented new constitutions in 1961 and 1982, designed to keep Islamist political parties in check. The 2008 *Ergenekon* and 2010 *Sledgehammer* trials, pushed by the AKP that resulted in hundreds of senior officers being jailed for coup plotting prior to 2007, weakened the military even more.[7]

However, the sidelining of the military did not mean an end to Turkey's political turmoil. Instead, once free of the military, differences over policy issues caused Erdoğan and his long-time political ally, Fetullah Gülen, to turn on each other. Gülen, a Turkish Islamic scholar living in self-imposed exile in the United States since 1999, manages a network of world-wide schools and businesses with millions of followers in Turkey, many of whom had risen to prominence in government as part of one of the most influential Islamic movements in the world. In early 2012, in a direct challenge to Erdoğan's efforts to seek a peaceful resolution with the PKK, Gülen's followers in the judiciary issued a subpoena to Hakan Fidan, the chief of Turkey's national intelligence organization, regarding secret negotiations he had conducted earlier with the PKK. If the aim was to embarrass or damage Erdoğan, it was a spectacular failure, and as events progressed, he would eventually respond by purging the judiciary and police of Gülen supporters and closing down Gülenist schools, businesses, and media outlets in Turkey such as the newspaper *Zaman*.[8]

While the political infighting between Erdoğan and Gülen was underway, a wave of demonstrations and civil unrest also began in May 2013. The Gezi Park protests, as they quickly became known, soon turned from a simple sit-in to protest urban development plans for Istanbul's Taksim Gezi Park to nationwide protests directed against the AKP government and its policies. The catalyst for the wider demonstrations was the police crackdown on the Gezi Park protestors. For the government, however, the protests were simply seen as an attempt by its opponents to topple them from power, and before long it became impossible to hold street protests of any kind.[9] "The violence practiced by the police," said Ece Temelkuran when commenting on the protests, "had nullified Turkey's chances of being a democratic or even a liberal model for the Middle East."[10] Indeed, the response to the Gezi Park protests was a clear indication, noted a Washington-based think tank, that since coming to power the AKP had moved from a broadly supported right-wing, centre-right political party to a traditional illiberal Turkish model.[11]

The political struggle between Erdoğan and Gülen reached a high point on 17 December 2013, a day that "will be long remembered in Turkish politics, as it launched an unprecedented chain of events."[12] As part of a major corruption investigation, the police launched raids that implicated the sons of three Turkish Cabinet ministers. Several days later the three Cabinet ministers resigned. Erdoğan eventually described events as "a very dirty operation" carried out by a parallel organization that had infiltrated state institutions and was now attempting to topple the government.[13] His response was to remove the public prosecutor overseeing the corruption case and get rid of any Gülen-linked police chiefs and police officers involved in the corruption investigation. On 10 August 2014, Erdoğan, following Turkey's first ever open election for the post, became Turkey's president. For him, the win was also seen as a political green light to hasten the dismantling of the Gülen movement. On 1 September the corruption probe targeting the government was closed down.

The final stage of the Erdoğan-Gülen conflict came during the late evening hours of 15 July 2016, when, according to Turkish authorities, a group of Gülenist military officers attempted, but ultimately failed, to overthrow the government. Dubbing themselves the "Peace at Home Council," their aim was to remove Erdoğan from power and, according to their declaration, reinstate constitutional order, human rights and freedoms, the rule of law, and general security. On the other hand, Gülen and his followers were quick to say that the coup attempt was a controlled coup contrived by Erdoğan to give him a free hand in silencing his opponents once and for all.

While the coup attempt did not succeed, 253 people lost their lives and 2,740 people were injured.[14] In the aftermath, a state of emergency was soon implemented, and the government suspended or sacked some 150,000 public employees with alleged ties to the Gülen movement, including thousands of university professors, judges, and prosecutors. Nearly 200 media outlets were also shut down.[15] Although the state of emergency was eventually lifted in July 2018, many of its provisions were written into law and the Turkish government continued to show little tolerance for its critics.

The Turkish government has become increasingly illiberal on human rights and freedom of expression and of the press. As Amnesty International reported in 2018, criticism of the government in the traditional and print media had largely disappeared, with Turkey rated 154th out of 180 countries in the 2020 World Press Freedom Index.[16] The *Guardian* reported that after winning the April 2017 constitutional referendum and also presidential and parliamentary elections in June 2018, President Erdoğan had "taken a giant step towards one-man rule in Turkey." Though Turkey was not yet a dictatorship, the newspaper concluded, it had become "an illiberal democracy" in which the president had cowed the opposition, judiciary, human rights organizations, and media and could now rule by decree.[17] The result was that in 2018, *Freedom House* declared Turkey "not free."[18]

That Erdoğan has survived in office speaks to his ability to consistently gather coalitions around him, depending on the political circumstances. As Soner Cagaptay noted in 2017, Erdoğan is one of Turkey's most "memorable, effective, and influential leaders."[19] Yet since the attempted coup, Erdoğan's political future seems less certain. Economically, growth fell from 7.5 per cent in 2017 to 0.9 per cent in 2019.[20] There has also been speculation that Turkey might need to ask for financial assistance from the IMF, although Erdoğan has since ruled out this possibility. Indeed, IMF loans are a very sensitive matter for him, given that Turkey paid down its IMF debt in May 2013, and the country took great pride in doing so. And, as Erdoğan is well aware, "the IMF has been very clear about its preferred solutions to Turkey's crisis: tight monetary policy, tight bank supervision, complete deregulation of the labor market, severe austerity, [and] high interest rates."[21] As for the PKK, Remzi Kartal, its co-chair, announced in 2019 that there could be no renewal of the peace process while the AKP and its far-right Nationalist Movement Party (MHP) coalition allies remain in power.[22]

Unlike many states in the Middle East, Turkey cannot rely on oil revenues to buy political loyalty; as such, well-functioning, stable domestic and regional markets are essential in order to develop the country. Any move away from peace, order, and good government, as has been recently witnessed, comes with an economic and political price. This was certainly so after ballots were counted following the 31 March 2019 municipal elections in Turkey that demonstrated that despite its grip on power, the AKP was still "vulnerable to economic and political undercurrents, just as should be the case in a normal democracy."[23]

President Erdoğan is also well aware that Turkey's Kurdish minority is growing and could one day hold the balance of political power. In June 2015, and for the first time in Turkey's history, the Kurdish-based Peoples' Democratic Party (HDP) entered Parliament passing the 10 per cent proportional election threshold and winning 80 seats in the 550-seat parliament. Even under tremendous pressure by the government, including the arrest of the party's co-leaders in November 2016, the HDP held on, taking 59 seats in a November 2015 snap election and sixty-seven seats after the June 2018 election.[24] The Kurdish vote was also a key factor behind Ekrem İmamoğlu, the opposition candidate, winning the Istanbul mayoral race in March 2019 by a slim, contested margin and a subsequent re-run, by a significantly larger one, in June 2019.[25] It is also worth noting that all these recent elections have taken place in an environment far from even the minimum standards expected in a liberal democracy. And despite the many coup-proofing actions taken by the government after July 2016, the Turkish authorities have continued to arrest military personnel for their alleged ties to the Gülen movement. The most recent wave of arrests occurred in July 2021 , indicating that the government is likely still concerned about the loyalty of some members of the armed forces.[26]

Canada-Turkey Relations

In Baskin Oran's comprehensive examination of Turkish foreign policy between 1919 and 2006, Canada merits only a single entry, on Ottawa's flooding the international market with surplus wheat in the 1950s, which drove down the value of Turkish wheat exports.[27] More recently, relations between the two countries have been driven largely by business interests, amounting to approximately $3.6 billion in annual two-way trade in 2019.[28] In bilateral relations, a major stumbling block has been Canada's 2004 recognition of the Armenian genocide. At the time, and in the years that followed, the Turkish Ministry of Foreign Affairs (MFA) was clear that "Canadian politicians had fallen prey to the pressures of an intensely hostile Armenian-Canadian community," and that the result could only be a "stagnation in bilateral relations."[29] But since 2004, many other governments have also passed resolutions recognizing the Armenian genocide, somewhat reducing Ankara's pointed frustration with Ottawa, as reflected in a general toning down of the criticism levelled at Canada. Today, for example, the MFA website simply notes that "the Canadian government's position and the resolutions adopted by both Chambers of the Canadian Parliament regarding the events of 1915 which contradict the historical facts, *had* [emphasis added] an adverse effect on the bilateral relations between the two countries."[30]

The unveiling of the Monument to Fallen Diplomats in Ottawa in September 2012 also improved relations between Canada and Turkey, especially concerning Canada's position on the Armenian genocide. Although the monument was dedicated to all public servants and diplomats who had been killed while serving overseas, there was a Turkish connection. The monument itself was a gift from the Turkish government, created by Turkish artists and sculptors, and unveiled by Ahmet Davutoğlu, then Turkey's minister of foreign affairs. As a special tribute, it was also placed close to where Colonel Atilla Altıkat, the Turkish military attaché to Canada, was assassinated while driving to work in 1982.[31] Although the perpetrators of the attack were never apprehended, it is widely believed to have been the work of the now-disbanded Armenian terrorist group ASALA.

Although Canadian diplomat Louis Delvoie wrote in 2011 that Canada and Turkey had "historically enjoyed a relationship largely devoid of bilateral substance,"[32] matters looked more promising following a visit to Turkey by the Standing Senate Committee on Foreign Affairs and International Trade in June 2013. Their report, *Building Bridges: Canada-Turkey Relations and Beyond*, noted that Turkey "was a country on the move," and a model democracy for the region with "ambitious foreign policy aspirations."[33] Canadians, they continued, needed to "engage politically, commercially and interpersonally" with their Turkish counterparts in order to create "a rewarding, long-term Canada–Turkey relationship."[34]

However, in the report there were warnings from witnesses who "pointed to the detention and imprisonment of thousands of Turks, including journalists, under anti-terrorism and other legislation as troubling signs that freedoms of expression and the media in Turkey [were] being repressed."[35] Nevertheless, the report recommended that the Canadian government should continue engaging with the Turkish government "at the highest political levels in order to develop a new and more significant bilateral relationship," and that a free trade agreement (FTA) with Turkey be fast tracked.[36]

Although an FTA between Canada and Turkey has not been forthcoming, the two countries did sign a Joint Economic and Trade Committee agreement in 2019, designed to further expand trade and investment.[37] There have also been several high-level visits between Turkey and Canada in recent years, although the onset of the COVID-19 pandemic meant that travel for in-person meetings was not possible. However, in January 2018, for example, Canada's parliamentary secretary to the minister of foreign affairs, Omar al-Ghabra, visited Turkey and met with the deputy minister of justice, the director-general of consular affairs at the Turkish Foreign Ministry, and the chief ombudsman of the Turkish Parliament.

George Furey, Canada's Speaker of the Senate, also visited Turkey in May 2019, and met with President Erdoğan and the Speaker of the Turkish Grand National Assembly. Izmir Deputy, former Speaker of the Parliament, and the last prime minister of Turkey, H.E. Binali Yıldırım, paid a similar visit to Canada in September 2019.[38]

However, the crackdown on the Gülen movement by the Turkish government, after its National Security Council labelled the movement the Fetullah Terrorist Organization (FETÖ) in May 2016 has had an impact on bilateral relations. After the attempted coup, Ankara began pressuring many countries to hand over alleged members of FETÖ while also flooding Interpol with notices seeking detention of 60,000 people allegedly connected to the Gülen movement.[39] In Canada, the number of Turkish citizens granted refugee status surged, and while not every Turkish refugee accepted by Canada self-proclaimed to be a Gülenist, the assumption was that "the Immigration and Refugee Board of Canada takes it as a given that Turks affiliated with Gülen will be at risk if they return to Turkey."[40] Prior to 2016, it was rare for Turks to claim refugee status in Canada, although some did after the 2013 Gezi Park protests. But following the July 2016 failed military coup attempt, which the Turkish government blamed on followers of Turkish Islamic cleric Fetullah Gülen, matters changed dramatically. Between 2017 and 2019, for example, 4,697 Turkish citizens were granted refugee status by Canada, the highest number of accepted claims from any country.[41]

After the coup attempt, the Turkish government also set out to make life as "miserable" as possible for Gülenists everywhere, including Canada.[42] Ankara urged Ottawa to close the Nile Academy, a private Gülen-affiliated school in Toronto. Gülen followers in Canada also reported that the Turkish government was spying on them and family members in Turkey were consistently harassed by the police. Gülen-inspired organizations such as the Anatolian Heritage Foundation and the Intercultural Dialogue Institute, "founded by Turkish Canadians inspired by the teachings and example of Fethullah Gülen," adopted a much lower profile.[43] Other organizations such as the Turkish Canadian Chamber of Commerce, associated with the Gülen movement, appear to have ceased operations in 2016.[44] More recently, in July 2020, the *Globe and Mail* reported that fifteen Canadian citizens, who also hold Turkish citizenship, had been named as suspects in a Turkish government-led anti-terrorist investigation and that Turkey's national intelligence agency had compiled files on all of them based on their alleged links to Gülen organizations in Canada. As for Turkey's position, the Turkish ambassador to Canada, Kerim Uras, defended Turkey's actions as perfectly reasonable, comparing the monitoring of Gülenists in Canada to the same way "the

Canadian embassy in Ankara pays attention to Canadians who travelled to Syria and Iraq to join the Islamic State."[45]

Another issue of concern for the Turkish government is international support to the PKK, which Canada also considers a terrorist organization. According to the 2016 Statistics Canada census, 63,955 people reported their ethnic origin as Turkish and 16,315 as Kurdish.[46] On the latter designation, it is not possible to tell how many, if any, who report their ethnic origin as Kurdish are actually Turkish-born Kurds or Kurds from another country. As for support to the PKK in Canada, it appears to be limited to websites and Facebook accounts such as the one belonging to the Democratic Kurdish Federation of Canada, which contains postings critical of the Turkish government.[47] However, in March 2019, the Canada Revenue Agency did remove the Toronto-based Anatolia Cultural Foundation's charitable status after it determined that $160,000 had been directed towards "groups or individuals associated with, or supportive of, the PKK," and the charity was "advancing and promoting a political ideology associated with the PKK."[48]

The most recent cause of friction between Canada and Turkey has its roots in Turkey's Operation Peace Spring. This October 2019 cross-border military incursion into north-eastern Syria has been focused on pushing back the Kurdish-dominated Syrian Democratic Forces (SDF) and creating a safe zone along the Turkish-Syrian border, where some of the 3.6 million Syrian refugees hosted by Turkey could be resettled. The Turkish government regards the SDF as a cover for the Syrian-Kurdish People's Protection Units (YPG), which it considers an extension of the PKK. While SDF officials deny any links to the PKK, there is plenty of evidence to suggest otherwise. Until 1999, the PKK was based largely in Syria and Syrian-controlled Lebanon, and more recently an Atlantic Council study noted that between January 2013 and January 2016, Turkish Kurds comprised 49.24 per cent of the YPG's self-reported casualties.[49] And SDF units often display flags with the face of imprisoned PKK leader Abdullah Öcalan on them.[50]

However, as a result of Operation Peace Spring, Canada and several other Western countries placed an arms embargo on Turkey. This was a significant move, because in Canada's international arms trade, Turkey ranked in fourth place behind the United States, Saudi Arabia, and Belgium in 2018, with sales to Ankara of almost $116 million. Now any new permit requests to export military items to Turkey, said the Canadian government, would be "presumptively denied."[51]

In addition, while the website of the Canadian Embassy in Turkey still paints an optimistic picture of current issues in the country and region, the Canadian government's travel advisory is more cautious. Visitors are advised to exercise a high degree of caution in Turkey "due to the threat of terrorist attacks and the possibility of demonstrations," to avoid all travel to the border with Syria and all non-essential travel to the southeast. "Turkish authorities," the advisory adds, "have detained and prosecuted people over social media posts criticizing the government, state officials, president, military operations. You could be subject to scrutiny even if a post was published years ago or outside of Turkey."[52]

Given the current state of affairs, an important question for Canada is in which direction will Turkey go. Will it become more authoritarian and move away from the West? The 2019 municipal election setback for the AKP has caused some commentators to suggest that Erdoğan might soften his stance, but this is likely wishful thinking.[53] The 2023 national election, which coincides with the 100th anniversary of the Turkish Republic, is not an election he will want to lose. Therefore, the most probable path is a continuation of the current political polarization and impasse with an ineffectual opposition unable to dislodge an increasingly controlling president.

Even if Erdoğan left politics, it is doubtful any post-Erdoğan government would do things differently. The main opposition parties in Turkey, less the Kurdish-based HDP, are led by aging nationalists who have struggled to come up with any sort of policy alternatives to those of the AKP. None challenge fundamental state principles, such as denial of the Armenian genocide. They also have little to say on Turkey's regional military operations or how the military is organized and structured, and offer no policy alternatives to address Kurdish issues. In short, it is important for Canadian policymakers to realize that there are few policy differences, economic or otherwise, between the main political parties on Turkey's chief domestic and foreign policy issues.

Regionally, and in the wake of the Arab uprisings, Turkey's ambitious foreign policy aspirations have also been held in check. During the early days of the Arab uprisings, Erdoğan aligned with the Muslim Brotherhood (MB) and supported Egyptian President Mohammed Morsi, but he was removed from power in July 2013 by General Abdel Fattah al-Sisi (see the chapter by Allam). Sudanese dictator Omar al-Bashir suffered the same fate in April 2019. Turkish support for the MB, Hamas in Gaza, and Brotherhood-linked opposition groups in Syria also led to a falling-out with Saudi Arabia and the United Arab Emirates, who regard the MB as a security threat. Ankara's attempt to topple Bashar al-Assad in Syria also failed, resulting in millions of Syrians seeking refuge in Turkey, and the Turkish presence in northern Syria is an ongoing economic burden. Turkey's military support, along with that of Sudan and Qatar, to the National Salvation Government in Tripoli, Libya, is yet another costly decision, with Turkey increasingly being drawn further into a civil war that it cannot afford.[54] Apart from Qatar, it would seem that Turkey has few friends in the region today.

Conclusion

Since its foundation in 1923, Turkey has been surrounded by neighbours where political convulsions are the norm and avoiding collateral damage often impossible. Turks have also witnessed numerous humiliations: The piecemeal destruction of the Ottoman Empire, the foreign-led Ottoman Public Debt Administration, which essentially ran the economy between 1881 and 1914, defeat in the First World War, the end of the Ottoman Empire, frequent weapons boycotts and political interventions by its closest allies, punishing economic downturns requiring IMF loans, and a consistent cold-shouldering by the EU. It is no wonder that Turkish governments, regardless of their political leanings, are hypersensitive to any sort of foreign criticism and just as quick to respond in kind.

In addition, Turkey is the only NATO country confronting a destructive and demoralizing domestic insurgency that has ebbed and flowed over thirty-five years and the only European country whose people defiantly stared down an attempted military coup in 2016. The recent cultivation of deeper economic and military ties with Russia, on the cusp of Turkey shooting down a Russian jet fighter in November 2015 and the assassination of the Russian ambassador in Ankara in December 2016, is just one example of Turkey having to swiftly pivot to protect its interests. Turkey, although often criticized by the United States for its close relations with Russia and Iran, really has little choice in the matter, as both countries are the main source of Turkey's domestic energy needs.

Looking back, Turkey's founder, Mustafa Kemal Atatürk, sought to modernize Turkey without Islam, and in the hands of the secularists, nationalism became the primary tool holding the country together. Then again, said Pankaj Mishra in 2013, those wishing for a supposed return to a previous golden age of democracy in Turkey had forgotten "Turkey's long history with plenty of rich and powerful secularists – but no democracy and human rights."[55] During its early years in power, the AKP relied upon democratic and economic reforms, mixed with religious propaganda and government largesse to maintain its grip on power. More recently, in the search for votes, it has relied upon whipping up Turkish nationalism with military deployments in Syria, Libya, and Azerbaijan, pursuing the PKK in Iraq, and, in the search for exploitable natural resources, expanding its naval presence in the Eastern Mediterranean.

But in the absence of economic growth, Erdoğan and the AKP can no longer paper over the cracks in Turkish society. The first sign of growing voter apathy for the AKP came during the June 2015 national election when the government lost its parliamentary majority for the first time since coming to power. Although regaining a majority in November 2015, political survival in the aftermath necessitated an alliance with the MHP, whose political fortunes were also in decline. Kemal Karpet was well ahead of his time when he wrote in 1961 that "the average voter in Turkey is affected less by religious propaganda than in the past, and casts his vote according to other more vital considerations."[56] Such is the case today, as the AKP has discovered.

COVID-19 has also exposed widespread economic weaknesses in most countries, including Turkey. As the World Bank noted in its April 2020 update, Turkey's overall macroeconomic picture was already "uncertain, given rising inflation and unemployment, contracting investment, elevated corporate and financial sector vulnerabilities, and patchy implementation of corrective policy actions and reforms."[57] On the other hand, Turkey's recovery after its own 2001 economic collapse and the 2008 global financial crisis points to a certain resiliency.

Whether it be an increasingly illiberal Turkey, an economically collapsing Turkey, or both at the same time, the impact on the region will be significant. Indeed, Turkey's political and economic stability is vitally important for the overall stability of the Middle East. However, there is little that Canada can do to steady the political and economic situation in Turkey by itself, and although it is not a complete bystander when it comes to Turkish politics, Canada has little direct influence in Ankara. That's not to say that the bilateral relationship with Turkey is not important. It is, but political and economic relations essentially remain on autopilot, unless temporarily disturbed by particular events such as Canada's recent arms embargo on Turkey.

NOTES

1 Government of Canada (GoC), "Canada-Turkey Relations," June 2019, accessed June 9, 2020, https://www.canadainternational.gc.ca /turkey-turquie/bilateral_relations_bilaterales/canada-turkey-turquie .aspx?lang=eng#:~:text=Bilateral%20Relations,-Canada%20and%20 Turkey&text=In%201944%2C%20Turkey%20opened%20an,%2C%20 strategic%2C%20and%20security%20partners.

2 GoC, Immigration and Refugee Board of Canada, "Refugee Claims Statistics," 17 May 2019, https://irb-cisr.gc.ca/en/statistics/protection/Pages /index.aspx.

3 GoC, "Enhancing the Security and Stabilization of Iraq, Syria, Jordan and Lebanon," 7 September 2021, https://www.international.gc.ca/world -monde/international_relations-relations_internationales/mena-moan /strategy-strategie.aspx?lang=eng#a3.

4 Louis A. Delvoie, *Canada and Turkey: Rethinking the Relationship* (Kingston, ON: Centre for International and Defence Policy, Queen's University, 2012), 8.

5 Freedom House, *Freedom in the World 2018 Turkey Profile*, 2019, accessed 27 March 2019, https://freedomhouse.org/country/turkey/freedom -world/2018.

6 Dexter Filkins, "Letter from Turkey: The Deep State," *New Yorker*, 12 March 2012, 46.

7 Most officers were later released when much of the evidence against them was deemed to have been fabricated by the Gülen movement.

8 Dexter Filkins, "Turkey's Thirty-Year Coup," *New Yorker*, 17 October 2016, https://www.newyorker.com/magazine/2016/10/17/turkeys-thirty -year-coup.

9 Cagri Özdemir, "What's Left of Turkey's Gezi Protest Movement?," *Deutsche Well*, 31 May 2017, https://www.dw.com/en/whats-left-of-turkeys-gezi -protest-movement/a-39049440.

10 Ece Temelkuran, *Turkey: The Insane and the Melancholy* (London: Zed Books, 2016), 230.

11 Soner Cagaptay, *The New Sultan: Erdogan and the Crisis of Modern Turkey* (London, I.B. Tauris, 2017), 125.

12 Turkey Task Force, "Erdogan's War against the Gülen Movement: Hate Speech and Beyond," *2015 Turkey Country Report*, Washington, DC: Rethink Institute, 2015, 25.

13 Turkey Task Force, "Erdogan's War, 26.

14 Republic of Turkey, *15 July Coup Attempt and the Parallel State Structure* (Ankara: Department of Corporate Communications, October 2016), 3.

15 Stephen Kinzer, "Turkey's 'Anti-Erdoğan' Deserves Nobel Peace Prize," *Politico*, 21 January 2019, https://www.politico.eu/article/turkey-activist -osman-kavala-anti-erdogan-deserves-nobel-peace-prize/.

16 Amnesty International, "2020 World Press Freedom Index, 2020," accessed 9 June 2020, https://rsf.org/en/ranking.

17 *Guardian*, "The Guardian View on Erdoğan's Turkey: Illiberal Democrat Takes Power," editorial, 25 June 2018, https://www.theguardian.com /commentisfree/2018/jun/25/the-guardian-view-on-erdogans-turkey -illiberal-democrat-takes-power.

18 Freedom House, *Freedom in the World 2018*.

19 Cagaptay, *New Sultan*, 5.

20 World Bank, *The World Bank in Turkey*, 16 April 2020, https://www.worldbank .org/en/country/turkey/overview.

21 Güney Işıkara, Alp Kayserilioğlu, and Max Zirngast, "Discontent Is Brewing in Erdoğan's Turkey," *Jacobin*, 20 March 2019, https://jacobinmag .com/2019/03/erdogan-akp-turkey-local-elections.

22 Ferhat Deniz, "No Peace Process in Turkey while Erdoğan in Charge, PKK Co-chair Says," *Ahval*, 31 May 2019, http://ahval.co/en-49114.

23 Sinan Ülgen, "Turkish Democracy Is the Winner in These Momentous Local Elections," *Guardian*, 3 April 2019, https://www.theguardian .com/commentisfree/2019/apr/03/turkey-democracy-local-elections-akp -erdogan?CMP=share_btn_link.

24 The number of parliamentarians increased to 600 following constitutional changes that were approved in a referendum held on 16 April 2017.

25 *Ahval*, "Pro-Kurdish Party Campaigns for Turkish Opposition in Istanbul Mayor Vote," 31 May 2019, http://ahval.co/en-49103.

26 *Ahval*, "Turkey Arrests 125 people for Alleged Gülen Movement Links," 12 July 2021, https://ahvalnews.com/gulen-operations-turkey/turkey-arrests -125-people-alleged-gulen-movement-links.

27 Baskin Oran, *Turkish Foreign Policy: 1919–2006, Facts and Analysis with Documents* (Salt Lake City: University of Utah Press, 2010), 333.

28 GoC, "Canada-Turkey Relations."

29 Republic of Turkey, "Turkish Canadian Relations, 20.3.2019," Republic of Turkey Embassy in Ottawa, http://ottava.be.mfa.gov.tr/Mission /ShowInfoNote/355137.

30 Republic of Turkey, "Relations between Turkey and Canada," Ministry of Foreign Affairs, n.d., http://www.mfa.gov.tr/relations-between-turkey -and-canada.en.mfa.

31 GoC, "Monument to Fallen Diplomats," 2017, https://www.canada.ca/en /canadian-heritage/services/art-monuments/monuments/fallen -diplomats.html.

32 Delvoie, *Canada and Turkey*, 11.

33 Standing Senate Committee on Foreign Affairs and International Trade, *Building Bridges: Canada-Turkey Relations and Beyond*, June 2013, vii, https:// sencanada.ca/content/sen/Committee/412/aefa/rep/rep02nov13-e.pdf.

34 Ibid. Standing Senate Committee on Foreign Affairs and International Trade, *Building Bridges*, vi.

35 Standing Senate Committee on Foreign Affairs and International Trade, *Building Bridges*, 17.

36 Standing Senate Committee on Foreign Affairs and International Trade, *Building Bridges*, 39–49.

37 Burak Bir, "Turkey, Canada Sign MoU on Economic, Trade Cooperation," *Anadolu Agency*, 8 June 2019, https://www.aa.com.tr/en/energy/energy -diplomacy/turkey-canada-sign-mou-on-economic-trade-cooperation /25690.

38 GoC, "Canada-Turkey Relations."

39 Claire Sadar, "Turkey May Be World's Most Prolific Abuser of Interpol Red Notices," *Ahval*, 27 April 2019, http://tinyurl.com/y3v96jb2.

40 Patrick Martin, "Turkey's Gülen Crackdown Hits Canada," *Globe and Mail*, 30 September 2016, https://www.theglobeandmail.com/news/world /turkeys-gulen-crackdown-hits-canada/article32191633/.

41 GoC, Immigration and Refugee Board of Canada, "Refugee Claims Statistics," 22 May 2020, accessed 9 June 2020, https://irb-cisr.gc.ca/en /statistics/protection/Pages/index.aspx.

42 Martin, "Turkey's Gülen Crackdown Hits Canada."

43 Anatolian Heritage Foundation, "About Us," n.d., https://anatolianheritage .ca/about-us/. See also Intercultural Dialogue Institute, GTA, "About Us," accessed 25 May 2019, https://toronto.interculturaldialog.com /category/upcomingevents/.

44 Turkish Canadian Chamber of Commerce, "About Us," n.d., https:// tcccommerce.com/about-u/.

45 Mark Mackinnon, "Fifteen Canadians Named in Turkish 'Terrorism' Probe Linked to President Erdogan's Rival," *Globe and Mail*, 6 July 2020, https:// www.theglobeandmail.com/world/article-fifteen-canadians-named-in -turkish-terrorism-probe-linked-to/#comments.

46 GoC, Statistics Canada, "Census Profile, 2016 Census – Ethnic Origin," 3 April 2019, https://www12.statcan.gc.ca/census-recensement/2016 /dp-pd/prof/details/page.cfm?Lang=E&Geo1=PR&Code1=01&Geo2 =PR&Code2=01&Data=Count&SearchText=Canada&SearchType=Begins &SearchPR=01&B1=Ethnic+origin&TABID=1.

47 Facebook, "Democratic Kurdish Federation of Canada," https://www .facebook.com/pg/canadakurds/about/?ref=page_internal.

48 Stewart Bell, "Toronto Foundation Stripped of Charity Status after Audit Finds Alleged Links to Kurdish Guerrillas," Global News, 5 March 2019, https://globalnews.ca/news/5013722/toronto-foundation -charity-guerrillas/.

49 Aaron Stein and Michelle Foley, "The YPG-PKK Connection," Atlantic Council, 26 January 2016, https://www.atlanticcouncil.org/blogs /menasource/the-ypg-pkk-connection/.

50 For more on the ties between the SDF/YPG and the PKK, see Barak Barfi, "Ascent of the PYD and the SDF," Washington Institute for Near East Policy, Research Notes, no. 32, April 2016, https://www.washingtoninstitute.org /policy-analysis/ascent-pyd-and-sdf.

51 GoC, "Notice to Exporters: Export of Items Listed on the Export Control List to Turkey," 16 April 2020, https://www.international.gc.ca/trade -commerce/controls-controles/notices-avis/992.aspx?lang=eng. On the other hand, the notice to exporters did add that if exceptional

circumstances warranted, especially in relation to NATO cooperation programs, a permit could be issued, and permits issued prior to 11 October
2019 would remain valid. However, the decision on 16 April 2020 by the
Canadian government to extend the ban on arms sales to Turkey until further notice was not well received in Ankara.

52 GoC, "Turkey: Travel Advisory," 16 August 2021, https://travel.gc.ca
    /destinations/turkey.
53 Soner Cagaptay, "Erdogan Should Seize the Chance for Change in Turkey,"
    Washington Post, 5 April 2019, https://www.washingtonpost.com
    /opinions/2019/04/05/erdogan-should-seize-chance-change-turkey
    /?utm_term=.edaef7a35bfc.
54 Amberim Zaman, "Turkey Entrenches Further into Libya as Rivals Strike
    Back," Al-Monitor, 6 July 2020, https://www.al-monitor.com/pulse
    /originals/2020/07/turkey-libya-role-war.html#ixzz6SCaSKEMy.
55 Pankaj Mishra, "The Rumble in Istanbul: It's Not about Religion," iPolitics,
    24 June 2013, https://ipolitics.ca/2013/06/24/the-rumble-in-istanbul
    -its-not-about-religion/.
56 Kemal H. Karpet, "The Turkish Election of 1957," *Western Political Quarterly*
    14, no. 2 (June 1961): 444.
57 World Bank, *World Bank in Turkey*.

9 Responding to Political Islam: Egypt's Muslim Brotherhood and Islam in Canada

NERMIN ALLAM

The short-lived victory of the Muslim Brotherhood in Egypt symbolized the rise and fall of Islamist politics in the Middle East following the Arab uprisings. Former prime minister Stephen Harper described the ousting of the Muslim Brotherhood president, Mohamed Morsi, as a "return to stability."[1] According to Harper, Morsi and the Muslim Brotherhood attempted to use their electoral victory as a means "to achieve what was in fact going to be an authoritarian Islamic state."[2] Harper's statement reflects the suspicion and animosity that has traditionally marked Canada's approach towards Islamist politics.

Canada has generally lacked a coherent policy towards Islamist political groups. Canadian governments have maintained limited engagement with Islamist politics and have kept Islamist groups at arm's length (see the Kilford chapter in this volume on Turkey). However, with the election of the Muslim Brotherhood candidate, Mohammed Morsi, in Egypt's first presidential elections in 2012, Canada had to engage with and respond to Islamist politics. This chapter examines how Canadian governments responded to the rise and fall of the Muslim Brotherhood during and after 2011. Canada's reaction to the participation of the Muslim Brotherhood in the 2011 Egyptian uprising and the group's ascension to power displayed vague suspicion, arguably a function of Canadian foreign policy more generally and its traditional lack of engagement in the Middle East and with Islamist politics. It was also due, in part, to how conversations over political Islam in the media as well as in policy debates often reduced Islamist politics to militant violent extremism and ignored the diverse trajectories of different groups.

The chapter adopts a threefold approach. First, surveying major theories on the relationship between the West and Islamist politics helps to situate Canada's approach to Islamist politics within the literature. Second, examining Canada's foreign policy in the Middle East and its engagement with other Islamist parties in the region highlights how national discussions on political Islam often figured in debates surrounding Canada's involvement in the so-called war on terrorism, the prospect of introducing sharia law in family matters, and the veil debate in Canada. The skewed view of Islamist politics found in these national Canadian debates had set the stage for Canada's response to the rise and fall of the Muslim Brotherhood in Egypt. Third, Canada's response to the electoral success of Islamist politics in Egypt following the uprising and the response by the Justin Trudeau government to the targeting and execution of Muslim Brotherhood leaders after the ousting of Mohamed Morsi and the election of the current president, Abdel Fattah al-Sisi, emphasize how current discussions on Islamist politics cut across foreign and national debates. The ousting of the Muslim Brotherhood and their failed policies in Egypt, moreover, are often used to justify the surveillance and targeting of Muslim associations and communities in Canada.

Islamist Politics and the West

Islamist groups are diverse in their structures, strategies, and political orientations. Beyond the common goal of disseminating the religion of Islam, these diverse groups do not subscribe to the same religious interpretations or share the same views about the use of violence, democracy, and pluralism.[3] For instance, while the Islamic Action Front (IAF) in Jordan, the Yemeni Congregation for Reform (the Islah Party) in Yemen, and Hamas in the Palestinian territories are grouped under the banner of the Muslim Brotherhood, they embody diverse political orientations and relationships. Jillian Schwedler astutely argues in her comparative study of Islamist parties in Jordan and Yemen that the IAF in Jordan became more "moderate" while Islah did not, as the IAF cooperated with other parties and participated in pluralist political processes.[4] Other groups, Janine Clark notes, such as Hamas in Gaza and Hizbullah in Lebanon have had different trajectories as they emerged from the military resistance to Israeli occupation.[5] The Islamic character of various groups influences their legal status and ideology, but so does the nature of the regime in power and its political strategies.[6]

Scholars have posited a number of theories to understand Western countries' relationships to political Islam. Some ground their explanations in culture,[7] while others explain Western governments' suspicion of Islamist groups as a function of strategic interest,[8] and others still trace it to the influence of the political process.[9] Whether extensively critiqued by scholars or "implicitly praised" by right-wing politicians,[10] Samuel Huntington's clash of civilizations thesis has been influential in debates on Islam in Western societies. Building on the work of Bernard Lewis, Huntington argues that post–Cold War conflict will be between civilizations, and mostly between the West and the Muslim world.[11] The distinction between Islam and Islamist politics is glossed over in these discussions.

Since Huntington presented his theory, scholars have extensively critiqued his claims of Islam versus the West.[12] Edward Said infamously described the theory as a "clash of ignorance" perpetuating conflict and misunderstanding, and grounding its assumptions within orientalist views and misconceptions about the Middle East and its people.[13] In his study of American foreign policy on political Islam, Fawaz Gerges argues that US hostility towards Islamist politics is not based on cultural animosity but rather on a clash in strategic interests.[14] Graham Fuller and Ian Lesser further refute the clash of civilizations thesis, arguing that Western societies' views of political Islam are largely a function of "perceptions and grievances on both sides involving historical, political, economic, cultural, psychological, and strategic elements."[15] While the "clash of interests"[16] approach is useful in partially understanding Western engagement with Islamist politics, other authors highlight its inability to explain variations in the ways in which different leaders pursue similar interests.

Several scholars have thus shifted their attention to the political process to explain Western polices towards Islamist groups, arguing that they are largely a consequence of the policymaking process itself.[17] Lorenzo Vidino, in his study of Muslim Brotherhood politics in the West, argues that barriers to information and the absence of nuanced understandings of Islam and Islamist groups influence governments' response to Islamist politics.[18] This approach has its own limitations, as Steven Brooke astutely points out in his study of the Muslim Brotherhood in Egypt.[19] According to Brooke, while leaders are constrained by the political process, bureaucracy, and domestic opinion, the strategic choices of the elected leaders do play an influential role in setting policy. I argue that in addition to the political process, domestic opinion, and leaders' strategic preferences, Canada's response to Islamist politics is also a result of its limited engagement in the Middle East and skewed view of political Islam.

Canada, the Middle East, and Islamist Politics

Canada's foreign policy in the Middle East is a surprisingly understudied topic. Apart from a number of analyses of Canada's role in the Israeli-Palestinian peace process,[20] its military interventions in the region,[21] and more recently its response to the 2010/11 Arab uprisings,[22] the issue remains largely under-researched. The limited scholarly work reflects Canada's indecisive role in the region. While Canada traditionally had limited engagement with Middle Eastern politics, the war on terrorism in the post-9/11 landscape created new interests and priorities in the region, as Marie-Joëlle Zahar observes in her study of Canada's foreign policy in the Arab world.[23] Canada came to identify "Islamist-inspired violence"[24] as a key threat to regional and international security. In addressing it, the Canadian government ostensibly displayed contradictory attitudes. On one hand, through its former international development agency, the Canadian International Development Agency (CIDA), the government funded initiatives and programs that promoted Islamist inclusion, thus reflecting the broader view that inclusion and governance reform could help curb radicalization. On the other hand, the government established alliances with regimes that were fighting Islamist groups and criticized those who supported Islamist extremism such as the regime in Iran and Hamas in Gaza. For instance, the diplomatic tension between Canada and the Islamic Republic of Iran escalated over the years. Similarly, following the electoral victory of Hamas in the Palestinian Legislative Council elections in 2006, the Canadian government cut off its funding to the Palestinian Authority, citing Hamas's militant activities and its refusal to recognize Israel.[25]

Although Islamist groups in the region do not share the same strategies or subscribe to the same religious interpretations, Canadian foreign policymakers have broadly refrained from engaging with Islamist parties. Canada's general distrust of Islamist parties has been in part a function of the sustained anti–Muslim Brotherhood campaign carried out by some autocracies and monarchies in the Middle East. For example, the United Arab Emirates, the Kingdom of Saudi Arabia, Egypt, and later Algeria frame the group as a threat to the region's stability and thus largely exclude it from politics. The Canadian government has displayed a similar approach, even with Islamist groups permitted to function in the region. For example, while the IAF in Jordan runs for elections in coalitions with secular candidates and even describes itself as a "loyal opposition"[26] to the monarchy, Canada does not seem to have a clear approach on how to engage with the group. Beyond Canada's general suspicion of political Islam, there are no official statements on how Canada treats Islamist political parties that are permitted to function in autocratic and semi-autocratic regimes such as Morocco or Jordan.

Canada's disengagement with Islamist political parties, Janine A. Clark argues in her study of Canada's promotion of democracy in the Middle East, "makes Canada hypocritical and undermines its programs, credibility, and values, and potentially the meaning of democracy itself."[27] In line with Clark, this chapter argues that Canada's disengagement undermines its foreign policy principles. While the commitment of Islamist groups to democracy continues to be contested, it is counterproductive to dismiss their voices, since Islamist groups often present the most significant oppositional forces to autocratic regimes and are integral to civil society.[28] These groups and movements have also addressed the needs of the poor and the middle classes and provide social welfare institutions such as schools and hospital, thus offering what "their governments could not or would not do."[29]

Canadian policy towards Islamist politics is thus shaped by international factors, but this chapter goes further and notes that it is also influenced by domestic politics in Canada that frame Islam as a threat. Canadian foreign policy has often demonstrated little interest in the Middle East and viewed Islamist politics with vague distrust; this attitude is evident in the ways in which national conversations over political Islam in media and policy debates often reduce Islamist politics to militant violent extremism and ignore the diverse trajectories of different groups. Discussion of Islamist politics in media and policy debates also reflects the ideological and political media ecosystems in the West, especially the emergence of a right-wing narrative that frames Islam as a threat.

Islamist politics also often figure in national discussions of Canada's involvement in the so-called war on terrorism, the prospect of introducing sharia law in family matters, and the veil debate. These discourses illustrate how Islamist politics were viewed at the national level and in the media in the period prior to the Arab uprisings. While politicians stressed that Islam and Muslims were not "the enemy," beneath this rhetoric, many had entangled Islamist politics with political violence and overlooked the diverse trajectories of different groups.

In justifying Canada's participation in the so-called war on terrorism, many politicians represented Islamist groups as a threat not only to regional and international security but also to Western culture. Similarly, in the ongoing debate over the veil in Quebec and faith-based arbitration in 2004–5, the official response and public debate in Canada reproduced the view of Islam as a threat to the West and its norms and values. State reaction to the prospect of introducing sharia law in family matters, Sherene Razack argued in her study of the war on terror discourse, had reproduced the "eternal triangle" of the "imperiled Muslim woman" who needs to be saved from "the dangerous Muslim man" by the civilized West.[30] Underlying this triangle is a "moral panic"[31] over the influence of Islam and a concern that it will take over Western societies. The same rationale underpinned the debate over banning the niqab – a face veil covering the face and leaving only the eyes exposed – and the burka – a one-piece veil covering the whole body, and the face with a cloth mesh covering the eyes. Critics argued that Quebec's Bill 94 and Bill 62 – also known as the religious neutrality bill – espoused a view of Islam as one entangled with extremism and militant Islamism. Bill 21 banned public workers and those receiving government services in Quebec from wearing a niqab or burka. It was further expanded by banning some public sector employees from wearing religious symbols at work. Civil liberties activists viewed the ban as predominantly targeting Muslim women who wear a face veil and stripped Muslim women of their agency and justified Islamophobia against the Muslim community.[32]

This securitization of Islam in Canadian politics demonstrates the ways in which some politicians' views of political Islam have been shaped by fears of militant Islamists. It reflects a concern over proponents of Islamist politics and their perceived challenges to liberalism, democracy, and the rights of women and minorities. These same concerns figured prominently in Canada's response to the participation of the Muslim Brotherhood in the 2011 Arab uprisings and its rise to power that followed. The Canadian government's response was due in part to how Islamist politics were discussed at the national level in the period prior to the Arab uprisings.

Canada and the Rise and Fall of the Muslim Brotherhood

The Canadian government's initial response to Egypt's revolution reiterated its foreign policy and democratic principles. In its official statements, the government closely aligned itself with its commitment to diplomacy and humanitarian principles. Prime Minister Stephen Harper stressed that "following President Mubarak's announcement today that he will not seek re-election, Canada reiterates its support for the Egyptian people as they transition to new leadership and a promising future."[33] He emphasized that "Canada supports universal values – including freedom, democracy and justice – and the right to the freedom of assembly, speech and information ... We stand by the people of Egypt, young Egyptians in particular, for their steadfast support for the fundamental values that Canadians profoundly share with them."[34]

While declaring its support for a transition, the Canadian government expressed its concerns over the implications for Egypt's peace with Israel. In the final days of Mubarak's regime, Foreign Minister Lawrence Cannon emphasized that Canada's main concern was securing an "orderly" transition, one that does not create a power vacuum and that protects Egypt's peace treaty with Israel.[35] Indeed, Jonathan Paquin observes in a study documenting the responses of Canada and the United States to the Arab uprisings that the issue of stability and the need to safeguard Israel figured most prominently in Canada's response to the Egyptian revolution.[36] The Canadian government reproduced the same stability versus democracy discourse put forward by Mubarak's government by emphasizing the need for an orderly transition, warning against a power vacuum, and sometimes supporting Mubarak's proposition for a gradual transition. Underpinning the stability versus democracy discourse is a concern that political Islam will take over and threaten the geopolitical interests of Western governments in the region. The Canada-Israel Committee in Ottawa echoed the same concern and lobbied members of Parliament to advocate for a slow change in Egypt, warning that the Muslim Brotherhood would hijack political power.[37]

The Muslim Brotherhood is historically the largest oppositional force in Egypt. While the group was formally banned under Mubarak's regime, its supporters often ran as independent candidates and secured seats in Parliament. Notwithstanding the ban, the group also managed a wide network of welfare services. Observers often viewed these services as a means to secure electoral gains and political mobilization.[38] Following the 2011 revolution, the ban on the Muslim Brotherhood came to an end and the group formally established itself as the Freedom and Justice party (FJP). Its members secured a majority in the 2011–12 parliamentary elections, and FJP candidate Mohamed Morsi was elected president in 2012. As Islamists ascended to power, Canada seemed to display anxiety, particularly over the relationship between Egypt and Israel, the treatment of religious minorities, and the protection of women's rights.

In the evolving political landscape that marked Egypt's transitional period and particularly following the rise of the Muslim Brotherhood to power, the Canadian government as well as major political parties in Canada frequently emphasized their continued support of Israel. It also highlighted the need to adhere to the 1979 Camp David accord that set peace terms between Egypt and Israel.[39]

Another central issue that marked the Canadian government's engagement with Islamist politics in Egypt was the question of Egypt's religious minorities. In defining its foreign policy, the Harper government emphasized its commitment to promoting religious freedom and diversity. In line with this image, the government established the Office of Religious Freedom in 2013. The office – which was dissolved by the Trudeau government in 2016 – had an overarching mandate of promoting the protection of religious communities and Canadian values of pluralism around the world.[40] Canadian governments have consistently condoned attacks against religious minorities in Egypt. Following the Arab uprisings, Canada's Parliament reiterated its position but linked new attacks to the rise of the Muslim Brotherhood in Egypt. A 2013 report by the Standing Committee on Foreign Affairs and International Development warned that "repression of the Copts had increased under the Muslim Brotherhood–led government, raising concern within the Coptic community."[41] Framing the attacks as a function of Islamist politics and the Muslim Brotherhood in power ignored decades-long legacies of oppression and persecution carried out by Egypt's secular regimes against Coptic communities. It is grounded in anxiety over the rise of political Islam and Islamist politics.

Following the 2012 election of the Muslim Brotherhood, the agenda of women's rights indeed had suffered in Egypt. The Canadian government produced generic and generalized statements supporting women's rights – among other groups – in Egypt. Statements by the Canadian government, however, were seldom backed by policies to address the problem. The government did little to address new challenges – represented in the election of the Muslim Brotherhood – and overlooked the more entrenched inequalities that existed prior to the Muslim Brotherhood. In the media, the Muslim Brotherhood's missteps and the ways in which they dismantled former advancements in women's rights reinforced the discourse of political Islam as a threat to women and to gender equality. While discourses that place Islam in opposition to gender equality already existed in Canadian media prior to the election of the Muslim Brotherhood, they gained prominence following the uprising. During Egypt's presidential election in May 2012, the *Globe and Mail* warned that the Muslim Brotherhood will "repeal laws" that advance women's rights.[42] The Muslim Brotherhood's missteps in the agenda of women's rights solidified this discourse and justified its use in Canadian media. Media coverage thus frequently invoked the same old representation of political Islam as a threat to women's rights and gender equality, and it did not address the more entrenched inequalities that existed prior to its rise. Canadian media did not go beyond surface arguments to discuss and highlight long-standing political factors that challenged and hindered women's rights in Egyptian society under different secular regimes.

Framing Islamist politics in Egypt as threats to democracy and stability continued to shape the debate and the representation of the Muslim Brotherhood following their short-lived victory. This emphasis shaped and influenced Canada's response to the ousting of Mohamed Morsi and the violent persecution of the Muslim Brotherhood that followed. In 2013, the army ousted President Morsi amid mass demonstrations protesting his government's failure to address the deteriorating economic and political situation. The army and security forces dispersed pro-Morsi supporters in Rabaa, a public square in Cairo, killing at least 817 protestors.[43] The Canadian government refrained from condemning the Egyptian state's violence in dispersing Morsi's supporters. Instead, Foreign Minister John Baird merely called upon all parties to refrain from the use of violence and to engage in political dialogue.[44]

The brutal dispersal of the Rabaa sit-in marked the beginning of a violent campaign targeting Muslim Brotherhood members and supporters. The Egyptian government banned the Brotherhood's party in September 2013 and later designated it a terrorist group. Under the new regime of Abdel Fattah al-Sisi – former defence minister in Morsi's government – members of the Muslim Brotherhood were persecuted along with other opposition groups and human rights activists.

The Harper government celebrated the election of Sisi in 2014. As Sisi prepared to run for the presidency, Harper voiced his support, describing the ousting of Morsi as a "return to stability."[45] Harper described Morsi's electoral victory as a means "to achieve what was in fact going to be an authoritarian Islamic state."[46] Foreign Minister Baird similarly lauded Sisi's government, highlighting "the significant leadership that the new government of Egypt is taking first in confronting the terrorist acts of the Muslim Brotherhood."[47]

A source of friction in relations between Canada and Egypt was the imprisonment of Canadian journalist Mohamed Fahmy, who was charged with terrorism because of his coverage for Al-Jazeera in Egypt and was sentenced to three years in prison. He was pardoned and released in 2015 after spending 400 days behind bars.[48] Fahmy's controversial charges and trial were part of a wider move by Sisi's regime to silence and crush dissent. However, the Canadian government refrained from situating Fahmy's case within the wider systemic repression carried out by the Egyptian government, as that would have meant condemning Sisi's regime.

The Muslim Brotherhood did engage in repression; Morsi's government did target and persecute political opposition during his short-lived presidency. Furthermore, following the ousting of Morsi and the persecution of the group's members and supporters, the group carried out violent attacks against the regime and society. Harper seemed to imply that a secular authoritarian state was a better and safer option for Egyptians than an Islamic authoritarian state, not that both were equally problematic. His statement raises the question of whether Islamist politics are viewed with suspicion because they are perceived as anti-democratic or just because they are Islamist. Harper's statement seemed to suggest the latter, especially when he asserted, "While we need to continue to pressure the Egyptian government to move in the right direction, we also need to make sure that as they do that transition it's done in a way that will strengthen over the long term the forces of modernization and progress rather than what could happen, simply forces from the street that run out of control."[49]

Harper's discourse reproduces orientalist views of Middle Eastern societies as backward and of Islamist politics as regressive and undemocratic. This view not only affects foreign relations but also animates and shapes local policies.

For instance, in 2014 the government of Canada listed the International Relief Fund for the Afflicted and Needy-Canada (IRFAN-Canada) as a terrorist entity. The Canada Revenue Agency revealed that IRFAN-Canada had transferred approximately $14.6 million worth of resources to organizations linked with Hamas.[50] In 2015, the *Toronto Sun* reported that the Muslim Association of Canada (MAC) provided $296,514 between 2001 and 2010 to IRFAN-Canada.[51] However, no charges were laid. More recently, in 2017, US President Donald Trump unsuccessfully pressured the State Department to designate the Muslim Brotherhood as a Foreign Terrorist Organization. But the State Department refused, given that the group is not a unitary organization and does not have an established pattern of violence.[52] While the Canadian government did not designate the Brotherhood a terrorist organization, some media outlets raised concerns about the group and its presence in Canada.

Media coverage of investigations surrounding the funding and operations of some Muslim associations in Canada has displayed a "moral panic" over what some view as the growing influence of Islamist political groups, especially the Muslim Brotherhood, in Canadian society. Media reports of these investigations frequently highlight their links to the Muslim Brotherhood.[53] They cite the ban on the Muslim Brotherhood in Egypt to underscore the potential threat of Islamist politics.[54] In so doing, such coverage overlooks the diversity of the different organizations and loosely affiliated groups under the banner of the Muslim Brotherhood.[55] The analysis presented in this section does not aim to condone these organizations, but draws attention to the different ways in which the ban was used in some media coverage and analysis to create a politics of fear.

Right-wing analysts especially sought to perpetuate Islamophobic discourses. Tom Quiggin, for example, described the Muslim Brotherhood as the "antithesis" of Canadian laws and values, representing "a greater existential threat to North American civilization than violent extremist movements such as al-Qaeda."[56] Quiggin warned against the significant presence of Muslim Brotherhood supporters and affiliated organizations in Canada. Major national media outlets such as the CBC have covered his writings.[57] Conservative media outlets such as the *Toronto Sun* have frequently echoed concerns cited in Quiggin's report[58] and even used his finding to explain attacks on Muslim communities in Canada.[59] In a *Toronto Sun* opinion piece published in 2018 on the first anniversary of the attack on the Islamic Cultural Centre of Quebec City, Quiggin seemed to suggest that the mosque was attacked because it was associated with the Muslim Brotherhood. The Brotherhood and its goal to dominate, he explained, "has the consequence of putting Muslim Brotherhood followers into conflict and competition with those who do not submit to their cause."[60] Yet his analysis ascribed a false identity to the victims. Investigations into the shooter's motivation highlighted that he was an "avid follower" of right-wing groups,[61] and there was no evidence that the victims were Muslim Brotherhood followers. This discourse of fear in media risks vilifying Muslims in the West as a whole.

Canada's foreign policy towards Islamist politics in Egypt did not drastically change under Justin Trudeau, notwithstanding his ideological differences with Harper. The government remained timid and refrained from criticizing Sisi's regime, even with highly controversial trials and executions of Muslim Brotherhood supporters. Despite the Trudeau government's disengaged position on Islamist politics, Trudeau has been increasingly criticized by right-wing groups and in conservative media outlets, who argue that he is supporting the Muslim Brotherhood and providing a safe haven for their operations.[62] They often cite Trudeau's visit to a mosque in Surrey, British Columbia, in 2013 as proof of his soft policies on Islamist politics.[63] Far-right groups, such as La Meute or Wolfpack in Quebec, blame Trudeau's immigration policies for the rise in the number of Muslim Brotherhood members in Canada.[64]

Current discussions in Canada on Islamist politics cut across foreign and national policies, as the ousting of the Muslim Brotherhood and its failed politics in Egypt are often used to justify the targeting of Muslim communities in Canada. The present debate over Muslim associations and Islam in Canada resembles earlier conversations over political Islam in the media and policy debates prior to the 2011 uprising. On both occasions, the media reproduced moral panic over the influence of political Islam and a concern that it would take over Western societies. This view underpinned the response of two different Canadian governments to the rise and fall of the Muslim Brotherhood in Egypt. Canada's response was also a function of its foreign policy and its traditional disengagement from Islamist politics. Canada's conservative approach towards the region and Islamist politics continued under the current prime minister Justin Trudeau, notwithstanding his liberal credentials.

Conclusion

This chapter examined how Canadian governments responded to the rise and fall of the Muslim Brotherhood during and after the 2011 uprisings in Egypt. Canadian governments reacted to the participation of the Muslim Brotherhood in the 2011 protests and their subsequent rise to power with suspicion and animosity. Canada's response was a function of its foreign policy in the Middle East and traditional lack of engagement with Islamist politics. It was also due in part to how conversations about political Islam in media and policy debates often reduce Islamist politics to militant violent extremism and ignore the diverse trajectories of different groups.

At the time of the uprising, Harper's government reproduced the stability-versus-democracy discourse introduced by Egyptian President Hosni Mubarak. Underpinning that position is a concern that political Islam will take over and threaten the geopolitical interests of Western governments. Following the election of the Muslim Brotherhood, Canada expressed concerns over relations between Egypt and Israel, the treatment of religious minorities, and the protection of women's rights. Framing Islamist politics in Egypt as threats to democracy and stability continued to shape the debate and the representation of the Muslim Brotherhood following its short-lived victory. It was rooted in years of a sustained anti-Brotherhood campaign by monarchies and autocracies in the region and influenced Canada's response to the ousting of Mohamed Morsi and the violent persecution of the Muslim Brotherhood.

Prime Minister Trudeau broadly maintained the same conservative approach that marked Harper's disengagement with Islamist politics in Egypt. Notwithstanding the Sisi government's violent crackdown on the Muslim Brotherhood, Canada refrained from condemning the new regime. Similarly, media coverage of the investigation into Muslim associations in Canada displayed a "moral panic" over what was perceived as the growing influence of Islamist political groups in Canada. Media reports of the investigation and public discussion frequently highlighted their link to the Muslim Brotherhood and cited the ban on the movement in Egypt to underscore the potential threat of Islamist politics.

Similar to other Western countries, Canada continues to be vaguely suspicious of Islamist politics broadly and the Muslim Brotherhood more specifically. While this attitude is often justified in part because the commitment of some Islamist groups to democracy and women's rights is questionable, Canada's response to Islamist politics runs the risk of also vilifying Muslims in Canadian society. In this environment, debates over political Islam reduce Islamist politics to militant violent extremism and ignore differences across groups. This skewed view of Islamist politics can also be used to justify the surveillance and targeting of Muslim communities in Canada. It limits the conditions under which Muslims are accepted in the nation and reproduces a politics of fear.

NOTES

1 YouTube, "Honorary Degrees Conferment Ceremony, the Right Honoura-ble Stephen Harper," 23 January 2014, https://www.youtube.com/watch?v=Dd7eDi7osX0.

2 YouTube, "Honorary Degrees."

3 Amy Hawthorne, "Is Civil Society the Answer?," in *Uncharted Journey: Promoting Democracy in the Middle East*, ed. Thomas Carothers and Marina Ottaway (Washington, DC: Carnegie Endowment for International Peace, 2005), 85.

4 Jillian Schwedler, *Faith in Moderation: Islamist Parties in Jordan and Yemen* (Cambridge: Cambridge University Press, 2007).

5 Janine A. Clark, "Canadian Interests and Democracy Promotion in the Middle East," in *Canada and the Middle East: In Theory and Practice*, ed. Paul Heinbecker and Bessma Momani (Waterloo, ON: Wilfrid Laurier University Press, 2007), 103.

6 See also the chapter by Kilford in this volume for more on Canada's rela-tions with Turkey, which have been by the Justice and Development Party since 2003.

7 Samuel P. Huntington, *The Clash of Civilizations and the Remaking of World Order* (New York: Touchstone, 1997).

8 Fawaz A. Gerges, *America and Political Islam: Clash of Cultures or Clash of Inter-ests?* (Cambridge: Cambridge University Press, 1999).

9 Lorenzo Vidino, ed., *The West and the Muslim Brotherhood after the Arab Spring* (Dubai, United Arab Emirates: Al Mesbar Studies & Research Centre, 2013).

10 Jeffrey Haynes, "Introduction: The 'Clash of Civilizations' and Relations between the West and the Muslim World," *Review of Faith & International Affairs* 17, no. 1 (2 January 2019): 1–10, https://doi.org/10.1080/15570274.2019.1570756.

11 Huntington, *Clash of Civilizations.*

12 Graham E. Fuller and Ian O. Lesser, *A Sense of Siege: The Geopolitics of Islam and the West* (Boulder, CO: Westview, 1995); Gerges, *America and Political Islam*; Vidino, *The West and the Muslim Brotherhood*; Steven Brooke, *Winning Hearts and Votes: Social Services and the Islamist Political Advantage* (Ithaca, NY: Cornell University Press, 2019).

13 Edward W. Said, "The Clash of Ignorance," *Nation*, 4 October 2001, http://
www.thenation.com/article/clash-ignorance.

14 Gerges, *America and Political Islam.*

15 Fuller and Lesser, *Sense of Siege.*

16 Gerges, *America and Political Islam.*

17 Lorenzo Vidino, *The New Muslim Brotherhood in the West* (New York: Columbia University Press, 2010).

18 Lorenzo Vidino, *The New Muslim Brotherhood in the West* (New York: Columbia University Press, 2010), 103–10.

19 Steven Brooke, "US Policy and the Muslim Brotherhood," in Vidino, *The
West and the Muslim Brotherhood*, 6–31.

20 Paul Heinbecker and Bessma Momani, eds., *Canada and the Middle East: In
Theory and Practice* (Waterloo, ON: Wilfrid Laurier University Press, 2007);
Fen Osler Hampson and Bessma Momani, "Lessons for Policy," in *Arab
Spring: Negotiating in the Shadow of the Intifadat*, ed. William Zartman, 439–63
(Athens: University of Georgia Press, 2015).

21 Andrew F. Cooper and Bessma Momani, "The Harper Government's Messaging in the Build-up to the Libyan Intervention: Was Canada Different
than Its NATO Allies?," *Canadian Foreign Policy Journal* 20, no. 2 (4 May
2014): 176–88, https://doi.org/10.1080/11926422.2014.934855.

22 Jonathan Paquin, "Is Ottawa Following Washington's Lead in Foreign
Policy?: Evidence from the Arab Spring," *International Journal* 67, no. 4 (1
December 2012): 1001–28, https://doi.org/10.1177/002070201206700409;
Marie-Joëlle Zahar, "Navigating Troubled Waters: Canada in the Arab
World," in *Elusive Pursuits: Lessons from Canada's Interventions Abroad*, ed.
Fen Osler Hampson and Stephen M. Saideman, 35–58 (Waterloo, ON:
CIGI, 2015).

23 Zahar, "Navigating Troubled Waters."

24 Zahar, "Navigating Troubled Waters," 45.

25 Clark, "Canadian Interests and Democracy Promotion."

26 Clark, "Canadian Interests and Democracy Promotion," 103.

27 Clark, "Canadian Interests and Democracy Promotion," 110.

28 Clark, "Canadian Interests and Democracy Promotion," 104–10.

29 Clark, "Canadian Interests and Democracy Promotion," 104.

30 Sherene Razack, *Casting Out: The Eviction of Muslims from Western Law and
Politics* (Toronto: University of Toronto Press, 2008), 146.

31 Razack, *Casting Out*, 149.

32 Reuters, "Quebec Law Banning Hijab at Work Creates 'Politics of Fear,'
Say Critics," *Guardian*, 17 June 2019, https://www.theguardian.com/
world/2019/jun/17/quebec-law-hijab-ban-religious-symbols-public
-employees.

33 "Statement by the Prime Minister of Canada on Recent Events in Egypt," Global Affairs Canada, 2011, https://www.international.gc.ca/.

34 "Statement by the Prime Minister of Canada on Recent Events in Egypt," Global Affairs Canada, 1 February 2011, https://www.canada.ca/en/news /archive/2011/02/statement-prime-minister-canada-recent-events-egypt .html.

35 Campbell Clark, "In Break with US, Ottawa Backs Gradual Handover in Egypt," *Globe and Mail*, 3 February 2011, https://www.theglobeandmail. com/news/politics/in-break-with-us-ottawa-backs-gradual-handover -in-egypt/article564884/.

36 Paquin, "Is Ottawa Following Washington's Lead?"

37 Alex Wilner, "Canada and the Arab Islamists: Plus Ça Change …," in Vidino, *The West and the Muslim Brotherhood*, 56–67.

38 Carrie Rosefsky Wickham, *The Muslim Brotherhood: Evolution of an Islamist Movement* (Princeton, NJ: Princeton University Press, 2013).

39 Wilner, "Canada and the Arab Islamists."

40 Global Affairs Canada, "Evaluation of the Office of Religious Freedom," May 2016, https://www.international.gc.ca/gac-amc/publications /evaluation/2016/eval_eorf-eblr_eval.aspx?lang=eng.

41 Standing Committee on Foreign Affairs and International Development, *Securing the Human Rights of Coptic Christians in Egypt after the Arab Spring: A View from Canada's Parliament*, 1st sess., 41st Parliament, May 2013, publications.gc.ca/pub?id=9.576695&sl=0.

42 Patrick Martin, "Will Egypt Finish the Islamist Arc, or Be the First to Buck the Trend?," *Globe and Mail*, 26 May 2012, https://www.theglobeandmail. com/news/world/will-egypt-finish-the-islamist-arc—or-be-the-first -to-buck-the-trend/article4216542/.

43 Human Rights Watch, "Egypt: No Justice for Rab'a Victims 5 Years On," 13 August 2018, https://www.hrw.org/news/2018/08/13/egypt-no-justice -raba-victims-5-years.

44 Global Affairs Canada, "Canada Deeply Concerned by Deadly Violence in Egypt," 14 August 2013, https://www.canada.ca/en/news/archive/2013/08 /canada-deeply-concerned-deadly-violence-egypt.html.

45 YouTube, "Honorary Degrees."

46 YouTube, "Honorary Degrees."

47 Aaron Mate, "Canada's Government Is Getting Cozy with Egypt's Increasingly Repressive Regime," Vice (blog), 29 January 2015, https://www.vice .com/en_ca/article/nnk9gm/canadas-government-is-getting-cozy-with -egypts-increasingly-repressive-regime-998.

48 CBC News, "Mohamed Fahmy, Canadian Journalist, Pardoned by Egyptian President, Released from Prison," 23 September 2015, https://www.cbc.ca /news/world/mohamed-fahmy-pardoned-egypt-1.3239822.

49 YouTube, "Honorary Degrees."

50 Public Safety Canada, "Government of Canada Lists IRFAN-Canada as Terrorist Entity," news release, 29 April 2014, https://www.canada.ca/en/news/archive/2014/04/government-canada-lists-irfan-canada-terrorist-entity.html.

51 Brian Daly, "Canadian Muslim Group Funnelled $300K to Hamas-Linked Charity: Documents," *Toronto Sun*, 28 January 2015, https://torontosun.com/2015/01/28/canadian-muslim-group-funnelled-300k-to-hamas-linked-charity-documents/wcm/2b8e3db1-fd84-4173-bb83-e8b3cce0cb6d (page discontinued).

52 Daniel Benjamin and Jason Blazakis, "The Muslim Brotherhood Is Not a Terrorist Organization," *Foreign Affairs*, 17 May 2019, https://www.foreignaffairs.com/articles/2019-05-17/muslim-brotherhood-not-terrorist-organization.

53 Tarek Fatah, "Doors Open for Muslim Brotherhood?," *Toronto Sun*, 2 June 2014, https://torontosun.com/2014/06/01/doors-open-for-muslim-brotherhood/wcm/c6c78d35-4c7a-48c6-8a8f-eda237f62a40 (page discontinued); Thomas Quiggin, "The Muslim Brotherhood in North America (Canada/USA)," Terrorism and Security Experts of Canada Network, 27 May 2014, https://d3n8a8pro7vhmx.cloudfront.net/truthmustbetold/pages/93/attachments/original/1443021805/The_Muslim_Brotherhood_in_North_America.pdf?1443021805; Candice Malcolm, "Another Controversial Islamic Group Gets Summer Jobs Grant Funding," *Toronto Sun*, 4 May 2018, https://torontosun.com/opinion/columnists/malcolm-another-controversial-islamic-group-gets-summer-jobs-grant-funding.

54 Malcolm, "Another Controversial Islamic Group."

55 Benjamin and Blazakis, "Muslim Brotherhood Is Not a Terrorist Organization."

56 Quiggin, "Muslim Brotherhood in North America (Canada/USA)," 7.

57 CBC News, "Muslim Brotherhood Activities in Canada Need to Be Probed, Report Says," 27 May 2014, https://www.cbc.ca/news/canada/muslim-brotherhood-activities-need-to-be-probed-in-canada-report-says-1.2654636.

58 Fatah, "Doors Open for Muslim Brotherhood?"; Malcolm, "Another Controversial Islamic Group."

59 Thomas Quiggin, "The Quebec Mosque Story Has Many Layers," *Toronto Sun*, 3 February 2018, https://torontosun.com/opinion/columnists/quiggin-the-quebec-mosque-story-has-many-layers.

60 Quiggin, "Quebec Mosque Story."

61 Jonathan Montpetit, "Quebec City Mosque Shooting," *The Canadian Encyclopedia*, 25 April 2019, https://www.thecanadianencyclopedia.ca/en/article/quebec-city-mosque-shooting.

62 Malcolm, "Another Controversial Islamic Group"; Dale Hurd, "As Trudeau Makes Nice with ISIS, Canada Becoming Potential Base for Terror Attack on US," CBN News, 14 January 2019, https://www1.cbn.com/cbnnews /world/2018/november/canada-becoming-a-potential-base-for-terrorists -to-attack-the-us-nbsp.

63 Jonathan Halevi, "Is Canada's Justin Trudeau the Great Reformer of Islam?," Jerusalem Center for Public Affairs, 18 November 2018, http:// jcpa.org/is-canadas-justin-trudeau-the-great-reformer-of-islam/.

64 Craig S. Smith, "In Canada, Where Muslims Are Few, Group Stirs Fear of Islamists," *New York Times*, 22 December 2017, https://www.nytimes .com/2017/04/05/world/canada/la-meute-muslims-quebec.html.

10 Promoting Human Rights: Canada's Confused Policies in the Middle East

DAVID PETRASEK

Since the late 1970s, all Canadian governments have claimed the promotion of human rights as a key foreign policy goal. This position is so entrenched in thinking about Canadian foreign policy that it is rarely challenged. And indeed such posturing has widespread public support.

Yet even to casual observers, it must be obvious that the promotion of human rights abroad is contingent on Canada's ability to do so in ways that do not undermine other foreign policy objectives, including enhancing trade, strengthening security, and maintaining good relations with allies. Occasionally, Canadian political leaders assert the primacy of human rights, but only rarely do they pursue a human rights principle *abroad* that carries significant costs *at home*.[1] In this respect, Canada is like most governments that include human rights objectives in their foreign policy: whatever the rhetoric, the pursuit of human rights abroad has always involved trade-offs.

This is perhaps especially true in the Middle East, where shortcomings on human rights are so apparent and other foreign policy concerns are evident – as will be discussed below. These affect Canadian human rights policy towards the Middle East. Moreover, human rights policy must be placed within Canada's overall foreign policy on the region, and this in itself lacks clarity, or at least a coherent and consistent narrative. Also, unlike the United States and the European Union (or even particular European countries), Canada lacks the trade and/or military relationships in the region that would give us the clout to make a real difference on human rights – at least acting alone. This weakness affects not just our ability to make an impact with our human rights policies, but also our willingness to try to do so.

The result is something of a muddle. Canada has a stated commitment to promote human rights but in an unstable region where our overall foreign policy is confused, and where human rights concerns compete with other priorities – and where there is little incentive to sort it out, since Canada can have little impact.

Nevertheless, while the overall picture is unclear, it is possible to discern common underlying factors, or *drivers* of Canada's human rights policies in the Middle East. First, however, some attention should be given to the general place of human rights in Canadian foreign policy.

Human Rights in Canadian Foreign Policy

The conventional wisdom is that Canada has always sought to support human rights abroad through its foreign policy, or at least since 1945 when the UN Charter proclaimed the promotion of human rights as a key goal of the organization.[2] In fact, Canada played little or no role in the momentous negotiations in the UN Commission on Human Rights in the 1950s and 1960s that led to the adoption of the two International Covenants (on civil and political, and economic and social rights, respectively) and in the ground-breaking Convention on the Elimination of Racial Discrimination, which formed the foundation for treaties on women's rights, children's rights, and torture that followed in the 1970s and 1980s.[3] There are several reasons for this initial ambivalence, but from the late 1970s onwards Canada did explicitly embrace human rights as a foreign policy goal.[4] It sought membership on the UN Commission on Human Rights and chaired that body from 1979 to 1981, and from that period onwards Canadian foreign ministers began much more routinely to acknowledge human rights as an issue of concern in bilateral relations and in multilateral diplomacy.

Yet despite the prominence given – at least rhetorically – to the place of human rights in Canadian foreign policy, there has been surprisingly little study of the subject, until recently. In the past decade, two monographs have sought to analyse the issue. Both place the question of consistency front and centre: in practice, does Canada pursue the promotion of rights that it claims it is committed to? The first, more theory-driven account seeks to answer that question within the framework of debates about realism and other influences in foreign policymaking.[5] The second, more historical work looks back at forty years of Canadian participation in UN human rights debates, in search of a guiding narrative.[6] Though the two works are very different in orientation, they reach a similar, somewhat predictable conclusion: for Canada the goal of promoting and protecting rights abroad is often over-ridden by other objectives – trade relationships, security concerns, marching in step with key allies, or indeed shielding Canada from UN scrutiny. Although Canada has often acted to uphold human rights or, to capture the title of one book, been "on the side of the angels," its record is hardly consistent. At times Canada has led efforts to advance human rights, yet at other times it has been ambivalent or even explicitly obstructionist.

The value of both accounts, and the broader historical record, is that they point to the largely *contingent* nature of Canadian human rights policy abroad: despite the rhetoric, the pursuit of these policies depends less on over-riding moral imperatives, and more on the exigencies of any given situation.[7]

However, although these accounts are largely true to the historical record, their conclusions do not sufficiently illuminate the underlying factors that *drive* foreign policy in this area. We are left with a picture of human rights being briefly ascendant, only to give way to some other concern, and then ascendant again, and so on, in an endless idealist/ realist see-saw. Why has Canada taken the lead each year since 2003 in marshalling support at the UN for a resolution condemning Iranian human rights practices, but remained mute about remarkably similar practices in other countries in the region? Why has Canada generally sought to be aligned with European allies on Middle East human rights policy, except in the Israeli-occupied Palestinian territories? Why was Canada so enthusiastic about joining the NATO coalition to protect civilians in Libya in 2011, but so disengaged from subsequent efforts to support democracy and human rights in the country? The diplomatic history of our UN engagement is of limited use in answering such questions, and so too are broad, theoretical conclusions about the relative prominence of idealism or realism in foreign policy; hence the emphasis in this chapter on identifying the range of factors that drive human rights concerns in foreign policy. The hope is that such an itemization might make it easier to identify the role of each in specific policies.

Before turning to look at these factors, it is worthwhile to consider briefly the question of implementation: whatever the policy, what are the *means* through which Canada can advance human rights objectives in the Middle East? There are two broad fields of implementation: at the multilateral level, primarily through the United Nations, Canada can bring pressure to bear through a variety of international mechanisms on individual countries. But it can also do so bilaterally, through its own relationships with the country in question. At the multilateral level, the main venue for Canadian action is through the intergovernmental UN Human Rights Council (HRC – or its predecessor until 2006, the UN Commission on Human Rights), which may pass resolutions critical of a country's human rights record or mandate various forms of UN scrutiny of a particular country. The UN General Assembly may take similar action while, in exceptional circumstances, a country's human rights record may be considered by the UN Security Council. Canada, of course, votes in the General Assembly, but can do so in the Human Rights Council or Security Council only when it is a member. But even lacking membership in these bodies, it can throw its diplomatic weight behind HRC resolutions or join calls for action at the Security Council. Perhaps the most prominent, consistent Canadian action via the UN on human rights in the region is our leadership each year to pass at the UN General Assembly a resolution condemning Iran's human rights record.[8]

At the bilateral level, Canada may express its concern on human rights issues through public or private means, through action on individual cases of concern, and it may choose to consider human rights concerns in trade, aid, and security relationships. A prominent recent example of possible Canadian bilateral action is the dispute over whether the government should block the sale of military equipment to Saudi Arabia, given that country's human rights record (see the chapter by Pederson in this volume).

Factors Driving Canadian Human Rights Policy in the Middle East

The Middle East poses particular human rights challenges. There is a depressing homogeneity in the authoritarian character of most governments in the region; there are only a handful of democracies, and even these are deeply flawed. Political repression, limited press freedom, arbitrary imprisonment, systematic torture, gender discrimination, religious persecution, attacks on minorities, gross inequalities in access to basic rights, and a threatened civil society are defining features of most countries in the region. The Middle East also continues to be racked by conflict, with over 40 per cent of regional countries experiencing armed conflict, generating a significant proportion of the world's refugees and displaced people. Although most Middle Eastern countries fall into the middle tier on the UN's development scale (only Yemen is classified as a "least developing country"), many face grave economic, social, and environmental problems, including mass youth unemployment, burgeoning slum populations, and stagnant economic growth. There are also dangerous rivalries in the region, contributing to its overall instability and insecurity.

Therefore promoting human rights in the Middle East is no easy task, and for Canada it is doubly difficult, as our levers of influence are limited. But if no clear, overall picture emerges of Canada's approach to promoting human rights in the Middle East, one can still discern the key elements driving decisions on when and how to take a stand. There are four key factors at play that might influence policymaking and specific interventions concerning Canada's position on human rights in the region. First, the position of our friends and allies in Europe, and of course also the United States, has an impact on when and how we promote and speak out for human rights in the Middle East. Second, since 2001, the war on terror has had a dramatic impact on Canadian foreign policy in the region, also evident in how we approach human rights issues. Third is the perceived influence of diaspora communities in Canada and how they might play a role in shaping human rights policy abroad. And fourth, there is the role played by particular Canadian governments and/or individual ministers, who on occasion have given prominence to particular human rights concerns in the region.

In addition to these four general factors (discussed below), there is also the fact that Canada has for many years given *particular* attention to human rights issues in two situations in the region: Iran, and the Israeli-occupied Palestinian territories. Although to some extent the factors above might influence the Canadian position on these countries, the human rights policy on each has its own momentum. Moreover, because these situations figure prominently in Canada's posture on human rights in the region, they have an impact on policies that might be pursued in other countries. For example, the general disinclination of Canadian governments to join in UN criticism of Israeli practices in the occupied territories arguably undermines other Canadian human rights approaches made in the region. Similarly, Canada's consistent hard line against Iran's human rights record has consequences beyond Iran. These two country situations are also considered in more depth below.

Better Together

When Canada acts publicly to criticize or sanction the human rights practices of Middle Eastern countries, it prefers to do so alongside its allies. Recent scholarship has pointed to the substantial alignment between Canada's voting record in the UN General Assembly and that of European governments, and to the weaker though still strong alignment with the United States.[9] The broader reasons for this can be debated, but in the context of Canadian action on human rights in the Middle East, such alignment makes practical and political sense. It is a sensible approach, as Canada's lack of clout in the region means that it has little influence when it acts alone. And it makes political sense because collective action on human rights – for example, a resolution passed by the Human Rights Council – means there is less likely to be any serious diplomatic cost when Canada's position is buried amongst those of its US and European allies. Further, and not to be under-estimated, there is also little diplomatic *energy* required, as in most cases one of our allies will be leading the effort and Canada need only sign on to a prepared text. This is much more likely to be a pro forma exercise when we are voting alongside our friends and allies, requiring little if any ministerial consultation. Canada's votes and statements at the UN condemning the human rights situation in Syria (or support for such resolutions), in Iraq at the height of the civil war there, in Libya, or the joint statement on the killing of Saudi journalist Jamal Khashoggi, are all examples of policy positions taken alongside those of our European and American friends.[10]

The importance of acting with others is perhaps best illustrated when we do not do so. In August 2018, Foreign Minister Freeland tweeted her displeasure at the Saudi detention of women activists and called for their release. The Saudi response was unexpectedly strong, denouncing the tweet as a blatant interference in Saudi internal affairs. The Saudis also took a series of economic and other measures in explicit retaliation, including halting all new Saudi investment in Canada, expelling the Canadian ambassador, and recalling Saudis studying in Canada. Although she did not admit it publicly, the minister undoubtedly felt exposed and a good deal of (largely wasted) effort was put into getting ex post facto European and US support for Canada's position. The episode proved the point about the risks of unilateral action. Under Crown Prince Mohammed bin Salman, the Saudis were marketing a vision of a new Saudi Arabia, opening movie theatres, allowing women to drive, and making other reforms. Pointing to the indefensible detention of these women undermined this image, and the strong Saudi reaction was undoubtedly intended to send a message – and not only to the Canadians. But precisely because Canada has a weak hand to play with the Saudis and in the region, it was an easy target for Saudi retaliation. The incident might have strengthened the hand of those inside government and the diplomatic corps who caution against strong, independent action by Canada on human rights in the region.

War on Terror

Since 2001, Canadian policy towards the Middle East has been heavily influenced by our interest in countering the rise of Islamist violence in the region, and its potential spillover effects in Canada. Pursuing this policy includes three sub-objectives, all of which have an impact on any human rights initiative we might pursue in the region. First, there is a perceived need to maintain good relations with key regional countries in order to allow for the military and security co-operation that is crucial to counterterrorism efforts; bilateral or multilateral criticism of human rights practices might undermine good relations. Counterterrorism concerns are likely to weigh heavily in decisions on whether to speak out publicly about human rights concerns or initiate or join multilateral action on human rights practices in a particular country.

Second, Canadian policy – and Western policy generally – in the region seeks to keep Islamists out of power (see the Allam chapter in this volume). The authoritarian and repressive nature of several secular Middle Eastern regimes is thus tolerated or even tacitly supported out of the concern that, were they to fall, the alternative might be worse. This concern necessarily affects the extent to which Canada might publicly push for democratic reform and political freedoms.[11]

Third, as part of its effort to counter Islamist violence, Canada has participated in the military coalition that since 2014 has been fighting the Islamic State (IS) in Syria and Iraq. Originally involving both combat aircraft and support to local anti-IS forces, the Canadian effort as of 2019 is largely focused on training local forces.[12] But it remains a significant Canadian engagement in the region, and it has had important ramifications for our foreign policy, including in relation to human rights. In particular, it has somewhat affected the extent to which Canada is willing to highlight human rights abuses in Middle Eastern partners in the anti-IS coalition, such as in Jordan or the Kurdish Regional Government in northern Iraq.

A clear example of the importance of the "war on terror" factor in driving human rights policy concerns Egypt. The eventual rise to power of President Abdel Fattah el-Sisi in Egypt, in the wake of the Arab uprisings, was accompanied by mass human rights abuses perpetrated by Egyptian security forces, including the arbitrary detention and torture of thousands of real and perceived political opponents, the massacre of hundreds (perhaps thousands) of unarmed civilians, and the closure of virtually all space for independent civil society. Yet neither Canada nor its allies have prioritized human rights in their relations with the Sisi regime. Although bilaterally Canada might have made known some concerns, it made a decidedly lacklustre effort on behalf of Canadian journalist Mohamed Fahmy, unjustly imprisoned in Egypt.[13]

Diaspora Concerns and Public Opinion

A further factor influencing Canadian human rights policy in the Middle East is whether the Canadian public supports particular policies. This is a difficult factor to consider, as polling data are imprecise or contradictory. A majority of Canadians want the government to accord a high priority to human rights in foreign policy; a majority also favour strong counterterrorism efforts. Interestingly, in a recent poll, a majority of Canadians favoured suspending arms sales to Saudi Arabia because of its dismal human rights record.[14] But there is little evidence to suggest Canadian governments are much driven by general public opinion in deciding on human rights policies in the Middle East.

On the other hand, some argue that Canadian foreign policy is driven, at least partially, by the concerns of particular segments of the public, namely diaspora communities.[15] Governments may respond to the persistent lobbying of such communities, or government may seek to win favour with those communities for electoral purposes. Thus, for example, some argue the Harper government's strong stance in support of Israel, including siding against UN resolutions critical of Israeli human rights practices in the occupied territories, was driven by the desire to win support, including electoral support, from Jewish-Canadians.[16] Yet again, there is little evidence to suggest that this was the Harper government's intention; certainly, if it was, it proved unsuccessful, as in the 2015 election it lost to the Liberals those seats where Jewish-Canadians were widely represented. And if electoral politics were guiding decisions on whether or not to condemn Israeli human rights practices in the occupied territories, what of the views of Arab-Canadians (or Canadian Muslims)? Both significantly outnumber Jewish-Canadians (for more on this issue, see the chapter by Boily in this volume).

Diaspora communities are not a bloc and will not all be in agreement on how best to deal with human rights issues in their homeland or country of emigration. Many Iranian-Canadians are likely to agree with the Canadian government's criticism of Iran's disregard of human rights. At the same time, in breaking off diplomatic relations, Canada makes it much harder for these Iranian-Canadians to maintain close links to relatives in Iran and creates additional risks for them if they choose to visit Iran. Outside of the Middle East, the same observation might be made about the significant Chinese-Canadian community, who by no means share one view on how Canada ought to deal with the human rights situation in China.

Nevertheless, although the evidence is mixed at best on the actual (as opposed to perceived) influence of diaspora communities on Canada's human rights foreign policy, it is undoubtedly a relevant factor, sometimes indirectly so. For example, Canada may take a certain position for another reason (solidarity with allies), and individual politicians may cite solidarity with the diaspora because it appears convenient to do so politically.

A Concerned Government

While the influence of allies, security concerns, and diasporas might all be relevant in influencing Canada's human rights policy in the Middle East, so too might the proclivities of a particular government. That is, although the general factors tend to persist across time and therefore appear as constants, regardless of who is in power in Ottawa, it is apparent that a change in government might significantly alter Canada's posture on human rights in the region. This was made clear in the approach taken to human rights in the Middle East by the Conservative governments led by Prime Minister Stephen Harper from 2006 to 2015, and in particular in the period 2011–15 when the Conservatives held a majority in Parliament and John Baird was foreign minister.

The Harper Conservatives took a number of distinct steps that marked a departure for Canadian policy in the region: they cut diplomatic relations with Iran, in part because of its human rights record; they resolutely voted against or condemned UN resolutions criticizing Israeli practices in the occupied territories; and they failed to articulate long-standing Canadian policy opposed to Israeli settlement policies.[17] The prime minister also strongly supported the UN-authorized NATO air campaign in Libya, justified on human rights grounds,[18] quickly contributing Canadian warplanes and a Canadian general to lead the NATO mission. Similarly, Harper promptly ensured a Canadian contribution to the anti–Islamic State coalition (although the prime justification was anti-terrorism, protecting human rights was also cited in support of Canada's role in the coalition).

Some might argue that the Conservatives' positions on Iran and Israel were broadly consistent with both prior and successor Liberal governments, and there is some truth in this.[19] Already under Paul Martin's government, Canada had begun to differ with its European allies (though not the United States) in opposing certain UN resolutions critical of Israel. And the annual UN General Assembly resolution condemning Iran's human rights record was first launched by Paul Martin's Liberal government in 2003, three years before the Conservatives took power. Yet the Conservatives amplified these positions. Moreover, their anti-Iran position also appears to have silenced them vis-à-vis human rights abuse in neighbouring (and anti-Iran) Gulf countries. Foreign Minister Baird made several trips to these countries without raising (at least publicly) any human rights concerns.[20] The Conservatives' pro-Israel policy led them to deny support to efforts to find a role for the International Criminal Court in conflicts in Syria and the occupied Palestinian territories, a court Canada did much to bring into being.[21]

Further, the Conservatives' willingness to commit military means to humanitarian objectives in the region – in particular in NATO's Libya campaign – remains distinctive. It is far from certain that a Liberal government under Justin Trudeau would have made the same commitment, notwithstanding its strong support for NATO.

Specific Country Concerns

As noted above, Canada has taken a consistent, decided, and firm position on human rights in regard to only two countries in the region: Israel and Iran. In the case of the latter, Canada has taken the lead each year since 2003 in the UN General Assembly to negotiate and win support for a resolution condemning the human rights situation in Iran. This has been a largely successful effort, in that the resolution is passed, year after year, notwithstanding the changes in government in Canada and in Iran, or the changing views among our allies about fuller engagement with Iran. On this effort, a few points stand out.

First, the human rights record of the Iranian regime deserves condemnation. It is characterized by widespread political repression, restrictions on free speech, assembly, and religious rights, torture and an unfair justice system, and discrimination against women and minorities. Having said that, these are abuses found to a greater or lesser extent in many countries in the region, and certainly among Iran's neighbours in the Gulf, including Saudi Arabia. Second, Canada's leadership role in singling out Iran for condemnation in the General Assembly has continued through both Liberal and Conservative governments. Third, although the effort to pass the resolution each year requires considerable diplomatic effort, there is little diplomatic cost. Canada has had strained or no diplomatic relations with Iran throughout the period, and there is virtually no trade or other relationship that might be harmed by taking such a prominent position on the human rights issue.

The strong position on Iran is not easily explainable by the influences already discussed. It is supported by our allies, but Canada has pursued it with vigour, even when they were lukewarm. There is no pressing security concern (for Canada) to justify singling out Iran, nor is there a strong domestic lobby pushing for Canadian action. The Conservatives were especially vocal in their condemnation of Iran's human rights record, but as noted it was a Liberal government that first took leadership on the issue. The best explanation for why Canada continues to lead efforts in the General Assembly each year might simply be that it is expected of us – or, less charitably, that Canada can find no credible way to step back from its leadership on the issue at the UN.

The second country in the region where human rights issues play a prominent role in foreign policy is Israel, and in particular in the Israeli-occupied Palestinian territories. For the past several years, dating back to the Liberal government of Paul Martin, Canada has regularly abstained or voted against UN resolutions condemning Israeli human rights practices in the occupied territories. Canada has also been reluctant to criticize Israeli violations of international humanitarian law in its numerous military engagements in Gaza, southern Lebanon, and the West Bank in the past twenty years.

Canada's official position is that Israel's human rights record receives excessive or unbalanced criticism, not that it has an unblemished record. And there is some truth in this. Israeli practices in the West Bank, Golan Heights, or vis-à-vis Gaza are subject to multiple critical resolutions at both the Human Rights Council and the General Assembly. At the Human Rights Council, there is a stand-alone agenda item to deal with these issues; no other country is similarly treated. It is worth pointing out, however, that all of these resolutions deal with human rights in the *occupied territories*. No UN resolution has ever singled out for criticism the human rights situation in Israel itself (i.e., in its pre-1967 borders). This is a partial explanation, but it does not fully deal with the Canadian concern. Although few in number, there are other situations of occupation that get little or no attention by UN human rights bodies (e.g., Western Sahara).

As with Iran, Canada's strong and consistent stance on Israel is not fully explainable by the factors above. It often places us at odds with our European allies and is not justified by security or anti-terrorism concerns. Although Canadian statements on the issue often affirm Israel's right to defend itself from terrorist attacks, Canada has not (at least publicly) endorsed arbitrary detention, house demolition, the blockade of Gaza, settlement activity, or myriad other abuses as legitimate means to that end. Some argue the strong stance on Israel aims to capture the electoral support of Jewish-Canadians, but as noted above the evidence is mixed. The Conservatives did pursue the pro-Israel policy with particular vigour, but under Justin Trudeau's government, Canada's voting record at the UN on the Israel resolutions has not changed. In short, the stance taken on Israel's human rights record in the occupied territories has its own dynamic, and this will likely continue.

Conclusion

As the promotion of human rights abroad remains a key foreign policy objective for Canadian governments, one would hope policies towards that goal would be designed to appear credible and consistent to those whom they are intended to influence. Perhaps this is particularly true in the pursuit of such policies in the Middle East, where rivalries, conflicts, and foreign interference give rise to high levels of distrust and ill will. As this chapter has argued, the diverse factors actually driving such policies vary in importance over time, and from one country to another. The result, regrettably, is that too often, Canadian positions on the human rights situation in a Middle Eastern country is seen not as the legitimate defence of universal values (that those countries have often pledged to uphold), but rather as driven by other, less laudable and defensible goals. This is hardly a revelation to the diplomats who must implement such policies. But the fact that our influence and role in the region is negligible limits any ambition to sort it out.

NOTES

1 In the wake of the hostile Saudi reaction to Foreign Minister Chrystia Freeland's criticism of arbitrary detention in the country, she refused to back down, claiming, "I will say Canada is very comfortable with our position. We are always going to speak up for human rights; we're always going to speak up for women's rights; and that is not going to change" ("Freeland Defends Canada's Stance on Saudi Arabia amid Sanctions," CBC News, 6 August 2018, https://www.cbc.ca/news/politics/canada-saudi-diplomacy-reaction-1.4775545). In fact, the incident was one of the very few when Canada, under any government, publicly denounced human rights abuses in Saudi Arabia.
2 That claim figures prominently on Global Affairs Canada's web page introducing its human rights policy. Global Affairs Canada, "Canada's Approach to Advancing Human Rights," http://international.gc.ca/world-monde/issues_development-enjeux_developpement/human_rights-droits_homme/advancing_rights-promouvoir_droits.aspx?lang=eng.
3 Indeed, Canada at first abstained (alone among Western powers) and then only reluctantly voted in favour of the Universal Declaration of Human Rights in the UN General Assembly in 1948. See William A. Schabas, "Canada and the Adoption of the Universal Declaration of Human Rights," *McGill Law Journal* 43, no. 2 (1998): 403–41.
4 Dominique Clement, "Human Rights in Canadian Domestic and Foreign Politics: From 'Niggardly Acceptance' to Enthusiastic Embrace," *Human Rights Quarterly* 34 (2012): 751–78.
5 Andrew Lui, *Why Canada Cares: Human Rights and Foreign Policy in Theory and Practice* (Montreal and Kingston: McGill-Queen's University Press, 2012).
6 Andrew S. Thompson, *On the Side of Angels: Canada and the UN Commission on Human Rights* (Vancouver: UBC Press, 2017).

7 This was also the conclusion of earlier efforts to assess Canada's human rights foreign policy; see Robert Matthews and Cranford Pratt, "Human Rights and Foreign Policy: Principles and Canadian Practice," *Human Rights Quarterly* 7 (1985): 159–88.

8 For an account of the origins of this resolution, see Robert J. Bookmiller, "Canada, Iran and 'Controlled Engagement': A New Start with Afghanistan?," *Canadian Foreign Policy Journal* 17, no. 1 (2011): 23–37.

9 Srdjan Vucetic and Bojan Ramadanovic, "Canada in the UN General Assembly from Trudeau to Trudeau," paper presented at Women in International Security Conference, Toronto, 5 March 2019.

10 For a full text of the statement, see H.E. Harald Aspelund, "Statement under Agenda Item 2: Interactive Dialogue with the High Commissioner," statement, 40th Session of the UN Human Rights Council, 9 March 2019, https://www.government.is/library/01-Ministries/Ministry-for-Foreign-Affairs/Myndir/Joint%20Statement%20on%20Saudi%20Arabia%20-%207%20March%202019.pdf.

11 Thomas Juneau, "A Realist Foreign Policy for Canada in the Middle East," *International Journal* 72, no. 3 (2019): 411.

12 See the chapter in this volume by Massie and Munier.

13 Amnesty International, "Open Letter to Prime Minister Stephen Harper on Mohamed Fahmy's Case," 16 January 2015. For more on how Canada approached Sisi's Egypt, see the chapter by Allam in this volume.

14 Steven Chase, "Majority Rank Human Rights above Job Creation in Saudi Arms Deal: Poll," *Globe and Mail*, 5 February 2016, https://www.theglobeandmail.com/news/politics/majority-rank-human-rights-above-job-creation-in-saudi-arms-deal-poll/article28588950/.

15 A range of views on the subject can be found in David Carment and David Bercuson, eds., *A World in Canada: Diaspora, Demography and Domestic Politics* (Montreal and Kingston: McGill-Queen's University Press, 2008).

16 Donald Barry, "Canada and the Middle East Today: Electoral Politics and Foreign Policy," *Arab Studies Quarterly* 32, no. 4 (2010): 191–217.

17 On human rights policy under the Conservatives, see David Petrasek, "Human Rights in Conservative Party Foreign Policy, 2006–15," *Canadian Yearbook of Human Rights* 1, no. 1 (2015): 7–18.

18 Andrew F. Cooper and Bessma Momani, "The Harper Government's Messaging in the Build-up to Libyan Intervention: Was Canada Different Than Its NATO Allies?," *Canadian Foreign Policy Journal* 20, no. 2 (2014): 176–88.

19 Steven Seligman, "Canada and the UN General Assembly (1994–2015), Continuity and Change under the Liberals and Conservatives," *Canadian Foreign Policy Journal* 22, no. 3 (2016): 276–315; Seligman, "Canada's Israel Policy under Justin Trudeau: Rejecting or Reinforcing the Legacy of

Stephen Harper?," *American Review of Canadian Studies* 48, no. 1 (2018): 80–95.

20 David Petrasek, "On Human Rights, Baird Leaves a Troubled Legacy," CIPS Blog, 3 February 2015, https://www.cips-cepi.ca/2015/02/03/on-human -rights-baird-leaves-a-troubled-legacy/.

21 Peter Stoett and Mark Stefan Kersten, "Beyond Ideological Fixation: Ecology, Justice and Canadian Foreign Policy," *Canadian Foreign Policy Journal* 20, no. 2 (2014): 229–32.

11 Selling Weapons: Saudi Arabia and the Trudeau Government's Feminist Foreign Policy

JENNIFER PEDERSEN[1]

Between 2015 and 2021, the Liberal government's handling of Canada's controversial relationship with Saudi Arabia was met with intense criticism from human rights activists, political opponents, and a good percentage of the Canadian public: why would Canada continue to supply weapons to a country that Amnesty International calls "a kingdom of cruelty"?[2] This issue became a tricky foreign policy challenge for Prime Minister Justin Trudeau, particularly as his government publicly promoted its feminist foreign policy and respect for human rights – prompting some to ask whether Canada is "a nation of feminist arms dealers."[3]

In this chapter I examine the Trudeau government's approach to Canadian arms sales to Saudi Arabia between 2015 and 2021, with particular focus on the $15 billion contract to supply the kingdom with light-armoured vehicles (LAVs) built by General Dynamics Land Systems of Canada (GDLS-C) in London, Ontario. As discussed elsewhere,[4] this was a highly political and partisan debate: the Liberal government faced significant public opposition to the deal, the NDP opposition was vocal in Parliament (while the Conservatives remained relatively silent), and a nervous defence industry insisted on the importance of the deal to the Canadian economy. Two points demonstrate that the Trudeau government's rhetoric on arms sales did not match the reality of its actions. First, its reluctance to cancel the deal, even in the face of egregious human rights violations by Saudi Arabia, called into question its commitment to a feminist foreign policy and to human rights. Second, contrary to the government's claims to have fixed Canada's arms export controls via Bill C-47 and accession to the Arms Trade Treaty, many loopholes remain.

Table 11.1. Largest Exporters of Major Arms and Their Main Client, 2014–2018

Rank	Exporter	Share of arms exports (%)	Main client
1	United States	36.0	Saudi Arabia
2	Russia	21.0	India
3	France	6.8	Egypt
4	Germany	6.4	South Korea
5	China	5.2	Pakistan
6	United Kingdom	4.2	Saudi Arabia
...	...	...	...
16	Canada	0.6	Saudi Arabia

Source: SIPRI Arms Transfers Database, March 2019.
Note: Canadian data may not include figures for 2018, which were released to
Parliament in the 2018 Report on the Export of Military Goods in June 2019, several
months after the release of the Stockholm International Peace Research Institute report.

Canadian Arms Sales to the Middle East

Compared to most other G7 countries, Canada is not a big arms sup-
plier, ranking sixteenth globally in the four-year period of 2014–18 (see
table 11.1). Canada produces less than 1 per cent of the world's weapons; in comparison, the United States produces 36 per cent. The Middle
East is a rapidly growing destination for the world's arms producers; between 2009–13 and 2014–18, arms imports by states in the Middle East
increased by 87 per cent. Saudi Arabia is now the world's largest importer
of arms, supplied by many of the world's main producers, including the
United States, France, and the United Kingdom.[5]

An estimated half of all Canadian arms exports are to the United
States, but the Canadian government does not collect data on the majority of these as the result of a long-standing agreement between the two
countries. In 2019, Canada's exports of military goods and technology to
countries other than the United States reached a record high of $3.757
billion (see table 11.2). The vast majority of these exports were LAVs
destined for Saudi Arabia, part of a $15 billion, fourteen-year contract
negotiated by the Conservative government in 2014.[6]

The Canada-Saudi trade and defence relationship goes back decades.
While Saudi Arabia is Canada's largest trading partner in the Middle
East and its second-largest buyer of military equipment, it is Canada's
seventeenth-largest trading partner overall. Notably, it is not one of Canada's top foreign policy priorities. As Thomas Juneau argues, Canada
and Saudi Arabia until recently enjoyed "cordial but limited relations."[7]
In addition to this limited trade in goods, Saudi Arabia also sends thousands of students to Canadian universities annually.

Table 11.2. Canada's Top Five Non-US Destinations for Military Goods and Technology, 2019

Destination	Total value ($)	%
Saudi Arabia	2,863,785,168	76.21
Belgium	151,658,040	4.04
Turkey	151,428,455	4.03
United Kingdom	116,349,158	3.10
Australia	61,399,886	1.63

Source: Global Affairs Canada, *Report on Exports of Military Goods from Canada, 2019*, Government of Canada, June 2020.

Canada's Defence Industry

Though Canada is not a major arms exporter in global terms, the Canadian defence industry does employ an estimated 60,000 workers and contributes close to $6.2 billion to the national economy.[8] The industry spans all regions of Canada, and a number of Canadian manufacturers have lucrative contracts destined for the Middle East.

The $15 billion GDLS-C LAV deal with Saudi Arabia, brokered by the Canadian Commercial Corporation – a federal Crown corporation – is the largest and most important arms export deal in the history of Canada's defence industry. The deal provides thousands of long-term, well-paid jobs over the fourteen-year duration of the contract, based at the GDLS-C plant in London, Ontario, and at suppliers across the country. In addition to the manufacturing of the LAVs, the contract includes long-term maintenance and support to the Saudis.[9] The contract's importance to Canada's defence industry cannot be understated; in 2019, the exports of these vehicles to Saudi Arabia amounted to over 70 per cent of Canada's military exports to countries other than the United States, at a value of nearly $3 billion for that year alone.[10]

GDLS-C is but one Canadian company exporting to Saudi Arabia; Terradyne manufactures its Saudi-bound Gurkha armoured vehicles in Newmarket, Ontario, and Winnipeg-based PGW has seen its rifle sales to Saudi Arabia rise sharply in recent years, while Quebec is home to a number of aeronautical companies with significant contracts to Middle East buyers.

Canada's defence industry also contributes a number of goods, software, and training to the Middle East that are not included in Global Affairs Canada's annual *Report on the Export of Military Goods from Canada*. Details about such exports are hard to come by; media reports over the past few years have revealed that the Canadian aeronautical industry has supplied Saudi Arabia, the UAE, Egypt, and Jordan with millions of dollars' worth of airplanes, airplane engines, drones, munitions, and helicopters. Many of these items are exported as civilian goods – meaning they are not covered by arms export rules and do not require export permits signed by the minister of foreign affairs – and are later modified by European and American companies for combat.[11] The Canadian defence industry is also active in training foreign pilots; for example, CAE Montreal has trained Emirati drone pilots, Kuwaiti pilots, and American pilots who refuel Saudi fighter jets during bombing raids in Yemen. Canadian companies are also contracted to repair Saudi military aircraft, and the GDLS-C LAV contract includes servicing of vehicles post-export.

The Debate on Arms Exports, 2015–2020

Within months of the 2015 election, the Liberal government was forced to defend the LAV deal inherited from the Conservatives as reports of human rights abuses in Saudi Arabia mounted. Their management of the issue relied at first on rhetoric that blamed the previous Conservative government for the problem, suggesting that the contract was a "done deal" and that their hands were tied. Foreign Affairs Minister Stéphane Dion claimed that the sale of the LAVs was private, downplaying the government's crucial role in negotiating the deal via the Canadian Commercial Corporation (CCC),[12] and argued that if Canada did not sell weapons to Saudi Arabia, others would.[13] Dion's comments earned the ire of human rights defenders; as former United Nations High Commissioner for Human Rights Louise Arbour argued, the idea that others will sell these arms is "the least convincing (argument), not infused with moral, ethical values."[14]

Export controls in place at the time of the negotiation of the LAV deal included a key requirement that Global Affairs Canada conduct a human rights assessment prior to the issue of an export permit. At that point, if there were any reasonable risk that violations of human rights would occur, the minister could refuse to issue a permit. A human rights assessment was not conducted for Saudi Arabia in the years in which the Saudi LAV deal was negotiated, however.[15]

In April 2016, the *Globe and Mail* revealed that Minister Dion had approved a number of export permits for the LAV deal, thereby giving a green light to send vehicles to Saudi Arabia. Questioned by the NDP in Parliament,[16] Prime Minister Trudeau defended the government's position, arguing that "the principle at play here is that Canada's word needs to mean something in the international community."[17] The government's main argument centred on Canada's trade reputation and Canadian jobs; in Parliament, they frequently pivoted from opposition questions on human rights by emphasizing the importance of the defence industry and the needs of workers in London, Ontario, where the LAVs were manufactured.

Nonetheless, Minister Dion promised that, "should I become aware of credible information of violations related to this equipment, I will suspend or revoke the permits."[18] This promise was tested a number of times but did not result in the suspension or cancellation of any export permits, with one brief exception. In 2017, the *Globe and Mail* revealed that Canadian-made Terradyne Gurkha vehicles were used by Saudi security forces in a crackdown on dissidents in Eastern Province, a fact publicly confirmed days later by the Saudi ambassador to Canada. The government launched an investigation into the allegations and temporarily suspended Terradyne's export permits. But in February 2018, the minister of foreign affairs, Chrystia Freeland, announced that her department's investigation had found "no conclusive evidence" of misuse of those vehicles and that the export permits had been reinstated.[19]

For critics, this argument was problematic. The standard for revisiting export permits is not *conclusive evidence* of misuse, but *reasonable risk*. The government's insistence that it did not find conclusive evidence of misuse was, in the opinion of one of Canada's leading disarmament experts, Cesar Jaramillo, "a perversion of both domestic and international arms control standards."[20]

A partially redacted copy of a Global Affairs Canada memorandum for action from October 2017, released via an Access to Information request months later, revealed more insights into the government's position. The memorandum, which appeared to rely heavily on Saudi government sources, showed that the Canadian government considered the guidelines of reasonable risk less important than whether the Saudi operations were considered "legitimate security operations" with "appropriate" use of force.[21] Moreover, it highlighted Saudi Arabia's role as a "regional leader and bulwark against terrorism, including Daesh," as well as the importance of the Saudi commercial relationship with Canada. (This language echoed the government's legal defence in a challenge brought before the Federal Court by Université de Montréal professor Daniel Turp in 2016, where Canada argued that the GDLS-C LAVs would "help" the Saudis, a "key military ally," to fight instability in Yemen.[22])

The Terradyne case is one of the few opportunities we have to look beyond the talking points of the government to examine its internal communications on Saudi Arabia. The language used in the memorandum is very different from the language the government used in Parliament or its media communications, which downplayed the importance of Canada's relationship with Saudi Arabia. Moreover, critics like the NDP and disarmament expert Jaramillo argued that the government's reliance on Saudi assurances, and its stringent insistence on conclusive evidence, represented "willful blindness."[23]

The Terradyne investigation also illustrates the Trudeau government's approach to transparency. This case was one of four separate allegations between 2015 and 2018 that Canadian-made weapons were used either against Saudi civilians or in the war in Yemen. Of those four cases – GDLS-C LAVs spotted in Yemen in 2015,[24] Winnipeg-made PGW sniper rifles seen in Yemen in 2016, the Terradyne Gurkha allegations in 2017, and an extensive list revealed in the *National Observer* in 2018[25] – the Canadian public know the result of only one government investigation, which resulted in no permanent cancellation of export permits.

Other actions by the Trudeau government also call into question its claims to be fully transparent. In 2017, the government twice refused to increase parliamentary oversight of Canadian arms sales, rejecting NDP motions to establish a parliamentary committee on arms exports similar to one in the United Kingdom.[26] In 2018, the government rejected NDP amendments to Bill C-47 that would have ensured arms exports to the United States be included annually in the *Report on Export of Military Goods*; the government argued that the United States was a trusted trading partner and the proposed changes would create an undue burden on the defence industry. In 2019, following the murder of Jamal Khashoggi, the government refused for months to answer questions about the status of its "review" of existing arms permits to Saudi Arabia, including on review criteria.[27] Important details about the nature of Canada's arms exports are often revealed only via media reports; for example, the fact that the LAV deal included "heavy assault" vehicles (not "jeeps" as Trudeau had earlier called them), and that the contract contained potential billions of dollars in penalties were revealed via Canadian media.

Canada and the War in Yemen

The conduct of the Saudi Arabia–led coalition in the Yemen war has contributed to the world's worst humanitarian crisis. International legal experts and human rights activists have repeatedly argued that Canada is potentially complicit in violations of international law in the conflict in Yemen by continuing to supply arms to a coalition of nine countries, including Saudi Arabia and the United Arab Emirates, fighting the Houthi rebels. Partly as a result of the war, more than 24 million people – about 80 per cent of the country's population – are in need of humanitarian assistance. Widespread violations of international law continue to lead to destruction of infrastructure, while indiscriminate airstrikes by the Saudi-led coalition have caused massive civilian casualties, hitting markets, hospitals, and homes, leading the UN to condemn the coalition for potential war crimes.[28]

While Canada has provided its fair share of humanitarian assistance to the crisis, it has mostly stayed silent on the role of Saudi Arabia and its coalition allies. A review of official Canadian statements on the Yemen conflict from 2017 to 2019 shows that Canada has consistently avoided calling out the Saudis by name. Rather, the government has referred to "all parties" and called for "an end to hostilities," but it has specifically named the Houthis, including in a statement in March 2018 condemning a Houthi missile attack on Saudi Arabia.[29] At no time has Canada named Saudi Arabia or its coalition partners, even when the Saudi-led coalition has attacked schools and hospitals. Moreover, critics have repeatedly questioned the contradictions inherent in providing humanitarian assistance to the people of Yemen on the one hand, and arming its abusers on the other.[30] As Jaramillo has argued, "It's a bit like helping pay for somebody's crutches after you've helped break their legs."[31]

Diplomatic Fallout and the Khashoggi Murder

The Canada-Saudi relationship began to publicly fall apart in the summer of 2018 after Canada issued tweets in support of Samar and Raif Badawi, human rights activists imprisoned in the kingdom. The Saudi reaction was unexpected: Canada's ambassador was expelled from the country; Canada no longer had access to military bases; Canadian companies were no longer permitted to bid on projects in Saudi Arabia; food and medication from Canada were banned; and Saudi students studying at Canadian universities were told to come home. Canada scrambled to find reassurance from Saudi allies in the Middle East, including the UAE, that others would not follow the kingdom's example, given billions of dollars in investment at risk.[32]

Saudi Arabia's foreign minister demanded that Canada apologize for its actions, suggesting Canada had likened his country to "a banana republic."[33] Publicly, Minister Freeland insisted that she was "comfortable" with Canada's position: "We are always going to speak up for human rights, we are always going to speak up for women's rights and that is not going to change." Privately, though, Freeland was quietly trying to repair the relationship,[34] and the LAVs continued to ship.

More than the humanitarian crisis in Yemen or other Saudi human rights abuses, the October 2018 murder of *Washington Post* columnist

Jamal Khashoggi spurred many governments to rethink their relationships with Saudi Arabia. In the weeks following the murder, Germany suspended its arms deals with Saudi Arabia and called on its allies to do the same.[35] American politicians from both major parties took action in Congress to demand their government stop supporting Saudi Arabia and its war in Yemen.[36]

In Canada, the Trudeau government faced renewed calls from political commentators, human rights activists, and the NDP to suspend the LAV deal. Within weeks, Trudeau announced an active review of existing export permits to the kingdom and the suspension of any new permits – though the LAV contract would continue, with the prime minister confirming for the first time publicly that penalties for cancellation of the LAV contract could be "in the billions of dollars."[37]

The decision to suspend future permits but continue the LAV deal was a clear attempt by the government to balance competing concerns of human rights and jobs. This decision was generally consistent with Canadian public opinion; a poll conducted by Angus Reid a few weeks after Khashoggi's murder showed that Canadians overwhelmingly agreed that future sales to Saudi Arabia should be stopped but were evenly divided over suspending the LAV deal.[38] As the global controversy continued, Canada also imposed sanctions on seventeen Saudi nationals suspected of involvement in Khashoggi's murder, though Mohammed bin Salman, the crown prince widely believed to have ordered the murder, was not on the list.

In November 2018, a report published in the *National Observer* revealed a number of points of evidence that Canadian weapons, including armoured vehicles and rifles, were being used in the war in Yemen. Canadian researcher Anthony Fenton provided detailed evidence found on social media of "Saudi selfies" with Canadian-made weapons or "bling videos."[39] These revelations strengthened critics' argument that there was high risk of misuse of Canadian weapons in the war in Yemen. The government replied by arguing that all permits were under review – though they provided no details of what the review entailed. By December, Trudeau was openly suggesting that Canada was looking for a way "of no longer exporting these vehicles to Saudi Arabia."[40] Yet shipments of arms continued unabated; in 2019, Canada exported over $2.4 billion in LAVs as part of the GDLS contract, nearly $20 million in aircraft equipment, and over $6 million in rifles to the kingdom.[41]

At the same time as the Trudeau government was under pressure from critics and a public increasingly critical of Canada's ties to Saudi Arabia, it was also under pressure from the defence industry to continue the contract. Lobbying records show that between August and December

2018, GDLS-C representatives met with the most senior political advisors in the Prime Minister's Office and the departments of Global Affairs, National Defence, and Finance a total of thirty-nine times to pressure the government not to cancel the LAV deal.[42] In March 2019, the Saudi minister of foreign affairs publicly stated that Trudeau's comments about cancelling the contract "are for domestic consumption ... [W]e see the Canadian government going ahead with the deal."[43] Repeated requests from the media, civil society, and the NDP for information on the status of Canada's review of export permits, including direct questions to Minister of Foreign Affairs Chrystia Freeland at an appearance before the House of Commons Foreign Affairs Committee, went unanswered in the months following Khashoggi's murder,[44] even after a United Nations special rapporteur found Saudi officials had planned and carried out the murder.[45]

In April 2020, the Trudeau government quietly announced at the beginning of a holiday weekend that it had lifted the suspension of new export permits to Saudi Arabia. While new permits would be approved on a "case-by-case basis," media reports indicated the government already had four dozen export permits waiting to be signed as soon as the suspension was lifted. Foreign Affairs Minister François-Philippe Champagne also announced Canada had renegotiated the LAV contract with Saudi Arabia, allowing the government to speak more freely about it, and confirmed that penalties for its cancellation could amount to up to its full $15 billion value.[46] The renegotiation also included a faster payment schedule from the Saudis, a fact celebrated by General Dynamics in a subsequent call to its shareholders.[47]

The minister also announced a change in Canada's export control process: the creation of a new arm's-length expert panel to advise the minister on best practices, in an attempt to ensure Canada's controls were "as robust as possible." Details of who would be on this panel, or how soon it would be formed, were not publicly released.[48]

The Debate over Bill C-47 and Changes to Canada's Arms Export Controls

Since its election in 2015, the Liberal government has frequently argued that its changes to arms export controls and accession to the Arms Trade Treaty (ATT) would hold Canada to a higher standard. In April 2017, Minister Freeland introduced Bill C-47, *An Act to Amend the Export and Import Permits Act*, that in principle was to amend Canada's arms export controls in order to accede to the treaty, which the previous Conservative government had refused to sign.

Civil society groups like Project Ploughshares, Amnesty International, Oxfam, and Control Arms – who had all campaigned for the treaty – were critical of Bill C-47 from the outset, arguing that the bill did not reflect the spirit or the letter of the ATT; among their concerns was the government's choice to include ATT assessment criteria – such as consideration of human rights, humanitarian rights law, peace and security, and gender-based violence – in regulations and not in the legislation proper.[49] After a number of committee testimonies to this effect, the government agreed to amend the legislation to legally require the minister of foreign affairs to consider ATT assessment criteria before issuing an export permit.

But the government would not budge on civil society's second major concern, which was, in the words of Project Ploughshares' Jaramillo, "a loophole you could drive a tank through":[50] the continued exemption of Canadian exports to the United States from licensing and reporting requirements. Such exemptions are prohibited by the treaty, but the government argued there was no harm in continuing a Canada-US Defence Production Sharing Agreement that dates back to the 1950s. Critics, however, pointed out that over 50 per cent of Canadian arms exports (an estimated $2 billion or more per year) go to the United States, and very little of this is tracked or reported publicly. Some of these weapons, parts and components are re-exported onward to third countries, including Saudi Arabia, but Canadians have no way to access this information. Anecdotal reports suggest that Canadian manufacturers contribute to a number of systems exported from the United States that may end up in the hands of human rights–abusing governments; for example, in 2017, the *Globe and Mail* revealed that engines made by Pratt & Whitney in Quebec are part of a US$593-million deal to export warplanes from the United States to Nigeria, a sale that alarmed human rights groups.[51]

The United States is not a state party to the Arms Trade Treaty and crucially, under President Donald Trump, its arms export controls have been watered down – a decision that has troubled arms control experts in the United States.[52] While the Canadian government argues that it considers exports to the United States to be low risk, the United States remains the world's largest exporter of weapons to Saudi Arabia and has provided significant military support to the coalition in the war in Yemen, including refuelling the same Saudi jets that have bombed school convoys and hospitals.

The Canadian government's reluctance to fix the US loophole may be explained partly by the influence of the defence industry. During government consultations, industry representatives expressed concern that the government would consider a country's entire human rights record rather than the potential human rights impact of a single exported item. They worried that manufacturers would be held accountable for misuse of the weapons they produced and also argued that additional reporting would present a burden to arms manufacturers – a perplexing argument, given that companies already keep internal records; their reluctance to share these records with the government and the Canadian public is more about commercial confidentiality than it is about the effort required to report.[53]

The government attempted to balance the concerns of civil society and industry by introducing a new general export permit for full systems to the United States, which will slightly improve public reporting in the future. However, parts and components are not included under this permit, and Canadians will still have very little information about where these weapons go after export, or how they are used.

Ongoing Concerns about Canadian Arms Exports

The Canadian debate has focused largely on the LAV deal, to the detriment of other important issues related to Canadian arms exports. The Trudeau government's changes to Canada's arms export controls did little to address questions surrounding the role of the Canadian Commercial Corporation (CCC), a Crown corporation that facilitates trade on behalf of Canadian industry with foreign governments. The CCC negotiated the $15 billion LAV contract as well as a controversial $234 million helicopter deal with the Philippines that was cancelled in 2018 by Rodrigo Duterte's government, following public outcry in Canada over his human rights record. Importantly, that deal did not require an export permit, as the helicopters were classified for civilian use, even though the recipient was the Philippines Air Force. The CCC, moreover, does not conduct human rights assessments, nor does it conduct follow-ups to ensure that exported Canadian equipment is not used to abuse human rights.[54] These weaknesses were noted in 2020 by Canada's auditor general, who criticized the absence of "a formal process to identify and mitigate the risks related to human rights when doing business with foreign governments."[55]

An additional concern stems from Canadian companies operating overseas outside of Canadian arms export controls. Allegations of Streit Group's sanctions-busting in 2016, in which Canadians learned that UAE-based but Canadian-owned Streit had sold armoured vehicles to Libya, Sudan, and South Sudan in contravention of UN sanctions, have not resulted in fines or charges in Canada.[56] In comparison, the US government fined Streit Group for illegal export of vehicles to Nigeria, the UAE, Iraq, and Afghanistan in 2015. While Bill C-47 made changes to brokering laws requiring Canadian citizens to apply for brokering permits, even if working outside of Canada, the effect of these changes on companies like Streit Group is unclear. There is no indication, in addition, that the Canadian government will increase resources to the RCMP to investigate violations of Canadian law abroad.

How the Debate Affects Canada

This complicated issue has broader implications for future Canadian governments as they navigate diplomatic and trade relationships in the Middle East, particularly with Saudi Arabia. Any future government will be forced to find a delicate balance between supporting the Canadian defence industry – including the lucrative jobs that come with it – and upholding Canada's human rights obligations. They will also need to pay close attention to the global conversation on arms exports and the Middle East.[57]

Canada is certainly not alone in navigating these challenges; Canada operates within a global context in which the arms trade affects foreign policy decisions in a number of countries. Disagreements over arms sales to Saudi Arabia have led to tensions within and even between arms-producing states. For example, after Germany suspended its arms sales to Saudi Arabia, the United Kingdom and France pleaded with the Merkel government to change its position, arguing that Germany's position was putting European arms sales at risk. Germany later relaxed its position to allow existing joint projects with European partners destined for Saudi Arabia to continue.[58]

Domestically, the debate in the United States has grown increasingly tense; in an unprecedented action in April 2019, Congress voted to end American military assistance for the war in Yemen. Despite bipartisan support for the resolution, President Trump vetoed the bill a few days later.[59] Spain, Norway, France, Australia, and other countries have also grappled with the ethics of continuing to sell weapons to Saudi Arabia as the war in Yemen continues. Several countries, Canada included, have also faced labour actions as dock workers refuse to load and unload weaponry destined for Saudi Arabia.[60]

Governments are also vulnerable to legal challenges. While Daniel Turp's legal challenge did not move forward in Canada, a decision by the UK Court of Appeal in 2019 had serious implications for the British government's policy. In response to a challenge by the Campaign against Arms Trade, the court ruled that British ministers had not properly assessed threats to civilians when approving arms sales to Saudi Arabia in

2016, nor had they considered past and current violations of international humanitarian law committed by the Saudi-led coalition in Yemen. The British government was forced to suspend arms export licences to Saudi Arabia while seeking to overturn the decision.[61]

Canada may also be affected by decisions made by other governments. Canada's third-largest destination for arms exports is Belgium; following an investigation that found Belgian arms were used in Yemen, Belgium's State Council suspended arms licences to Saudi Arabia dating back to 2017, including licences granted to CMI Defense, which supplies gun systems for the GDLS LAVs.[62] At the time of writing, and with several years left on the contract, it is unclear whether decisions made in Belgium could delay deliveries of Canadian LAVs to Saudi Arabia.

Conclusion

That the Trudeau government has continued to export arms to Saudi Arabia is not surprising; Vucetic has argued that there is little difference between Liberal and Conservative governments in exporting arms to human rights violators.[63] Further, the 2019 decision by Canada's Supreme Court *not* to hear Turp's challenge on the legality of arms exports to Saudi Arabia has made the legal argument against exporting these weapons weaker. But concerns about reasonable risk of misuse, transparency, and human rights still stand. Gutterman and Lane have questioned whether Canada should continue to support the defence industry's efforts to sell to certain countries, given known corruption in the Saudi arms industry, Canada's poor record of prosecuting corruption, and the overwhelming evidence that the arms trade fuels violence and corruption.[64] In addition, arms control experts Thrall and Dorminey have argued that arms sales might actually embolden states like Saudi Arabia to commit violations and create a host of unintended negative consequences.[65] These questions deserve further consideration.

The government's half-hearted changes to Canada's arms export system do not make up for the facts that significant loopholes are still unaddressed, and arms still flow to Saudi Arabia, while the country continues to wage war in Yemen and imprison women's rights activists like Nobel Peace Prize nominee Loujain al-Hathloul, a graduate of Canada's University of British Columbia.[66] While stopping the Canadian LAV sale would do little to end Saudi Arabia's violations of international law, as Momani[67] and others have argued, the questions of complicity in violations of international law and of continuing to enable the Saudi regime in the name of the Canadian public also matter.

NOTES

1 I am grateful to the editors and to Cesar Jaramillo for constructive comments on earlier drafts of this chapter.
2 Amnesty International, "Saudi Arabia: 10 Things You Need to Know about a Kingdom of Cruelty," 23 October 2018, https://www.amnesty.org/en /latest/news/2018/10/saudi-arabia-10-things-you-need-to-know -about-a-kingdom-of-cruelty/.
3 Srdjan Vucetic, "A Nation of Feminist Arms Dealers? Canada and Military Exports," *International Journal* 72, no. 4 (2017): 503–19, https://doi.org /10.1177/0020702017740156.
4 Jennifer Pedersen, "We Will Honour Our Good Name: The Trudeau Government, Arms Exports, and Human Rights," in *Justin Trudeau and Canadian Foreign Policy*, ed. Norman Hillmer and Philippe Lagasse, 207–32 (London: Palgrave, 2018).
5 Stockholm International Peace Research Institute, "Trends in International Arms Transfers, 2018," March 2019, https://www.sipri.org/sites/default /files/2019–03/fs_1903_at_2018.pdf.
6 Thomas Juneau, "Canada and Saudi Arabia: A Deeply Flawed but Necessary Partnership," Canadian Global Affairs Institute, July 2016, https://www .cgai.ca/canada_and_saudi_arabia#LAV; Ellen Gutterman and Andrea Lane, "Beyond LAVs: Corruption, Commercialization and the Canadian Defence Industry," *Canadian Foreign Policy Journal* 23, no. 1 (2017): 77–92.
7 Thomas Juneau, "A Surprising Spat: The Causes and Consequences of the Saudi-Canadian Dispute," *International Journal* 74, no. 2 (2019): 313–23.
8 These figures are from 2016. Canadian Association of Defence and Security Industries, "State of Canada's Defence Industry," (2018), https://www .mynorthmyhome.ca/wp-content/uploads/2018/05/State_of_Canadas _Defence_Industry-2018_Report.pdf.
9 Norman De Bono, "$15B General Dynamics Deal Means Big Things for London Workers," *London Free Press*, 5 April 2018, https://lfpress.com /news/local-news/maintenance-on-gdlss-saudi-contract-boosts-long -term-job-security/.
10 Government of Canada, *Report on Exports of Military Goods from Canada, 2019*, June 2020.
11 Hugo Joncas, "Fabriqués ici pour tuer," TVA, 12 January 2019, https:// www.tvanouvelles.ca/2019/01/12/fabriques-ici-pour-tuer-1; Martin Lukacs, "Is Saudi Arabia Deploying Canadian-Made Weapons in Yemen?," *National Observer*, 30 November 2018, https://www.nationalobserver .com/2018/11/30/news/experts-say-theres-proof-canadian-made-weapons -are-being-used-saudi-war-yemen.

12 Justin Ling, "Exclusive: Canada Isn't Being Totally Honest about Its Plan to Sell Weapons to Saudi Arabia," Vice News, 12 July 2016, https://news .vice.com/en_us/article/bjkkg4/exclusive-canada-isnt-being-totally-honest -about-its-plan-to-sell-weapons-to-saudi-arabia.

13 Murray Brewster, "Canada's Arms Deal with Saudi Arabia Is Shrinking," CBC, 10 September 2018, https://www.cbc.ca/news/politics/saudi-arabia -arms-canada-1.4815571; Steven Chase, "Cancelling Saudi Arms Deal Would Have No Effect on Human Rights: Dion," *Globe and Mail*, 29 March 2016, https://www.theglobeandmail.com/news/politics/cancelling-saudi -arms-deal-would-have-no-effect-on-human-rights-dion/article29427814/.

14 Chase, "Cancelling Saudi Arms Deal."

15 Steven Chase, "Canada Not Tracking Saudi Rights Record Despite 15-Billion Arms Deal," *Globe and Mail*, 20 May 2015, https://www .theglobeandmail.com/news/politics/canada-not-tracking-saudi-rights -record-despite-15-billion-arms-deal/article24506186/.

16 Of the parties in the 42nd Parliament, the opposition New Democrats were the most vocal in demanding cancellation of the LAV deal and an end to arms sales to Saudi Arabia, raising concerns about Saudi Arabia 179 times in the House of Commons, including 77 times in Question Period alone.

17 Ryan Maloney, "Trudeau Says Honouring Saudi Arms Deal a 'Matter of Principle,'" *Huffington Post*, 14 April 2016, https://www.huffingtonpost .ca/2016/04/14/trudeau-saudi-arms-deal-london_n_9693112.html.

18 Quoted in Pedersen, "We Will Honour Our Good Name."

19 Steven Chase, "Saudi Arabia Defends Use of Canadian-Made Armoured Vehicles against Civilians," *Globe and Mail*, 16 August 2017, https://www .theglobeandmail.com/news/politics/saudi-arabia-defends-use-of -canadian-made-armoured-vehicles-against-civilians/article36007932/.

20 Cesar Jaramillo, "Canada and Saudi Arabia: An Arms Deal No Matter What," *Ploughshares Monitor* 39, no. 1 (Spring 2018), https://ploughshares .ca/pl_publications/canada-and-saudi-arabia-an-arms-deal-no-matter-what/.

21 Global Affairs Canada, "Memorandum for Action: Export Permit Suspension: Munitions List Item to Saudi Arabia," BPTS:03120-2017, 10 October 2017, https://www.international.gc.ca/controls-controles/assets /pdfs/documents/memorandum-memo.pdf.

22 Justin Ling, "Canada Admits the Weapons It Sells to Saudi Arabia Could Be Used in Yemen's Civil War," Vice News, 20 December 2016, https://news .vice.com/en_ca/article/mb9mvp/canada-admits-the-weapons-it-sells-to -saudi-arabia-could-be-used-in-yemen-civil-war.

23 Cesar Jaramillo, "Latest Saudi Behaviour Another Reason to Cancel Arms Deal," OpenCanada, 10 August 2018, https://www.opencanada.org /features/latest-saudi-behaviour-another-reason-cancel-arms-deal/.

24 Steven Chase and Robert Fife, "Saudis Appear to Be Using Canadian-Made
    Combat Vehicles against Yemeni Rebels," *Globe and Mail*, 22 February 2016,
    https://www.theglobeandmail.com/news/politics/saudi-arms-used
    -against-yemeni-rebels-seem-to-match-canadian-lavs/article28846678/.
25 Lukacs, "Is Saudi Arabia Deploying Canadian-Made Weapons."
26 Steven Chase, "Liberals Reject NDP Motion to Increase Scrutiny of Arms
    Exports," *Globe and Mail*, 4 October 2016, https://beta.theglobeandmail
    .com/news/politics/liberals-reject-ndp-motion-to-increase-scrutiny
    -of-arms-exports/article32252484/.
27 Samantha Wright Allen, "Arms Exports to Saudi Arabia Reach $1.2 Billion
    in 2018, Despite Calls for Canada to Suspend Permits," *Hill Times*, 3 July
    2019.
28 ACAPS, "Yemen," 2019, https://www.acaps.org/country/yemen; United
    Nations Human Rights Council, "Yemen: United Nations Experts Point to
    Possible War Crimes by Parties to the Conflict," 28 August 2018.
29 See Global Affairs Canada, "Canada Calls for an End to the Conflict in Yemen,"
    1 November 2018, https://www.canada.ca/en/global-affairs/news/2018/11
    /canada-calls-for-an-end-to-the-conflict-in-yemen.html; Global Affairs Canada,
    "Canada Encouraged by UN-Sponsored Peace Consultations on Yemen," 15
    December 2018, https://www.canada.ca/en/global-affairs/news/2018/12
    /canada-encouraged-by-un-sponsored-peace-consultations-on-yemen.html;
    Global Affairs Canada, "Canada Calls for Humanitarian Access and De-
    escalation of Violence in Yemen," 6 December 2017, https://www.canada.ca
    /en/global-affairs/news/2017/12/canada_calls_forhumanitarianaccessandde
    -escalationofviolenceinye.html; Global Affairs Canada, "Statement by Foreign
    Affairs Minister on Missile Attack in Saudi Arabia," 27 March 2018, https://
    www.canada.ca/en/global-affairs/news/2018/03/statement-by-foreign-affairs
    -minister-on-missile-attack-in-saudi-arabia.html.
30 New Democratic Party of Canada, "NDP Calls on Liberals to Follow Yemen
    Humanitarian Assistance with a Halt in Arms Exports to Saudi Arabia,"
    28 February 2019, https://www.ndp.ca/news/ndp-calls-liberals-follow
    -yemen-humanitarian-assistance-halt-arms-exports-saudi-arabia.
31 Brendan Kennedy and Michelle Shephard, "Canada's Dual Role in Yemen:
    Arms Exports to Saudi Coalition Dwarf Aid Sent to War-Torn Country,"
    Toronto Star, 30 April 2018, https://www.thestar.com/news/investigations
    /2018/04/30/canadas-dual-role-in-yemen-arms-exports-to-saudi-coalition
    -dwarfs-aid-sent-to-war-torn-country.html.
32 Evan Dyer, "Canada Will Meet with Saudis to Discuss Diplomatic Rift:
    Freeland," CBC News, 25 September 2018, https://www.cbc.ca/news
    /politics/freelant-to-meet-saudi-regime-1.4837033; Murray Brewster,
    "Canada Risked Losing More Than $7B in Investment over Saudi Spat,
    Documents show," CBC News, 15 March 2019, https://www.cbc.ca/news

/politics/saudi-arabia-canada-direct-investment-1.5057144; Jacques Marcoux and Caroline Barghou, "How Events Unfolded after Foreign Affairs Minister Sent Tweet Rebuking Saudi Arabia," CBC News, 6 December 2018, https://www.cbc.ca/news/canada/how-events-unfolded -after-foreign-affairs-minister-sent-tweet-rebuking-saudi-arabia-1.4935735.

33 Marcoux and Barghout, "How Events Unfolded."

34 Evan Dyer, "Canada Will Meet with Saudis to Discuss Diplomatic Rift: Freeland," CBC News, 25 September 2018, https://www.cbc.ca/news /politics/freelant-to-meet-saudi-regime-1.4837033.

35 Rick Noack, "Germany Halts Arms Deals with Saudi Arabia, Encourages Allies to Do the Same," *Washington Post*, 22 October 2018, https://www .washingtonpost.com/world/2018/10/22/germany-its-allies-well-halt-future -arms-sales-saudi-arabia-until-we-have-clarity-khashoggi-so-should-you/.

36 Mark Weisbrot, "Congress Is Finally Pushing the US to Withdraw from Yemen. It's about Time," *Guardian*, 30 November 2018, https://www .theguardian.com/commentisfree/2018/nov/30/congress-finally -pushing-us-withdraw-yemen.

37 Reuters, "Canada's Trudeau Says Reviewing Saudi Arms Export Permits," 25 October 2018, https://ca.reuters.com/article/topNews /idCAKCN1MZ2OA-OCATP.

38 Angus Reid Institute, "Nine-in-Ten Canadians Say 'No' to Future Arms Deals with Saudi Arabia; Divided over Cancelling Current One," 6 November 2018, http://angusreid.org/saudi-arabia-canada-khashoggi/.

39 Lukacs, "Is Saudi Arabia Deploying Canadian-Made Weapons."

40 Steven Chase, "Trudeau Says Canada Trying to End Arms Contract with Saudi Arabia," *Globe and Mail*, 16 December 2018, https://www .theglobeandmail.com/politics/article-trudeau-says-canada-trying -to-end-arms-export-deal-to-saudi-arabia/.

41 "Canadian International Merchandise Trade Database," Statistics Canada, https://www5.statcan.gc.ca/cimt-cicm/home-accueil?lang=eng.

42 Information from the Office of the Commissioner of Lobbying of Canada, Lobbycanada.gc.ca.

43 Jesse Ferreras, "Saudi Arabia Expects Canada to Proceed with $15B Arms Deal, but There's 'No Final Decision,'" Global News, 5 March 2019, https://globalnews.ca/news/5021709/saudi-arabia-canada-arms-deal/.

44 Samantha Wright Allen, "Arms Exports to Saudi Arabia Reach $1.2 Billion in 2018, Despite Calls for Canada to Suspend Permits," *Hill Times*, 3 July 2019.

45 Office of the United Nations High Commissioner for Human Rights, "Khashoggi Killing: UN Human Rights Expert Says Saudi Arabia Is Responsible for 'Premeditated Execution,'" 19 June 2019, https://www .ohchr.org/EN/NewsEvents/Pages/DisplayNews.aspx?NewsID =24713&LangID=E.

46 Levon Sevunts, "Canada Cuts New Deal with Saudi Arabia, Clearing Way for More Arms Sales," Radio Canada International, 10 April 2020, https://www.rcinet.ca/en/2020/04/10/canada-cuts-new-deal-with-saudi-arabia-clearing-way-for-more-arms-sales/.

47 Joe Gould, "General Dynamics Saw $1 Billion Bump after Canada-Saudi Accord," Defense News, 6 May 2020, https://www.defensenews.com/congress/2020/05/07/general-dynamics-saw-1-billion-bump-after-canada-saudi-accord/.

48 Government of Canada, *Report on Exports of Military Goods from Canada, 2019*, June 2020.

49 Amnesty International et al., "Bill C-47 and Canadian Accession to the Arms Trade Treaty: Civil Society Concerns and Recommendations," Submission to the House of Commons Standing Committee on Foreign Affairs, October 2017, https://www.ourcommons.ca/Content/Committee/421/FAAE/Brief/BR9214271/br-external/AmnestyInternational-e.pdf.

50 Cesar Jaramillo, "Canada's ATT Legislation Has a Loophole You Could Drive a Tank Through," *Huffington Post*, 6 July 2017, https://www.huffingtonpost.ca/cesar-jaramillo/canadas-arms-exports_a_22533341/.

51 Geoffrey York, "Canadian Firms Part of Arms Sales to Nigeria," *Globe and Mail*, 13 September 2017, https://www.theglobeandmail.com/news/world/canadian-firms-part-of-us-arms-sales-to-nigeria/article36256222/.

52 William Hartung, "Weapons for Anyone: Donald Trump and the Art of the Arms Deal," CounterPunch, 2 April 2018, https://www.counterpunch.org/2018/04/02/weapons-for-anyone-donald-trump-and-the-art-of-the-arms-deal/.

53 Global Affairs Canada, "Global Affairs Canada's Proposed Strengthening of Canada's Export Controls Program: What We Heard, Summary Report," April 2019.

54 David Pugliese, "Lucrative Arms Deals Provide Little Incentive for Canadian Commercial Corp. to Scale Back on Defence Market," *National Post*, 28 May 2018, https://nationalpost.com/news/canada/lucrative-arms-deals-provide-little-incentive-for-canadian-commercial-corp-to-scale-back-on-defence-market.

55 Auditor General of Canada, *Special Examination Report: Canadian Commercial Corporation*, July 2020, https://www.oag-bvg.gc.ca/internet/English/parl_oag_202007_04_e_43575.html.

56 Murray Brewster, "Feds Want RCMP to Look into Canadian Firm's Armoured Car Shipments to War-Torn Libya," CBC News, 15 August 2016, https://www.cbc.ca/news/politics/streit-libya-un-rcmp-brewster-1.3722409.

57 On the difficult balance between human rights and other considerations in Canada's Middle East policies, see also the chapter by Petrasek in this volume.

58 Patrick Wintour, "Jeremy Hunt Urges Germany to Rethink Saudi Arms Sales Ban," *Guardian*, 20 February 2019, https://www.theguardian.com/world /2019/feb/20/jeremy-hunt-urges-germany-to-rethink-saudi-arms-sales-ban.

59 Ed Pilkington, "Dismay as Trump Vetoes Bill to End US Support for War in Yemen," *Guardian*, 17 April 2019, https://www.theguardian.com/us -news/2019/apr/16/trump-yemen-war-veto-military-aid.

60 Simon Black and Anthony Fenton, "Canada's Labour Movement Must Take a Stand against the Saudi Arms Deal," Conversation, 25 June 2019, http:// theconversation.com/canadas-labour-movement-must-take-a-stand-against -the-saudi-arms-deal-118510.

61 Dan Sabbagh, "UK Ministers Challenge Court Ruling on Saudi Arabia Arms Sales," *Guardian*, 8 July 2019, https://www.theguardian.com/politics/2019 /jul/08/uk-ministers-challenge-court-ruling-on-saudi-arabia-arms-sales.

62 Belga, "Le Conseil d'État annule les licences d'exportations d'armes wallonnes en Arabie saoudite," Radio Télévision Belge Francophone, 14 June 2019, https://www.rtbf.be/info/belgique/detail_le-conseil -d-etat-annule-les-licences-d-exportations-d-armes-wallonnes-en-arabie -saoudite?id=10246413.

63 Vucetic, "Nation of Feminist Arms Dealers?"

64 Gutterman and Lane, "Beyond LAVs."

65 A. Trevor Thrall and Caroline Dorminey, "American Weapons in Yemen: A Cautionary Tale," CATO Institute, 5 February 2019, https://www.cato .org/blog/american-weapons-yemen-cautionary-tale.

66 Al-Hathloul was released in early 2021 but remains subject to a travel ban. Jillian Kestler d'Amours, "Saudi Human Rights Defender Gets Backing for Nobel Peace Prize," Middle East Eye, 6 February 2019, https://www .middleeasteye.net/news/saudi-human-rights-defender-gets-backing-nobel -peace-prize.

67 Bessma Momani, "Cancelling Canada's Saudi Arms Deal Would Merely Be a Feel-Good Measure," *Globe and Mail*, 18 December 2018, https://www .theglobeandmail.com/opinion/article-cancelling-canadas-saudi-arms -deal-would-merely-be-a-feel-good/.

12 Supporting Mediation: Canada as Peacemaker in the Middle East

PETER JONES

Many Canadians take pride in their country being a "helpful fixer" in world affairs; a notion of Canada as a "good state" has acquired a powerful constituency in the country. It holds that such states pursue an expansive conception of self-interest, defined by advancing broader goals of justice and peace than those associated with more traditionally realist policies. Of course, not everyone agrees.[1] For those who do subscribe to the "good state" idea, niche activities such as peacekeeping and mediation have been identified as an integral part of this vocation.[2]

This chapter discusses Canada's role as a peacemaker in the Middle East. It identifies three distinct eras of Canadian involvement as a Middle East peacemaker and explores them. It also examines Canada's role in the context of aspects of the conflict resolution literature, specifically whether the objective is to manage, resolve, or transform a situation. The chapter holds that Canada's actions have been tentative and motivated primarily by a desire to be seen as a "good ally" of the United States and other NATO partners. It explores meanings of the term "impartial" as they pertain to Canada's actions over the years and argues that, while Canada's supposed impartiality in specific regional disputes has been touted as a reason why it is well suited to peacemaking, Canada has not always been impartial. Even when Canada has been even-handed in its approach to disputes, its desire to uphold a regional order that is largely to the benefit of key allies raises questions of whether Canada's actions as a peacemaker have really been as "impartial" as it often argues.

Peacemaking in the Middle East: Canada's Approach over the Years

This chapter argues that Canada's involvement as a peacemaker in the Middle East has gone through three broad phases since the Second World War. The longest was from the 1950s to the early 2000s, when

Canada portrayed itself as an "honest broker" and a "peacekeeper," around the world, and in the Middle East in particular. This activity was usually undertaken within a multilateral framework and took many forms.[3] One of these was the oft-cited "invention" of peacekeeping by Lester Pearson and Canada's involvement in virtually every regional peacekeeping mission for most of these decades.[4] Canada was also active in the search for an Arab-Israeli peace agreement, most publicly as a "gavel holder" of one of the multilateral groups of the Middle East peace process and contributor to others (see the Musu chapter in this volume).[5] Throughout all of this, Canadian politicians were eager to proclaim that Canada was a uniquely placed and motivated country, which sought compromise and peace without the venal ambitions and interests that characterized others.[6]

A significant element in all this was Canada's self-proclaimed "impartiality" in regional disputes, which, it was argued, made Canada "acceptable" as an intervenor to a wide variety of interested states and players. After all, Canada had little investment in the region, and trade with it was marginal (though immigration from the region took place at an increasing rate over these years, so that its concerns steadily also became a part of the Canadian political landscape).[7] In addition to official actions as a peacemaker, Canada also occasionally sponsored unofficial dialogues explore the possible terrain of compromise. One of the best known of these was the Jerusalem Old City Initiative (JOCI), which gathered Israeli, Palestinian, and international experts to explore whether a new approach might be taken to the contentious issue of the Old City of Jerusalem.[8] Finally, though far less well-known and documented, Canada frequently served as a "helpful fixer" – a quiet actor behind the scenes, helping to facilitate contacts and smooth transactions that could not easily be done directly or in the light of day.[9]

The second phase occurred during the prime ministership of Stephen Harper (2006–15). It was, publicly at least, largely a rejection of the first phase, whose ongoing and, with the end of the Cold War, increasingly bloody conflicts had caused many in Canada to wonder whether automatic involvement in peacekeeping missions in which there was no peace to keep was desirable. In reality, much of the groundwork for what became the second phase, identified in this chapter as the Harper years, was laid during the administration of Paul Martin (2003–6). Indeed, after the Cold War, Canada's commitment to peacekeeping declined precipitously as it joined other forms of international military actions, often coercive and without a UN mandate. Some had been questioning much earlier whether Canada's automatic involvement in peacekeeping had not become a substitute for thought.[10] Beyond the issue of "peacekeeping" specifically, the Harper people questioned "impartiality" as a virtue in itself.[11]

Some Canadian foreign policy analysts and commentators supported the Harper government's line that Canada's image of itself as a "peace-maker" and an "honest broker" was largely mythic.[12] The Harper government itself characterized the previous era of "going along to get along" as a shameful period in which Canada had cravenly failed to stand up for its values in the misguided hope of currying favour with reprehensible regimes. As Foreign Minister Baird put it, "After the Second World War, some decision makers lost sight of our proud tradition to do what is just and right. Some decided it would be better to paint Canada as a so-called honest broker. I call it being afraid to take a clear position."[13] Harper himself said in 2011 that Canada would "*no longer* [seek] to please every dictator with a vote at the United Nations ... I confess that I don't know why past attempts to do so were ever thought to be in Canada's national interest."[14] Obviously, all of this was a direct rebuke of the notion of peacemaking, both in the region, and more broadly, based on impartiality as a Canadian value.

The Harper government believed strongly that Canada should side overtly with those (in the Middle East and elsewhere) who, they believed, typified Canada's commitment to freedom and democracy, particularly in the post-9/11 era. These values were characterized as being based on "Judeo-Christian" principles. For example, an Office of Religious Freedom was established within Foreign Affairs, which the Liberal government subsequently closed. More concretely, during the 2006 Israel invasion of Lebanon, and its 2008 attacks on Gaza, while most of the international community argued that Israel's use of force was not proportionate, the Canadian government unstintingly supported Israel and placed blame for the fighting squarely on Israel's enemies, drawing considerable notice for its new stance at home and abroad (see the Boily chapter in this volume).[15] As the Arab uprisings broke out and swept the region, Canada was one of the few Western governments who followed the Israeli government in lamenting the fall of regimes such as that of Hosni Mubarak in Egypt, and their (often brief) replacement with more populist governments as being potentially not in Israel's interests (see the Allam chapter in this volume). Canada's actions in subsequent episodes (for example, in Libya and Syria) during this time reflect a growing ambivalence over support for regime change and a recognition of the costs of direct involvement.[16]

However, even though much of this period was characterized by rhetoric that sought to distance Canada from the previous era, the Harper government was not immune to the need to support key allies in the region, and particularly the United States. Thus, even though the Harper government vocally supported those in Israel who cast doubt on many of the compromises necessary to achieve a so-called two-state solution to the Israeli-Palestinian issue, it never completely turned its back on this objective, and even (for a time) continued to support initiatives, such as JOCI, which were appreciated by the US government as a means to keep dialogue channels alive on key issues. Moreover, even though some in the Harper government vocally supported the efforts of the Israeli right, led by Prime Minister Benjamin Netanyahu, to advocate an attack on Iran's nuclear program, the fact that the American government was opposed meant that official Canadian policy on the matter never went so far. Nor did Canada officially abandon its position that Israeli settlements on occupied land are illegal. Indeed, one cannot help but think that the Harper government's policy of vocally supporting the Israeli right, while quietly toeing the line with US policy, amounted to an attempt to have it both ways: loudly catering to its pro-Israeli political base, while quietly not offending its closest ally.[17]

The third phase began when, upon assuming office in 2015, the Trudeau government issued instructions to the new minister of foreign affairs (re-named "Global Affairs") that efforts be made to recapture Canada's place as an active player in international mediation, peacekeeping, and conflict resolution.[18] The new government stated that it was determined to recapture the proud tradition of the pre-Harper years, but to do so in a way that also highlighted new priorities, such as women's rights and the environment.[19] While these broader policies were not Middle East–centric as such, they informed Canada's actions in that region as in all others. It is still not clear what the ultimate impact of this new approach to old priorities will be, but the Trudeau government's commitment to human rights and other such norms has embroiled it (somewhat reluctantly, at first) in controversies over the contradictory pressures inherent in such activities as arms sales and support for human rights, both generally and in Saudi Arabia in particular (see the Pederson chapter in this volume).[20]

Here again, the question of "impartiality" arises, though not in the way traditionally thought of in contexts such as mediation. It is also notable that Canada has yet to take on any official role as a mediator or peacekeeper in the region since the election of the Trudeau government, nor has established the mechanisms to do so.[21] This may be because it fears the domestic repercussions of talking with those who violate human rights and other norms, which one must do as a mediator.[22] However, the Trudeau government has recommitted Canada to a more "balanced" approach to the Arab-Israeli dispute and sought to quietly re-enter the business of supporting efforts at the unofficial level to keep dialogue alive on the "two-state solution," particularly in an era when US government support for that goal seemed to be slipping under President Donald Trump.

Impartiality

Each of these three eras has seen Canada take a different approach to "impartiality" as it affects the ability to be a peacemaker. Explicit in the Harper government's criticism of the "helpful fixer" role, for example, is the notion that it requires nations to essentially remain silent on their fundamental values so as not to offend questionable regimes in order to be acceptable as a mediator; to "go along to get along." The alternative view is that countries that aspire to a mediating role need not abandon their values, though it may be necessary to temper one's public utterances occasionally.

Moreover, those who disagree with the Harper line take the view that Canada's actions as a "helpful fixer" during the first era of Canadian peacemaking in the Middle East were based not on "impartiality" or even a misguided altruism, but rather on a hard-headed and realist analysis of interests. These were held to be promoting a rules-based, multilateral international order that would offer protections to smaller countries against unilateral actions by the bigger ones, and (during the Cold War) help to smooth over rough patches and crises that threatened the solidarity of the Western alliance. Indeed, in the words of one architect of Canada's postwar foreign policy, this supposedly altruistic approach was always based on a "hard-boiled calculation of the Canadian national interest."[23]

Canada's involvement in peacekeeping missions throughout the Cold War was usually motivated by a desire to tamp down regional conflicts before they could threaten bipolar stability. Most such missions, for example, saw Canada informally "twinned" with a nation from the Warsaw Pact for the sake of balance. Moreover, the primary motivator of Canada's involvement in the creation of the first peacekeeping force in 1956 in Suez was not "peace" as such, but to help extricate Britain and France from a foreign policy misadventure that threatened the stability of NATO and the crucial relationship between the United Kingdom and the United States. The essentially realist nature of Canada's actions during this era (as opposed to the naive idealism charged by those who supported the ambitions of the Harper era) is illustrated by the fact that, in the service of its goals, "Canada, whether explicitly or implicitly, adopted contradictory policies in supporting regimes throughout the Middle East that often had little regard for fundamental Canadian values."[24]

As the Trudeau government launched the third era of Canadian peacemaking in the Middle East, it has found that it confronts issues far beyond simply recapturing the Pearsonian "golden era." Notably, while it is willing to speak in terms of the rhetoric of the Pearsonian era of peacemaking (which implies the need to speak to all sides in a conflict), the Trudeau government is having great difficulty confronting the domestic political consequences of engaging with actors who abuse human rights, whether to promote compromise or sell weapons. The Trudeau government has made the promotion of such norms a particular part of its approach to international affairs and has had some difficulty squaring the circle of its own actions when they appear to contradict its rhetoric. In particular, though the sale of LAVs to Saudi Arabia was an initiative of the Harper era, the Trudeau government initially supported it (and the jobs it created) and accepted the need to examine a reversal of this policy only after much delay and under pressure (see the chapters by Pedersen and Petrasek in this volume for more on this issue).

It must thus be noted that in none of the eras discussed in this chapter was Canada's involvement in peacemaking crucial to the outcome of such efforts, nor was it "impartial" in the sense that it was undertaken without reference to, or in the absence of, a careful consideration of Canadian interests. The key to understanding these different eras is that various Canadian governments defined their interests differently, and not necessarily in the context of the specific dispute upon which they were acting as peacemakers. In the Cold War, these interests were defined as being the need to play a modest but at times important role in promoting a stable, bipolar international order and prevent the erosion of the Western alliance; in the Harper era, they were defined as being the need to loudly promote "Judeo-Christian" values and assist Israel in standing up to threats from "extremism," though without actually taking steps directly counter to the United States on crucial issues; and in the Trudeau era they are defined as finding a way forward that sees Canada promote stability and peace, while also promoting a human rights–based foreign policy agenda, but without damaging commercial interests, wherever possible. This agenda will embroil Canada in conflicts with human rights advocacy groups and authoritarian regimes in regions such as the Middle East.

Fundamental to any analysis of all of this is thus the concept of "impartiality" as it relates to peacemaking.[25] The field of conflict resolution has debated the question of whether an impartial mediator is better than a partial one. Indeed, the very concepts of "neutrality" or "impartiality" are subtly different. The International Committee of the Red Cross (ICRC) has defined impartiality as non-discrimination in responding to humanitarian needs: aid is provided to all who need it, regardless of race, religion, or political affiliation. At the same time, neutrality is a conscious stance that takes no sides and makes no attempt to engage in the political issues motivating the conflict.[26] Other groups in the field have found it more difficult to adhere to these strict guidelines and do take sides when they see atrocities committed.[27] This is a point of considerable contention between the conflict-resolution community and the community committed to international legal processes devoted to the punishment of war crimes, often expressed as "the well-known tensions between stability and justice."[28]

Beyond the question of whether a mediator can deplore the actions of a party to the conflict and still remain a mediator, the issue of whether a mediator should be politically neutral generates great discussion.[29] It has been believed within the field that, in the words of Kleiboer, "mediator impartiality is crucial for disputants' confidence in the mediator which, in turn, is a necessary condition for his gaining acceptability which, in turn, is essential for mediation success to come about."[30] Others have studied the techniques of mediators and found that "unbiased" mediators were more likely to use techniques that produced agreements, while "biased" mediators selected techniques more likely to favour a particular outcome.[31]

Other scholars and practitioners believe that biased mediators can be more effective, as they are more likely to be personally invested and, therefore, to devote themselves over the long term.[32] In a study of mediator bias in the outcome of 124 peace agreements between 1989 and 2004, Svensson found that "biased mediators positively affect the likelihood of institutional arrangements in peace agreements ... [while] neutral mediators tend to lead to outcomes without provisions for political and territorial power sharing, third-party security guarantees, government-sided amnesties and repatriation of civilians."[33]

In other words, while some argue that unbiased mediators have more "success" in number of conflicts "resolved," others argue that they pursue resolutions that are not likely to last long, as they do not address deep-seated problems. Biased mediators, on the other hand, will try to address these problems, as they have a higher personal commitment to pursue a genuine resolution of the situation, although Beber questions whether those making this claim suffer from a selection bias in how they frame the question and finds that unbiased mediators are better.[34]

This debate thus invites a more complete discussion of what "impartial" means when acting as an international mediator. Most obviously, impartiality means taking no overt position between the *sides* in a dispute. But impartiality in mediation can also be thought of as taking no overt position on the *actions* of those involved in the fighting. Though the difference between the two interpretations of impartiality may appear subtle, it is important; one may decline to publicly take a side on the specific positions taken by the actors in a dispute, but this does not mean that one accepts the actions taken by either or both protagonists if they violate international law or one's values. Impartiality may thus be thought of as a matrix, with one axis, or side, relating to whether or not one is partial on the positions or objectives of the parties or sides in the dispute, and the other axis relating to whether or not one is partial on the actions that have been taken by the parties in the dispute as they relate to cherished norms and values; in a sense, the degree to which a potential mediator is sensitive to such issues.

As the matrix in figure 12.1 points out, a country that is willing to be impartial (or has a low level of partiality, as the matrix puts it) along both axes of the matrix – the lower left-hand box – is likely able to become involved as a mediator in the maximum number of disputes, without particular concerns for the positions of either side or the actions they have taken during the conflict. Following Svensson's analysis, they are also likely to push for any outcome that stops or moderates the fighting, even if it does not address longer-term issues and, therefore, is more likely to lead to a resumption of the conflict down the road. A mediator in the upper left-hand box will favour one party over another in their positions in dispute, but has low concerns about the actions taken by either or both of the parties in the conflict. A mediator in the lower right-hand box will be sensitive to whether either or both parties have violated international norms, but not particularly partial to the position or objectives of any of the parties. Finally, a mediator in the upper right-hand box will be sensitive to the implications of the conduct of the parties, and also to the question of which one succeeds.

Observations for Canada

Applying the matrix to Canada's actions as a peacemaker in the Middle East leads to interesting conclusions. In the first era, Canada's peacemaking was motivated largely by considerations in the lower left-hand box of the matrix – we were prepared to become involved in peacemaking without significant biases over the positions of the parties involved in the disputes or their actions. To the extent that Canada was responding to any imperatives, they were outside the matrix and had to do with the desire to play a constructive role in supporting stability within the bipolar global order and supporting the alliances of which Canada was a part. In many respects, this was the most "straightforward" era of Canadian

Figure 12.1. The Impartiality Matrix

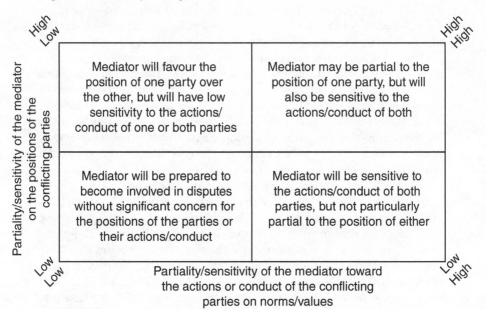

peacemaking in the region and, despite criticisms, the least ideological in terms of what the fundamental goals were.

In the second era, the Harper government and its supporters made rhetorical statements that were popular with their domestic political base and seemed to place it in a version of the upper left-hand box of the matrix: favouring the positions of Israel while having low sensitivity to its conduct (because Israel was "defending democracy"), while simultaneously not favouring those of the Palestinians and having great concerns over their conduct (because they were "supporting terror"). But one may question whether Canada's actions really bore this out. In particular, Canada was careful to never cross any US red lines on Middle East issues, nor did it actually abandon its legal position on matters such as Israeli settlements. Far from being an era when Canada ditched the "shameful" practice of "going along to get along," this was an era when the Harper government strove to appear to do so, for the benefit of its standing with its ideological and electoral base, without really carrying through.[35]

The third era, in which we are now located, seems to see Canada migrating, somewhat uncomfortably at times, to the upper right-hand box of the matrix: sensitivity to both the positions and the actions of the parties. In both the Israeli-Palestinian conflict and other issues such as the Saudi-Iran dispute, the Yemen conflict and internal conflicts in the region, the Trudeau government has stated that it will be motivated primarily by considerations such as human rights. Though Canada's commitment to these rights has been slow at times, particularly when they have conflicted with other imperatives such as trade, there does seem to be a clear trend in this direction, for now. Perhaps not coincidentally, there is also a trend in favour of not really becoming directly involved as a peacemaker, at least officially, in spite of rhetorical suggestions that Canada is "back" as a peacemaker. This is hardly surprising, as the upper right-hand box of the matrix presents by far the most difficulties to a state that wishes to be a mediator in terms of the barriers to entry that a potential peacemaker places upon itself. Put simply, it is hard to be a mediator if one is unwilling to talk to those who have been doing the fighting for fear that their actions in violating cherished norms might offend other constituencies one wishes to cultivate.

Canadian Peacemaking in the Three Eras: Management, Resolution, or Transformation?

A final framework from the conflict-resolution literature can be introduced to offer perspective on the evolution of Canada's approach to peacemaking in the Middle East. In defining ways in which peacemakers can approach a conflict, the field has generally developed a typology:[36]

- Conflict *management* is a set of approaches that assume that the conflict is not "ripe" to be resolved, but rather must be managed to prevent it from worsening and to set the stage for eventual progress. Conflict management tends to assume that the reality of the conflict, such as the leadership on each side, is not likely to change soon and must be worked with.
- Conflict *resolution* is oriented towards an assumption that the conflict may be capable of resolution and that the approach of the peacemaker should be to encourage it. Conflict resolution is not necessarily in favour of changing the conflict reality, if peace can be achieved within it, but recognizes that it may have to change to achieve peace and does not shy away from this approach.
- Finally, conflict *transformation* holds that the fundamentals of the conflict are the problem in themselves and that the underlying situation must be transformed if there is to be real peace. This approach is thus concerned with advocating transformative change, often to sweep away the prevailing order.

On the basis of this typology, it can be said that Canada's approach to peacemaking in the Middle East during the first era was focused squarely on conflict management in support of preserving international stability and upholding its "side" in the bipolar order. To the extent Canada supported efforts to resolve conflict in the region, it did so in support of the US lead, and to help preserve a Middle East order to America's liking and, by extension, that of the West generally. This often meant turning a blind eye to regimes that broke international norms with which Canada was associated in favour of maintaining "stability" in the region. In this, even though it proclaimed its impartiality as a reason why it was acceptable to all as a peacekeeper and peacemaker, Canada was, in fact, deeply partial in a larger sense to the kind of Middle East it wished to see.

The second era, the Harper years, represented a moment when Canada's efforts seemed to turn, rhetorically at least, towards a more decisive approach to the region and Canada's involvement in it. When taken to its logical conclusion, the policies of the Harper government called for resolution of the Arab-Israeli dispute, but firmly along lines that favoured the positions of the Israeli right wing and the promotion of a regional status quo accepting the need to work with regimes that were systematic violators of human rights in the service of a regional stability favourable to Israel and good for business in Canada. In reality, however, policies of the Harper government were not so very different from those of the previous era, particularly in the sense of a deep reluctance to take actions that would upset American efforts to manage the region and its problems. Canada was thus deeply partial in the kind of Middle East it wanted to see overall. But, rhetorically at least, it also showed partiality towards Israel on the key dispute in the region. It made little difference, however.

Today's third era is yet to be fully shaped. Though the Trudeau government has indicated that it wishes to follow a foreign policy informed by a desire to transform the international agenda on issues such as the environment, human rights generally, and women's rights in particular, it has also said that it wishes to recapture a role as an international peacemaker. Thus, the Trudeau government has not been eager to confront the hard choices when acting as a peacemaker – generally and in the region. The case of arms sales to a country embroiled in regional conflicts and suppression at home, Saudi Arabia, is a case in point; the government did change its arms sales policies, but only reluctantly and after public outcry forced it to. More broadly, the stated desire of the government to reassert Canadian leadership as a peacemaker around the world has not been forcefully acted on, at least not yet. This is largely the result of an unwillingness to confront the hard choices between involvement in deeply messy situations (and the moral compromises required) and the fact that key elements of the Liberal base seem uncomfortable with such actions.

That said, the broad contours of the Trudeau government's approach to the region seem to suggest an inversion of the Harper era's rhetorical approach. On the one hand, Canada is regaining, at least rhetorically, a sense of impartiality on the positions of each side in the Israeli-Palestinian dispute after years of a vocal pro-Israeli stance. On the other, it is perhaps beginning to take a partial stand (albeit reluctantly at times) in favour of a transformative agenda towards the question of what kind of region it wishes to see develop – a stand that, if followed through, may see it increasingly at odds with the United States.

Conclusion

Of course, the political landscape of the region has changed dramatically over the decades. Much of the peacemaking activities of the "golden era" took place when the region was emerging within the wider post-colonial, Cold War framework. Though the Middle East had its own history and particularities, much of the action was between the emerging states, backed by their Cold War patrons, and over questions posed by such problems as boundaries. Today, non-state extremist actors have arisen as combatants to a degree previously unknown and are fighting for agendas far less amenable to mediation in any classic sense. Moreover, several small regional states have themselves sought to fashion a role as mediators of the region's problems (Qatar, Oman, and Kuwait, for example). To some extent, Canada's ability to insert itself into the peacemaking niche in the region, even if it really wanted to, is diminished by these developments.

At the least, if Canada really does want to play this role, which is far from certain (rhetoric about renewed "Pearsonianism" aside), it will require new approaches that recognize at least two factors. First, on the question of impartiality, the Trudeau government's positions on human rights and related issues place it at a different position on the "impartiality matrix" than previous governments have occupied, and this has significant implications for Canada's ability to act as a mediator. While the Trudeau government no longer seeks to support the Israeli right wing, as did the Harper government, and can therefore claim to have "recaptured" a degree of impartiality, its positions on other issues make it difficult for this government to interact with players who have violated cherished norms of conduct on human rights. This is a different kind of "partiality," but it affects Canada's ability to play a role as a mediator, and the Trudeau government has yet to find a way forward, beyond supporting, financially and otherwise, others who play the mediator role.

Second, there are fundamentally new regional realities. These include the emergence of new players as protagonists in regional conflicts and potential partners in regional peacemaking. Gone are the days when peacemaking in the Middle East involved Western diplomats (usually Americans) shuttling between regional capitals to persuade strongmen to accept this deal or that. The role of countries such as Canada in this reality was supportive, but not decisive. Today's reality is one in which sub-state actors with religious and ideological agendas must be included in such peacemaking discussions, while others refuse to recognize the validity of these discussions altogether. Perhaps a new mediation role is emerging that is opening doors to conversations with new constellations of actors and issues that lie beyond the reach of traditional diplomacy, and working with regional actors in doing so. This would require an approach that supports quiet discussions on multiple levels, including unofficial discussions where official ones are not yet possible. If Canada were to embrace this role, it would be working on behalf of something potentially transformative.

In summary, Canada's role in Middle East peacemaking has both evolved and remained consistent. Canada has been content to play a junior role, which was intended to smooth regional problems, where possible, and buttress its status as a loyal ally; a country willing to help the Western alliance in promoting its interests in a particular kind of state-centred stability within the region. For much of the past sixty years, the latter objective – helping allies to achieve and defend regional stability – was of at least as much importance in policy terms as helping to actually make peace. Where Canada has sought to play a role consistent with a particular philosophical view of regional issues, as during the Harper era, its actions were far less strident than its words. It still remains to be seen if the Trudeau era will see a re-engagement with Canadian peacemaking in the Middle East and elsewhere, and if that is even possible, given changing realities in the region and this government's desire to advocate views and causes in such areas as human rights and feminist issues that are not widely shared by many in power in the region. It is thus an open question as to whether Canada's actions in this space will really be as transformative as the Trudeau government would like or whether, like the Harper era, the Liberals will say all the "right" things for their domestic base, while continuing to quietly help Canada's allies to manage a region that has always seen fit to reject its good ideas. Unless the Trudeau government can summon the courage to play a really transformative role, history would suggest the Canada's role will be the latter, whatever its rhetoric might suggest.

NOTES

1 For more, see P. Lawler, "The 'Good State' Debate in International Relations," *International Politics* 50, no. 1 (2013): 18–37; M. Mazower, "Paved Intentions: Civilisation and Imperialism," *Orbis* (Fall 2008): 72–84.

2 See A.F. Cooper, ed., *Niche Diplomacy: Middle Powers after the Cold War* (London: Macmillan, 1997). See particularly A.K. Henrikson, "Middle Powers as Managers: International Mediation within, across and outside Institutions," 47–72; and G. Hayes, "Canada as a Middle Power: The Case of Peacekeeping," 73–89. Henrikson defines mediation to include the ways in which middle powers try to "manage" the international system to their liking, but he also discusses more traditional mediation as a role of middle powers.

3 See D. Dewitt and J. Kirton, "Canadian Policy towards the Middle East," in *Canada as a Principal Power*, ed. D. Dewitt and J. Kirton, 355–401 (Toronto: J. Wiley and Sons, 1983).

4 For more on Canada and peacekeeping generally during these years, see Hayes, "Canada as a Middle Power."

5 For more on Canada's role in the peace process, see R. Brynen, "Canada's Role in the Israeli-Palestinian Peace Process," in *Canada and the Middle East*, ed. P. Heinbecker and B. Momani, 73–90 (Waterloo, ON: Wilfrid Laurier Press, 2007). On the multilateral groups of the peace process, see J. Peters, *Building Bridges: Arab-Israeli Multilateral Talks* (London: Royal Institute of International Affairs, 1994); and D.D. Kaye, *Beyond the Handshake: Multilateral Cooperation in the Arab-Israeli Peace Process: 1991–1996* (New York: Columbia University Press, 1991). Also, interviews with former Canadian diplomats involved in this work. The author was involved in this activity when he served with the then Department of Foreign Affairs.

6 See, for example, A. Chapnick, "The Canadian Middle Power Myth," *International Journal* 55, no. 2 (June 2000): 188–206.

7 See D. Taras and D. Goldberg, *Domestic Battlegrounds: Canada and the Arab-Israeli Conflict* (Montreal and Kingston: McGill-Queen's University Press, 1989); and D. Barry, "Canada and the Middle East Today: Electoral Politics and Foreign Policy," *Arab Studies Quarterly* 32, no. 4 (2010): 191–217.

8 For more on JOCI, see T. Najem, M. Molloy, M. Bell, and J. Bell, eds., *Track Two Diplomacy and Jerusalem: The Jerusalem Old City Initiative* (London: Routledge, 2017).

9 I am grateful to Dennis Horak, Michael Molloy, Michel de Salaberry, and Mark Bailey, all former Canadian ambassadors in the region, for pointing this out.

10 See J.L. Granatstein, "Peacekeeping: Did Canada Make a Difference? And What Difference Did Peacekeeping Make to Canada?," in *Making a*

Difference? Canada's Foreign Policy in a Changing World Order, ed. J. English and N. Hilmer (Toronto: Lester Publishing, 1992).

11 The following analysis of the Harper government's approach draws on Peter Jones, "Middle Power Liberal Internationalism and Mediation in Messy Places: The Canadian Dilemma," *International Journal* 74, no. 1 (March, 2019): 119–34.

12 "The notion advanced by some that Canada's position as an 'honest broker' is now deeply compromised is a partisan fiction … We never were, and never will be." Fen Hampson quoted in M. Blanchfield and L. Goodman, "Harper's Israel, Jordan Visit More Likely to Resonate at Home Than in the Middle East," *Ottawa Citizen,* 25 January 2014. "A nostalgia for some romantic view of Canada as a peace-maker is misplaced. It describes a very brief period in the fifties and sixties." Quote from Janice Stein in interview on "Power and Politics," CBC News Network, 19 December 2013. Conrad Black: "We have finally got beyond the self-righteous fairy tales about peacekeeping and 'soft power.'" Conrad Black quoted in C. Black, "A Great Moment for Canada," *National Post,* 25 January 2014. These quotes may be found in R. Paris, "Are Canadians Still Foreign Policy Internationalists? Foreign Policy and Public Opinion in the Harper Era," *International Journal* 69, no. 3 (2014): 285.

13 John Baird, "Address by Minister Baird at Religious Liberty Dinner," Washington DC, 24 May 2012.

14 Implying, of course, that Canada's policy had been to appease dictators up to that point. Quoted in P. Wells, "Why Harper Wants to Take On the World," *Maclean's,* 15 July 2011 (emphasis added). For further discussion of the Harper government's belief that Canada's foreign policy should eschew the "honest broker" idea, see A. Chapnick, "Middle Power No More? Canada in World Affairs since 2006," *Seton Hall Journal of Diplomacy and International Relations* (Sumer/Fall, 2013): 101–10.

15 See D. Dewitt and B. Momani, "Canada and the Middle East: Working within Multilateralism," in *Beyond Afghanistan: An International Security Agenda for Canada,* ed. J. Fergusson and F. Furtado (Vancouver: UBC Press, 2017), 169–70.

16 See Dewitt and Momani, "Canada and the Middle East," 172–4.

17 Point supported by interviews, conducted under the Chatham House Rule, with several senior Canadian government officials directing Middle East policy at this time.

18 The mandate letter of the first Trudeau-era foreign minister said that one of his priorities was to "increase Canada's support for United Nations peace operations and its mediation, conflict-prevention, and post-conflict reconstruction efforts." Though the letter speaks of mediation in the UN context, this has been interpreted as a call for Canada to be more involved in mediation generally (confidential interviews with officials implementing

Canadian mediation policy). For the text of the letter, see Justin Trudeau, "Minister of Foreign Affairs Mandate Letter," Office of the Prime Minister, 13 December 2019, http://pm.gc.ca/eng/minister-foreign-affairs-mandate-letter. There has been discussion of whether Canada should develop mediation as part of its foreign policy. For more, see Peter Jones, "Canada and Mediation: Issues and Considerations," Policy Update, Canadian Global Affairs Institute, January, 2017, https://d3n8a8pro7vhmx.cloudfront.net/cdfai/pages/1458/attachments/original/1485392280/Canada_and_Mediation_Issues_and_Considerations.pdf?1485392280; Jones, "Canada and International Conflict Mediation," *International Negotiation* 18, no. 2 (2013): 219–44; F. Storie, "A Canadian International Mediation Capacity," CIIAN News, Summer 2006, http://www.ciian.org/assets/newsletters/CIIAN-Newsletter-Summer2006.pdf; and "Canada and Mediation," *Canadian Foreign Policy Journal*, special issue 19, no. 1 (2013).

19 The "feminist foreign policy" has been a particular aspect of the Trudeau government's approach to the world. For more, see "Address by Minister Freeland on Canada's Foreign Policy Priorities," speech, 6 June 2017, https://www.canada.ca/en/global-affairs/news/2017/06/address_by_ministerfreelandoncanadasforeignpolicypriorities.html; and Global Affairs Canada, "Canada Launches New Feminist International Assistance Policy," news release, 9 June 2017, https://www.canada.ca/en/global-affairs/news/2017/06/canada_launches_newfeministinternationalassistancepolicy.html.

20 For more on what happened when the Trudeau government's desire to promote a new agenda clashed with imperatives such as economic growth through arms sale, see Srdjan Vucetic, "A Nation of Feminist Arms Dealers? Canada and Military Exports," *International Journal* 72, no. 4 (December 2017): 503–19. See also the chapter by Pedersen in this volume.

21 For example, Canada does not seem to have put mechanisms in place within Global Affairs that would allow it to nimbly respond to mediation requests, as have countries like Norway and Switzerland. For more on what Canada might do if it seriously wished to play a greater role as an international mediator, see Jones, "Canada and International Conflict Mediation"; Storie, "Canadian International Mediation Capacity"; Jones, "Canada and Mediation; and "Canada and Mediation," special issue, *Canadian Foreign Policy Journal* 19, no. 1 (2013).

22 For more on the Trudeau government's unwillingness to take on actual mediation roles despite its commitment to the matter. see Peter Jones, "Middle Power Liberal Internationalism and Mediation in Messy Places: The Canadian Dilemma," *International Journal* 74, no. 1 (March 2019): 119–34.

23 J.W. Holmes, *Canada: A Middle-Aged Power* (Toronto: McClelland and Stewart, 1976), 6. For more contemporary examples of this argument, see Paris,

"Are Canadians Still Foreign Policy Internationalists?"; and P. Heinbecker, *Getting Back in the Game: A Foreign Policy Playbook for Canada* (Toronto: Key Porter Books, 2010).

24 Dewitt and Momani, "Canada and the Middle East," 165.

25 This discussion draws on Jones, "Middle Power Liberal Internationalism and Mediation."

26 See D. Forsythe, *Humanitarian Politics: The International Committee of the Red Cross* (Baltimore, MD: Johns Hopkins University Press, 1977).

27 See the discussion in O. Ramsbotham, T. Woodhouse, and H. Miall, *Contemporary Conflict Resolution*, 3rd ed. (Cambridge: Polity, 2011), 320–1.

28 Ramsbotham et al., *Contemporary Conflict Resolution*, 210. See also the collection of essays in M. Abu-Nimer, ed., *Reconciliation, Justice, and Coexistence: Theory and Practice* (Lanham, MD: Lexington, 2001); and M. Deutsch, "Justice and Conflict," in *The Handbook of Conflict Resolution: Theory and Practice*, 2nd ed., ed. M. Deutsch, P.T. Coleman, and E.C. Marcus, 43–68 (San Francisco: Jossey-Bass, 2006). See also E.F. Babbitt, "Conflict Resolution and Human Rights: The State of the Art," in *The Sage Handbook of Conflict Resolution*, ed. J. Bercovitch, V. Kremenyuk, and I.W. Zartman (Thousand Oaks, CA: Sage Publishers, 2009), 619. This is not just theoretical. See E. Aspinall, "Peace without justice? The Helsinki Peace Process in Aceh," *HD Report*, April 2008, which looks at whether efforts to bring peace had come too much at the expense of justice for the victims of the fighting in Aceh.

29 For example, A. Kydd, "Which Side Are You On? Bias, Credibility and Mediation," *American Journal of Political Science* 47, no. 4 (2007): 597–611.

30 M. Kleiboer, "Understanding the Success or Failure of International Mediation," *Journal of Conflict Resolution* 40, no. 2 (1996): 369.

31 S.E. Gent and M. Shannon, "Bias and Effectiveness of Third Party Conflict Management Mechanisms," *Conflict Management and Peace Science* 28, no. 2 (2011): 124–44.

32 For more on these arguments, see, for example, Kydd, "Which Side Are You On? P. Wehr and J.P. Lederach, "Mediating Conflict in Central America," *Journal of Conflict Resolution* 53, no. 3 (2009): 446–69; and B. Savun, "Information, Bias and Mediation Success," *International Studies Quarterly* 52 (2008): 25–47.

33 See I. Svensson, "Who Brings Peace? Neutral Versus Biased Mediation and Institutional Peace Arrangements in Civil Wars," *Journal of Conflict Resolution* 53, no. 3 (2009): 446–69. For others who challenge the traditional notion that mediators should be "neutral," see B. Mayer, *Beyond Neutrality: Confronting the Crisis in Conflict Resolution* (San Francisco: Jossey-Bass, 2004); S. Cobb, and J. Rifkin, "Practice and Paradox: Deconstructing Neutrality in Mediation," *Law and Social Inquiry* 16, no. 1 (1991): 35–62; and T. Princen,

Intermediaries in International Conflict (Princeton, NJ: Princeton University Press, 1992).

34 See B. Beber, "International Mediation, Selection Effects, and the Question of Bias," *Conflict Management and Peace Science* 29, no. 4 (2012): 397–424.

35 It is interesting to speculate on what might have happened had President Trump been in power during the Harper years, and if the need not to get too far out of step with US policy had not been a restraint. One surmises that the Canadian embassy to Israel may well have moved to Jerusalem quickly, once the American embassy had done so.

36 On the sometimes difficult debate in conflict resolution over difference between "management," "resolution," or "transformation" and what is the appropriate role, see E. Babbitt and F.O. Hampson, "Conflict Resolution as a Field of Inquiry: Practice Informing Theory," *International Studies Quarterly* 13, no. 1 (2011): 46–57. See also J.P. Lederach, *The Moral Imagination: The Art and Soul of Building Peace* (Oxford: Oxford University Press, 2010); and P. Gamaghelyan, "Towards an Inclusive Conception of Best Practices in Peace and Conflict Initiatives," *International Negotiation* 26, no. 1 (2021): 121–50.

13 Balancing Canada's Role in the Arab-Israeli Peace Process

COSTANZA MUSU

This chapter analyses Canada's policy towards the Arab-Israeli conflict, with a focus on the post 9/11 era. To this end, the chapter will examine the fundamental tenets of Canada's policy towards the conflict, and will also put them in the broader context of Canada's policy towards the Middle East and of the priorities that affect the government's decision-making in this region.

Canada's history of global engagement has always included a commitment to address the Israeli-Palestinian conflict, which has consistently been a source of tension for the international community. Since Canada's initial participation in the drafting of the 1947 United Nations Partition Plan to divide the British Mandate of Palestine into a state of Israel and an Arab state,[1] Canada's official policy on the Arab-Israeli conflict has remained fairly consistent, continuously expressing support for the existence and security of the Israeli state, and the right of self-determination for the Palestinian people.

Canada's official policy in support of a "two-state solution" has persisted even in light of geopolitical changes in the region, international developments, and domestic electoral shifts. This has earned Canada the reputation of being a "balanced broker," if perhaps not a powerful one. Since 2004, however, this reputation has been challenged as some rhetoric and some substance of Canada's policy shifted towards a more partisan approach in support of Israel, which might cause Canada to lose the limited role it holds in the peace process.[2]

To best understand the evolution of Canada's stance towards the conflict, this chapter will focus first on the broad lines of Canada's Middle East policy, looking not only at the peace process but also at Canada's relations with Arab states and with Israel, trying to identify the priorities that drive Ottawa's policymaking in the region. Second, the chapter will place Canada's policy towards the Middle East in the context of Canada's broader priorities, particularly its relations with the United States and other important allies, its commitment to multilateralism, and its reliance on international law. These considerations are balanced with an overview of Ottawa's explicit economic and security priorities. Third, the chapter will analyse the instruments at Canada's disposal in the formulation of its policy towards the peace process, with specific reference to "large fora" diplomacy (e.g., its votes at the United Nations and role in the official peace process), bilateral diplomacy, track-two diplomacy, and economic diplomacy.

The conclusion will draw these threads together and attempt to answer some relevant if uncomfortable questions: Does Canada truly *want* a significant role in the Middle East peace process? If it does, does it have something substantial to offer? Can it develop any kind of meaningful role without harming its other interests? And if Canada has limited resources and limited interest in the peace process, how can it best maximize the impact of its policy?

Is There a Canadian Middle East Policy?

The broader Middle East, the region that includes the Maghreb, the Mashreq, and the Gulf, is of importance to Canada for the same reasons it is of importance to the rest of the world: parts of the region possess vast energy resources, and regional governments can therefore influence global oil prices; economic underdevelopment and job scarcity cause social instability and uncontrolled migration flows; authoritarian governments, endemic corruption, and sectarianism all contribute to a fertile breeding ground for terrorism; and of course the unresolved Arab-Israeli conflict is a further source of tension and instability.[3] All these factors make it arduous for any country, no matter how geographically distant, to ignore the region and its issues, and that is certainly the case for Canada.

It is difficult, however, to identify a coherent Canadian "Middle East policy." Ottawa has rarely attempted to forge an overall policy for the region, incorporating political, security, and economic interests into an overarching strategy. This lack of a strategic vision can be ascribed partly to the fact that the region itself is very diverse, with the sub-regions (Maghreb, Mashreq, and Gulf) presenting distinct challenges, but also to the fact that successive Canadian governments have preferred developing bilateral relations with individual countries, often based primarily, if not exclusively, on economic interests.

In 1980, a government-commissioned study laid down what became the guidelines of Ottawa's policy towards the broader Middle East for years to come, based on the pursuit of economic interests through bilateral relations and continued focus on the Arab-Israeli conflict in general, and the Israeli-Palestinian issue in particular.

Robert Stanfield, former Conservative Party leader and author of the report, described what he saw as Canada's priorities quite clearly:

> While Canada has important economic interests in the area, our most fundamental goal there is to contribute to a just and lasting peace. My reasons for adopting this attitude are straight forward. The dispute between Arabs and Israelis has resulted in the disruption and uprooting of peoples and an immense and wasteful diversion of scarce resources to military expenditures. It has caused great suffering on both sides. It has also been a source of continuing world tension and uncertainty, and carries the threat of wider conflict which could engulf the entire international community ...
>
> I have tried to put forward positions and recommendations which could be considered by the Government as a basis for Canadian policy in the area. In doing so I have borne in mind that Canada is not a major world power like the United States. The Americans have had and will continue to have a particular responsibility in fostering the peace process in the Middle East. While Canada's influence on events is necessarily limited this does not mean that we cannot be effective ...
>
> Our strong support for Israel does not mean that we cannot maintain and further develop good relations with the Arab peoples ... After concluding my visits to the Middle East and North Africa I am convinced that bilateral relations between Canada and the countries of these areas can be broadened substantially ...
>
> Broad and systematic contact must be maintained between the Governments and peoples of the region and of Canada if we are to pursue our commercial interests, develop closer relations in areas of cultural understanding and technological and development assistance, and contribute fully to the resolution of disputes and conflicts: our most basic interest in the region.[4]

Following publication of the report, there was growth in the web of relations between Canada and several Arab countries: new embassies were opened in the region, including in Jordan and Syria, and trade overall benefited. It should be emphasized, however, that the volume of Canada's trade with the broader Middle East remained relatively small, compared to the total volume of its foreign trade, reaching barely 0.6 per cent of the total of Canadian exports and 0.8 per cent of the total of Canadian imports in 2000.

The Stanfield Report also underlined the importance of Canada's relations with Israel but identified several key policies in which Canada stood in clear disagreement with Tel Aviv, including the development of settlements in the West Bank and the annexation of East Jerusalem. The document reiterated Canada's support for a two-state solution to the Arab-Israeli conflict and emphasized the desire of the Palestinian people to give political expression to their identity, referring to Palestinian "rights" rather than only to Palestinian "aspirations." As Michael Bell, a former Canadian ambassador to Jordan, Egypt, and Israel, noted, Canada was interested in being "fair-minded" rather than simply "neutral" – an attitude that denoted concern for moral considerations and value-based positions, and the desire to promote Canadian values such as tolerance, democracy, respect for diversity, and the rule of law.[5] In this framework, there was no contradiction between supporting Israel and its quest for security as well as the right of Palestinians to self-determination. In fact, they were viewed as two sides of the same coin and, crucially, mutually reinforcing.

For the following years, Canada's policy towards the Middle East remained essentially characterized by the same objectives: the development of bilateral relations with countries in the region, ad-hoc decision making to address specific crises, and a continued effort to maintain some level of involvement in the Arab-Israeli issue, as will be discussed later in the chapter.

Overall, however, Canada remained a minor actor in the region, a fact that can be best explained through an analysis of Ottawa's sometimes clashing policy priorities, and the balancing act conducted by successive Canadian governments in an effort to protect these priorities.

Canada's Foreign Policy Priorities

To better understand Canada's policy towards the Middle East, and more specifically towards the Arab-Israeli conflict and the Israeli-Palestinian dispute, it is necessary to ask a crucial question: To what degree is the Middle East really a priority for Canada? And how does it fit with Ottawa's more pressing priorities?

Discussions of Canada's priorities cannot escape considerations of its relationship with the United States (for more on this dimension, see the chapter by Sabet in this volume). Politically and economically, a country like Canada simply cannot avoid putting its relationship with its behemoth neighbour to the south at the centre of most policies. Canada's security and prosperity depend in large measure on ensuring the continuation of this relationship, and very few circumstances warrant endangering it.[6]

A few figures can help give the measure of this necessity. As of the year 2000, trade with the United States accounted for 87 per cent of

Canadian exports (for a value of C$358.3 billion), and 64 per cent of Canadian imports (C$229.7 billion). In 2018 the figures were 75 per cent of exports (C$437.9 billion) and 51 per cent of imports (C$304.6).[7] By comparison, as already mentioned, the volume of Canada's trade with the broader Middle East is minuscule, in the year 2000 reaching barely 0.6 per cent of the total of Canadian exports (C$2.3 billion) and 0.8 per cent of imports (C$2.9 billion), and in 2018 1.2 per cent of the total of Canadian exports (C$7.2 billion) and 1.6 per cent of imports (C$9.3 billion).[8] Bilateral economic relations with Washington, as well as participation in the North American Free Trade Agreement (NAFTA), remain the centre of gravity of Canada's economic priorities, as the frenzy generated by US President Donald Trump's decision in 2017 to renegotiate the agreement illustrated.

From a security policy standpoint, Canada is equally focused on its relations with Washington. Being considered a good ally by the United States and maintaining an active participation in the North Atlantic Treaty Organization (NATO) are the twin pillars of Canada's security architecture (see the chapter by Massie and Munier in this volume), to which we can add membership in the intelligence partnership known as the Five Eyes (comprising Australia, Canada, New Zealand, the United Kingdom, and the United States) and participation in UN-endorsed missions through either military or financial contributions.

After the terrorist attacks of 11 September 2001, Canada, following intense pressure from the United States, adopted stringent domestic measures to ensure airport and border security in line with new American expectations and standards. While this generated an intense debate on how to simultaneously protect national security and civil rights and liberties, Ottawa had no real alternative but to follow the desires of its main ally and trade partner and introduce new counterterrorism measures, while reinforcing intelligence-sharing and working towards the harmonization of security policies.[9] In the years following 9/11, Canadian foreign policy emphasized support for the US-led "War on Terror"; in recognition that terrorist violence also posed a significant threat to Canadian national security, Canada supported its ally in its quest to identify and confront terrorist organizations that posed a threat to Western security. In this context, the importance of Israel as a reliable partner in the hunt for jihadist terrorists grew significantly, together with the feeling that there were many similarities between the suicide bombings that targeted Israel regularly and the ones that threatened the West.

The Liberal government's decision in 2003 not to join the United States in the war against Iraq in the absence of a UN Security Council resolution authorizing it underlined Canada's reliance on international law

and multilateral organizations, and caused a significant, though temporary, cooling of relations with Washington. Nevertheless, supporting an-
ti-terror coalitions and operations, primarily in cooperation with crucial
allies, remained a clear priority for successive Canadian governments,
both Conservative and Liberal.

Indeed, this is one of the most complex Gordian knots of Canada's
foreign and defence policy. Following the Second World War, Canada
became a committed supporter of the creation of a multilateral institution tasked with protecting international peace and security, and became
a founding member of the United Nations. Canada's support for, and
participation in, the United Nations represents a desire for recognition
and influence: participation in the United Nations allows for a more
distinctly Canadian voice to be projected internationally and gives credibility to the promotion of Canadian interests and foreign policy goals
to a wider, global audience, with an emphasis on negotiation, communication, and cooperation. On many important issues, including policy
towards the Arab-Israeli conflict, Canada finds itself aligned (both at the
UN and outside) with like-minded countries such as northern European
countries, as well as Australia and New Zealand. On many occasions, however, this convergence of political beliefs and views (including a reliance
on multilateralism and international law) has to be balanced with the
inescapable importance afforded to the relationship with Washington.

The push and pull of these sometimes-conflicting priorities is often reflected in the contradictory policies adopted by many Canadian governments, as well as the discrepancies between political rhetoric and actual
decision making, as will be illustrated below. In few areas is this tension
as evident as it is in Canada's policy towards the Middle East, especially
the Israeli-Palestinian conflict.

Forging Canada's Policy towards the Arab-Israeli Peace Process: Instruments and Limitations

Canada has long been involved in the Middle East, notably through its
development assistance to a number of states in the region and, more
recently, its participation in the international fight against terrorism, including in the context of the international coalition against the Islamic
State (see the Massie and Munier chapter in this volume).[10]

Furthermore, the Canadian Armed Forces contribute to three multinational missions in the Middle East crucial for the Arab-Israeli peace
process: one that supports security assistance to the Palestinian Authority
through the United States Security Coordinator for Israel and the Palestinian Authority; another that implements the security provisions of the

Egyptian-Israel Treaty of Peace through the Multinational Force and Observers mission based in the Sinai Peninsula; and a third that monitors compliance with the United Nations Disengagement Observer Force in the Golan Heights and the United Nations Internal Force in Lebanon.[11]

The peace process has indeed occupied a central place in Canada's Middle East policy. As mentioned, Ottawa has long seen itself as an "honest broker" in the Israeli-Palestinian peace process, not as powerful as the United States but able to offer to the two sides of the conflict a balanced and fair approach.[12] Support for Israel has been a constant of Canadian governments since the creation of the State of Israel, underpinned by sympathy for the Jews in the wake of the Holocaust and by empathy for a fellow democratic country struggling in a hostile region. This support, especially since 1967, has been coupled with recognition of the national aspirations of the Palestinian people. As Robert Stanfield put it in his 1980 report, "Canada's commitment to friendship with Israel and to that country's well-being cannot be subject to question. Our close ties with Israel should remain a fundamental cornerstone of Canadian Middle East policy ... Our respect and affection for the Israelis is not diminished by our concern for the Palestinians ... I recommend support for a homeland for the Palestinians."[13]

While not a major player in the peace process, Canada has at its disposal a number of instruments in forging its policy. These instruments can thus be categorized: large-fora diplomacy; bilateral diplomacy; track-two diplomacy; and economic diplomacy.

Large-fora diplomacy is conducted essentially through two channels: participation in United Nations debates and votes, and in the multilateral track of the official Arab-Israeli peace process started in 1991 at the Madrid Peace Conference.

For a long time, Canada's voting choices at the United Nations have been characterized by an attempt to maintain a balanced approach that would recognize Israel's security concerns and Palestinian grievances and desire for self-determination. Canada would support Palestinian aspirations but insist on resolutions that would highlight the responsibility of both parties in each flare-up of violence, speaking out against resolutions that would single out exclusively the use of force by Israel. For a long time, Ottawa's position at the UN could be placed somewhere between that of the United States and that of Europe. Canada's vote was often aligned with that of several European countries, but overall Canada tried to avoid being more than one step away from America's votes on issues related to the Arab-Israeli conflict (for example, abstaining on a resolution where Washington voted against, or voting in favour where Washington abstained).

This strategy allowed Canada to carve a role for itself in the peace process, distinct from that of the United States but not at odds with it. Diplomacy at the United Nations was supplemented with participation in the official peace process negotiations started at the Madrid Peace Conference of 1991. In particular, at Washington's request Canada became "gavel holder" of the Refugees Working Group (RWG), trying to give a constructive contribution to the Middle East peace process working on one of the most intractable issues that divides Israelis and Palestinians.[14] The RWG was active for several years, and Canadian diplomats, praised for their balanced approach, were able to keep open the dialogue on the thorny issue of Palestinian refugees, their status, and their future. While it was not possible to come to a resolution of the dispute, Canada helped bring the problem to the attention of the international community, and to secure financial support for humanitarian initiatives.[15] This official involvement tapered off with the paralysis of the multilateral track of negotiations following the beginning of the Second Intifada in 2000, but the "unofficial," or track-two, channels of diplomacy continued their work on the refugees and Jerusalem issues (see the chapter by Peter Jones in this volume).

Starting in 2004, however, during the Liberal Paul Martin government, Canada's traditional voting behaviour on Middle East issues at the UN started to move towards a more open support of Israel. This policy shift became all the more evident with the arrival to power of Stephen Harper in 2006, who expanded the scope of his Conservative government's support for Israel to include not only UN votes but also strong public rhetoric and direct diplomatic initiatives (see the Boily chapter in this volume). At the United Nations, this translated into consistent voting aligned with the United States and Israel, and in direct opposition to what had previously been Canada's traditional allies at the UN on these issues, particularly Western Europe. The focus of the government changed from the Palestinian-Israeli issue to primarily the tightening and strengthening of relations with Israel, and support for the legitimacy of Israel and for its security needs turned into support of most policies of the Israeli government. In its official policy, delineated in various documents and on the Government of Canada's website, Canada continued to support the two-state solution and to oppose the construction of settlements, but the political message coming from the government after 2006 focused on Israeli priorities and preoccupations. This policy shift created tensions with Washington, especially when Prime Minister Harper's positions turned out to be at odds with President Obama's policy and with his efforts to restart peace negotiations. The diplomatic impasse at the 2011 G8 meeting in France offers a perfect example of these tensions, when Prime Minister Harper, standing alone amongst other members of the G8, blocked efforts to mention the importance of a solution to the Israeli-Palestinian conflict based on the 1967 borders in a joint communiqué.

While many anticipated that the election of Justin Trudeau's Liberal government in 2015 might bring a shift back to the previous voting pattern at the UN, these expectations were not fulfilled during Trudeau's first term, as by and large Canadian votes have thus far remained aligned with American votes. Arguably, this can be explained partly with the tensions between the two countries since the election of Donald Trump as US president in 2016, and his decision to renegotiate the NAFTA agreement. As Canadian diplomacy has been massively concentrated on ensuring that Canada's interests be protected as much as possible in the course of the "NAFTA 2.0" negotiations, avoiding further tensions with the volatile American president became a high priority, obscuring the Liberals' declared desire to re-engage Canada in multilateralism and UN diplomacy, which they argued had been neglected during the Harper years.

Furthermore, unlike President Obama, President Trump himself embraced a strong rhetoric of support for most policies of the government of Israel, as highlighted by his announcement in 2017 that the United States recognized Jerusalem as the capital of Israel, and would therefore move the American embassy there from Tel Aviv.

Canada's official policy on Jerusalem has consistently been, and remains, as of late 2020, that "the status of Jerusalem can be resolved only as part of a general settlement of the Palestinian-Israeli dispute. Canada does not recognize Israel's unilateral annexation of East Jerusalem."[16] In line with this policy, Prime Minister Trudeau did not join the United States in moving the location of the embassy from Tel Aviv to Jerusalem; however, Canada abstained when the UN General Assembly voted 128 to 9 in favour of a resolution declaring the US recognition of Jerusalem as the Israeli capital to be null and void; the United Kingdom, France, and Germany were among the 128 countries that voted in favour of the resolution.[17] The incident once again underlined the pressures to which Canada is subject: on the one hand, the need to maintain coherence to its own declared policy and principles (support for a two-state solution, support for Israel's security but also for the Palestinians' right of self-determination, support for international law and UN resolutions); on the other, the necessity to try to avoid tension with Washington, especially when crucial economic interests are threatened.

In the use of bilateral diplomacy in the Middle East, Canada has developed strong relations with Israel. In 1996 the two countries signed a free trade agreement, which entered into effect in 1997. This was supplemented by an Agreement on Bilateral Cooperation in Industrial Research and Development signed in 2012, a Convention for the Avoidance of Double Taxation, and an Air Transportation Agreement (2016). Canada's already close political, economic, social, and cultural ties with Israel have also been strengthened with the signing in 2014 of a Canada-Israel Strategic Partnership Memorandum of Understanding, which "touches on energy, security, international aid and development, innovation, and the promotion of human rights globally."[18]

As for the Palestinians, Canada has developed a cordial relationship with the Palestinian Authority (PA), but it maintains no relations with Hamas, which it considers – as do all its Western allies – a terrorist organization. A Joint Canadian-Palestinian Framework on Economic Cooperation and Trade was approved in 1999, confirming the PA's approval of applying preferential tariffs and any future concessions under the Canada-Israel Free Trade Agreement to goods produced in the West Bank and Gaza. Canada also supports reform in the Palestinian security sector through Operation PROTEUS, which aims to build the capacity of Palestinian security forces, and through the deployment of Canadian police officers to the European Union Co-ordinating Office for Palestinian Police Support. Canada also supports justice sector reform in order to improve the rule of law in the Palestinian territories.

An important component of Canada's policy has been the provision of aid through the United Nations Relief and Works Agency (UNRWA) and other organizations located in the West Bank and Gaza. Since 1993, Canada has also been a member of the Ad Hoc Liaison Committee, the principal policy-level coordination mechanism for development assistance to the Occupied Palestinian Territory, which promotes coordination and coherence of foreign aid and donations to Gaza and the West Bank. In the years since 1993, Canada has channelled over US$600 million, making Canada one of the most important donor to Palestinians.

However, relations between Canada and UNRWA have been strained at times, especially following accusations that the agency maintains ties with Hamas and fuels the conflict between the Palestinians and Israel by promoting hatred against the Jewish state. In 2010, notably, Prime Minister Harper ended all funding to UNRWA – a decision that paradoxically was not met with favour by Israel.[19] While Israel has often criticized the UN agency and the way it uses its funds, it has at the same time recognized UNRWA's importance in sustaining a viable Palestinian Authority, preventing the spiralling of a humanitarian crisis into a full-blown uprising. Trudeau's Liberal party promised to restore funding to UNRWA if elected, underlining the vital role played by the UN agency in providing aid to over five million Palestinian refugees in Syria, Lebanon, Jordan,

Gaza, and the West Bank. The funding was restored in 2016, and Canada has since committed $110 million to the agency, despite the leaking of a damning internal report, sent to the UN secretary general in December 2018 and obtained by the press in the summer of 2019, which alleged that senior UNRWA management engaged in "sexual misconduct, nepotism, retaliation, discrimination and other abuses of authority, for personal gain, to suppress legitimate dissent and to otherwise achieve their personal objectives." The report came on the heels of the announcement of a decision by the United States to cut its funding to the agency and, in November 2019, led to the resignation of UNRWA's commissioner-general, Pierre Krahenbuhl.

At the time of writing, the Canadian government has not announced changes to its plans to continue its contributions to UNRWA's general fund. However, the problems surrounding funding of UNRWA perfectly encapsulate the dilemma that Canada regularly faces in its policy towards the peace process, torn between different and often diverging priorities: protecting human rights, maintaining the primacy of international law and UN decisions, ensuring the security of Israel, promoting Palestinian self-determination, developing policies in harmony with like-minded nations, and last but certainly not least, ensuring minimal fall-out onto relations with the United States in the case of disagreement with Washington over any peace process–related issue.

Conclusion

In the introduction, this chapter posed a set of questions: Does Canada truly *want* a significant role in the Middle East peace process? If it does, does it have something substantial to offer? Can it develop any kind of meaningful role without harming its other interests? And if Canada has limited resources and limited interest in the peace process, how can it best maximize the impact of its policy?

What has emerged from the analysis is an essentially contradictory policy. On the one hand, Canada has tried to contribute to the peace process by emphasizing the importance of negotiations between the parties, of international law, and of multilateralism, as well as condemning violence and unilateral decisions. It has established a cordial relation with the Palestinian Authority and developed strong ties with Israel, all the while working on increasing its political and economic relationships in the broader Middle East region. It offers financial assistance to the Palestinian people and contributes to initiatives that strengthen the institutions of the Palestinian Authority and, along with it, the likelihood that a viable two-state solution to the conflict will one day be reached.

On the other hand, all these initiatives are carefully crafted to minimize harm to relations with the United States. Ottawa is acutely aware of its limited margin of manoeuvre in the peace process. Successive American presidents, as well as European and Middle East regional powers, have tried to influence the peace process with limited to no results. Interests of the United States in the region remain strong, even if its military presence has diminished somewhat, and American dominance, further complicated by the recently increased presence and influence of Russia and China, determines to a large extent how great a role other actors can play.

In this context, Canada has to craft a balancing act between the pursuit of its sincerely held vision for an equitable resolution to the Israeli-Palestinian conflict and the inescapable priority that needs to be accorded to the relationship with Washington. Even accounting for the variations in policies and rhetoric between successive Conservative and Liberal governments, discussed in this and other chapters in this volume, this balancing act remains at the core of Canada's policy towards the peace process, and will continue to limit the potential for further Canadian involvement for the foreseeable future.

NOTES

1 Hassan Husseini, "'Middle Power' in Action: Canada and the Partition of Palestine," *Arab Studies Quarterly* 30, no. 3 (2008): 41–55.

2 Marie-Joëlle Zahar, "Navigating Troubled Waters: Canada in the Arab World," in *Elusive Pursuits: Lessons from Canada's Interventions Abroad,* ed. Fen Osler Hampson and Stephen M. Saideman, 35–58 (Waterloo, ON: CIGI, 2015); Jerome Klassen and Yves Engler, "What's Not to Like? Justin Trudeau, the Global Disorder, and Liberal Illusions," in *Justin Trudeau and Canadian Foreign Policy,* ed. Norman Hillmer and Philippe Lagassé, 55–82 (London: Palgrave Macmillan, 2018); Srdjan Vucetic and Bojan Ramadanovic, "Canada in the United Nations General Assembly from Trudeau to Trudeau," *Canadian Journal of Political Science* 53, no. (2019): 1–20.

3 Costanza Musu, "Canada and the MENA Region: The Foreign Policy of a Middle Power," *Canadian Foreign Policy Journal* 18, no. 1 (2012): 65–75.

4 Stanfield Report, 1980.

5 Michael Bell, "Practitioners' Perspectives on Canada–Middle East Relations," In *Canada and the Middle East,* ed. P. Heinbecker and B. Momani (Waterloo, ON: Wilfrid Laurier University Press, 2007), 8.

6 Kim Nossal, Stephane Roussel, and Stephane Paquin, "International Policy and Politics in Canada," *Pearson Canada Inc.* (2011).

7   Data retrieved on 5 November 2019, from the website of Statistics Canada.
8   The figures refer to the sum of exports and imports from Saudi Arabia, United Arab Emirates, Turkey, Israel, Egypt, Bahrein, Kuwait, Iraq, Oman, Ethiopia, Lebanon, Qatar, Iran, Jordan, Libya, Sudan, Syria, Yemen, Cyprus, Somalia, and Eritrea. Data retrieved 5 November 2019 from Statistics Canada.
9   A.H. Kilic, "Continuities and Changes in Canada's Middle East Policies during the Chrétien Era," In *Canada–Middle East Relations during the Chrétien Era*, ed. T.A. Jacoby and A.H. Kilic, Bison Paper 10, Centre for Defence and Security Studies (University of Manitoba, 2007), 27.
10 Thomas Juneau, "A Realist Foreign Policy for Canada in the Middle East," *International Journal* 72, no. 3 (2017): 401–12.
11 See Embassy of Canada to Israel, "Canada–Israel Relations," *Government of Canada*, accessed 25 October 2019, https://www.canadainternational.gc.ca /israel/bilateral_relations_bilaterales/index.aspx?lang=eng.
12 For a discussion on the idea of "impartiality" see Peter Jones's chapter in this volume.
13 Stanfield Report, 1980.
14 Rex Brynen, "Canada's Role in the Israeli-Palestinian Peace Process," *Canada and the Middle East: In Theory and Practice* (Waterloo, ON: Wilfrid Laurier University Press, 2007).
15 A. Robinson, "Canada's Credibility as an Actor in the Middle East Peace Process: The Refugee Working Group, 1992–2000," *International Journal* 66, no. 3 (2017): 695–718.
16 See "Canadian Policy on Key Issues in the Israeli-Palestinian Conflict," *Government of Canada*, 19 March 2019, https://www.international.gc.ca /world-monde/international_relations-relations_internationales/mena -moan/israeli-palistinian_policy-politique_israelo-palestinien.aspx?lang =eng#a04.
17 See Amanda Connolly, "Canada among 35 Abstaining from UN Vote Condemning American Embassy Move to Jerusalem," Global News, 22 December 2017, https://globalnews.ca/news/3929255/canada-abstains-un -vote-american-embassy-jerusalem/.
18 "Canada-Israel Strategic Partnership MOU," news release, *Government of Canada*, 21 January 2014, https://www.canada.ca/en/news/archive/2014 /01/canada-israel-strategic-partnership-mou.html.
19 Steven Seligman, "Canada and the United Nations General Assembly (1994–2015): Continuity and Change under the Liberals and Conservatives," *Canadian Foreign Policy Journal* 22, no. 3 (2016): 276–315.

14 Navigating Ideology and Foreign Policy: Canadian Prime Ministers and Israel

FRÉDÉRIC BOILY[1]

At first glance, dilemmas and conflicts involving Israel, even those relating to Canadian foreign policy, are far from the thoughts of Canadian voters during an election period. Issues such as the economy, health-care spending, or the leadership factor are the dimensions with which voters distinguish one party from another when determining their allegiance.[2] Furthermore, on economic policy, Canada generally does not have important relationships with the Middle East.[3] Nonetheless, debates surrounding Canada's role on the international scene and its foreign policy are not completely absent from political contests, especially with regard to Israel.

Most issues touching Israel quickly stimulate strong debates and criticism. For example, former Bloc Québécois MP Maria Mourani found herself in a difficult position when she described Israeli military operations in Lebanon in 2006 as "war crimes," and she had to retract her statements quickly.[4] In recent years, the Boycott, Divestment, and Sanctions movement has created some controversy, on university campuses and elsewhere, putting pressure on the Liberal government of Justin Trudeau to endorse the movement (which it did not do, as discussed below).[5] In recent years, conservative critics have decried the movement as a home for anti-Semites,[6] as was the case when several groups, including the Conservative government, questioned the legitimacy of the Mapping Conference at York University.[7]

This chapter analyses the ideological and non-ideological foundations of Canadian foreign policy towards Israel. While this objective may appear simple, in practice it requires nuance. How can we reliably identify the source of policies advocated for Israel? What are the imprints of ideology upon foreign policy? Looking at Justin Trudeau as well as at his four predecessors, this chapter seeks to draw out the motivations behind current Canadian foreign policy towards Israel by comparing it to that of previous prime ministers.

While the question of Israeli politics is not of primary concern for Canada's major political parties, it nonetheless constitutes a differentiating element between the parties, through which they may position themselves in reference to each other as well as reinforce their specific identity. The chapter focuses quite narrowly on the role of prime ministers, although many other determinants would ultimately require attention.[8] The first objective is to present the differing views held by successive Canadian prime ministers on Israel, then to identify the motivations behind them. For example: Is the position of Stephen Harper on Israel purely ideological? Or does it perhaps represent partisan pragmatism? What is the basis for Liberal (Jean Chrétien and Justin Trudeau) positions regarding Israel?

For this purpose, the first section discusses the importance of political leaders in determining policy towards Israel by proposing an analytical framework that identifies four distinct ideal-typical positions. The second section provides a brief historical review of the positions of three prime ministers (Brian Mulroney, Jean Chrétien, and Paul Martin). This leads, in the third section, to the identification and comparison of the positions of the two most recent prime ministers, Stephen Harper and Justin Trudeau.

Understanding the Relationship between Ideology and Canadian Foreign Policy: A Framework

Political and electoral specialists typically place little emphasis on the impact of foreign policy upon voter behaviour in Canada. From one election to another, there are plenty of other elements to explain voter choice. Nevertheless, foreign policy remains an important factor through which political parties strive to distinguish themselves from one another. For the Middle East specifically, a multitude of factors explain foreign policy;[9] this analysis adopts the individualist approach, focusing on the prime ministers themselves. Indeed, even when a prime minister does not determine policy alone, he maintains a dominant role nevertheless. This was the case with Liberal Prime Minister Paul Martin, who during his brief tenure as head of government emerged as his own de facto foreign minister.[10] Moreover, in a system of government where the prime minister has a key impact on policies at all levels,[11] it is essential to first understand the legacy of past political leaders.

To this end, this chapter uses a framework of Weber-inspired analysis, drawing on his ideal type method, to categorize the positions of each prime minister, which are reviewed in more detail in the third section of this chapter. This method can be used as an instrument of analysis and comparison that helps to understand better some phenomena that are not defined precisely in other typologies. Max Weber gave the following definition of the ideal type: "An ideal type is formed by the one-sided *accentuation* of one or more points of view" according to which "*concrete individual phenomena* ... are arranged into a unified analytical construct" (*Gedankenbild*); in its purely fictional nature, it is a methodological "utopia [that] cannot be found empirically anywhere in reality."[12]

Keenly aware of its fictional nature, the ideal type never seeks to claim its validity in terms of a reproduction of or a correspondence with reality. Its validity can be ascertained only in terms of adequacy, which is too conveniently ignored by the proponents of positivism.[13]

This chapter identifies four ideal-type positions: two of an ideological nature and two of a more pragmatic and partisan form. Before going further, it is necessary to explain how these four types were determined, as well as clarify what is meant by "ideological" and "pragmatic." To build these ideal types, we analysed research focused on Israel and anti-Semitism, some chosen deliberately for its polemical character. The mixture of academic research and polemical essays was instrumental in clarifying the ideological tenets of the Right and the Left.[14]

Our conception of ideology considers neither morals nor irrationality. Rather, the approach rests on the premise that ideology is largely unavoidable in politics: "They [ideologies] offer decision-making frameworks without which political action cannot occur."[15] This is not to say that any position is essentially ideological, but that certain political programs and behaviours result from an ideological standpoint rigidly affirmed by political actors, as opposed to other cases where decisions result instead from electoral pragmatism that changes along with partisan coalitions. As Giovanni Sartori has observed, "Whenever ideology and pragmatism are confronted dichotomously, and thereby conceptualized as polar types, ideology is a belief system based on i) fixed elements, characterized by ii) strong affect and iii) closed cognitive structure. Pragmatism is, conversely, a belief system based on i) flexible elements characterized by ii) weak affect and iii) open cognitive structure."[16] While a pragmatist position remains a cognitively open structure, likely to vary according to observed reality, ideology is a slanted outlook, closed to reality: "Indeed, ideologies are nearly always partial."[17]

This typology combines the ideology/pragmatism dichotomy with the Left/Right political spectrum (see figure 14.1). The ideological Left

Figure 14.1. Four Ideal Type Positions

Ideological Left	Ideological Right
- Israel is a colonialist and apartheid regime - The Israeli extreme Right has a constant and nefarious presence - Islamophobia has replaced anti-Semitism - Occult influence of Jewish lobbies	- Israel is the sole democracy in the Middle East - Israel is under perpetual threat - Anti-Zionism is a mask for anti-Semitism - Fundamental struggle against terrorism
Partisan/Pragmatic Left	**Partisan/Pragmatic Right**
- Prefers a social approach based on humanitarian positions - Assures the development of NGOs in the area - Positive electoral impact in several districts (principally in Ontario and Quebec) - Response to social actors and interest groups	- Economic interest with political actors in the area - Priority on saving jobs - Positive electoral impact in several districts (principally in Montreal, Winnipeg, and Toronto) - Response to economic actors and interest groups

assumes that Israel is a colonial state that oppresses Palestinians, at its extreme going as far as comparing present-day Israel to Nazi Germany. According to this view, Israeli initiatives in the region are de facto illegitimate. At the opposite end of the spectrum, the ideological Right views Israel as a beacon of democracy surrounded by aggressive neighbours, and actors critical of the Jewish state are decried as anti-Semitic. On the other side of this dichotomy, the pragmatic Left supports humanitarian organizations in the region, in response to Canadian interest groups, hoping to reap electoral favour with Canadian pro-Palestinian groups. The pragmatic Right, for its part, champions the economic and job-saving benefits of working relationships with Israel as well as with its neighbours. On both the Right and the Left, pragmatic political leaders may respond to pressure from either side of the ideological divide, shifting their position one way or the other to maximize the electoral potential of either group.

Finally, this interpretive framing aims not to make recommendations but rather to understand the respective positions of Canadian prime ministers. It is not the intent here to prescribe or promote any particular position for the Canadian government towards Israel, which would be analysis of an altogether different order.

Brian Mulroney, Jean Chrétien, and Paul Martin on Israel (1984–2006)

Canadian foreign policy rarely takes centre stage in shaping voter preferences. This is not to say, however, that external issues are entirely absent from political debates. While the Canadian position on Israel may be far from the forefront of most voters' consideration, it remains an object of ideological struggle and debate on the political scene. A contentious issue that tends to inflame passions, the Israeli question continually requires the attention of political contenders and leaders. For this reason, this section examines the positions held by Prime Ministers Brian Mulroney, Paul Martin, and Jean Chrétien as necessary background before shifting to those of Stephen Harper and Justin Trudeau.

Brian Mulroney, Defender of Israel

Upon his retirement from politics in February 1993, Progressive Conservative leader Brian Mulroney was hailed by Jewish organizations for having been responsive to the needs of their communities. The president of the Canadian Jewish Congress recalled at the time a number of initiatives taken by Mulroney and his government.[18] The organization cited the former prime minister's unwavering commitment to Israel as well as his clear approach to the peace process, unmatched by any other Western leader.

After leaving active politics, Mulroney continued to show his support for Israel by condemning, notably in the *National Post*, the rising threat of anti-Semitism.[19] He also spoke at a conference at Toronto's Munk Centre about the disturbing resurgence of anti-Semitism. He explained that although this form of discrimination had markedly declined after 1945, it had returned at the dawn of the twenty-first century. He departed the conference in protest following the denunciation of Israel.[20] According to Mulroney, anti-Semitism was rising again, masquerading as anti-Zionism.

Mulroney recently addressed this issue (March 2019), reiterating his "unshakeable support for the state of Israel" as well as his "extremely strong stand" against anti-Semitism, presently and as he had while in office.[21] B'nai Brith published an article lauding both Mulroney's speech and his devotion to the community.[22] This consistency over time attests to the basis for the former Conservative prime minister's intellectual and political position regarding Israel and the Jewish community in Canada. This would suggest that the Conservatives' approach to these issues goes beyond electoral considerations, as it appears firmly rooted in the tenet of the ideological Right.

Jean Chrétien and Paul Martin: Pragmatism and Stability

Jean Chrétien is often seen as a pragmatist for whom politics is just as much sport – where winning matters most of all – rather than a political figure preoccupied by big questions. Nevertheless, Chrétien was indeed guided by a sort of philosophy, a quasi-instinctive priority placed on political and constitutional stability.[23] Some would describe him as a "passive internationalist" whose foreign policy "was driven by domestic priorities and foremost among these was the deficit."[24]

Chrétien believed that Canada had "a more modest role to play internationally,"[25] including in the Middle East. His journey to the region, in April 2000, was particularly difficult, to the point of being dubbed "Chrétien's terrible trip" by a journalist.[26] "Responding to questions from Canadian reporters, he appeared to endorse the threat of a unilateral declaration of independence as a legitimate negotiating tactic by the Palestinians in peace talks with Israel."[27] Like many Liberals, Chrétien believed that the West had done irreparable damage to the Middle East. He argued as much in a 2014 piece that justified his refusal to participate in the war in Iraq in 2003 while criticizing Stephen Harper's *va-t-en-guerre* approach: "The legacy of colonialism in the Middle East had not been forgotten and was only exacerbated by the Western military intervention in Iraq in 2003, with the consequences we face today. Unfortunately, Mr. Harper did not understand that history in 2003, and he does not understand it today … The Islamic State's atrocities must be stopped. But Western countries must be cognizant of the region's history in deciding how to act."[28]

Indeed, Chrétien was critical of US interventions in the Middle East, most clearly through his refusal to participate in the Iraq war in 2003.[29] Historical sensibilities notwithstanding, however, this decision appears to have been driven by domestic politics most of all: on one hand, to appeal to the Quebec and Ontario electorates and, on the other, to play the anti-American card, through which some members of his party distinguished themselves from Preston Manning's Reform Party and from Western-Canadian intellectuals who were pro-American. These actions, in contrast to Brian Mulroney's staunch ideological motivations, ascribe Jean Chrétien to the pragmatic/electoralist-Right ideal type.

In an effort to distance himself from Jean Chrétien, Paul Martin shifted towards policies more favourable to Israel.[30] At that time, a number of

Liberal MPs (*Liberals for Canada*) allegedly exerted pressure within the party to steer the Liberal government's policy in favour of Israel. As a result, for example, Cabinet and caucus both sought to reorient Canada's voting at the United Nations.[31] Nonetheless, Paul Martin drew the ire of the Jewish community when he allowed Foreign Minister Pierre Pettigrew to attend Yassir Arafat's funeral in November 2004, a gesture that B'nai Brith denounced as "scandalous."[32]

Israel through the Eyes of Stephen Harper and Justin Trudeau (2006–2019)

Stephen Harper: Israel and the Fight against Islamic Extremism

When Prime Minister Harper travelled to the Middle East in January 2014, his visit to Israel was particularly revealing. The visit reaffirmed the Conservative departure from Canada's past policies. Prior to Harper's trip, a number of events had already signalled this diplomatic realignment. For example, as soon as the Conservative government came to power, Minister of Foreign Affairs Peter MacKay cut Canadian ties with the Palestinian Authority, citing the presence of members of Hamas within its government (March 2006). A year later (January 2007), the minister met with Israeli Prime Minister Ehud Olmert but refused to do the same with Palestinian Foreign Minister Mahmoud Zahar, a member of Hamas. Equally indicative of the new Conservative policy was MacKay's speech, again in 2007, at the annual Herzliya conference in Tel Aviv. On this occasion, the minister reaffirmed the government's commitment to keep its distance from Hamas's leadership.[33] Nevertheless, Stephen Harper offered substantial aid to the president of the Palestinian Authority during his visit to Israel, which is discussed further below.[34]

Notwithstanding this offer, Harper's position remains fully informed by his unchanging ideological viewpoint, as evidenced by, to cite only a few examples, his defence of Israeli strikes on Lebanon in the summer of 2006 and his refusal to recognize the observer status of Palestine at the United Nations. The question of why Harper would take such a strong stand remains the subject of multiple interpretations, some observers going as far as flirting with conspiracy theories involving Jewish lobbies or Christian Evangelicals.[35] Most analyses fall into one of two large families, one leaning towards ideology and religion,[36] the other seeing an electoral calculation performed by the prime minister and his team.

When invoking the economic ties uniting Canada and Israel, Harper justified his support for Israel on moral rather than economic grounds, as he made clear during his 2014 visit to Israel, which he had been hoping to make since 2008.[37] In this regard, his speech to the Knesset, the Israeli parliament, where he discussed the "special relationship" between the two countries is indicative. After mentioning that Jews had been established in Canada for 250 years, Harper insisted on the necessity to support Israel specifically because of its history of persecution:

> It is right to support Israel because, after generations of persecution, the Jewish people deserve their own homeland and deserve to live safely and peacefully in that homeland. Let me repeat that: Canada supports Israel because it is right to do so. This is a very Canadian trait, to do something for no reason other than it is right, even when no immediate reward for, or threat to, ourselves is evident. On many occasions, Canadians have even gone so far as to bleed and die to defend the freedom of others in far-off lands.[38]

This would suggest that a moral imperative is likely the primary reason for supporting Israel. And if the Jewish state is not entirely beyond reproach, criticism of Israel too easily slides from moral relativism to anti-Semitism:

> Unfortunately, ladies and gentlemen, we live in a world where that kind of moral relativism runs rampant. And in the garden of such moral relativism, the seeds of much more sinister notions can be easily planted. And so we have witnessed, in recent years, the mutation of the old disease of anti-Semitism and the emergence of a new strain. We all know about the old anti-Semitism. It was crude and ignorant, and it led to the horrors of the death camps. Of course, in many dark corners, it is still with us. But, in much of the western world, the old hatred has been translated into more sophisticated language for use in polite society. People who would never say they hate and blame the Jews for their own failings or the problems of the world, instead declare their hatred of Israel and blame the only Jewish state for the problems of the Middle East.[39]

In this regard, the Conservative party's position is based on recent conservative tradition. Both Mulroney and Harper founded their intellectual convictions on ideological bases from which to validate their position against an existential menace. Harper, like Mulroney, defended Israel with an emphasis on its being the only democracy in the Middle East. Both feared the resurgence of anti-Semitism and viewed anti-Zionism as its new face.[40]

The relationship between Stephen Harper and Brian Mulroney was not amicable during Harper's terms in government. Nonetheless, in their respective policies concerning Israel, there are important parallels to be found in a shared ideological approach.

Justin Trudeau: Closer to Harper or Chrétien?

In the days following the Liberal victory of 19 October 2015, a kind of media euphoria was sweeping through Canada, and many observers hailed a new beginning after the Conservative era. At last, it was believed, "Canada was back," especially in foreign policy. During the 2015 campaign, Justin Trudeau and the Liberals promised to bring Canada back to the forefront of nations and to return to its past internationalist role.[41] Strictly speaking, Canada had of course not disappeared from the international scene during the Conservative mandate. Implicit in this idea was that Canada had abandoned its traditional role as an honest middleman to adopt positions that appeared to turn their back to those of the past, including in the Middle East.[42] Thus, with the Liberals of Justin Trudeau, Canada would again be seen internationally as an "honest broker" that would not strictly align with US policy and defend the state of Israel unconditionally. But what exactly does the idea of a "returning" Canada mean for the Middle East?

One journalist wrote that Justin Trudeau differed greatly from Jean Chrétien and that the current prime minister was closer to his Conservative predecessor than to the former Liberal prime minister: "His policies on Israel closely track Mr. Harper's, though without the snarky rhetoric attached."[43] How do we situate Justin Trudeau here? He is certainly more discreet than Stephen Harper and he does not broach the question of Israel with the same vigour. Yet, if one looks to the political background of Justin Trudeau's positions, it is not immediately clear whether the difference is one of nature or degree.

Early in Trudeau's mandate, one could have expected the difference to be one of nature. In the lead up to the 2019 federal election, however, the Liberal and Conservative parties were competing to present themselves as the better friend of Israel to Canada's Jewish voters. This could be observed in the *Canadian Jewish News*, as both parties defended their respective voting records at the United Nations. Liberal MP Anthony Housefather (who notably represents the riding of former Liberal MP Irwin Cotler, who was well known for his efforts against anti-Semitism) wrote an editorial in the *Canadian Jewish News* to promote and defend his party's voting record on UN actions regarding Israel. Housefather noted increasing opposition to resolutions condemning Israel under the Liberals compared to Harper's Conservatives (voting against 87 per cent of resolutions as opposed to 61 per cent).[44] Conservative Senator Linda Frum responded to Housefather's editorial in the same paper, pointing to two resolutions on which Canada had abstained, including condemnation of the American embassy's move to Jerusalem.[45] Previously, in the same newspaper, a political scientist noted that Trudeau had mostly upheld Harper's support of Israel, while also condemning the Liberal government's funding of the United Nations Relief and Works Agency, which it held to be harmful to Israel.[46]

Trudeau addressed the Boycott, Divestment, and Sanctions campaign at a town hall in January 2019. He both echoed and differed from Mulroney's rhetoric; like Mulroney, he gave weight to the resurging menace of anti-Semitism, all the while maintaining that it was only healthy to criticize some actions of the Jewish state, as Israeli opposition parties do every day. Trudeau also rejected the BDS movement because it singularly and unfairly targeted Israel: "But when you have movements like BDS that single out Israel, that seek to delegitimize and in some cases demonize, when you have students on campus dealing with things like Israel apartheid weeks that make them fearful of actually attending campus events because of their religion in Canada, we have to recognize that there are things that aren't acceptable, not because of foreign policy concerns, but because of Canadian values."[47]

Noteworthy here is the reference to Canadian values that underpinned Trudeau's response, an attempt to depoliticize the issue and anchor it instead to the realm of values. It should be understood that the Canadian values to which Trudeau appealed here were vastly different from the moral values on which Harper based his own support for Israel.

Even though Trudeau's position appears more ideological than Chrétien's, he has also shown, on occasion, a distinctly pragmatic bent. A telling example is Trudeau's response to the shooting of a Canadian doctor, Tarek Loubani, by Israeli security forces during the Gaza border protests of May 2018. After the shooting, Trudeau declared that he was "appalled,"[48] and his foreign minister Chrystia Freeland affirmed that "an independent investigation at an international level remains necessary. Canada will continue to work with our international partners in order to set that up."[49] Yet Canada did not appear to support the UN Human Rights Council's efforts to establish such an investigation[50] and abstained from voting on a UN resolution condemning the Israeli Defense Forces' use of force against civilians (including medical personnel) during these protests.[51] Here Trudeau appeared to be navigating the electorate "pragmatically," moderating his position for the Canadian media all the while reassuring those who would pay close attention to Canada's pro-Israel voting record at the UN. Indeed, the Center for Israel and Jewish Affairs seemed quite satisfied with Trudeau's response.[52]

To be sure, the Liberals under Justin Trudeau have made obvious efforts to reassure the Jewish community that they need not fear a softening of Canada's support for Israel under their government. As Housefather noted, "During the last election campaign, the Conservatives repeatedly warned our community that terrible things would happen if a Liberal government was elected. We stated the contrary, that if elected we would work tirelessly to have Israel's back and advocate for Canada's Jewish community."[53] Trudeau's opponents have observed the same: in the controversial work of journalist Eric Walberg, for example, Justin Trudeau is deemed to be quite different from Jean Chrétien and much too close to Israel.[54] Indeed, for those who believe that Canada has been too favourable to Israel, Trudeau has become a bitter disappointment.

This is the case because Justin Trudeau is, on that issue, not far from Stephen Harper and shares with him an ideologically Right position. To be sure, this position is not argued as vocally as with the Conservatives, to the point of having announced a meeting with Benjamin Netanyahu only *after* it had taken place.[55] In the same vein, there was no mention of Israel in the Liberal program (*Forward. Everyone*) for the 2021 election, to the disappointment of some.[56] Nonetheless, there are no profound differences between Trudeau and Harper on this issue, with both leaders corresponding to the ideological Right ideal type.

Finally, there remains the question of Canada's vote at the United Nations for the recognition of the right of the Palestinian people to self-determination (18 November 2019). It is not yet clear whether this position represents a significant and durable shift in Canada's position on the Middle East. While the Israelis were "very disappointed," [57] this vote may have been a one-time attempt to distinguish Canadian policy from that of the Trump administration, or to garner additional votes – unsuccessfully – to regain a seat on the UN Security Council. Indeed, on the occasion of the menorah lighting on Parliament Hill, Trudeau reaffirmed his support for Israel,[58] such that it is not yet clear whether this vote was an expedient tweak or a major readjustment.

Conclusion

For Conservatives Brian Mulroney and Stephen Harper, ideology appears central to their foreign policy on Israel. As we have argued in our previous work,[59] Harper holds a clearly conservative (albeit not apocalyptic) view that radical Islamism in all its forms constitutes a rising neo-totalitarianism that threatens world democracies, Israel at the forefront. "So much of the Conservative government's foreign policy was driven by domestic political calculations. The Middle East was different. Ideology, not domestic political considerations, was the prime driver there."[60] Ideology, in the case of Stephen Harper in particular, was proclaimed loudly as the central priority of Middle East policy.

For the Liberals of Jean Chrétien and Justin Trudeau, the situation is a little less clear. Jean Chrétien was more concerned with domestic politics, and his stance on Israel was not firmly anchored in any particular ideology. Nevertheless, some ideological elements, corresponding to the ideological Left type, can be discerned under Chrétien. Yet in toto neither the Liberal approach generally nor Jean Chrétien's more specifically is firmly backed by an ideological position like that of Stephen Harper, or even of Paul Martin, who expressed themselves more candidly on the issue.

While ideology appears to be a greater factor in Justin Trudeau's case, he remains, if we follow Jocelyn Coulon, closer to the pragmatic type, certainly when compared to Harper.[61] It is true that Justin Trudeau seems less enthusiastic about foreign policy[62] and is less Manichean than Harper on these issues. Yet he too has adopted the position that the state of Israel is not only an ally but also a friend, as he said on Twitter during the official visit of Israeli President Reuven Rivlin.[63] The Israeli president took the opportunity not only to give Trudeau colourful socks but especially to praise the efforts of the Canadian government in the fight against anti-Semitism, as well as Canadian positions on Iran and the condemnation of the BDS movement.[64] Similarly, the apology given by Justin Trudeau in November 2018, for the Canadian government's refusal to admit 907 Jewish refugees in 1939, was well received.[65] Trudeau's ideological moorings nevertheless appear tempered by some degree of Right pragmatism. Indeed, it seems unlikely that Trudeau, given his lack of enthusiasm for the topic, would carry the same zealous ideological mantle as Harper and the retired Mulroney.

In sum, Brian Mulroney, Stephen Harper, and Justin Trudeau represent a continuity marked with significant differences of emphasis and degree in their support of Israel. It is rather Jean Chrétien (and, to a lesser degree, Paul Martin) who seems the most pragmatic, he for whom foreign trade missions mattered more than major statements of principle, including with Israel. He was not entirely without vision, yet he rarely expressed as much. In short, Chrétien stands apart from the other three prime ministers.

NOTES

1 I would like to thank Le Bureau de la Recherche (Faculté Saint-Jean, University of Alberta) for supporting this research, my research assistant Timothy van den Brink for the constructive help and translation, and Natalie Boisvert for revisions and translation.

2 Gidengil Elisabeth, Neil Nevitte, André Blais, Joanna Everitt, and Patrick Fournier, *Dominance and Decline: Making Sense of Recent Canadian Elections* (Toronto: University of Toronto Press, 2012), 158–66.

3 Bessma Momani and Agata Antkiewiecz, "Canada's Economic Interests in the Middle East," *The Centre for International Governance Innovation*, working paper no. 26 (June 2007), 1.

4 *Radio-Canada*, "Revirement de Maria Mourani," 30 August 2006, https://ici .radio-canada.ca/nouvelle/319948/mourani-se-retracte.

5 Julien Bauer, "Consensus, Trade Unions, and Intellectuals for Hamas," in *Anti-Zionism on Campus: The University, Free Speech, and BDS*, ed. Andrew Pessin and Doron S. Ben-Atar, 58–65 (Bloomington: Indiana University Press, 2018).

6 Robert Fulford, "The BDS Movement, Where the Anti-Semites Find Room to Flourish," *National Post*, 30 November 2018, https://nationalpost.com /opinion/robert-fulford-the-bds-movement-where-the-anti-semites-find -room-to-flourish.

7 Frank Iacobucci, "The Mapping Conference and Academic Freedom: A Report to President Mamdouh Shoukri from the Honorable Frank Iacobucci," March 2010, http://www.yorku.ca/acreview/iacobucci_report.pdf.

8 Brian W. Tomlin, Norman Hillmer, and Fen Olser Hampson, *Canada's International Policies: Agendas, Alternatives, and Politics* (Don Mills, ON: Oxford University Press, 2008), 13.

9 Rex Brynen, "Canada's Role in the Israeli-Palestine Peace Process," in *Canada and the Middle East: In Theory and Practice*, ed. Paul Heinbecker and Bessma Momani (Waterloo, ON: Wilfrid Laurier University Press, 2007), 82.

10 Adam Chapnick, "A Question of Degree: The Prime Minister, Political Leadership, and Canadian Foreign Policy," in *The World in Canada: Diaspora, Demography, and Domestic Politics*, ed. David Carment and David Bercuson (Montreal and Kingston: McGill-Queen's University Press, 2008), 17–18.

11 Donald J. Savoie, *Governing from the Centre: The Concentration of Power in Canadian Politics* (Toronto: University of Toronto Press, 1999).

12 Sung Ho Kim, "Max Weber," *The Stanford Encyclopedia of Philosophy*, last modified 27 November 2017, https://plato.stanford.edu/archives/win2017 /entries/weber/.

13 Kim, "Max Weber."

14 Pierre-André Taguieff, *Judéophobie: La dernière vague* (Paris: Fayard, 2018); Deborah Lipstadt, *Antisemitism: Here and Now* (New York: Schocken Books, 2019); *Dictionnaire historique et critique du racisme*, ed. Pierre-André Taguieff (Paris: Les Presses Universitaires de France, 2013); Norman G. Finkelstein, *The Holocaust Industry: Reflections on the Exploitation of Jewish Suffering* (London: Verso, 2000); John J. Mearsheimer and Stephen M. Walt, *The Israel Lobby and US Foreign Policy* (Toronto: Penguin Canada, 2007); Yakov Rabkin, *Comprendre l'État d'Israël. Idéologie, religion et société* (Montréal: Ecosociété, 2014); Daniel Freeman-Maloy, "Organizing the Canada-Israel Alliance," *Canadian Dimension*, 29 October 2006, https://canadiandimension.com/articles/view /organizing-the-canada-israel-alliance-daniel-freeman-maloy.

15 Michael Freeden, *Ideology: A Very Short Introduction* (Oxford: Oxford University Press, 2003), 127.
16 Giovanni Sartori, "Politics, Ideology, and Belief Systems," *American Political Science Review* 63, no. 2 (June 1969): 405.
17 John Plamenatz, *Ideology* (London: MacMillan, 1970), 18.
18 *Daily News Bulletin*, "Mulroney Announcing Resignation, Is Hailed by Canadians Jews as Friends," 26 February 1993, https://www.jta.org/1993/02/26/archive/mulroney-announcing-resignation-is-hailed-by-canadian-jews-as-friend.
19 Brian Mulroney, "Canada and the Jews," *National Post*, 7 June 2010, https://nationalpost.com/full-comment/brian-mulroney-canada-and-the-jews.
20 Brian Mulroney, "Anti-Semitism: An Enduring Reality," in *Contemporary Antisemitism: Canada and the World*, edited by Derek J. Penslar, Michael R. Marrus, and Janice Gross Stein, 15–25 (Toronto: University of Toronto Press, 2005).
21 Brian Mulroney, "Brian Mulroney: New Steps Must Be Taken to Combat Anti-Semitism," *Montreal Gazette*, 14 March 2019, https://montrealgazette.com/opinion/brian-mulroney-new-steps-must-be-taken-to-combat-anti-semitism.
22 Mike Cohen, "Brian Mulroney Remains Devoted Supporter of Jewish Community and Israel," B'nai Brith, 26 March 2019, https://www.bnaibrith.ca/brian_mulroney_remains_devoted_supporter_of_jewish_community_and_israel.
23 Brooke Jeffrey, *Divided Loyalties: The Liberal Party of Canada, 1984–2008* (Toronto: University of Toronto Press, 2010), 241.
24 Tom Keating, "A Passive Internationalist: Jean Chretien and Foreign Policy," *Review of Constitutional Studies* 9, no. 1 & 2 (2004): 118.
25 Kim Richard Nossal, Stéphane Roussel, and Stéphane Paquin, *Politique internationale et défense au Canada et au Québec* (Montréal: Les Presses de l'Université de Montréal, 2007), 306.
26 Jeff Sallot, "Chrétien's Terrible Trip: The Inside Story," *Globe and Mail*, 21 April 2000, https://www.theglobeandmail.com/news/national/chretiens-terrible-trip-the-inside-story/article25460512/.
27 Sallot, "Chrétien's Terrible Trip."
28 Jean Chrétien, "Canada's True Role in the Middle East Conflict," *Globe and Mail*, 17 October 2014, https://www.theglobeandmail.com/opinion/canadas-true-role-in-the-mideast-conflict/article21138349/.
29 Keating, "Passive Internationalist," 124.
30 Brynen, "Canada's Role in the Israeli-Palestine Peace Process," 78.
31 Donald Barry, "Canada and the Middle East Today: Electoral Politics and Foreign Policy," *Arab Studies Quarterly* 32, no. 4 (2010): 196.
32 Paul C. Merkley, "Reversing the Roles: How the Pro-Israeli Policy of Canada's Conservative Government May Be Moving Jewish Voters from Left to Right," *Jewish Political Studies Review* 23, no. 1–2 (2011): 42.

33 Mark MacKinnon, "MacKay Holds Firm on Hamas Policy," *Globe and Mail,* 23 January 2007, http://www.theglobeandmail.com/news/world/mackay -holds-firm-on-hamas-policy/article17989624/.

34 Canadian Press, "Stephen Harper Offers $66 Million in New Aid to Palestin-ians But Refuses to Criticize Israel during West Bank Visit," *National Post,* 20 January 2014, https://nationalpost.com/news/politics/stephen-harper -visits-west-bank-city-offers-66-million-in-new-aid-to-palestinians.

35 Eric Walberg, *The Canada-Israel Nexus* (Atlanta: Clarity, 2017).

36 Marci McDonald, *The Armageddon Factor: The Rise of Christian Nationalism in Canada* (Toronto: Random House Canada, 2010).

37 Merkley, "At Issue," 47.

38 CBC News, "Stephen Harper's Speech to the Israeli Knesset," 20 January 2014, https://www.cbc.ca/news/politics/stephen-harper-s-speech-to-the -israeli-knesset-1.2503902.

39 CBC News, "Stephen Harper's Speech."

40 Jocelyn Coulon, *Un selfie avec Justin Trudeau. Regard critique sur la diplomatie du premier ministre* (Montréal: Québec/Amérique, 2018), 118.

41 Frédéric Boily, *Trudeau de Pierre à Justin: Portrait de famille de l'idéologie libérale du Canada,* 2nd ed. (Québec: Les Presses de l'Université Laval, 2019), 197–200.

42 Frédéric Boily, "Les conservateurs canadiens, la question d'Israël et l'antisémitisme," *Études internationales* 45, no. 4 (décembre 2014): 579–600.

43 Konrad Yakabuski, "On Israel, Trudeau Is Harper's pupil," *Globe and Mail,* 10 May 2018, https://www.theglobeandmail.com/opinion/article-on -israel-trudeau-is-harpers-pupil/.

44 Anthony Housefather, "Liberal MP Defends His Party's Record on Israel and Jewish Community," *Canadian Jewish News,* 28 August 2018, https:// www.cjnews.com/perspectives/opinions/liberal-mp-defends-his-partys -record-on-israel-and-jewish-community.

45 Linda Frum, "Frum: The Conservative Party's Record on Israel Is Clear," *Canadian Jewish News,* 4 September 2018, https://www.cjnews.com/perspectives /frum-letter-in-response-to-editorial-by-anthony-housefather.

46 Steven Seligman, "How Far Apart Are Trudeau and Harper?," *Canadian Jewish News,* 13 June 2018, https://www.cjnews.com/news/canada/how-far -apart-are-trudeau-and-harper.

47 CJN Staff, "Justin Trudeau Defends His Opposition to BDS at Town Hall," *Canadian Jewish News,* 17 January 2019, https://www.cjnews.com/news /canada/justin-trudeau-defends-his-opposition-to-bds-at-town-hall.

48 Mike Blanchfield, "'Appalled' Trudeau Calls for Investigation into Shooting of Canadian Doctor in Gaza," Global News, 16 May 2018, https://globalnews .ca/news/4213402/appalled-trudeau-calls-for-investigation-into-shooting -of-canadian-doctor-in-gaza/.

49   Robert Fife, "Canadian Doctor Shot in Gaza Has Doubts about Israeli
      Probe, But Will Co-operate," *Globe and Mail*, 23 May 2018, https://www
      .theglobeandmail.com/politics/article-canadian-doctor-shot-in-gaza-has
      -doubts-about-israeli-probe-but-will/.

50   United Nations Human Rights Council Secretariat, Twitter post, 18 May 2018,
      10:35 a.m., https://twitter.com/UN_HRC/status/997485721056366592
      /photo/1?ref_src=twsrc%5Etfw%7Ctwcamp%5Etweetembed%7Ctwterm%
      5E997485721056366592&ref_url=https%3A%2F%2Fwww.aljazeera.com
      %2Fnews%2F2018%2F05%2Fvotes-send-war-crimes-investigators-gaza
      -180518142752946.html.

51   "General Assembly Adopts Resolution on Protecting Palestinian Civilians
      following Rejection of United States Amendment to Condemn Hamas
      Rocket Fire, "United Nations General Assembly resolution GA/12028, ES-10
      /L.23 (13 June 2018), https://www.un.org/press/en/2018/ga12028.doc.htm.

52   Michael Fraiman, "Canadian Officials React to the Violence in Gaza,"
      Canadian Jewish News, 15 May 2018, https://www.cjnews.com/news/canada
      /canadian-officials-react-to-the-violence-in-gaza.

53   Anthony Housefather, "Liberal MP Defends His Party's Record on Israel
      and Jewish Community," *Canadian Jewish News*, 28 August 2018, https://
      www.cjnews.com/perspectives/opinions/liberal-mp-defends-his-partys
      -record-on-israel-and-jewish-community.

54   Eric Walberg, *Canada-Israel Nexus*, 205–8.

55   CTV News, "Questions Raised as PM Trudeau Keeps Netanyahu Meeting
      Quiet," 25 January 2018, https://www.ctvnews.ca/politics/questions
      -raised-as-pm-trudeau-keeps-netanyahu-meeting-quiet-1.3773623.

56   Mark Schiffer, "#Election2021: Where the Canadian Parties and Leaders
      Stand on Israel," TheJ.ca, 1 September 2021, https://www.thej.ca/2021
      /09/01/election2021-where-the-canadian-parties-and-leaders-stand-on
      -israel/.

57   Raphael Ahren, "In Sudden Switch, Canada Backs Pro-Palestine UN
      Resolution," *Times of Israel*, 20 November 2019, https://www.timesofisrael
      .com/in-sudden-switch-canada-backs-pro-palestine-un-resolution/.

58   Canadian Press, "Recent UN Vote Not a Shift in Canada's 'Steadfast'
      Support for Israel: Trudeau," Global News, 9 December 2019, https://
      globalnews.ca/news/6275884/trudeau-un-vote-canada-israel/.

59   Frédéric Boily, *Stephen Harper, La fracture idéologique d'une vision du Canada*
      (Québec: Les Presses de l'Université Laval, 2016), 44–53.

60   Mike Blanchfield, *Swingback: Getting Along in the World with Harper and
      Trudeau* (Montreal and Kingston: McGill-Queen's University Press,
      2017), 155.

61   Coulon, *Un selfie avec Justin Trudeau*, 123.

62   Coulon, *Un selfie avec Justin Trudeau*, 30–1.

63 Justin Trudeau, "We have more than an ally in Israel, we have a trusted and longstanding friend," Twitter, 4 April 2019. https://twitter.com/justintrudeau /status/1113815203349762049?lang=en.

64 Jewish News Syndicate, "In Canada, Israel's President Thanks Trudeau for Battling Anti-Semitism, BDS," 1 April 2019, https://www.jns.org/in-canada -israels-president-thanks-trudeau-for-battling-anti-semitism-bds/.

65 Emily Rauhala, "Apologizing for Canada's Rejection of Jews in 1939, Trudeau Vows to Fight Anti-Semitism," *Washington Post*, 7 November 2018, https://www.washingtonpost.com/world/the_americas/trudeau-to -apologize-for-canadas-rejection-of-a-boat-full-of-jewish-refugees-in-1939 /2018/11/07/5462d53a-e1f9-11e8-a1c9-6afe99dddd92_story.html?utm _term=.10839d43d920.

15 Conclusion

NATHAN C. FUNK

As contributors to this volume have demonstrated, the study of Canada's Middle East policy is, in many respects, a study in continuities and constraints. Despite periodic changes in the ideological tone and tenor of Canadian leadership, certain patterns are recurrent. While it would be an overstatement and misjudgment to dismiss variations in policy and rhetoric among Canadian governments, there is still considerable validity to the assertion that Middle East policy is not an area in which most Canadian politicians and policymakers are inclined to pursue new agendas that appear costly, risky, or detached from a clear conception of Canada's interests, commitments, and capacities.

Nonetheless, fluctuations in significant aspects of Canadian policy towards the Middle East during recent decades testify to the decisive roles that political judgment and choice play in policy decisions and in the formulation of a strategic vision. Though influenced by the priorities of allies, Canadian decisions are not always made in lockstep with the policies of the country's southern neighbour or in deference to the articulated preferences of other influential states, within as well as beyond the region. Thus, there is clearly scope for critical re-evaluation of past choices, for reassessment of immediate as well as longer-term interests, and for judicious pursuit of initiatives that seek to leverage Canada's international "brand" identity and try to harmonize Canadian interests and values.

Indeed, the extent to which Canada will be seen as a valuable presence in the contemporary Middle East is to no small extent a function of the degree to which Canadian foreign policy leaders can communicate a message that credibly addresses valid concerns of traditional allies while also manifesting an agenda that is not only authentically internationalist but also well-informed about the complexities of the region, attuned to humanitarian priorities, and more inclined towards collaborative problem solving than ideological posturing. Though Canada's Middle East interests may seem modest in comparison to those of other major international actors, the limited nature of these interests can be construed in some respects as an advantage for a country that still has significant capacity for diplomatic engagement. Limited interests provide greater latitude for reinventing a traditional "helpful fixer" role in ways that are well-adapted to present needs, acceptable to multiple parties, and visionary in the sense that they seek to deepen regional dialogue, expand its time horizon and societal reach, and incrementally build consensus on responses to unmet challenges.

Continuities and Constraints

The geopolitical, governance, humanitarian, and sustainability challenges of the contemporary Middle East are daunting, and certain aspects of Canadian policy towards the region are extrinsically given or shaped. Moreover, to the extent that foreign policy is also a matter of domestic politics as well as international partnerships, choices are not neutral in their acceptability to a given political coalition or audience. Thus, Canadian Middle East policy is not infinitely malleable, nor are choices free of political costs. As most contributors to this volume have emphasized, there have been notable continuities in Canadian policies across multiple governments, and the real priorities of Canadian Middle East engagement have not always matched the national self-image of an internationalist middle power inclined towards impartiality and peacekeeping.

As Justin Massie and Marco Munier argue in their chapter, Canadian foreign policy in the Middle East is strongly influenced by alliance considerations, resulting in a high level of pressure to play the role of "steadfast ally" to the United States and other key states in situations that involve military force. The variety of intervention may vary, but demonstrating support has been a key consideration in Liberal as well as Conservative policies. Such observations carry the implication that, in turbulent and unsettled times, the most salient debates about Canadian involvement in the region are likely to be centred more on questions of security and maintenance of alliances than on forms of engagement or advocacy intended to shape outcomes in an innovative manner. Though writing specifically on the subject of modern Turkey and its role in Canadian diplomatic relations, Chris Kilford underscores the related point that certain regional realities and political trends are deeply rooted in history, and likely beyond Canada's limited capacity for independent influence.

As Mike Fleet and Nizar Mohamad note in their chapter, Canada has in recent years inclined towards programming that fits a "security aid paradigm." This prioritizes relatively low-cost and low-risk interventions that involve training military and police forces to advance professionalization as well as defence capacity. Policymakers have regarded such limited commitments as useful for signalling engagement to allies without jeopardizing domestic support.

Ezra Karmel similarly highlights the impact of a post-9/11 security framework on policy in his chapter. As he argues, Canadian-supported civil society programming more consistently aligns with a security/stability paradigm than with local concerns about corruption, accountability, and meaningful participation. In his judgment, this constitutes a "shift in development aid," which has had the effect of reorienting civil society organizations that once reflected more indigenous and independent concerns with democratization, "transforming them into intermediary organizations by recasting civil society as a tool for supporting good governance and stabilization."

Other chapters also point to the salience of stability concerns, alliance politics, relations with the United States, and anti-terrorism in Canada's Middle Eastern engagements, and highlight inconsistencies between proclaimed Canadian goals and the substance of actual policies. Costanza Musu acknowledges a policy shift towards "a more partisan approach in support of Israel" during the last two decades, while also flagging a desire to "minimize negative impacts on relations with the United States" as a formative factor in Canadian involvement with the Israeli-Palestinian conflict. David Petrasek raises additional concerns, emphasizing ways in which Canada's human rights record in the Middle East falls short of idealist aspirations. As he observes, policy alignment with allies (within as well as beyond the region) carries the cost of diminishing advocacy vis-à-vis states with discouragingly poor human rights records. By largely overlooking the deficiencies of regional allies and selectively focusing on Iran, Canada has moved towards a policy that lacks the credibility that might come with greater even-handedness. Although Canada admittedly has limited leverage in situations where its expressions of critique are not joined by other noteworthy international actors, the appearance of double standards is not helpful to Canada's reputation in the Middle East or in broader multilateral policy forums.

As Jennifer Pederson argues, commercial interests have also been a source of contradictions in regional policy, and have had the effect of undermining Canada's stated support for human rights and for multilateral instruments such as the Arms Trade Treaty. Pointing to the Liberal government's choice to continue implementing an arms deal with Saudi Arabia, Pedersen suggests that commercial interests have been prioritized over human rights values and commitments. She also highlights similarities between Canada's regional policy and the policies of other external countries, which similarly accept the "moral cost of jobs over human rights." In her judgment, this short-term calculus has longer-term (but seemingly indeterminate) impacts, and effectively ratifies the regional status quo by offering no real critique of authoritarian governments. While noting the potential for damage to Canada's brand and claims to a positive overall influence, Pedersen appears justified in her conclusion that the tension between Canadian values and expediency-based policies implicates Canada in regional problems.

Broader Canadian Interests and Opportunities for Choice

For Canadians who seek openings for constructive engagement in to-day's Middle East, many dynamics in the region appear sobering. Several key conflicts, from Yemen to the Syria-Iraq milieu to Libya, speak to the dangers of internationalized civil war in the wake of governance failures, with armed non-state actors assuming a major presence on a landscape marked by fractured national identities, mobilized communal identities, extremist forces, and regional as well as extra-regional geopolitical agendas. Such conflicts have profound human consequences and have generated millions of refugees and internally displaced peoples (IDPs). Despite the apparent incentives for intervention and multilateral solutions, addressing these conflicts has been rendered difficult by the disinclination of regional and global powers (including Russia and China) to elevate the arbitration of Middle Eastern conflicts as a strategic priority that would require coordination and compromise with other major players. Difficulties of navigating regional politics are further compounded by the diminished viability of a two-state solution in the Israeli-Palestinian conflict, the reinvigoration of tensions between the United States and Iran, the development of intensified rivalries among Arab Gulf monarchies, the annulment of Egypt's democratic experiment, and the decline of the "Turkish model" as an example for how regional states might explore pathways out of the sclerotic political structures that ignited the Arab uprisings.

Although some Canadian voices are inclined to frame these complex and painful realities as the consequences of a grand ideological struggle within which Canada must necessarily act as a partisan player, a more pragmatic and nuanced response appears to align more naturally with basic Canadian interests, values, and policy resources. As Amarnath Amarasingam and Stephanie Carvin suggest in their chapter, Canada has an interest in conflict mitigation and in elevating international law and order over more extreme narratives and strategies. In addition to providing a grounded assessment of real dangers posed by returning foreign fighters, Amarasingam and Carvin offer suggestions for a non-politicized response as well as a cautionary statement against threat inflation. The findings of this chapter also reinforce the point that aspiring towards peace and security in the Middle East is very much in line with Canadian interests and values. Although Canada's ability to independently advance this objective is modest, the enhancement of diplomatic capacity for the region should be central to Canada's strategic vision. Whereas a fragmented region riven by regional and great-power rivalries is likely to remain a seedbed for insurgent movements that thrive on narratives of victimization and struggle, the development of coherent multilateral approaches to regional problems is an important basis for reducing the appeal of radicalized groups over the long term.

While Canada has much at stake in its bilateral relations with the United States and in other strategic relationships, the significance of these relationships as determinants of Canadian Middle East policy can also be overstated. In his chapter, Farzan Sabet argues persuasively that "at least four" factors other than inherent security and economic interests play a central role in shaping the content of Canadian decisions and commitments: "upholding a rules-based international order; alliance management; bilateral relations with regional states; and the ruling party's electoral coalition and political ideology." Viewed through this lens, it becomes clear that the origins of Canadian policy cannot be reduced to a single variable, and that Canadian governments have some margin of manoeuvre when they choose how they engage allies, international organizations, and adversaries. At the time the Harper government cut diplomatic relations with Iran in 2012, for example, the United States was pursuing a different path involving diplomacy as well as economic sanctions. Likewise, it was not the Obama administration that inspired the same Canadian government to elevate "megaphone diplomacy" over the more traditionally favoured "honest broker" posture. Certain US initiatives may be difficult to refuse, yet Canadian leaders can and do make choices (including the refusal to join the US coalition of the willing against Iraq in 2003) in light of domestic, international, and ideological considerations.

Other contributors to this volume have also helped to establish that there is significant scope for choice and strategic vision in Canadian Middle East policy. As Massie and Munier note, different electoral strategies and coalitions are linked to distinguishable postures, with Liberal and NDP policies seeking to accentuate "international citizenship" commitments and Conservative policies placing greater emphasis on the "good ally" position in situations of escalating conflict. Frédéric Boily, in turn, explores how divergent ideological orientations have informed these different approaches. He argues that the Harper government's stances on the Israeli-Palestinian conflict and on the region more generally were inspired by an ideological framework that equated grievances towards the Israeli state with anti-Semitism and that perceived a threateningly coherent Islamic extremist stance in diverse regional groups, cases, and contexts. In contrast, more pragmatic Canadian leaders such as Jean Chrétien have argued that Middle Eastern politics must be understood from a perspective that comprehends the history and consequences of Western colonialism and interventionism, and that is less hasty to impose a Western narrative as the principal frame of reference for interpreting the varied goals and ideologies of regional movements. For example, one can abhor the ideology and methods of the Islamic State without presenting this organization's extremism as the "authentic face" of diverse movements expressing Islamic political identity and dissatisfaction with aspects of a local or regional status quo.

Moving towards a more distinctively Canadian Middle East policy that advances interests and values in an internationalist context will require greater attentiveness to complex dynamics within the region, as well as an ability to analyse the official conflict narratives of prominent actors within a larger regional and historical context. As Nermin Allam argues, Canadian disengagement from the Middle East is a significant source of misconceptions about the region, and leaves space for unhelpfully selective misrepresentations of Islamic political discourse. While the depth of commitment to democratic pluralism among Islamists varies, Allam offers relevant guidance in her assertion that "it is counterproductive to dismiss their voices because Islamist groups present the most significant oppositional forces in autocratic regimes and are [an] integral part of civil society." Policymakers would be wise to heed Allam's warning against "debates over political Islam [that] reduce Islamist politics to militant violent extremism and ignore the diverse trajectories of different groups," and to embrace a more nuanced policy recognizing religious and cultural specificities. Rather than construe stability and security in narrow terms that privilege rigidly authoritarian governments, Canadian interlocutors can play a more helpful role by reminding their partners that durable security needs to be built on an inclusive and equitable basis. In the absence of more participatory political structures and confidence-building among regional states, security will remain elusive.

Well-informed and broadly based Canadian engagement with Middle Eastern realities does not need to be excessively costly. As Fleet and Mohamad argue on the issue of security sector reform, there are opportunities not just to achieve professionalization but also to support human rights and democratization. A key to success, they propose, is tapping into suitable multilateral frameworks even when advancing modest, "tactical-level programs." Despite budgetary constraints and additional political considerations, this model may nonetheless be applicable to other relatively low-cost forms of activity that go beyond a transactional approach to foreign policy in which Canada aspires merely to be seen as "useful" while advancing ends that are largely congruent with or derivative from an ally's strategic priorities.

What then might a more forward-looking policy look like if it were to play to recognized areas of Canadian strength and to internationally recognized priorities such as sustainable development, human security, and peacebuilding? Can lessons be drawn from past Canadian experiences? In this regard, in his chapter Peter Jones helpfully identifies three eras of Canadian involvement: an era in which Canada sought to play an "honest broker" or peacekeeper role, within a framework of Cold War stability and conflict management; an era of open partiality towards specific actors and causes; and the current era in which Canada is once again projecting a more impartial stance, with a stated intent to engage on gender and human rights issues. There are many potential activities that might be pursued on the basis of the most recent stance, which offers scope for renewed problem-solving efforts: "Perhaps a new mediation role is emerging in terms of opening doors to conversations with new constellations of actors and issues who lie beyond the reach of traditional diplomacy, and working with regional actors in doing so. This would require an approach allowing for support of quiet discussions on multiple levels, including quiet support for non-official discussions where official ones were not yet possible."

As Jones argues, coupling traditional diplomacy with robust support for track-two or multi-track forms of sustained dialogue is a form of engagement that would bring transformative possibilities as well as modest risks. The current fragmentation of the region suggests that considerable staying power would be necessary to achieve positive results, and special engagement on signature issues like gender and human rights might need to be coupled with a careful selection of partners and attention to cultural resources for advancing such causes in a contextually resonant manner. A focus on these issues could also benefit from a larger, solution-oriented stance of "positive neutrality" towards important regional conflicts, animated by efforts to build trust among multiple parties and to support networks of regional actors with visions for longer-term change.

Can Canada Manifest a Larger Strategic Vision?

Insofar as Canadian policy is not simply a by-product of external pressures or of undisputed national interests, there is genuine scope for choice in Canadian Middle East policy, and for modest yet persistent efforts to advance a recognizably Canadian strategic vision. Such a vision need not be grandiosely conceived or overly ambitious in immediate goals and expectations, yet foregrounding certain "brand Canada" values and concerns has utility in collaborative efforts to construct platforms for future-oriented dialogue and scenario building. Given that the United States has lost considerable "soft power" and brand value in the region, recently through the embrace of nativism and restrictions on foreign travellers from multiple states, there is arguably an opening for enhanced Canadian involvement on signature issues such as peace and good governance, as well as on important areas of multilateral concern like the Sustainable Development Goals. By heightening engagement on these issues and adopting elements of the multi-level dialogue model proposed by Jones, Canada can enlarge its foreign policy footprint in the Middle East in ways that are likely to be recognized as positive by many thought leaders and forward-thinking civil servants in the region. There are also opportunities to partner more dynamically with European Union states and with agencies of the United Nations.

The relevance of such an approach is accentuated by a survey of the regional landscape. Four countries (Syria, Iraq, Yemen, and Libya) are in grave need of reconstruction. Regional fault lines pitting Arab Gulf states and Israel against Iran, together with rivalries among Arab Gulf states themselves, distract attention from looming challenges linked to demographics, climate change, poverty alleviation, public health, water security, and the human security of marginalized, suppressed, and displaced communities. The divergent political agendas of external great powers and of intra-regional contenders for influence consistently exacerbate armed conflicts and block paths to conflict resolution. The renewal of popular protests in many regional states, from Algeria to Iran, Iraq, Lebanon, Sudan, Tunisia, and Yemen, speaks to continuing youth-driven demands for change, accountability, and economic opportunity. The intensification of conflict between Jews and Arabs in the Israeli-Palestinian sphere also speaks to the need for discussion of alternatives to an unsustainable status quo.

Nawroos Shibli's chapter highlights this viability of fresh Canadian approaches. Focusing her analysis on Canada's response to the Syrian refugee crisis, Shibli underscores the potential for action, particularly in humanitarian areas. Contrasting the Trudeau government's welcoming of refugees to the response of the previous Harper government and to the policies of the Trump administration in the United States, Shibli emphasizes Canada's capacity for agency, leadership, and international citizenship within a broad multilateral framework. By relating the Syrian refugee policy to a deeper historical context, Shibli demonstrates that Canada's recent moves were not unprecedented and can be regarded as carrying forward previous welcomes extended to Hungarian, Ismaili, and Southeast Asian refugees from the 1950s through the 1970s. Though not risk-free from a domestic political perspective, Canada's actions on the refugee file were arguably consistent with these past efforts to engage as a principled state actor and can be interpreted as a "new pivot away from hard power strategies and active military entanglements in war zones towards standard-setting humanitarian assistance and traditional Canadian diplomacy." Given that Canada's "soft power" initiative on refugees was welcomed by many states, Shibli's argument invites further reflection about how a confident and well-thought-out approach to multilateral engagement might enhance Canada's standing while also furthering humanitarian objectives.

To carve out a coherent niche role that responds creatively to regional needs while also addressing shared interests in a more secure future, Canada will have to navigate competing pressures without being captured by narrow intra- or extra-regional agendas. To align contemporary policy with some of Canada's more notable historic contributions, it may be helpful to shift underlying policy metaphors from the domain of boxing kinetics ("punching above our weight") to feats of weightlifting (e.g., "lifting above our weight class") that are more reflective of current challenges. As a middle power, Canada has limited capacity to command attention or force change. Canada does, however, possess the reputational, diplomatic, political, and human resources to play a dynamic role in opening channels of dialogue, convening important voices, and helping to organize new initiatives. By aiming to build consensus on needed changes and supporting efforts to set them in motion, Canada can enact the "helpful fixer" role in ways that clarify and advance common interests. Accomplishing this is likely to require widening the conversation on regional peace and security and underscoring the need to ground stability in a more participatory, cooperative, and resilient regional order.

The case for such augmented forms of Canadian engagement becomes stronger when one considers the full range of relevant national assets. In addition to the obvious presence of diplomatic experience, Canada's historical record with Middle East refugee issues through UNRWA and the Madrid working group is worth noting, as is its lack of a colonial legacy in the region when compared to other actors. Past forays in the domain of public diplomacy may also be instructive, particularly considering Canada's impressive ability to tap diaspora knowledge and networks to enhance regional engagement. Such human capital might be particularly useful for exploratory discussions of Middle Eastern governance challenges and of ways in which Canada's distinctive federal governance profile may or may not speak to the realities of factionalized societies experiencing strong forms of regionalism. Despite its imperfections, the Canadian brand remains desirable in the Middle Eastern context. Canada's dearth of high-level regional interests may be a limiting factor in some respects, but in other ways it is a potential advantage. Similarly, "hard power" limitations and middle power status force clarity of thinking about where Canada's genuine strengths lie.

Low-profile official Canadian diplomacy, reinforced by the active use of public and track-two diplomacy initiatives to map complex issues and shape new policy options,[1] can provide constructive and relatively low-cost ways to explore concerns of regional peoples and not just governments. While still identifiably linked with other Western states and capable of calling in additional resources, Canada can offer forums for exploring conflict resolution and crisis management options as well as for drafting future-oriented agendas that are not overburdened with geopolitical baggage. There is also a need to connect regional security issues to matters of responsive governance, human development, and sustainability, as outlined in documents such as the Arab Human Development reports.

To the extent that they help to generate new options, initiatives for conflict de-escalation and resolution can favourably serve the Canadian interest in preventing the expansion of conflicts that might ultimately draw in allied as well as Canadian forces. Track-two diplomacy can also support dialogue on future governance scenarios for Yemen, Libya, and other states facing internal fragmentation. When convening dialogue on longer-term social and regional priorities, inclusion of youth, professionals, academics, civil society advocates, and religious leaders can provide a valuable counterpoint to potentially imbalanced and sometimes deficient perspectives gleaned through narrower engagement with governments and elite stakeholders. Learning from such dialogue can enhance insight into changing social trends, providing a more nuanced and textured understanding of demands for change and of the roles religious and cultural identities play in regional politics.

In taking on an enhanced but still unobtrusive diplomatic role, Canada can build on its past contributions to shaping the international human security agenda. Human security provides a potentially dynamic and non-partisan way of engaging genuine regional problems with political violence as well as the special vulnerabilities faced by displaced, vulnerable, and under-served population groups seeking dignity, avenues of participation, and government accountability. Human security may also prove relevant for decision-making amid the moral and political complexities posed by the protracted Israeli-Palestinian conflict.

In addition to conflict management, efforts to support the gradual emergence of greater consensus on longer-term goals for the Middle East are needed. Sustained dialogue that engages creative thinkers from across the region – inside as well as outside governments – can help set the agenda for addressing issues not yet at the forefront. These issues include implementing the UN's Sustainable Development Goals and disaster risk-reduction frameworks, meeting the challenges of climate change, promoting norms of accountable governance, meeting the needs of refugees and internally displaced peoples, and pursuing reconstruction and peacebuilding in areas riven by conflict. Canada's foreign policy emphases on gender equity and human rights can be brought to the table of such discussions, for example in exploring the different impacts of armed conflict on women and children and in highlighting vital roles played by women in reconstruction.

New Forms of Engagement

Taken together, the chapters of this volume underscore the difficulty of defining Canadian Middle East policy. As many observers have noted, direct and immediate gains from heightened engagement in the region are by no means guaranteed, and yet Canada does arguably have a stake in processes that help to build more durable regional security, founded on resilient and functional socio-political systems as well as on more effective conflict management measures. In the absence of sustained, constructive processes that advance these priorities, the chances that Canada might be drawn into regional conflicts affecting key allies remain significant. More proactive involvement in public and second-track diplomacy is therefore congruent not just with past Canadian foreign policy traditions and values, but also with tangible, present-day Canadian interests and with trends in thinking about collaborative approaches to international engagement.[2] Relevant expertise – substantive as well as procedural – already exists within Canadian governmental, academic, diaspora, and civil society networks, and can be mobilized without great expense or major shifts in the architecture of government institutions.

By strengthening commitments to such processes, as well as to other practical, constructive, and low-cost forms of engagement analysed by contributors to this volume, Canada has the ability to "lift above its weight class," provide meaningful support to multilateralism, and model a quiet form of leadership in which Canadian citizens can take pride. Despite constraints, there is scope for choice and initiative in Canadian Middle East policy through intentional efforts to reinforce and project values that align with the country's basic and enduring interests. These are admittedly aspirational values that are not fully realized even in Canada. Nonetheless, they are dynamically relevant to building networks of confidence, cohesion, and cooperation amid the many centrifugal forces that perpetuate conflict and insecurity.

NOTES

1 Peter Jones, *Track Two Diplomacy in Theory and Practice* (Stanford, CA: Stanford University Press, 2015).
2 R.S. Zaharna, Amelia Arsenault, and Ali Fisher, *Regional, Networked, and Collaborative Approaches to Public Diplomacy: The Connective Mindshift* (New York: Routledge, 2013).

Contributors

Nermin Allam is an assistant professor of politics at Rutgers University–Newark. Allam holds a PhD in international relations and comparative politics from the University of Alberta. Her research interests include social movements, gender politics, Middle Eastern and North African studies, and political Islam. She is the author of *Women and the Egyptian Revolution: Engagement and Activism during the 2011 Arab Uprisings* (2017). Allam held a Social Science and Humanities Research Council postdoctoral fellowship at Princeton University.

Amarnath Amarasingam is an assistant professor in the School of Religion, and is cross-appointed to the Department of Political Studies, at Queen's University, Ontario. He is also a senior fellow with the International Centre for the Study of Radicalization. His research interests are in terrorism, radicalization and extremism, online communities, diaspora politics, post-war reconstruction, and the sociology of religion. He is the author of *Pain, Pride, and Politics: Sri Lankan Tamil Activism in Canada* (2015) and the co-editor of *Sri Lanka: The Struggle for Peace in the Aftermath of War* (2016). He has also published over forty peer-reviewed articles and book chapters, presented papers at over one hundred national and international conferences, and written for the *New York Times*, the *Monkey Cage*, the *Washington Post*, CNN, Politico, the *Atlantic*, and *Foreign Affairs*. He has been interviewed on CNN, PBS Newshour, CBC, BBC, and other media outlets. He tweets at @AmarAmarasingam.

Frédéric Boily is a Canadian and Quebec policy specialist, and a professor of political science at the campus Saint-Jean (University of Alberta). His research focuses on the right, conservatism, and populism in Canada and Quebec. He is the author of several books, including *Le fédéralisme selon Harper* (2014) and *Droitisation et populisme. Canada, Québec, États-Unis*

(2020). He is also an associate researcher at the Centre of Expertise and Training on integrisms.

Stephanie Carvin is an associate professor at the Norman Paterson School of International Affairs, Carleton University. She holds a PhD in international relations from the London School of Economics and is the author of *Stand on Guard: Reassessing Canadian National Security* (2021), *Prisoners of America's Wars: From the Early Republic to Guantanamo* (2010), and *Law, Science, Liberalism and the American Way of Warfare: The Quest for Humanity in Conflict* (2015). She is the co-author of *Intelligence Analysis and Policy Making: The Canadian Experience* (2021) and co-editor of *Top Secret Canada: Understanding the Canadian Intelligence and National Security Community* (2021). Between 2012 and 2015 she worked as a national security analyst for the Government of Canada.

Mike Fleet is a senior analyst with the Government of Canada, where he focuses on Iraq. He previously worked as a senior researcher with the Institute on Governance on the Iraq Team that implemented the Fiscal Decentralization and Resiliency Project. His research focus is on Iraqi politics, federalism, state-building, and conflict dynamics. He tweets at @MikeFleet23. The views and opinions expressed in his chapter are those of the authors alone and do not reflect the views of their employers or of the Government of Canada.

Nathan C. Funk is an associate professor of peace and conflict studies at the University of Waterloo. He has served on the boards of two Canadian NGOs, Project Ploughshares and Peacebuild: The Canadian Peacebuilding Network, and acts as a board member for the Peace and Conflict Studies Association of Canada. He has written on peacebuilding and international conflict resolution, with a special focus on the contemporary Middle East, Islamic-Western relations, identity conflict, sustained dialogue, and the role of cultural and religious factors in localized peacebuilding and social change. His publications include *Islam and Peacemaking in the Middle East* (2009) and *Ameen Rihani: Bridging East and West* (2004).

Peter Jones is an associate professor at the University of Ottawa. He is also executive director of the Ottawa Dialogue, a university-based organization that runs Track 1.5 and Track Two Dialogues around the world. Before joining the University of Ottawa, he served as a senior analyst for the Security and Intelligence Secretariat of the Privy Council of Canada. Previously, he held positions related to international affairs and security at the Department of Foreign Affairs, the Privy Council Office, and the Department of

National Defence. He served on the Canadian delegation to the multilateral talks of the Middle East Peace Process and led the Middle East Security and Arms Control Project at the Stockholm International Peace Research Institute in Sweden in the 1990s. He is the author of *Track Two Diplomacy: In Theory and Practice* (2015), published by the Stanford University Press.

Thomas Juneau is an associate professor at the University of Ottawa's Graduate School of Public and International Affairs. His research focuses on the Middle East (in particular Iran and Yemen) and on Canadian foreign, national security, and defence policy. He is the author of *Squandered Opportunity: Neoclassical Realism and Iranian Foreign Policy* (2015) and *Le Yémen en guerre* (2021), co-author of *Intelligence Analysis and Policy Making: The Canadian Experience* (2021), editor of *Strategic Analysis in Support of International Policy Making: Case Studies in Achieving Analytical Relevance* (2017), and co-editor of *Top Secret Canada: Understanding the Canadian Intelligence and National Security Community* (2021), *Canadian Defence Policy in Theory and Practice* (2019), and *Iranian Foreign Policy since 2001: Alone in the World* (2013). From 2003 until 2014, he worked with Canada's Department of National Defence. He tweets at @thomasjuneau.

E.J. Karmel is a PhD candidate at the University of Guelph. His research focuses on public policy and decentralization in the Middle East. Alongside his research, he has been working with national and international development organizations in Jordan since 2013.

Chris Kilford served for thirty-six years in the Canadian Army, in Canada, Germany, Afghanistan, and Turkey in command, instructional, staff, and defence attaché roles. He obtained his PhD at Queen's University (2009), where he focused on civil-military relations in the developing world in the post-colonial period. Today he is an external fellow at the Queen's Centre for International and Defence Policy; a part-time assistant professor at the Canadian Forces College; president of the Canadian International Council, Victoria Branch; and a member of the national board. His articles on Canadian defence and foreign policy issues as well as Turkish and Middle Eastern matters have appeared in numerous Canadian and international publications, and he is a frequent media commentator.

Justin Massie is a full professor of political science at the Université du Québec à Montréal and co-director of the Network for Strategic Analysis. His research focuses on the global power transition, multinational military coalitions, and Canadian foreign and defence policy. He is the author of *Francosphère: l'importance de la France dans la culture stratégique* *du Canada* (Presses de l'Université du Québec, 2013) and co-editor of *Paradiplomatie identitaire: Nations minoritaires et politique extérieure* (Presses de l'Université du Québec, 2019) and *America's Allies and the Decline of U.S. Hegemony* (Routledge, 2019).

Nizar Mohamad is an independent analyst based in Toronto, who focuses on Middle Eastern politics and security. Nizar's research interests centre on the politics of the Levant, with a focus on Syria and Iraq. In particular, Nizar has spent years studying the changing dynamics of the security climate in both countries, with an analytical emphasis on the formation of paramilitary mobilizations by the state within the theatres of conflict that have dominated their respective political landscapes. Specifically, he has been attempting to assess the implications of these substate actors on future political settlements, as well as what this entails for regional security arrangements, particularly given the extensive role that they continue to play across the region. His thesis focuses on the link between regime (in)security in Iraq and Syria and the outsourcing of operations to actors outside of the official security apparatus of the state, as well as the corresponding implications for state sovereignty.

Bessma Momani is a full professor of political science at the University of Waterloo, a senior fellow at the Centre for International Governance and Innovation, and a non-resident fellow at the Arab Gulf States Institute in Washington, DC. She was a non-resident senior fellow at both the Brookings Institution and Stimson Center in Washington, DC; a consultant to the International Monetary Fund; and a visiting scholar at Georgetown University's Mortara Center. She was a 2015 fellow of the Pierre Elliott Trudeau Foundation and now sits on its board of directors. She is also a Fulbright scholar. Momani has written and co-edited ten books and over eighty scholarly, peer-reviewed journal articles and book chapters that have examined international affairs, diversity and inclusion, Middle East affairs, and the global economy. She is recipient of a number of research grants from the Social Sciences and Humanities Research Council, International Development Research Council, and the Department of National Defence. Dr. Momani is a regular contributor to national and international media on global security and economic policy issues. She has written editorials for the *New York Times*, the *Economist*, the *Globe and Mail*, the *Toronto Star*, *Newsweek*, and *Time*.

Marco Munier is a PhD student in political science at Université du Québec à Montréal and a doctoral researcher at the Network for Strategic Analysis and the Canadian network for research on terrorism, security, and society. His research focuses on intelligence issues and defence and national security policies of Western countries, especially Canada, France, Italy, Australia, and the United States. He also published a paper on Canada's national intelligence culture in *International Journal* and is the author of several entries in the dictionary *Relations internationales: Théories et concepts*, fourth edition.

Costanza Musu is an associate professor at the Graduate School of Public and International Affairs at the University of Ottawa. She obtained her PhD in international relations from the London School of Economics and Political Science. Subsequently she was a Jean Monnet Fellow at the European University Institute in Florence and an assistant professor of international relations at Richmond University (London-UK). She has been a consultant for the Military Center for Strategic Studies – Center for Advanced Defense Studies, the think tank of the Italian Ministry of Defence. She has published extensively on Western policies towards the Middle East. Her current research, supported by a SSHRC Insight Grant, focuses on the fight against the illicit trafficking of antiquities looted from conflict areas in the Middle East.

Jennifer Pedersen works at the intersection of politics and policy. Her past roles have included senior humanitarian policy advisor for a Canadian non-governmental organization. She spent seven years working on the Foreign Affairs and International Development files with the New Democratic Party of Canada. She holds a PhD in international politics from Aberystwyth University and has published on women and war, the arms trade, peace activism in Liberia, and tribal conflict and mediation in Yemen.

David Petrasek was an associate professor at the University of Ottawa. Formerly special adviser to the secretary-general of Amnesty International, David worked extensively on human rights, and humanitarian and conflict resolution issues, including for Amnesty International (1990–6), for the Office of the UN High Commissioner for Human Rights (1997–8), for the International Council on Human Rights Policy (1998–2002), and as director of policy at the HD Centre (2003–7). He has taught international human rights and/or humanitarian law courses at the Osgoode Hall Law School; the Raoul Wallenberg Institute at Lund University, Sweden; and at Oxford University. David also worked as a consultant or adviser to several NGOs and UN agencies. His research interests included conflict mediation in theory and practice, strengthening international human rights law, human rights and poverty, human rights and armed conflict, and human rights in Canadian foreign policy.

Farzan Sabet is a researcher in the Middle East WMD-Free Zone Project at the United Nations Institute for Disarmament Research. He was a postdoctoral fellow at the Global Governance Centre of the Graduate Institute Geneva, a nuclear security predoctoral fellow at the Centre for International Security and Cooperation at Stanford University, and a visiting fellow in the Department of Government at Georgetown University. Farzan holds a PhD and an MA in international history from the Graduate Institute Geneva and a BA in history and political science from McGill University. His research focuses on Middle East politics, nuclear non-proliferation, and economic sanctions. Farzan speaks English, French, and Persian.

Nawroos Shibli is a PhD candidate in global governance at the Balsillie School of International Affairs (BSIA) at the University of Waterloo (UW), where her research focuses on institutional legal responses to Islamophobia in Europe and their human rights implications. She also holds an MA in global governance from UW. Nawroos recently served as the support officer for the Global Justice and Human Rights Research Cluster at the BSIA, and she was a senior research fellow at the Canadian Arab Institute, where her work centred on immigration settlement processes in Canada for Arab communities. Previously, she served as an editorial assistant for *Stability: International Journal of Security and Development* and was a program assistant for the International Law Research Program at the Centre for International Governance Innovation.

Index

Figures and tables are indicated by page numbers in italics.

Abadi, Haidar al-, 54
Abbas, Mahmoud, 57
Abu Huzayfah, 67
Abu Muhandis (Jamal Ja'afar al-Ibrahim), 61
Abu Muslim (André Poulin), 70
Abu Ridwan al-Kanadi, 72
Abu Usamah (Farah Shirdon), 70, 72
Ad Hoc Liaison Committee, 215
aeronautical industry, 171–2
Afghanistan, 69, 73, 179
Afghanistan War, 21, 24, 27, 40
aid. *See* civil society organizations
AKP (Justice and Development Party), 123–5, 126, 131, 132–3
Algeria, 141, 243
alliance management: Canada's Middle East policies and, 7, 41, 49–50, 237; Global Coalition against the Islamic State and, 33–4, 40, 58; NATO Mission–Iraq and, 58, 59
Altıkat, Atilla, 128
Amman-6, 60
Amnesty International, 126, 169, 178
Anatolia Cultural Foundation, 130
Anatolian Heritage Foundation, 129
anti-Semitism, 223, 226, 228
Antkiewicz, Agata, 19–20
Arab-Israeli peace process, 211–16; about, 8, 11–12, 206–7, 216–17; bilateral diplomacy, 214–15; Camp David accord, 144; Canada's human rights policy and,

159, 165; Canada's Middle East policy and, 189, 212; capacity building and, 50–3, 56–8, 61; Deal of the Century, 61; and electoral coalitions and party ideology, 20–1; Harper government and, 16, 191, 213–14, 215; Jerusalem status and, 214; large-fora diplomacy, 212–14; Martin government and, 213; multilateral missions, 211–12; Oslo Accords, 57; Roadmap to Peace, 51, 57; scholarship on Canada and, 4; Stanfield Report on, 208–9, 212; track-two diplomacy, 213; Trudeau government and, 191–2, 214, 215–16; two-state solution, 56, 57, 61–2, 191, 192, 206, 209, 213, 216, 239; United States and, 50–1, 61, 213, 214, 216, 217; UNRWA and, 215–16. *See also* Israel
Arab Spring. *See* Arab uprisings
Arab uprisings: Canada's response, 4, 190; in Jordan, 112; regional impact of, 5; scholarship on Canada and, 4, 140; in Syria, 85, 86 (*see also* Syrian refugee crisis); Turkey and, 131
Arafat, Yassir, 225
Arbour, Louise, 172
Armenian genocide, 127
armoured neoliberalism, 106
arms sales, 170, *170*, *171*, 179–80. *See also* Saudi Arabia, arms sales to
Arms Trade Treaty (ATT), 177–8. *See also* Bill C-47

ASALA, 128
Aspinall, E., 204n28
Assad, Bashar al-, 131
asymmetrical interdependence, 17, 18
Atatürk, Mustafa Kemal, 132
Australia: alignment with Canada, 211; arms sales and, *171*, 180; in Five Eyes, 210; Global Coalition against the Islamic State and, 32, 33, 36, 38–9; return of foreign fighters, 68; Syrian refugee crisis and, 95

Badawi, Raif, 175
Badawi, Samar, 175
Baghdadi, Abu Bakr al-, 79
Baird, John, 146, 163, 190
Bashir, Omar al-, 131
Belgium, 34, 38, 70, *171*, 181
Bell, Michael, 209
Bell, Stewart, 67
Bergen, Candice, 67
bilateral diplomacy, 22, 157, 158, 214–15
Bill C-47 (*An Act to Amend the Export and Import Permits Act*), 169, 174, 177–80
bin Salman, Mohammed, 160, 176
Black, Conrad, 202n12
blended Visa Office–referred refugees (BVORR) programs, 93, 94
blowback, 73
Bow, Brian, 16
Boycott, Divestment, and Sanctions movement (BDS), 219, 228, 230. *See also* sanctions
Britain. *See* United Kingdom
Brooke, Steven, 140
Building Bridges (Standing Senate Committee on Foreign Affairs and International Trade), 128
burka, 142–3
Bush, George W. (Bush administration), 27, 28

CAE Montreal, 172
Cagaptay, Soner, 126
Callimachi, Rukmini, 67
Campaign against Arms Trade, 180
Camp David accord, 144
camps: for foreign fighters, 67–8; for Syrian refugees, 87, 88, 89
Canada: arms sales by, 170, *170*, *171*; citizenship, 76, 83n40; defence industry,

171–2; neoliberalism and the voluntary sector, 105–6; 2015 federal election, 22, 36–8, 41, 90–1, 92–3, 96–7, 162, 227; securitization of Islam in domestic politics, 142–3; trade with Middle East, 208, 210, 218n8; transnational ties to Middle East, 6
– foreign and defence policy: Cold War and, 14–15, 17, 192, 193, 242; functional principle, 14; global order changes and, 6; "good state" self-perception, 188; helpful fixer approach, 189, 192, 237, 244; human rights and, 156–8, 166n2, 246; megaphone diplomacy, 15, 16, 19, 240; multilateralism, 15–16, 18, 48–50, 157–8, 211; overview, 3; party ideology and, 18–19; peacekeeping, 15, 48, 189–90, 192; priorities, 209–11; selective power approach, 15; transformation post–Cold War, 15; unilateralism, 15, 160; United States and, 3, 16–17, 209–10, 240. *See also* alliance management; honest broker diplomacy; middle power
– Middle East foreign and defence policy: about, 3–4, 5, 8–12, 236–7, 246–7; broader interests and opportunities, 4, 19–20, 239–42; budget, 47, 62n2; Conservative vs. Liberal policies, 15–16, 18–19, 22–4, 90–3; continuities and constraints, 237–9; current strategy, 117n3; development post-9/11, 106–7; foreign policy priorities and, 209–11; future strategic vision, 242–6; gaps, 61, 103; geography and, 7; goals, 49–50; historical background, 207–9; Islamist political groups and, 141–3; misperceptions, 7–8; prime ministers' influence, 7; scholarship on, 4, 140–1; security lens, 5; stabilization focus, 115; transnational ties to Middle East and, 6; 2016–19 Middle East Strategy, 103, 107, 117n3, 118n29; United States and, 4, 6–7, 17–19. *See also* Arab-Israeli peace process; capacity building; civil society organizations; Global Coalition against the Islamic State; human rights; Islamic State foreign fighters; Islamist political groups; Israel; Jordan; Muslim Brotherhood; peacemaking; Saudi

Arabia, arms sales to; Syrian refugee crisis; Turkey; United States of America; *specific prime ministers*

Canada Border Services Agency (CBSA), 51, 76

Canada Centre for Community Engagement and Prevention of Violence, 78

Canada Fund for Local Initiatives (CFLI), 116

Canada Revenue Agency, 130, 147

Canadian Armed Forces (CAF), 49, 50

Canadian Commercial Corporation (CCC), 171, 179

Canadian International Development Agency (CIDA), 141

Canadian Jewish Congress, 223

Canadian Jewish News, 227–8

Canadian Security Intelligence Service (CSIS), 76, 77

Canadian Training Assistance Team–Jordan (CTAT-J), 55–6

Cannon, Lawrence, 143

capacity building (CB), 47–62; about, 7, 8–9, 47–8, 60–2, 241–2; challenges facing, 56–60, 61–2; in Iraq, 47, 53–5, 58–60, 61, 122–3; in Israel-Palestine, 50–3, 56–8, 61; in Jordan, 54, 55–6, 60, 107; middle power context and multilateral approach, 48–50; security aid paradigm, 50, 237–8. *See also specific operations*

Carignan, Jennie, 55

Carter, Ashton, 39

Center for Israel and Jewish Affairs, 228

Champagne, François-Philippe, 177

Chapnick, Adam, 16

Charlie Hebdo attack (2015), 78

Charter of Rights and Freedoms, 76, 83n40

children: of foreign fighter detainees, 67, 68, 74, 82n24; Syrian refugees, 88

China, 16, 17, 162, *170*, 217

Chrétien, Jean (Chrétien government): Iraq War and, 17, 23–4; on Israel, 230; Kyoto Protocol and, 19; on Middle East, 224, 241

citizenship, in Canada, 76, 83n40

civil society organizations (CSOs), 103–16; about, 7, 9–10, 103, 115–16, 238; bureaucratic restrictions, 107–8; Canada's support for, 103, 115–16;

first lady NGOs (FLANGOs), 119n34; governmental NGOs (GONGOs), 108, 110, 111; intermediary NGOs, 109–15; "local," claims to, and, 111–12, 120n47; neoliberalization of aid and, 104–6; regime NGOs (RENGOs), 108; royal NGOs (RONGOs), 108–9, 110, 111, 119n34; securitization of aid and, 104, 106–7

Clark, Janine A., 139, 141

clash of civilizations thesis, 139–40

CMI Defense, 181

Cold War, 14–15, 17, 192, 193, 242

Commission on Human Rights (UN), 156, 157

conflict management, 197, 198

conflict resolution, 197, 198

conflict transformation, 197, 198–9

Conservative Party, 169. *See also* Harper, Stephen (Harper government); Mulroney, Brian

Control Arms, 178

Convention on the Elimination of Racial Discrimination, 156

Cotler, Irwin, 227

Coulon, Jocelyn, 230

counterterrorism, 18, 58, 79, 107, 160–1, 162, 210

Counter-Terrorism Capacity-Building Training Program (CTCBP), 53, 55–6

counter-violent extremism (CVE) programs, 78, 79. *See also* Islamic State foreign fighters

COVID-19 pandemic, 59, 128, 133

Crosby, Ann Denholm, 104

Davutoğlu, Ahmet, 128

Dayton, Keith, 52–3, 58

defence industry, 169, 171–2, 178–9, 180. *See also* Saudi Arabia, arms sales to

Delvoie, Louis, 128

democracy and democracy promotion, 103, 104, 114–15, 141–2, 149. *See also* civil society organizations

Democratic Kurdish Federation of Canada, 130

Denmark, 32, 34, 38

Department of National Defence (DND): *Strong, Secure, Engaged* (2017 report), 49–50

Dermer, P.J., 53
diaspora communities, 6, 9, 24–5, 159,
    162, 228–9
Dion, Stéphane, 172–3
Dorminey, Caroline, 181
Duterte, Rodrigo, 179

Ecevit, Bülent, 123
Egmont Institute, 78
Egypt, 89, 141, 161, *170. See also* Muslim
    Brotherhood
11 September 2001 attack, 5, 17, 103, 106,
    210
Enhanced Opportunities Partners, 55
Erdoğan, Recep Tayyip, 123, 124, 125,
    126, 127, 129, 131, 133
European Union (EU), 56, 89, 123, 132,
    159
European Union Coordinating Office for
    Palestinian Police Support (EUPOL-
    COPPS), 48, 51, 52, 53
extremism. *See* counterterrorism; counter-
    violent extremism programs; Islamic
    State foreign fighters; terrorism; war on
    terrorism

Fahmy, Mohamed, 146, 161
Fatah, 51
Fayyad, Salam, 51
fear, politics of, 147–8, 150
feminist foreign policy, 105, 169, 203n19
Fenton, Anthony, 176
Fetullah Terrorist Organization (FETÖ),
    129. *See also* Gülen, Fetullah (Gülen
    movement)
Fidan, Hakan, 124
first lady NGOs (FLANGOs), 119n34
Five Eyes, 210
foreign aid: neoliberalization of, 104–6;
    securitization of, 104, 106–7. *See also*
    civil society organizations
foreign fighters. *See* Islamic State foreign
    fighters
France, 36, 38–9, 170, *170*, 180
Freedom and Justice Party (FJP), 144,
    146. *See also* Muslim Brotherhood
Freedom House, 123, 126
Freeland, Chrystia, 160, 166n1, 173, 175,
    177, 228

Frum, Linda, 227
Fuller, Graham, 140
functional principle, 14
Furey, George, 129

Gabryś, Marcin, 15
Gaza, 51, 131, 165, 190, 215–16
gender and gender equality: Canada's
    Middle East policy and, 242, 246;
    female capacity-building efforts, 52,
    56, 60; "imperiled Muslim woman"
    discourse and Quebec's burka/niqab
    ban, 142–3; Muslim Brotherhood and,
    145; Trudeau's feminist foreign policy,
    105, 169, 203n19
General Dynamics Land Systems of
    Canada (GDLS-C), 169, 171, 172, 173,
    174, 177
geography, 7
Gerges, Fawaz, 140
Germany, 39, *170*, 176, 180
Gezi Park protests (Turkey), 124–5, 129
Ghabra, Omar al-, 128
Global Affairs Canada (GAC): arms sales
    to Saudi Arabia and, 172; civil society
    organizations and, 115–16; foreign
    fighter returnees and, 76; on Global
    Coalition against the Islamic State, 39; on
    intermediary NGOs, 120n45; mediation
    and, 203n21; on Middle East strategy,
    118n29; Trudeau government and, 191
Global Coalition against the Islamic State,
    31–41; about, 7, 8, 31, 40–1; Canada's
    role, 4, 122–3, 161; capacity building in
    Iraq and, 47, 53–5, 58–60; expansion
    to Syria, 34–6; Harper government's
    joining, 22, 32–4, 163; party ideology
    and, 22–3; scholarship on Canada and,
    4; Trudeau government and, 22–3, 27,
    34, 37–40, 41, 58; 2015 federal election
    and, 22, 36–8, 41; US influence on
    Canada's participation, 21–2, 23, 27
global order, 6
"good state," Canada as, 188
governance, good, 103, 104–6, 114
governmental NGOs (GONGOs), 108,
    110, 111
government-assisted refugees (GAR), 93,
    94

Great Britain. See United Kingdom
Gül, Abdullah, 123–4
Gülen, Fetullah (Gülen movement), 124, 125–6, 127, 129–30, 134n7
Gulf War, 4
Gutterman, Ellen, 181

Hamas, 51, 131, 139, 141, 147, 215, 225
Hampson, Fen Osler, 202n12
Harper, Stephen (Harper government): Arab-Israeli peace process and, 213–14, 215; Arab uprisings and, 190; comparison to Trudeau foreign policy, 15–16, 164, 229; Egypt's political transition after Mubarak and, 138, 143–4, 146–7, 149; Global Coalition against the Islamic State, 22, 32–4, 34–6, 40–1, 163; human rights policy and, 163–4; Iran relations, 16, 25, 28, 163, 240; Iraq War and, 23–4, 27–8; Israel relations, 21, 162, 163, 190, 191, 196, 198, 205n35, 225–6, 229, 230, 240–1; Kanishka program, 79; Kyoto Protocol and, 19; Libya air campaign and, 163, 164; Office of Religious Freedom, 144, 190; Palestinian Authority and, 57; peacemaking and, 189–91, 192, 193, 196–7, 198, 202n12, 202n14; Syrian refugee crisis and, 90, 92–3, 96; Trump administration and, 205n35; 2015 federal election and war against Islamic State, 36–7, 38, 41; UNRWA and, 215
Hathloul, Loujain al-, 181
HDP (Peoples' Democratic Party), 127
Hegghammer, Thomas, 73–4
helpful fixer approach, 189, 192, 237, 244
Henrikson, A.K., 201n2
High-Risk Returnee Interdepartmental Taskforce (IDTF), 76
Hizbullah, 139
Al-Hol camp (Syria), 68
honest broker diplomacy: Arab-Israeli peace process and, 212; Harper government on, 15, 16, 190, 202n12; vs. megaphone diplomacy, 15, 16, 240; Middle East engagement and, 50; middle power and, 104; misperceptions of, 7; party ideology and, 19;

peacemaking and, 188–9; Trudeau government and, 15, 227
Hoop Messenger (app), 68
Housefather, Anthony, 227, 228–9
human rights, 155–66; about, 7, 10–11, 155–6, 165–6, 238; alignment with allies, 159–60; and arms exports and Canadian Commercial Corporation, 179; and arms sales to Saudi Arabia, 11, 158, 162, 172–3, 174–6, 238–9; in Canada's foreign policy, 156–7, 166n2, 246; Canada's Middle East policy and, 158–9; diaspora communities and, 159, 162; governments-in-power and, 159, 163–4; Iran and, 159, 164; Iraq and, 59; Israel-Palestinian conflict and, 159, 165; Jordan and, 60; Palestinian Authority and, 57; policy implementation approaches, 157–8; public support and, 155, 161–2; Saudi Arabia and, 160, 166n1; Syria and, 68; Universal Declaration of Human Rights, 166n3; war on terrorism and, 159, 160–1
Human Rights Council (HRC), 157, 158, 159, 165, 228. See also Commission on Human Rights
Human Rights Watch, 87
human security, 49, 104, 245
Huntington, Samuel, 139–40

Ibbitson, John, 16
Ibrahim, Jamal Ja'afar al- (Abu Muhandis), 61
ideal-type positions, ideological/pragmatic, 220–3, 222
ideology, party, 18–19, 22–4, 26, 27–8
İmamoğlu, Ekrem, 127
Immigration, Refugees and Citizenship Canada, 76
Immigration and Refugee Board of Canada, 129
immigration and refugee policy, 18. See also Islamic State foreign fighters; migration, global; Syrian refugee crisis
impartiality, 189, 190, 191, 192–5, 196, 199
India, 170
Individual Cooperation Program, 55
intelligence-sharing, 18, 210
Intercultural Dialogue Institute, 129

intermediary NGOs: about, 109–10; decline in democracy promotion, 113–15; donor relations, 112–13, 120n57; genesis of, 112; "local," claims to, 111–12, 120n47; professionalization and, 116; role of, 110–12, 120n45; staffing, 111. *See also* civil society organizations

International Committee of the Red Cross (ICRC), 193–4

International Criminal Court, 163

international law, 174–5, 210–11, 216, 239

International Monetary Fund (IMF), 123, 126, 132

International Police Peacekeeping and Peace Operations (IPP), 52

International Relief Fund for the Afflicted and Needy–Canada (IRFAN-Canada), 147

Iran: Canada's stance on Islamist groups and, 141; diaspora community and, 24–5, 162; Harper government and, 16, 25, 28, 163, 240; human rights and, 158, 159, 162, 164; Martin government and, 163; as perceived challenge to regional peace and security, 24; protests in, 243; Trudeau government and, 25, 26, 28; Turkey and, 132; US and Canada-Iran relations, 4, 25–7, 28

Iraq: arms sales and, 179; Canadian foreign fighters in, 69–70; capacity building in, 47, 53–5, 58–60, 61, 122–3; NATO Mission–Iraq (NMI), 31, 39–40, 53, 54–5, 58, 59, 64n29, 66n50; Operation IMPACT, 31, 32–4, 40, 53–4, 55, 59–60; protests in, 243; reconstruction needs, 243; scholarship on Canada and, 4; Syrian refugee crisis and, 89

Iraq War: Canada's position, 63n7, 210–11; Canada's response, 4, 17, 21, 23–4, 27–8; Chrétien on, 224; Islamic State and, 79

Islah Party (Yemeni Congregation for Reform), 139

Islamic Action Front (IAF), 139, 141

Islamic Cultural Centre shooting (Quebec City), 148

Islamic State (IS), and Syrian refugees, 86. *See also* Global Coalition against the Islamic State

Islamic State foreign fighters, 67–80; about, 7, 9, 67–8, 78–80, 81n15; blowback, 73; Canada's returnee policies, 75–8; children, 67, 68, 74, 82n24; counter-violent extremism (CVE) programs and, 78, 79; deaths and current status of, 72; in media propaganda, 70, 72; mobilization, 69, 72, 75; national debate on, 67, 78–9; number of Canadians, 67, 69–70, *71*, 72; potential non-violent activities by returnees, 74–5; research barriers, 82n28; retrieval from Kurdish detention, 67–8, 80; returnee definition, 72; return to home countries, 70, 72–3, 75–6; terrorism risks of returnees, 73–4, 78

Islamist political groups: about, 138–9, 241; Canada's approach to, 138, 141–3, 149–50, 161; diversity among, 139; Trudeau government and, 148; West and, 139–40. *See also* Muslim Brotherhood; Turkey

Israel, 219–30; about, 7–8, 12, 219–20, 229–30, 238; Canada relations overview, 20–1, 212, 214–15; Chrétien government and, 224, 230, 241; diaspora community and, 162, 165, 228–9; Egypt's political transition and, 143–4, 149; Harper government and, 16, 162, 163, 190, 191, 196, 198, 205n35, 225–6, 229, 230, 240–1; human rights and, 159, 162, 163, 165; ideal-type ideological/pragmatic positions and, 220–3, *222*; illegal settlements, 56–7, 65n35, 65n37; Martin government and, 21, 163, 165, 213, 224–5, 230; Mulroney government and, 223–4, 226, 228, 229, 230; Trudeau government and, 165, 227–9, 230

Israeli-Palestinian conflict. *See* Arab-Israeli peace process

Italian Institute for International Political Studies (ISPI), 73–4

Italy, 32, 39

Jaramillo, Cesar, 173, 174, 175, 178

Jerusalem, 205n35, 214

Jerusalem Old City Initiative (JOCI), 189, 191

Joint Comprehensive Plan of Action (JCPOA), 26, 28
Jordan: bureaucratic restrictions on civil society, 107–8; Canada's aid overview, 107; Canada's support for civil society organizations, 103, 115–16; capacity building in, 54, 55–6, 60, 107; first lady NGOs (FLANGOs), 119n34; intermediary NGOs, 109–15; Islamic Action Front (IAF), 139, 141; royal NGOs (RONGOs), 108–9, 110, 111, 119n34; Syrian refugee crisis and, 88–9, 95, 107; women in security forces, 56, 60
Juneau, Thomas, 19, 170
Justice and Development Party (AKP), 123–5, 126, 131, 132–3
Justice for Victims of Terrorism Act (JVTA), 25, 26

Kanishka program, 79
Karpet, Kemal, 133
Kartal, Remzi, 126
Kenney, Jason, 35, 54
Khashoggi, Jamal, 160, 174, 175–7
King, William Lyon Mackenzie, 14
Klassen, Jerome, 106
Kleiboer, M., 194
Kouachi brothers, 78
Krahenbuhl, Pierre, 216
Kurdi, Alan, 36, 89–90, 92
Kurdish Workers Party (PKK), 123, 124, 126, 130
Kurdistan Regional Government (KRG), 59
Kurds: Islamic State foreign fighters in custody of, 67–8; Peshmerga capacity building, 23, 33, 36, 47, 53–4, 58–9, 66n47; Turkey and, 123, 126, 127
Kuwait, 54, 172, 199
Kyoto Protocol, 19

Laforest, Rachel, 105–6
Lane, Andrea, 181
large-fora diplomacy, 212–14
law, international, 174–5, 210–11, 216, 239
Lawson, Tom, 35
Lebanon, 54, 55, 88, 243
Lesser, Ian, 140
Lewis, Bernard, 140
Liberal Party. See Chrétien, Jean (Chrétien government); Martin, Paul (Martin government); Trudeau, Justin (Trudeau government)
Libya, 4, 21, 131–2, 163, 164, 243, 245
Loubani, Tarek, 228

MacKay, Peter, 225
Madrid Peace Conference (1991), 213, 244
Maguire, John, 72
Manning, Preston, 224
Mapping Conference (York University), 219
Martin, Paul (Martin government): foreign policy transformation under, 15, 189; Israel and, 21, 163, 165, 213, 224–5, 230; Kyoto Protocol and, 19
mediation, 199–200, 201n2, 202–3n18, 203n21, 242
Mediterranean Dialogue, 55, 60, 62n3
megaphone diplomacy, 15, 16, 19, 240
MHP (Nationalist Movement Party), 126, 133
Middle East: overview of contemporary issues, 239, 243; trade with Canada, 208, 210, 218n8; transnational ties to Canada, 6. See also Arab-Israeli peace process; Canada, Middle East foreign and defence policy; capacity building; civil society organizations; Global Coalition against the Islamic State; human rights; Islamic State foreign fighters; Islamist political groups; Israel; Jordan; Muslim Brotherhood; peacemaking; Saudi Arabia, arms sales to; Syrian refugee crisis; Turkey; United States of America
middle power: Canada's foreign policy approach and, 7, 48–50, 61, 63n5, 97, 244; mediation and, 201n2; neoliberalism and, 104; vs. selective power, 15
migration, global, 6. See also immigration and refugee policy; Syrian refugee crisis
Military Training and Cooperation Program (MTCP), 55, 60, 61
Mishra, Pankaj, 132
Momani, Bessma, 19–20, 181
Monument to Fallen Diplomats (Ottawa), 128
Morsi, Mohammed, 131, 138, 139, 145

Mourani, Maria, 219
Mubarak, Hosni, 143–4, 149, 190
Mulcair, Tom, 36, 38
Mulroney, Brian, 223–4, 226, 228, 229, 230
multilateralism, 15–16, 18, 48–50, 157–8,
211. *See also* honest broker diplomacy;
peacemaking
Muslim Association of Canada (MAC), 147
Muslim Brotherhood, 143–8; about, 10,
138–9, 149; background, 144; Canada's
domestic politics and, 147–8; Erdoğan
and, 131; Harper on, 138, 146–7;
ousting and persecution of, 145–6;
religious freedom concerns and, 144–5;
rise to power after Mubarak regime,
143–4; women's rights and, 145. *See also*
Islamist political groups
Musu, Costanza, 20

Nationalist Movement Party (MHP), 126,
133
NATO (North Atlantic Treaty
Organization): Canada's involvement,
3, 40, 48, 210; Enhanced Opportunities
Partners, 55; Libya intervention, 4, 163,
164; Mediterranean Dialogue, 55, 60,
62n3; Trump on, 59; US-led military
interventions and, 21
NATO Mission–Iraq (NMI), 31, 39–40, 53,
54–5, 58, 59, 64n29, 66n50
neoliberalism, 103, 104–6, 108, 115
Nesser, Petter, 73–4
Netanyahu, Benjamin, 56, 191, 229
Netherlands, 32, 34, 36, 39
Neufeld, Mark, 104
neutrality, 193–4. *See also* impartiality
New Democratic Party (NDP): arms sales
to Saudi Arabia and, 169, 172, 174, 176,
177, 183n16; Global Coalition against the
Islamic State and, 33; Syrian refugee crisis
and, 36; 2015 federal election and, 37
New Zealand, 210, 211
Nigeria, 68, 178, 179
9/11 attack, 5, 17, 103, 106, 210
niqab, 142–3
non-governmental organizations
(NGOs). *See* civil society organizations;
intermediary NGOs
North American Free Trade Agreement
(NAFTA), 17, 210, 214

Norway, 180, 203n21
November 2015 Paris attacks, 74, 91, 92
Nuri, Ayub, 66n47

Obama, Barack (Obama administration):
Arab-Israeli peace process and, 213;
Canada-Iran relations and, 25, 26,
28, 240; Global Coalition against the
Islamic State and, 27, 32, 38; Syrian
refugee crisis and, 96
Occupied Palestinian Territories (OPT).
See Palestinians
Office of Religious Freedom, 144, 190
Olmert, Ehud, 225
Oman, 199
Operation ARTEMIS, *49*
Operation CALUMET, *49*
Operation CARIBBE, *49*
Operation CROCODILE, *49*
Operation DRIFTNET, *49*
Operation EDIFICE, *49*
Operation FOUNDATION, *49*
Operation FREQUENCE, *49*
Operation IGNITION, *49*
Operation IMPACT: about, 48, *49*, 122;
in Iraq, 31, 32–4, 40, 53–4, 55, 59–60; in
Jordan, 55–6, 60
Operation JADE, *49*
Operation KOBOLD, *49*
Operation NABERIOUS, *49*
Operation NEON, *49*
Operation OPEN SPIRIT, *49*
Operation Peace Spring, 130
Operation PRESENCE, *49*
Operation PROJECTION, *49*
Operation PROTEUS, 48, *49*, 51, 52, 53,
215
Operation REASSURANCE, *49*
Operation RENDER-SAFE, *49*
Operation Resolute Support, 40
Operation SNOWGOOSE, *49*
Operation SOPRANO, *49*
Operation UNIFIER, *49*
Oran, Baskin, 127
Oslo Accords, 57
Oxfam, 178

Pakistan, 69, 73, *170*
Palestinian Authority Security Forces
(PASF), 51, 52–3, 57–8

Palestinians: Canada relations with,
215; capacity building, 50–3, 56–8, 61;
Harper government and, 141, 225;
Trudeau government and, 229.
See also Arab-Israeli peace process;
Fatah; Gaza; Hamas; West Bank
Paquin, Jonathan, 143–4
Paris attacks (November 2015), 74, 91,
92
party ideology, 18–19, 22–4, 26, 27–8
Peace and Stabilization Operations
Program (PSOPS), 53
peace bonds, 77–8
peacekeeping, 15, 48, 189–90, 192
peacemaking, 188–200; about, 11, 188,
199–200, 242; Canada's motivations,
195–7; conflict management, 197,
198; conflict resolution, 197; conflict
transformation, 197, 198–9; future
considerations, 199–200; Harper
government and, 189–91, 192, 193,
196–7, 198, 202n12, 202n14; helpful
fixer approach, 189, 192, 237, 244;
historical overview, 188–92; impartiality
and, 189, 190, 191, 192–5, *196*, 199;
mediation, 199–200, 201n2, 202–3n18,
203n21, 242; peacekeeping, 15, 48,
189–90, 192; pre-Harper, 188–9, 192,
193, 195–6, 198; Trudeau government
and, 191–2, 193, 197–200, 202–3n18,
203n19; typology of, 197–8. *See also*
Arab-Israeli peace process; honest
broker diplomacy; multilateralism
Pearson, Lester, 189
Peoples' Democratic Party (HDP), 127
People's Protection Units (YPG), 82n24, 130
Pettigrew, Pierre, 225
PGW, 171, 174
Philippines, 179
PKK (Kurdish Workers Party), 123, 124,
126, 130
Poulin, André (Abu Muslim), 70
privately sponsored refugees (PSRs), 93,
94
professionalization, 116
Project Ploughshares, 178
public opinion: arms sales and, 176, 179;
human rights and, 155, 161–2; Syrian
refugee crisis and, 90, 91–2
Public Safety Canada, 69–70, 73, 76

al-Qaeda, 4, 5
Qatar, 54, 131–2, 199
Quebec, 24, 142–3
Quebec City: Islamic Cultural Centre
shooting, 148
Quiggin, Tom, 147–8

radicalization, 74–5
Radicalization Awareness Network (RAN),
73
Razack, Sherene, 142
realism, 63n5, 192
Red Cross, 193–4
Reform Party, 224
refoulement, 88
Refugee and Humanitarian Resettlement
Program, 95
Refugee Convention (1951), 87, 88
refugees, Turkish, 129. *See also* Syrian
refugee crisis
Refugees Working Group (RWG), 213
regime NGOs (RENGOs), 108
religious freedom, 144–5, 190
returnees. *See* Islamic State foreign
fighters
Rivlin, Reuven, 230
Royal Canadian Mounted Police
(RCMP): in Iraq, 53–5; Islamic State
foreign fighter returnees and, 73,
76–7; in Jordan, 55–6; resources to
investigate Canadian law violations
abroad, 180
royal NGOs (RONGOs), 108–9, 110, 111,
119n34
rules-based international order, 6, 22,
27
Russia, 17, 132, *170*, 217

Said, Edward, 140
Sajjan, Harjit, 39, 40, 55
sanctions, 18, 26–7, 176, 179–80. *See also*
Boycott, Divestment, and Sanctions
movement
Sartori, Giovanni, 221
Saudi Arabia: Canada relations, 170–1;
human rights and, 160, 166n1; Muslim
Brotherhood and, 141; Turkey and, 131
Saudi Arabia, arms sales to, 169–81;
about, 7, 11, 169, 181; arms export
controls and, 169, 174, 177–9; arms

Saudi Arabia, arms sales to, (*cont.*)
    imports overview, 170, *170, 171*;
    commercial interests vs. Canadian
    values, 238–9; contract with Canada,
    171; future implications, 180–1;
    human rights and, 11, 158, 162, 172–3,
    174–6, 238–9; Khashoggi murder and,
    175–7; NDP on, 169, 172, 174, 176,
    177, 183n16; transparency and, 174;
    Trudeau government on, 172–4, 193,
    198; Yemen war and, 174–5
Schwedler, Jillian, 139
Secure Air Travel Act, 76
securitization, of foreign aid, 104, 106–7
security aid, 50, 237–8. *See also* capacity
    building
security sector reform (SSR), 49, 50, 55,
    59, 106, 107. *See also* capacity building
selective power, 15
September 11, 2001, attack, 5, 17, 103,
    106, 210
Shirdon, Farah (Abu Usamah), 70, 72
Sisi, Abdel Fattah al-, 131, 139, 146, 148,
    149, 161
sleeper cells, 78
Soleimani, Qasem, 61
Soroka, Tomasz, 15
South Korea, *170*
Spain, 32, 180
stabilization, 115
Stairs, Denis, 17
Standing Committee on Foreign Affairs
    and International Development, 145
Standing Senate Committee on Foreign
    Affairs and International Trade:
    Building Bridges report, 128
Stanfield, Robert (Stanfield Report), 207–9,
    212
State Immunity Act, 25
Stein, Janice, 202n12
Streit Group, 179–80
Structural Adjustment Programs (SAPs),
    104
Sudan, 131, 243
Suez Crisis, 15, 48, 192
Sustainable Development Goals, 243, 246
Svensson, I., 194, 195
Switzerland, 203n21
Syria: Canadian foreign fighters in,
    67, 69–70, 75; civil war and human
    rights violations, 68, 85; expanding
    anti–Islamic State war to, 34–6; foreign
    fighter mobilization and civil war in,
    68, 69; Al-Hol camp, 68; reconstruction
    needs, 243; scholarship on Canada
    and, 4; Turkey and, 131.
    See also Syrian refugee crisis
Syrian Democratic Forces (SDF), 67, 130
Syrian refugee crisis, 85–97; about, 7, 9,
    85, 96–7, 122, 243–4; background, 86;
    Canada vs. US responses, 96; Canadian
    public opinion on, 90, 91–2; Harper
    government and, 90, 92–3, 96; journeys
    to Europe, 89–90; Kurdi, Alan, 36,
    89–90, 92; neighbouring countries and,
    87–9, 98n15; resettlement in Canada,
    93–5, *94*; Trudeau government and, 90–
    1, 92–3, 95, 96–7; 2015 federal election
    and, 36, 90–1, 92–3, 96–7; UNHCR's
    Regional Response Plan, 87

Telegram (app), 68
Temelkuran, Ece, 125
Terradyne, 171, 173–4
terrorism, 25, 73–4. *See also*
    counterterrorism; counter-violent
    extremism programs; Islamic State
    foreign fighters; war on terrorism
Thrall, A. Trevor, 181
threat inflation, 240
Thruelson, Peter Dahl, 66n50
Toronto Sun, 147–8
track-two diplomacy, 12, 213, 242, 245,
    246
trade, Canada–Middle East, 208, 209–10,
    218n8
transparency, 174
Transport Canada, 76
Trinidad, 68
Trudeau, Justin (Trudeau government):
    Arab-Israeli peace process and, 191–2,
    214, 215–16; Boycott, Divestment,
    and Sanctions movement and, 219,
    228; capacity building and, 54, 58;
    comparison to Harper foreign policy,
    15–16, 164, 229; feminist foreign
    policy, 105, 169, 203n19; foreign policy
    promises, 15, 227; Global Coalition
    against the Islamic State and, 22–3, 27,
    34, 37–40, 41, 58; Iran relations, 25,

26, 28; Islamic State foreign fighter
returnees and, 75; Islamist political
groups and, 148, 149; Israel relations,
165, 227–9, 230; Khashoggi murder
and, 175–7; Muslim Brotherhood and,
139; NATO Mission–Iraq, 54–5; Office
of Religious Freedom and, 144, 190;
peacemaking and, 191–2, 193, 197–200,
202–3n18, 203n19; Syrian refugee crisis
and, 90–1, 92–3, 95, 96–7; UNRWA and,
215–16; Yemen war and, 174–5.
See also Saudi Arabia, arms sales to
Trudeau, Pierre Elliott, 19, 96
Trump, Donald (Trump administration):
Arab-Israeli peace process and,
214; arms export controls and, 178;
assassinations in Iran ordered by, 61;
Canada-Iran relations and, 26, 28;
Harper government and, 205n35;
Muslim Brotherhood and, 147; NAFTA
renegotiation, 210, 214; on NATO, 59;
Syrian refugee crisis and, 96; Yemen war
and, 180
Turkey, 122–33; about, 7, 10, 122–3, 132–3,
237; Armenian genocide and, 127; arms
embargo on, 130, 136n51; arms sales
from Canada, *171*; bilateral discussions
and visits, 128–9; Canada relations, 122,
127–31, 133; Canadian foreign fighters
in, 69–70; future political directions, 131;
Gülen movement and, 124, 125–6, 127,
129–30, 134n7; Iran and, 132;
Kurds and, 123, 126, 127, 130;
Monument to Fallen Diplomats (Ottawa)
and, 128; Operation Peace Spring, 130;
parliament size, 135n24; political history
and recent illiberalism, 123–7, 132–3,
134n7; regional engagement by, 131–2;
Russia and, 132; Syrian refugee crisis
and, 87–8, 98n15; travel advisory on,
130–1
Turkish Canadian Chamber of Commerce,
129
Turp, Daniel, 173, 180, 181

unilateralism, 15, 160
United Arab Emirates (UAE), 131, 141,
172, 179
United Kingdom: arms sales and, 170,
170, 171, 180–1; capacity building
and, 48; in Five Eyes, 210; in Global
Coalition against the Islamic State,
34, 36, 39; Islamic State foreign
fighters and, 70; Syrian refugee crisis
and, 95
United Nations: Arab-Israeli peace
process and, 212–13; Canada and, 211;
Commission on Human Rights, 156,
157; Convention on the Elimination
of Racial Discrimination, 156; human
rights and, 156, 157–8; Human Rights
Council, 157, 158, 159, 165, 228;
Sustainable Development Goals, 243,
246; Universal Declaration of Human
Rights, 166n3
United Nations Emergency Force (UNEF),
48
United Nations High Commissioner for
Refugees (UNHCR), 86, 87, 96
United Nations Relief and Works Agency
(UNRWA), 215, 228, 244
United States of America, 14–28; about,
6–7, 8, 14, 27–8, 240; Arab-Israeli
peace process and, 50–1, 61, 213, 214,
216, 217; arms sales and, 170, *170*, 174,
178–9; asymmetrical interdependence
with, 17, 18; Canada-Iran relations
and, 4, 25–7, 28; Canada's foreign
policy and, 3, 16–17, 209–10, 240;
Canada's Middle East policy and, 4,
6–7, 17–19; Canada's participation in
US-led military interventions, 21–4;
in Five Eyes, 210; Global Coalition
against the Islamic State and, 32, 33,
35–6, 38, 39, 47; Iran and, 240; loss
of soft power, 243; party ideology
and Canada's foreign policy, 18–19,
27–8; Syrian refugee crisis and, 96;
trade with, 209–10; UNRWA and, 216;
Yemen war and, 180. *See also specific
presidents*
United States Security Coordinator (USSC),
50–1, 52
Universal Declaration of Human Rights,
166n3
Uras, Kerim, 129–30

Vidino, Lorenzo, 140
voluntary sector, 105–6
Vucetic, Srdjan, 181

Walberg, Eric, 229
war on terrorism: Canada and, 17, 141, 142, 210; human rights and, 159, 160–1; securitization of aid and, 106, 107
Washington consensus, 104
Weber, Max, 220–1
West Bank, 53, 56–7, 65n37
Wiktorowicz, Quintan, 107–8, 109
women. *See* gender and gender equality
World Bank, 133

Yemen: development status, 158; Islamic State foreign fighter returnees from, 73;

protests and reconstruction needs, 243; track-two diplomacy and, 245; war in, 172, 174–5, 178, 180
Yemeni Congregation for Reform (Islah Party), 139
Yıldırım, H.E. Binali, 129
York University: Mapping Conference, 219
YPG (People's Protection Units), 82n24, 130

Zahar, Mahmoud, 225
Zahar, Marie-Joëlle, 141